IMPROVING THE PRESUMPTIVE DISABILITY DECISION-MAKING PROCESS FOR VETERANS

Committee on Evaluation of the Presumptive Disability
Decision-Making Process for Veterans

Board on Military and Veterans Health

Jonathan M. Samet and Catherine C. Bodurow, *Editors*

INSTITUTE OF MEDICINE
OF THE NATIONAL ACADEMIES

THE NATIONAL ACADEMIES PRESS
Washington, D.C.
www.nap.edu

THE NATIONAL ACADEMIES PRESS 500 Fifth Street, N.W. Washington, DC 20001

NOTICE: The project that is the subject of this report was approved by the Governing Board of the National Research Council, whose members are drawn from the councils of the National Academy of Sciences, the National Academy of Engineering, and the Institute of Medicine. The members of the committee responsible for the report were chosen for their special competences and with regard for appropriate balance.

This study was supported by Contract No. V101 (93) P-2136 between the National Academy of Sciences and United States Department of Veterans Affairs. Any opinions, findings, conclusions, or recommendations expressed in this publication are those of the author(s) and do not necessarily reflect the view of the organizations or agencies that provided support for this project.

International Standard Book Number-13: 978-0-309-10730-3
International Standard Book Number-10: 0-309-10730-X

Additional copies of this report are available from the National Academies Press, 500 Fifth Street, N.W., Lockbox 285, Washington, DC 20055; (800) 624-6242 or (202) 334-3313 (in the Washington metropolitan area); Internet, http://www.nap.edu.

For more information about the Institute of Medicine, visit the IOM home page at: **www.iom.edu.**

Printed in the United States of America

The serpent has been a symbol of long life, healing, and knowledge among almost all cultures and religions since the beginning of recorded history. The serpent adopted as a logotype by the Institute of Medicine is a relief carving from ancient Greece, now held by the Staatliche Museen in Berlin.

Suggested citation: IOM (Institute of Medicine). 2008. *Improving the presumptive disability decision-making process for veterans*. Washington, DC: The National Academies Press.

"Knowing is not enough; we must apply.
Willing is not enough; we must do."

—Goethe

INSTITUTE OF MEDICINE

OF THE NATIONAL ACADEMIES

Advising the Nation. Improving Health.

THE NATIONAL ACADEMIES

Advisers to the Nation on Science, Engineering, and Medicine

The **National Academy of Sciences** is a private, nonprofit, self-perpetuating society of distinguished scholars engaged in scientific and engineering research, dedicated to the furtherance of science and technology and to their use for the general welfare. Upon the authority of the charter granted to it by the Congress in 1863, the Academy has a mandate that requires it to advise the federal government on scientific and technical matters. Dr. Ralph J. Cicerone is president of the National Academy of Sciences.

The **National Academy of Engineering** was established in 1964, under the charter of the National Academy of Sciences, as a parallel organization of outstanding engineers. It is autonomous in its administration and in the selection of its members, sharing with the National Academy of Sciences the responsibility for advising the federal government. The National Academy of Engineering also sponsors engineering programs aimed at meeting national needs, encourages education and research, and recognizes the superior achievements of engineers. Dr. Charles M. Vest is president of the National Academy of Engineering.

The **Institute of Medicine** was established in 1970 by the National Academy of Sciences to secure the services of eminent members of appropriate professions in the examination of policy matters pertaining to the health of the public. The Institute acts under the responsibility given to the National Academy of Sciences by its congressional charter to be an adviser to the federal government and, upon its own initiative, to identify issues of medical care, research, and education. Dr. Harvey V. Fineberg is president of the Institute of Medicine.

The **National Research Council** was organized by the National Academy of Sciences in 1916 to associate the broad community of science and technology with the Academy's purposes of furthering knowledge and advising the federal government. Functioning in accordance with general policies determined by the Academy, the Council has become the principal operating agency of both the National Academy of Sciences and the National Academy of Engineering in providing services to the government, the public, and the scientific and engineering communities. The Council is administered jointly by both Academies and the Institute of Medicine. Dr. Ralph J. Cicerone and Dr. Charles M. Vest are chair and vice chair, respectively, of the National Research Council.

www.national-academies.org

COMMITTEE ON EVALUATION OF THE PRESUMPTIVE DISABILITY DECISION-MAKING PROCESS FOR VETERANS

JONATHAN M. SAMET (*Chair*), Professor and Chair, Department of Epidemiology, Jacob I. and Irene B. Fabrikant Professor in Health, Risk, and Society, Johns Hopkins University, Bloomberg School of Public Health, Baltimore, MD

MARGARET A. BERGER, Suzanne J. and Norman Miles Professor of Law, Brooklyn Law School, NY

KIRSTEN BIBBINS-DOMINGO, Assistant Professor of Medicine and of Epidemiology, Biostatistics, University of California, San Francisco

ERIC G. BING, Endowed Professor of Global Health and HIV, Charles R. Drew University of Medicine and Science, Los Angeles, CA

BERNARD D. GOLDSTEIN, Professor of Environmental and Occupational Health, Graduate School of Public Health, University of Pittsburgh, PA

GUY H. McMICHAEL III, President, GHM Consulting, Washington, DC

JOHN R. MULHAUSEN, Director, Corporate Safety and Industrial Hygiene, 3M Company, St. Paul, MN

RICHARD P. SCHEINES, Professor and Head, Department of Philosophy, Carnegie Mellon University, Pittsburgh, PA

KENNETH R. STILL, President and Scientific Director, Occupational Toxicology Associates, Inc., Hillsboro, OR

DUNCAN C. THOMAS, Verna Richter Chair in Cancer Research, Professor, and Director, Biostatistics Division, Department of Preventive Medicine, Keck School of Medicine, University of Southern California, Los Angeles

SVERRE VEDAL, Professor, Department of Environmental and Occupational Health Sciences, University of Washington School of Public Health and Community Medicine, Seattle

ALLEN J. WILCOX, Senior Investigator, Epidemiology Branch, National Institute of Environmental Health Sciences, and Editor-in-Chief of Epidemiology, Durham, NC

SCOTT L. ZEGER, Frank Hurley-Catharine Dorrier Professor and Chair, Department of Biostatistics, Bloomberg School of Public Health, Johns Hopkins University, Baltimore, MD

LAUREN ZEISE, Chief, Reproductive and Cancer Hazard Assessment Branch, Office of Environmental Health Hazard Assessment, California Environmental Protection Agency, Oakland

Volunteer Scientific Consultant

MELISSA McDIARMID, Professor of Medicine, Occupational Health Program, University of Maryland School of Medicine, Baltimore

Consultant

ROBERT J. EPLEY, Independent Consultant, Waxhaw, NC

Staff

CATHERINE BODUROW, Study Director
MORGAN A. FORD, Program Officer (May-August 2007)
LESLIE SIM, Program Officer (February-May 2006)
ALICE VOROSMARTI, Research Associate (May-August 2007)
CARA JAMES, Research Associate (June 2006-May 2007)
ANISHA DHARSHI, Research Associate (June 2006-January 2007)
KRISTEN BUTLER, Research Assistant (March-July 2007)
KRISTEN GILBERTSON, Research Assistant (February-July 2006)
JON Q. SANDERS, Program Associate (March 2006-May 2007)
REINE Y. HOMAWOO, Senior Program Assistant (May-August 2007)
VERA DIAZ, Intern (February-April 2007)

BOARD ON MILITARY AND VETERANS HEALTH

ROBERT B. WALLACE (*Chair*), Professor of Epidemiology and Internal Medicine, and Director, Center on Aging, College of Public Health, University of Iowa, Iowa City
GEORGE K. ANDERSON, Executive Director, Association of Military Surgeons in the United States, Bethesda, MD
MICHAEL S. ASCHER, Senior Medical Advisor, Defense Biology Biosciences Directorate, Lawrence Livermore National Laboratory, Livermore, CA
ARTHUR J. BARSKY, Professor of Psychiatry, Harvard Medical School, and Director of Psychiatric Research, Brigham and Women's Hospital, Boston, MA
DIANA D. CARDENAS, Professor and Chair, Department of Rehabilitation Medicine, University of Miami, FL
LINDA D. COWAN, Professor, University of Oklahoma College of Public Health, Oklahoma City
TIMOTHY R. GERRITY, Senior Partner, Noventus Medical, Worcester, MA
KATHERINE L. HEILPERN, Acting Chair, Department of Emergency Medicine, Emory School of Medicine, Atlanta, GA
MYRON M. LEVINE, Head, Division of Geographic Medicine, and Director, Center for Vaccine Development, University of Maryland School of Medicine, Baltimore
SUSAN H. MATHER, Department of Veterans Affairs (Retired), Bowie, MD
MATTHEW L. PUGLISI, Director, Business Development, Aptima, Inc., Washington, DC
PHYLLIS W. SHARPS, Professor and Director, Master's Program, Johns Hopkins University School of Nursing, Baltimore, MD
ERNEST T. TAKAFUJI, Director, Office of Biodefense Research, National Institute of Allergy and Infectious Diseases, Bethesda, MD

Board Staff

FREDERICK ERDTMANN, Director
PAMELA RAMEY-McCRAY, Administrative Assistant
ANDREA COHEN, Financial Associate

IOM boards do not review or approve individual reports and are not asked to endorse conclusions and recommendations. The responsibility for the content of the reports rests with the authoring committee and the institution.

Reviewers

This report has been reviewed in draft form by individuals chosen for their diverse perspectives and technical expertise, in accordance with procedures approved by the National Research Council's Report Review Committee. The purpose of this independent review is to provide candid and critical comments that will assist the institution in making its published report as sound as possible and to ensure that the report meets institutional standards for objectivity, evidence, and responsiveness to the study charge. The review comments and draft manuscript remain confidential to protect the integrity of the deliberative process. We wish to thank the following individuals for their review of this report:

Dan G. Blazer, Duke University Medical Center
Mark R. Cullen, Yale University School of Medicine
Lynn R. Goldman, Johns Hopkins Bloomberg School of Public Health
Steven N. Goodman, Johns Hopkins University School of Medicine
Robert F. Herrick, Harvard School of Public Health
Susan H. Mather, Department of Veterans Affairs (Retired)
Francis L. O'Donnell, Department of Defense's Force Health Protection and Readiness Programs
Louise M. Ryan, Harvard School of Public Health
Patrick Ryan, PricewaterhouseCoopers
David A. Savitz, Mount Sinai School of Medicine
Harold C. Sox, American College of Physicians and Internal Medicine
Michael A. Stoto, Georgetown University

Judith P. Swazey, The Acadia Institute
Joseph Thompson, Aequus, Inc.

Although the reviewers listed above have provided many constructive comments and suggestions, they were not asked to endorse the conclusions or recommendations nor did they see the final draft of the report before its release. The review of this report was overseen by **Gilbert S. Omenn,** University of Michigan Medical School, and **Willard G. Manning,** University of Chicago. Appointed by the National Research Council and Institute of Medicine, respectively, they were responsible for making certain that an independent examination of this report was carried out in accordance with institutional procedures and that all review comments were carefully considered. Responsibility for the final content of this report rests entirely with the authoring committee and the institution.

Preface

This committee, the Committee on Evaluation of the Presumptive Disability Decision-Making Process for Veterans (Committee), was charged with describing the current process for how presumptive decisions are made for veterans who have health conditions arising from military service and with proposing a scientific framework for making such presumptive decisions in the future. Although an individual veteran can establish a direct service connection for an illness, the needed information on the responsible exposure received during military service may be unavailable or incomplete. Additionally, there may be scientific uncertainty as to whether the exposure is known to cause the health condition. To ensure that veterans are compensated when information for direct service connection is needed but unavailable, Congress or the Secretary of the Department of Veterans Affairs (VA) can decide to service connect entire groups of veterans for specific health conditions due to exposures received during service. This decision to compensate particular groups of veterans is called a presumptive disability service-connection decision or, simply, a presumption. A presumption may address unavailable or incomplete information on exposure or gaps in the evidence as to whether the exposure increases risk for the health condition.

Each veteran identified as eligible for coverage under a presumptive decision will have a separate, individual disability rating conducted by the VA and will be eligible for disability compensation based on the nature and severity of the health condition. That is, the presumptive disability service-connection decision is separate from the rating evaluation and compensation process.

The Committee took on the task of addressing presumptions while the United States was involved in conflict in Iraq and Afghanistan and veterans from prior conflicts were developing health conditions linked to service in Vietnam and the 1990 Persian Gulf War. The Committee's charge involved examination of the processes used by all participants in the presumptive disability decision-making process for veterans—Congress, VA, the National Academies (National Research Council [NRC] and Institute of Medicine [IOM]), veterans service organizations, and veterans. The Committee examined the processes used by the NRC and IOM to evaluate scientific evidence in support of presumptive disability decision-making by the VA and how the VA used the syntheses and scientific classifications of the NRC and IOM, along with other information, to establish presumptive decisions. The Committee was asked to describe the current process. The Committee's approach involved a series of case studies, intended to draw out "lessons learned" that would inform the development of a new approach. The case studies are not intended as criticisms about the work of past NRC or IOM committees or previously established presumptive decisions by Congress and VA. Rather the case studies serve as an appropriate and informative foundation for proposing an approach for the future.

The Committee concluded that the presumptive disability decision-making process should be based on evidence about veterans' health and how their health had been affected by military service. The Committee proposes a framework for the future that will be based on findings about the health of veterans that come from careful charting of Service member exposures during military service and tracking of their health at entry into, during, at separation from and after military service. The proposed framework may be applied to all types of exposures (e.g., chemical, biological, infectious, physical, and psychological); however, we recognize that characterizing psychological stressors, particularly under combat circumstances, is particularly difficult, although highly relevant to the chronic neuropsychiatric disorders faced by veterans. The Committee offers its framework for evaluation of the resulting evidence and for considering the evidence from studies of veterans in the context of all other relevant lines of scientific evidence. The Committee recommends a two-step approach for evaluation of scientific evidence on exposures of military personnel and risks to health. The first step is to determine the strength of evidence in support of causation and to classify the strength of the causal classification. The second step is to describe the magnitude of the disease burden caused by the exposure in a specific group of veterans.

Presumptive decisions, while based in evidence on risks to health status, are also affected by other considerations. The report acknowledges these considerations. The Committee recognizes that its proposed framework for the future will be applied in a context set by many considerations beyond the scope of scientific evidence and its classification with regard to the strength of evidence for causality. Nonetheless, the Committee respectfully hopes that the Veterans' Disability Benefits Commission will recommend and that Congress and the VA will adhere to an evidence-based approach for the future presumptive disability decision-making process for veterans.

I am highly appreciative of the dedication and work of the members of the Committee on Evaluation of the Presumptive Disability Decision-Making Process for Veterans. They willingly took on this important effort at a time when every American is aware of the great sacrifices that military service men and women and our veterans have and do make each day. The Committee addressed its charge with great dedication and worked tirelessly to consider all of the relevant information, to deliberate at length in committee meetings and conference calls. Of course, each committee member invested substantial time in this effort, reflective of its importance and of its challenging nature. The proposed scientific framework, levels for strength of evidence, and other recommendations in this report reflect the thoughtful and carefully considered conclusions of the Committee. The Committee wishes to express its appreciation for the valuable support of its dedicated staff directed by Catherine Bodurow. This report would not have been possible without their contributions.

Veterans have sacrificed a great deal for our nation. We owe them the best possible process for ensuring that those having service-related health conditions are properly identified, treated, and compensated.

Jonathan M. Samet, M.D., M.S.
Chair, Committee on Evaluation of the Presumptive Disability Decision-Making Process for Veterans

Acknowledgments

The Committee on Evaluation of the Presumptive Disability Decision-Making Process for Veterans (Committee) and Institute of Medicine (IOM) staff would like to thank many individuals for providing information, data, discussions, and comments throughout this study. The Committee and IOM staff are indebted to these individuals for their assistance and contributions.

The Committee and IOM staff would like to acknowledge and thank members of the Veterans' Disability Benefits Commission (VDBC) for taking time to attend and participate at the Committee's open session meetings. The commissioners include: James T. Scott (VDBC's Chairman), John Grady, Rick Surratt, and Joe Wynn. We would also like to recognize the VDBC Staff for their attendance and participation at the Committee's open session meetings as well as any needed technical assistance throughout the study. These individuals include: Ray Wilburn (VDBC's Executive Director), Jacqueline Garrick, Kathleen Greve, Steve Riddle, Jim Wear, and Donald Zeglin. IOM staff is appreciative of the assistance provided by Marcelle Habibion (Department of Veterans Affairs' [VA] Director of Program Evaluation Service in the Office of Policy and Planning) during the course of the study. Many others from VA also provided information, presented at Committee meetings or participated in meetings with the Committee Chair and IOM staff. They are recognized, as follows, in alphabetical order: David Barrans, Mark Brown, Douglas Dembling, Lawrence Deyton, Patrick Dunne (VA's Assistant Secretary for Policy and Planning), George Fitzelle, Duane Fleming, Bradley Flohr, Paul Hutter (VA's Acting General

Counsel), P. Craig Hyams, Patrick Joyce, Gordon Mansfield (VA's Deputy Secretary), David McLenachen, Thomas Pamperin, and Joseph Salvatore.

The Committee benefited greatly from the knowledge, information, and views of presenters and panelists at its three open session meetings. The Committee would like to recognize the following individuals from its open session meeting on May 31, 2006 (listed in order of their presentation): John Grady (VDBC), Rick Surratt (VDBC), Joe Wynn (VDBC), Ray Wilburn (VDBC), Thomas Pamperin (VA), David Barrans (VA), Mark Brown (VA), Patrick Joyce (VA), and Bradley Flohr (VA). The Committee would like to recognize the following individuals who presented at its second open session meeting on July 27, 2006 (listed in order of their presentation): Rose Marie Martinez (IOM), Han Kang (VA), Lawrence Deyton (VA), R. Craig Postlewaite (DoD), Jack M. Heller (DoD), John Seibert (DoD), Cathy Wiblemo (The American Legion), Leonard Selfon (United Spinal Association), Quentin Kinderman (Veterans of Foreign Wars of the United States), and Rick Weidman (Vietnam Veterans of America). Finally, the Committee would like to recognize the following individuals who presented at its third open session meeting on October 4, 2006 (listed in order of their presentation): Laura Petrou, Patrick Ryan, Edward Scott, Chris Yoder, Nhan Do (DoD), Cliff Freeman (VA), and James T. Scott (VDBC's Chairman). In addition, several congressional staffers joined a panel discussion in person or by phone. They are recognized in alphabetical order, as follows: William Brew, Kelly Craven, Mary Ellen McCarthy, Paige McManus, Dahlia Melendrez, Kingston Smith, Jon Towers, and Lupe Wissel.

Representatives of the Department of Defense (DoD) contributed to the Committee's efforts by attending and presenting at open session meetings, participating in conference calls, and providing written responses to Committee questions. The Committee and IOM staff would like to thank Ellen Embrey (DoD's Deputy Assistant Secretary of Defense for Force Health Protection and Readiness), along with Michael Kilpatrick and George Johnson of her office, for making the assistance and expertise of many in DoD available to the Committee and IOM staff. IOM staff would like to acknowledge Craig Postlewaite who facilitated and participated in each of the DoD, Committee, and IOM staff interactions. The following individuals (listed in alphabetical order) contributed substantial time and effort to providing the Committee documents, answers to questions and participating at panel discussions during open session meetings: Kenneth Cox, Donna Doganiero, Jack Heller, Brad Hutchens, Jack Jeter, Bill Monk, Christine Moser, John Seibert, Becky Sobel, and Hew Wolf.

Throughout the course of the study, the Committee received written comments from veterans service organizations, individual veterans, and the public. These comments served to heighten awareness of important issues that the Committee considered during its deliberations of the proposed levels for strength of evidence, proposed framework for the presumptive disability decision-making process, and recommendations. The Committee and IOM staff are grateful for the level of interest demonstrated and information that was shared.

IOM staff assembled an extensive electronic library of public laws, *Federal Register* notices, and all related presumptive disability decision documents with the assistance of librarians and experts at the Library of Congress. These individuals provided assistance in assembling an enormous knowledge base—from microfiche to electronic files—for the Committee, which was extensively researched and used throughout the study process. IOM staff is greatly indebted to the staff at the Library of Congress for these efforts.

The Committee was provided invaluable background information and expertise from IOM staff, including Rose Marie Martinez, David Butler, Jennifer Cohen, Carolyn Fulco, Abigail Mitchell, and Mary Paxton, during the course of the study. The Committee would like to thank these individuals for their contributions.

The Committee was fortunate to have the assistance of two knowledgeable consultants throughout the study. Melissa McDiarmid provided invaluable scientific input to the Committee's efforts. Robert Epley provided guidance on VA processes and background. The Committee is indebted to both of these individuals for the time and efforts they contributed.

Finally, the Committee would like to acknowledge the support of the IOM staff. The Committee would like to recognize, in particular, the efforts of Catherine Bodurow (Study Director) who worked tirelessly over the course of the study. The Committee is also particularly appreciative of the efforts of Morgan Ford (Program Officer), Alice Vorosmarti (Research Associate), and Reine Homawoo (Senior Program Assistant) who supported the study at its conclusion and delivered this report. The Committee would also like to recognize Frederick Erdtmann (Board Director) who attended each of the Committee meetings and provided assistance throughout the study. There were many who provided part-time staff support to the committee's efforts over the course of the study. These additional staff included: Leslie Sim (Program Officer), Cara James (Research Associate), Anisha Dharshi (Research Associate), Kristen Butler (Research Assistant), Kristen Gilbertson (Research Assistant), Jon Sanders (Program Associate), and Vera Diaz (Intern). Additional staff support included assistance from: Andrea Cohen (Financial Associate), Pamela Ramey-McCray (Administrative Assistant), Lara Andersen (Office of Reports and Communication), and Mark Goodin (Copyeditor). The staff would also like to acknowledge William McLeod (Senior Librarian, The National Academies) who provided invaluable support throughout the study.

Contents

Appendixes[1]

[1] Appendixes D-M can be found on a CD attached to the back of the report cover.

Tables, Figures, and Boxes

TABLES

FIGURES

BOXES

Acronyms and Abbreviations

ACB	Army Classification Battery
ACES-EM	Automated Civil Engineering System-Environmental Management
ACHRE	Advisory Committee on Human Radiation Experiments
ADA	American Diabetes Association
AEC	Atomic Energy Commission
AF	Attributable fraction
AF-EMIS	Air Force Environmental Management Information System
AFCESA	Air Force Civil Engineer Support Agency
AFHLTA	Armed Forces Health Longitudinal Technology Application
AFHS	Air Force Health Study
AFHSC	Armed Forces Health Surveillance Center
AHA	American Heart Association
AHLTA	Armed Forces Health Longitudinal Technology Application
AhR	Aryl hydrocarbon receptor
AIDS	Acquired immunodeficiency syndrome
AIS	Automated information systems
ALS	Amyotrophic lateral sclerosis (Lou Gehrig's disease)
AML	Acute myelogenous leukemia
ANG	Air National Guard
ANLL	Acute non-lymphocytic leukemia

APIMS	Air Program Information Management System
AS	Assigned share
ASTM	American Society for Testing and Materials
ATSDR	Agency for Toxic Substances and Disease Registry
BEIR	Biological Effects of Ionizing Radiation
BMI	Body mass index
C&P Service	Compensation and Pension Service
CCB	Configuration Control Board
CCS	Command Core System (Air Force)
CDC	Centers for Disease Control and Prevention
CDVA	Commonwealth Department of Veterans' Affairs
CERHR	Center for the Evaluation of Risks to Human Reproduction
CES-D	Centers for Epidemiological Studies-Depression Scale
CFR	Code of Federal Regulations
CHD	Coronary heart disease
CHF	Congestive heart failure
CHPPM	Center for Health Promotion and Preventive Medicine (Army)
CI	Confidence interval
CIA	Central Intelligence Agency
CIRRPC	Committee on Interagency Radiation Research and Policy Coordination
CLL	Chronic lymphocytic leukemia
CNS	Central nervous system
COPD	Chronic obstructive pulmonary disease
CRDP	Concurrent Retirement and Disability Payments
CRS	Congressional Research Service
CRSC	Combat-Related Special Compensation
CSM	Cerebrospinal malformation
CSP	Cooperative Studies Program
CVD	Cardiovascular disease
DALY	Disability-adjusted life year
DCI SCI	Director of Central Intelligence Sensitive Compartmented Information Programs
DECC-D	Defense Enterprise Computing Center-Detachment
DHHS	Department of Health and Human Services
DISA	Defense Information Systems Agency
DMDC	Defense Manpower Data Center

DMSS	Defense Medical Surveillance System
DNBI	Disease and nonbattle injury
DoA	Department of the Army
DoD	Department of Defense
DoDI	Department of Defense Instruction
DOE	Department of Energy
DOEHRS	Defense Occupational and Environmental Health Readiness System
DoL	Department of Labor
DSM-III-R	Diagnostic and Statistical Manual of Mental Disorders, Third Edition, Revised
DTAS	Defense Theater Accountability Software
EA	Exposure Assessment
EAR	Excess absolute risk
EEOICPA	Energy Employees Occupational Illness Compensation Program Act
EESOH-MIS	Enterprise Environmental Safety and Occupational Health-Management Information System
EO	Executive Order
EPA	Environmental Protection Agency
EPCRA	Emergency Planning and Community Right-to-Know Act
ERIC	Epidemiologic Research and Information Center
ERR	Excess relative risk
FECA	Federal Employees' Compensation Act
FERS	Federal Employees Retirement System
FHIE	Federal Health Information Exchange
FHP	Force Health Protection
fMRI	Functional magnetic resonance imaging
FN	False negative
FNR	False negative rate
FOUO	For official use only
FP	False positive
FPR	False positive rate
FR	Federal Register
FY	Fiscal Year
GAF	Global Assessment of Functioning
GAO	Government Accountability Office
GBD	General birth defect
GBS	Guillain-Barre syndrome

GPS	Global Positioning System
GT test	General Technical test
GW	Gulf War
Gy	Gray (measure of dose of irradiation)
HART	Health Assessment Review Tool
HCFA	Health Care Financing Administration
HEW	U.S. Department of Health, Education, and Welfare
HHIM	Health Hazard Information Module
HIV	Human immunodeficiency virus
HMMS	Hazardous Materials Management System
HUS	Hemolytic-uremic syndrome
IARC	International Agency for Research on Cancer
ICD	International Classification of Diseases
IH	Industrial hygiene
IHIMS	Industrial Hygiene Information Management System (Navy)
IOM	Institute of Medicine
IQ	Intelligence quotient
IREP	Interactive RadioEpidemiological Program
IU	Individual unemployability
LIMDIS	Limited Dissemination
LMF	Lovelace Medical Foundation
MDS	Myelodysplastic syndrome
MFUA	Medical Follow-up Agency
MMPI	Minnesota Multiphasic Personality Inventory
MOA	Memorandum of Agreement
MOS	Military occupational specialty
MRI	Magnetic resonance imaging
MS	Multiple sclerosis
MTF	Military Treatment Facility
NAS	National Academy of Sciences
NCEH	National Center for Environmental Health
NCHS	National Center for Health Statistics
NCI	National Cancer Institute
NEHC	Navy Environmental Health Center
NESHAP	National Emission Standards for Hazardous Air Pollutants
NHANES	National Health and Nutrition Examination Survey
NHL	Non-Hodgkin's lymphoma

NHLBI	National Heart, Lung, and Blood Institute
NHS	Nurses Health Study
NIH	National Institutes of Health
NIOSH	National Institute for Occupational Safety and Health
NOCONTRACT	Not releasable to contractors
NOED	Navy Occupational Exposure Database
NOFORN	Not releasable to foreign nationals
NPV	Negative predictive value
NRC	National Research Council
NTP	National Toxicology Program
NTS	Nevada Test Site
OEF	Operation Enduring Freedom
OEH	Occupational and environmental health
OEHHA	Office of Environmental Health Hazard Assessment
OEHS	Occupational environmental health and safety
OEL	Occupational exposure limit
OGC	Office of the General Counsel
OH	Occupational health
OHMIS	Occupational Health Management Information System
OIF	Operation Iraqi Freedom
OMB	Office of Management and Budget
OPHEH	Office of Public Health and Environmental Hazards
OPM	Office of Personnel Management
OR	Odds ratio
ORCON	Originator controlled dissemination and extraction of information
ORD	Office of Research and Development
OSHA	Occupational Safety and Health Administration
OSTP	Office of Science and Technology Policy
PAF	Population attributable fraction
PAR	Population attributable risk
PC	Probability of causation
PCB	Polychlorinated biphenyl
PDDM	Presumptive disability decision making
PHA	Periodic health assessment
PKDL	Post-kala-azar dermal leishmaniasis
PL	Public Law
POM	Program Objectives Memorandum
POW	Prisoner of War
PPB	Parts per billion
PPG	Pacific Proving Grounds

PPM	Parts per million
PPV	Positive predictive value
PSA	Prostate-specific antigen
PSG II	Professional Staffing Group II
PTF	Presidential Task Force
PTSD	Posttraumatic stress disorder
PY	Person-year
RADS	Reactive airways dysfunction syndrome
RCT	Randomized controlled/clinical trial
RD	Restricted data
ReA	Reactive arthritis
RECA	Radiation Exposure Compensation Act of 1990
RECAC	Radiation Exposure Compensation Act Committee
REVCA	Radiation-Exposed Veterans Compensation Act
RO	Rey-Osterreith Test
ROC	Receiver Operator Characteristics curve
RR	Relative risk/risk ratio
RTI	Research Triangle Institute
SAD	Service-attributable disease
SAF	Service-attributable fraction
SANG	Saudi Arabian National Guard
SAP	Special Access Program
SCI	Sensitive Compartmented Information
SCID	Structured Clinical Interview for Diagnostic and Statistical Manual of Mental Disorders
SCL	Symptoms Checklist
SEER	Surveillance Epidemiology and End Results
SEG	Similar exposure group
SES	Socioeconomic status
SF	Standard Form
SFFWG	Shared Functions Focus Working Group
SHAD	Project Shipboard Hazard and Defense
SMITREC	Serious Mental Illness Treatment Research and Evaluation Center
SMR	Standardized mortality ratio
SSA	Social Security Administration
SSDI	Social Security Disability Insurance
SSI	Supplemental Security Income
TBI	Traumatic brain injury
TCDD	Tetrachlorodibenzo-*p*-dioxin

TN	True negative
TNR	True negative rate
TP	True positive
TPR	True positive rate
UNSCEAR	United Nations Scientific Committee on the Effects of Atomic Radiation
USC	United States Code
USPSTF	U.S. Preventive Health Services Task Force
VA	Department of Veterans Affairs
VAO	Veterans and Agent Orange
VASRD	Veterans Administration Schedule for Rating Disabilities
VBA	Veterans Benefits Administration
VDBC	Veterans' Disability Benefits Commission
VDRECSA	Veterans' Dioxin and Radiation Exposure Compensation Standards Act
VES	Vietnam Experience Study
VET (registry)	Vietnam Era Twin (registry)
VHA	Veterans Health Administration
VHI	Veterans Health Initiative
VISTA	Veterans Health Information Systems and Technology Architecture
VOC	Volatile organic compound
VSO	Veterans Service Organization
WAIS-R	Wechsler Adult Intelligence Scale-Revised
WNINTEL	Warning notice, intelligence sources, and methods involved
WRIISC	War-Related Illness and Injury Study Centers
WWI	World War I
WWII	World War II
YLD	Years of life lived with disability
YLL	Years of life lost

General Summary

The United States has long recognized and honored the service and sacrifices of its military and veterans. Veterans who have been injured by their service (whether their injury appears during service or afterwards) are owed appropriate health care and disability compensation. For some medical conditions that develop after military service, the scientific information needed to connect the health conditions to the circumstances of service may be incomplete. When information is incomplete, Congress or the Department of Veterans Affairs (VA) may need to make a "presumption" of service connection so that a group of veterans can be appropriately compensated. The missing information may be about the specific exposures of the veterans, or there may be incomplete scientific evidence as to whether an exposure during service causes the health condition of concern. For example, when the exposures of military personnel in Vietnam to Agent Orange could not be clearly documented, a presumption was established that all those who set foot on Vietnam soil were exposed to Agent Orange.

The Institute of Medicine (IOM) Committee was charged with reviewing and describing how presumptions have been made in the past and, if needed, to make recommendations for an improved scientific framework that could be used in the future for determining if a presumption should be made. The Committee was asked to consider and describe the processes of all participants in the current presumptive disability decision-making process for veterans. The Committee was not asked to offer an opinion about past presumptive decisions or to suggest specific future presumptions. The Committee heard from a range of groups that figure into this decision-making process, including past and present staffers from Congress, the VA, the IOM, veterans service organizations, and individual veterans. The Department of Defense (DoD) briefed the Committee about its current activities and plans to better track the exposures and health conditions of military personnel. The Committee further documented the current process by developing case studies around exposures and health conditions for which presumptions had been made. The Committee also reviewed general methods by which scientists, as well as government and other organizations, evaluate scientific evidence in order to determine if a specific exposure causes a health condition.

The history of presumptions is a fascinating and complex story. In 1921 Congress empowered the VA Administrator (now Secretary) to establish presumptions of service connection for veterans. Only Congress and VA have the authority to establish presumptions for veterans. Since 1921, nearly 150 health outcomes have been service-connected on a presumptive basis by Congress and VA. This process has evolved over the years. The current process for making presumptions can be traced to the Agent Orange Act of 1991 (Public Law 102-4. 102d Cong., 2d Sess.), an act that established a model for decision making by VA that still stands today. In the 1991 Act, Congress asked VA to contract with an independent organization to review the scientific evidence on Agent Orange. VA turned to the IOM of the National Academy of Sciences to carry out these reviews. Subsequently, VA turned to IOM for issues arising from the 1990 Gulf War. Based on the work of a committee, IOM provides VA with reports that describe the strength of evidence that links agents of concern with specific health conditions. VA uses IOM reports and other information in an internal decision-making process to decide whether a presumption will be made.

The Committee carefully studied the current approach to presumptive disability decision making and examined a number of specific case examples. This assessment led to a number of recommendations to improve the process:

- As the case studies demonstrated, Congress could provide a clearer and more consistent charge on how much evidence is needed to make a presumption. There should be clarity as to whether the finding of an association in one or more studies is sufficient or the evidence should support causation.
- Due to lack of clarity and consistency in congressional language and VA's charges to the committees, IOM committees have taken somewhat varying approaches since 1991 in reviewing the scientific evidence and in forming their opinions on the possibility that exposures during military service contributed to causing a health condition. Future committees could improve their review and classification of scientific evidence if they were given clear and consistent charges and followed uniform evaluation procedures.

• The internal processes by which the VA makes its presumptive decisions following receipt of an IOM report have been unclear. VA should adopt transparent and consistent approaches for making these decisions.

• Complete exposure data and health condition information for military personnel (both individuals and groups) usually have not been available from DoD in the past. Such information is one of the most critical pieces of evidence for improving the determination of links between exposures and health conditions.

All of these improvements are feasible over the longer term and are needed to ensure that the presumptive disability decision-making process for veterans is based on the best possible scientific evidence. Decisions about disability compensation and related benefits (e.g., medical care) for veterans should be based on the best possible documentation and evidence of their military exposures as well as on the best possible information on any health conditions caused by these exposures. While it is impossible to provide certainty in every case, a fresh approach could do much to improve the current process. The Committee's recommended approach (Figure GS-1) has several parts:

• An open process for nominating exposures and health conditions for review; involving all stakeholders in this process is critical

• A revised process for evaluating scientific information on whether a given exposure causes a health condition in veterans; this includes a new set of categories to assess the strength of the evidence for causation, and an estimate of the numbers of exposed veterans whose health condition can be attributed to their military exposure

• A consistent and transparent decision-making process by VA

• A system for tracking the exposures of military personnel (including chemical, biological, infectious, physical, and psychological stressors), and for monitoring the health conditions of all military personnel while in service and after separation

• An organizational structure to support this process

To support the Committee's recommendations, we suggest the creation of two panels. One is an Advisory Committee (advisory to VA), that would assemble, consider, and give priority to the exposures and health conditions proposed for possible presumptive evaluation. Nominations for presumptions could come from veterans and other stakeholders as well as from health tracking, surveillance, and research. The second panel would be a Science Review Board, an independent body, which would evaluate the strength of the evidence (based on causation) that links a health condition to a military exposure and then estimates the fraction of exposed veterans

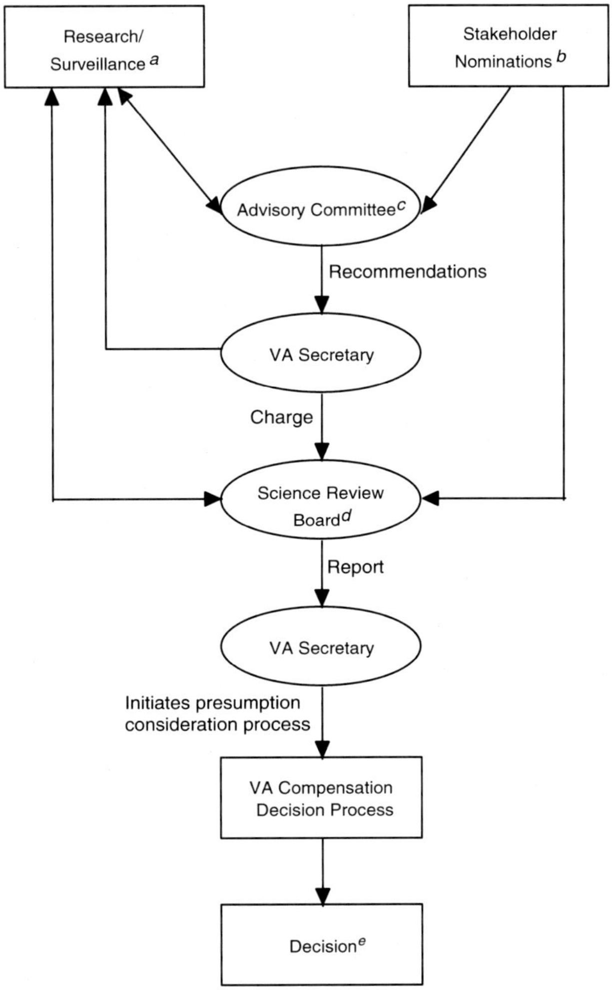

FIGURE GS-1 Proposed framework for future presumptive disability decision-making process for veterans.

[a] Includes research for classified or secret activities, exposures, etc.

[b] Includes veterans, Veterans Service Organizations, federal agencies, scientists, general public, etc.

[c] This committee screens stakeholders' proposals and research in support of evaluating evidence for presumptions and makes recommendations to the VA Secretary when full evidence review or additional research is appropriate.

[d] The board conducts a two-step evidence review process (see report text for further detail).

[e] Final presumptive disability compensation decisions are made by the Secretary, Department of Veterans Affairs, unless legislated by Congress.

whose health condition could be attributed to their military exposure. The Science Review Board's report and recommendations would go to VA for its consideration. VA would use explicit criteria to render a decision by the VA Secretary with regard to whether a presumption would be established. In addition, the Science Review Board would monitor information on the health of veterans as it accumulates over time in the DoD and VA tracking systems, and nominate new exposures or health conditions for evaluation as appropriate.

This Committee recommends that the following principles be adopted in establishing this new approach:

1. Stakeholder inclusiveness
2. Evidence-based decisions
3. Transparent process
4. Flexibility
5. Consistency
6. Causation, not just association, as the target for decision making

The Committee suggests that its framework be considered as the model to guide the evolution of the current approach. While some aspects of the approach may appear challenging or infeasible at present, feasibility would be improved with the full implementation of the Committee's recommendations, provision of appropriate resources to all of the participants in the presumptive disability decision-making process for veterans, and future methodological developments. DoD and VA have already been discussing various aspects of improving exposure and health tracking and how the two agencies can share data and information with each other. Veterans deserve to have these improvements accomplished as soon as possible.

Summary

INTRODUCTION

The United States has long recognized and honored military veterans' service and sacrifices. Veterans injured by their service, becoming ill while in service, or having an illness after discharge as a long-term consequence of their service have been given healthcare coverage and disability compensation. As the complexity of exposures during combat has increased, the list of service-connected illnesses has grown. The Department of Veterans Affairs (VA) now provides disability compensation to approximately 2.6 million veterans for 7.7 million disabilities annually, expending approximately $24 billion for this purpose (VBA, 2006, pp. 19, 24, 27).

Disability compensation for military veterans requires that there be a service connection. A medical illness or injury that occurred while a member was in military service is considered service connected whether caused by or aggravated by an exposure or event during service *or simply occurring coincidentally* with military service. However, if a medical condition appears after the period of military service and it is presumed to be caused by or aggravated by an exposure or an event that occurred during military service, then veterans may receive compensation based on that presumption (Pamperin, 2006).

In making a decision to provide compensation, VA needs to determine whether the illness of concern can generally be caused by exposures received during service and whether the illness in a specific claimant was caused by the exposure. The answer to the general question of causality comes from a careful review of all available scientific information, while the answer to the question of causation in a specific person hinges on knowledge of the exposure received by that individual and of other factors that may be relevant. If the scientific evidence is incomplete, there may be uncertainty on the question of causation generally; if there is limited or no information on exposure of individual claimants or if other factors also contribute to disease causation, there may be uncertainty on the question of individual causation.

To provide benefits to veterans in the face of these two broad types of uncertainty, Congress and VA make presumptive decisions that bridge gaps in the evidence related to causation and to exposure. Presumptions may relieve the veteran of persuading VA that the exposure produced the adverse health outcome and of proving that an exposure occurred during military service (Pamperin, 2006). Once a medical condition is service connected through presumptions, and the veteran can document military service consistent with having received the given exposure, the veteran only has to show the basic fact that he or she suffers from the condition in order to receive a disability payment and eligibility for medical care (Zeglin, 2006).

In 2004, Congress established the Veterans' Disability Benefits Commission (the Commission), which was charged with "studying the benefits provided to compensate and assist veterans for disabilities attributable to military service" (VDBC, 2006, p. 1; as found in Appendix A). The Commission identified the presumptive disability decision-making process as a topic needing assessment and asked the Institute of Medicine (IOM) to establish a committee for this purpose that would be funded by VA. The resulting committee, the Committee on Evaluation of the Presumptive Disability Decision-Making Process for Veterans (the Committee), was given the following charge by VA:

- Describe and evaluate the current model used to recognize diseases that are subject to service connection on a presumptive basis.
- If appropriate, propose a scientific framework that would justify recognizing or not recognizing conditions as presumptive.

The Commission further elaborated the charge, asking the Committee to "help ensure that future veterans are granted service connection under a presumptive basis based on the best scientific evidence available" (VDBC, 2006, p. 4; as found in Appendix A). The Commission asked the Committee to "evaluate the current model used to determine diseases that qualify for service connection on a presumptive basis, and if appropriate, propose improvements in the model" (VDBC, 2006, p. 1; as found in Appendix A). The Commission emphasized that "having a method of granting service connection quickly and fairly based on a presumption is of critical importance to our disabled veterans and their surviving spouses" and that "ensuring that future presumption processes reflect the then current medical knowledge about the causal relationship would benefit the entire veteran community" (VDBC, 2006, p. 4; as found in Appendix A). The Commission's summary statement further commented that "[t]o the extent possible, suggestions that will avoid the necessity for many future presumptions by ensuring that exposure of service members is documented and scientific evidence is made available would be important" (VDBC, 2006, p. 4; as found in Appendix A).

IOM appointed a 14-member committee that covered the broad scientific and medical areas of general, occupational, and psychiatric medicine; biostatistics; epidemiology; toxicology; industrial hygiene; and exposure and risk assessment. The Committee's members also brought expertise in law, philosophy, causal decision making, and policy as well as knowledge of the Department of Defense (DoD) and VA's approach to disability compensation.

THE COMMITTEE'S APPROACH TO ITS CHARGE

In fulfilling its charge, the Committee first investigated and attempted to characterize Congress' and VA's recent approach to presumptive disability decision making, and then developed a conceptual framework for a new, more evidence-based process. It then constructed a way to move forward that builds on the framework and addresses deficiencies of the current process.

The Committee held three open meetings to gather information on the current presumptive disability decision-making process. The Committee heard from past and present congressional staff members, representatives of VA, DoD, IOM, various stakeholder groups (e.g., veteran service organizations [VSOs]) and the general public. Committee members also participated in conference calls with DoD experts on medical surveillance and exposure data collection and exposure assessment systems.

The Committee reviewed extensive background information including: documents provided by the Commission, public laws and supporting House and Senate reports, *Federal Register* notices, VA documents (e.g., cost estimates, a white paper on VA's decision-making processes [found in Appendix G], and responses by VA to written questions from the Committee), DoD documents, and past IOM reports commissioned by DoD and VA. The Committee conducted 10 case study reviews—Mental Disorders' Presumptions, Multiple Sclerosis Presumption, Prisoners of War Presumptions, Amputees and Cardiovascular Disease Presumption, Radiation Presumptions, Mustard Gas and Lewisite Presumptions, Gulf War Presumptions, Agent Orange and Prostate Cancer Presumption, Agent Orange and Type 2

Diabetes Presumption, and Spina Bifida Program (not a presumption but a VA program area)—that cover a wide variety of circumstances for which presumptions have been established by Congress and VA since 1921. The case studies were a foundation for the Committee's efforts in understanding past practices of all participants in the presumptive disability decision-making process (see Appendix I).

The Committee also researched and considered capabilities and limitations of the exposure data and health outcome information available to DoD and VA for exposure assessment, surveillance, and research purposes. The Committee examined whether DoD and VA have a strategic research plan and vision for the necessary interface between the agencies, as well as with other, relevant research organizations.

The Committee considered the use of scientific evidence in guiding the process for making presumptive decisions that affect the compensation of veterans. Drawing upon the Committee members' expertise in epidemiology, medicine, toxicology, biostatistics, and causal decision making, the Committee covered the evaluation of evidence for inferring association and causation as well as methods for quantifying the contribution of an agent to disease causation in populations and extending this quantification to individuals. Using this framework, the Committee developed an evidence-based approach for making future decisions with regard to presumptions.

THE PRESUMPTIVE DISABILITY DECISION-MAKING PROCESS FOR VETERANS

In 1921 Congress empowered the VA Administrator (now Secretary) to establish presumptions of service connection for veterans. Only Congress and the VA Secretary have the authority to establish presumptions. Over time, presumptions have been made to relieve veterans of the burden to prove that disability or illness was caused by a specific exposure that occurred during military service (e.g., Prisoners of War). Since 1921, nearly 150 health outcomes have been service connected on a presumptive basis (see Appendix F). In February 2006, Congress codified all regulatory presumptions that VA had put in place to that time.

The current presumptive disability decision-making process for veterans involves several steps and several organizations. The process involves input from many parties—Congress, VA, the National Academies, and stakeholders (e.g., VSOs, advisory committees, and individual veterans) (Figure S-1). Congress has made presumptions itself. In the current model, Congress or stakeholders acting through Congress may call on VA to assess whether a presumption is needed. The VA turns to IOM for completion of a review of the scientific evidence. The findings of that evaluation are consid-

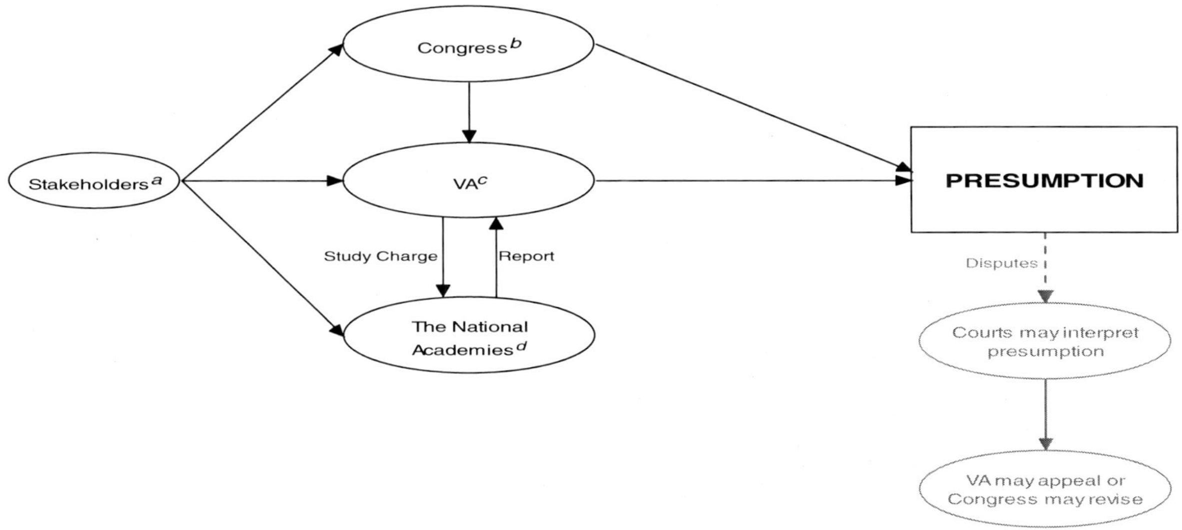

FIGURE S-1 Roles of the participants involved in the presumptive disability decision-making process for veterans.

[a] Stakeholders include (but are not limited to) veterans service organizations (VSOs), veterans, advisory groups, federal agencies, and the general public; these stakeholders provide input into the presumptive process by communicating with Congress, VA, and independent organizations (e.g., the National Academies).

[b] Congress has created many presumptions itself; in 1921, Congress also empowered the VA Secretary to create regulatory presumptions; on several occasions in the past, Congress has directed VA to contract with an independent organization (e.g., the National Academies) to conduct studies and then use the organization's report in its deliberations of granting or not granting regulatory presumptions.

[c] VA can establish regulatory presumptions; VA sometimes contracts with the National Academies to conduct studies and uses the organization's report in its deliberations of granting or not granting regulatory presumptions.

[d] The National Academies (Institute of Medicine and National Research Council) submit reports to VA based on requests and study charges from VA.

ered by VA in its presumptive disability decision-making process. Decisions made in the courts have also influenced the current presumptive process.

Three major legislative actions by Congress have influenced the recent presumptive decisions—the Radiation Exposed Veterans Compensation Act of 1988 (Public Law 100-321. 100th Cong., 2d Sess.), the Agent Orange Act of 1991 (Public Law 102-4. 102d Cong., 1st Sess.), and the Persian Gulf War Acts of 1995 (Veterans' Benefits Improvement Act of 1994. Public Law 103-446. 103rd Cong., 2d Sess.) and 1998 (Making Omnibus Consolidated and Emergency Appropriations for the Fiscal Year Ending September 30, 1999, and for Other Purposes. Public Law 105-277. 105th Cong., 2d Sess.). The concept of "at least as likely as not" with regard to exposure potential was introduced for radiation exposures and its use has since been continued. The Agent Orange Act (Public Law 102-4. 102d Cong., 1st Sess.) grew out of events following the Vietnam War, and its language expresses substantial and significant elements of the presumptive story. The presumptions put in place by Congress for Gulf War illnesses represent the first time that Congress produced a list of health outcomes that it defined as "undiagnosed illnesses" (Veterans Education and Benefits Expansion Act of 2001. Public Law 107-103. 107th Cong., 1st Sess.).

When Congress enacted the Agent Orange Act of 1991 (Public Law 102-4. 102d Cong., 1st Sess.), it started a model for a decision-making process that is still in place. Congress asked VA to contract with an independent organization—VA contracted with IOM—to review the scientific evidence for Agent Orange. Since 1994, IOM has produced biennial reports on Agent Orange for VA to use as it considers making presumptive decisions (IOM, 1994, 1996, 1999, 2001, 2003b, 2005b). IOM has also delivered five volumes on the Gulf War (IOM, 2000a, 2003a, 2005a, 2006, 2007). Congress requires VA to respond after receiving an IOM report with a determination as to whether VA will make a service connection for particular health outcomes on a presumptive basis. VA has described its internal decision-making processes to the Committee in a general fashion, and the Committee has reviewed VA's *Federal Register* notices and documents (see Chapter 3). However, it remains unclear to the Committee how VA makes particular determinations with regard to weighing strength of evidence for causation and exposure potential in making its presumptive decisions.

Analysis of the Agent Orange and Gulf War case studies (see Appendix I) shows important similarities and differences relevant to the overall presumptive process. One difference is that Agent Orange is a single product (actually a mixture of compounds that contains the contaminant dioxin), extensively researched for associated health outcomes, whereas the health consequences of the Gulf War are unlikely to be the result of any single agent. Military service men and women may have received a number of health-relevant exposures during service in the Persian Gulf, complicating the development of evidence reviews. For Agent Orange, there is one exposure of concern and a more constrained set of health indicators. There have been some differences in approaches of Agent Orange and Gulf War committees. The IOM Agent Orange reports (IOM, 1994, 1996, 1999, 2001, 2003b, 2005b) did not explicitly include a causal category in their evaluations whereas recent Gulf War reports (IOM, 2000a, 2003a, 2005a, 2006, 2007) did include a category for evidence sufficient to infer causation when characterizing the strength of evidence for agents evaluated. For neither set of reports does VA describe in its *Federal Register* notices how it accounted for exposure potential or magnitude in making its presumptive decisions.

FINDINGS OF CASE STUDIES

The case studies offered a diverse set of lessons learned and indicated elements of the current process that need to be addressed. In carrying out the case studies, this Committee had the opportunity to retrospectively examine the work of IOM committees as they grappled with the challenge of using uncertain evidence and of VA staff as they used the findings of IOM committees to make decisions about presumptions. The case studies demonstrate that the process has acted to serve the interests of veterans in many instances. Congress and VA have repeatedly acted to maximize the sensitivity of presumptive decisions so as to assure that no veteran who might have been affected is denied compensation. On the other hand, in maximizing sensitivity of presumptive disability decision making, substantial numbers of veterans whose illnesses may or may not have been actually service related are nonetheless compensated. There are both financial and nonfinancial costs to such decisions.

The case studies illustrate the use of presumptions to cover gaps in evidence, gaps that exist in part because of lack of information on exposures received by military personnel and inadequate surveillance of veterans for service-related illnesses. Secrecy is a particularly troubling source of incomplete information, as illustrated by the veterans who participated in studies of mustard gas and lewisite. Research carried out directly on the health of veterans has proved useful in some instances, leading to a decision, for example, on granting disability compensation for cardiovascular disease in amputees. But the research has not been systematic, and in the example of cardiovascular disease in amputees no further evidence relevant to a presumption made in 1979 has been collected. Research on radiation risks in veterans has been severely constrained by a lack of dose information, and the studies on radiation-exposed veterans have not been highly informative.

Across the case studies, the Committee found variable approaches to synthesizing evidence on the health consequences of military service. The inferential target of scientific evidence reviews has not been consistent and varied between causation (e.g., mustard gas and lewisite, Gulf War) and association alone (e.g., Agent Orange). The more recent IOM Agent Orange reports have emphasized findings of observational studies on association and interpretation that might have been enhanced by placing the findings within a biological framework strengthened by greater attention to other lines of evidence. In the Agent Orange case studies, the category "limited/suggestive" for classifying evidence for association has been used for a broad range of evidence from indicating the mere possibility of an association to showing that an association is possibly causal. The "limited/suggestive" evidence of association—on which the VA's presumptive decisions to compensate type 2 diabetes and prostate cancer were made—may be below the level of certainty needed to support causation absent strong mechanistic understanding or to meet the congressional language of "if the credible evidence for the association is equal to or outweighs the credible evidence against the association," which the Committee refers to "at least as likely as not."

Both prostate cancer and type 2 diabetes illustrate situations in which the contribution of military exposures should be assessed against a background of disease risk that has other strong determinants: age in the case of prostate cancer and family history and obesity in the case of type 2 diabetes, as indicated by the IOM committee in its report (IOM, 2000b). For both type 2 diabetes and prostate cancer, the magnitude of the relative risks observed for pesticide exposure implies that the contribution of military exposures is likely to be small in comparison to those of the other contributing factors. In such circumstances, an estimation of the proportion of cases attributable to military exposures could be helpful to the VA in considering whether or not to presumptively service-connect disabilities. The Committee recognizes that development of such estimations is a complicated process dependent on acquiring better exposure data, which may not be available for some period of time.

In the case studies, the Committee's analyses were based on the very general information provided by VA about its internal decision-making processes. The case studies and VA's decision to withhold documents related to specific decisions from the Committee did make clear, however, that these processes are not fully transparent. VA believes that access to predecisional documents by outside sources could stifle candid staff discussions on issues. Once IOM carries out its reviews and provides VA with reports documenting the extent of evidence available on associations, the internal processes of VA that follow are not fully open to scrutiny. This closed process could reduce trust of veterans in the presumptive disability decision-making process and may hinder efforts to optimize the use of scientific evidence. The Committee also found inconsistency in the decision-making process.

SCIENTIFIC FOUNDATION FOR PRESUMPTIVE DISABILITY DECISION MAKING

In developing a future approach for presumptive disability decision making, the Committee first gave extensive consideration to causal inference and the processes used to make causal judgments. In other words, the Committee considered how scientific evidence is used to determine *if* exposure causes some disease. These determinations are generally made by expert committees that examine all relevant evidence for strengths and weaknesses and then synthesize the evidence to make a summary judgment. The Committee defines "exposure" in a broad manner to include chemical, biological, infectious, physical, and psychological stressors. The Committee recognizes that psychological stressors may be particularly difficult to describe, let alone measure and quantify.

The Committee then considered the quantification of the contribution of a particular exposure to disease causation. This second issue addresses the question of *how much* of the observed disease in a group, in both absolute and relative terms, is caused by the exposure.

Provision of compensation to veterans on a presumptive basis, or to any other group that has been injured, requires a *general* decision as to whether the agent or exposure of concern has the potential to cause the condition or disease for which compensation is to be provided in at least some individuals, and a *specific* decision as to whether the agent or exposure has caused the condition or disease in a particular individual. The determination of causation in general is based in a review and evaluation of all relevant evidence including (1) data on exposures of military personnel during service; (2) evidence on risks for disease coming from observational (epidemiologic) studies of military personnel; (3) other relevant epidemiologic evidence, including findings from studies of nonmilitary populations exposed to the agent of interest or similar agents; and (4) findings relevant to plausibility from experimental and laboratory research. The determination of causation in a particular case is based first on the general determination as to whether the exposure can cause disease, then on information about the exposures of the individual being evaluated for compensation, and on any other relevant information about the individual.

The Committee considered the properties of a decision-making process, recognizing the possibility of two types of systematic errors: making a decision to compensate when the exposure has not caused the illness (false positive) and to not compensate when the exposure has actually caused the illness (false negative). The Committee recommends that any decision process consider the trade-off between these two errors and attempt to optimize both the sensitivity (i.e., minimize the false negatives) and the specificity (i.e., minimize the false positives). Generally, higher sensitivity cannot be achieved without lower specificity. These errors have costs. False positive errors result in the expenditure of funds for cases of disease not caused by military service while false negative errors leave deserving veterans uncompensated. The appropriate balancing of these costs also needs consideration.

The Committee considered ways to classify evidence, reaching the conclusion that a broader and more inclusive evidence review process is needed. It found that IOM reviews could be enhanced if a broader array of epidemiologic and other evidence (e.g., animal and mechanistic data) was considered. The Committee also found that the target of inference had varied from causation (e.g., mustard gas and lewisite, Gulf War) to association (e.g., Agent Orange). Consequently, the Committee recommends that categories of evidence for reviews be established to make clear those relationships that are at least as likely as not to be causal. The Committee has concluded that a categorization of evidence is needed that gives a scientifically coherent rendering of the language employed by Congress in calling for review of available scientific evidence. The Committee proposes a four-level hierarchy that classifies the strength of evidence for *causation, not just association,* and that incorporates the concept of equipoise: that is, whether the weight of scientific evidence makes causation at least as likely as not in the judgment of the reviewing group.

The Committee also gave consideration to the quantification of the burden of disease attributable to an exposure. This quantification would be made to provide an evaluation of the numbers of veterans to be compensated, but it would not be a component of the evidence evaluation for causation. For the purpose of quantification, the attributable risk, termed the *service-attributable fraction*, can be calculated if the needed information is available on the relative risk of disease among exposed individuals. For those exposures meeting the necessary level of evidence for compensation, the Committee recommends that the service-attributable fraction should be estimated overall and for subgroups of veterans, perhaps grouped by level of exposure, if the requisite data are available. Until more complete exposure information becomes available in the future, such calculations may not be possible for all conditions for which presumptions are made.

COMMITTEE'S RECOMMENDED APPROACH FOR THE FUTURE

Overview

The Committee's recommended approach for the future (Figure S-2) has multiple new elements: a process for proposing exposures and illnesses for review; a systematic evidence review process incorporating a new evidence classification scheme and quantification of the extent of disease

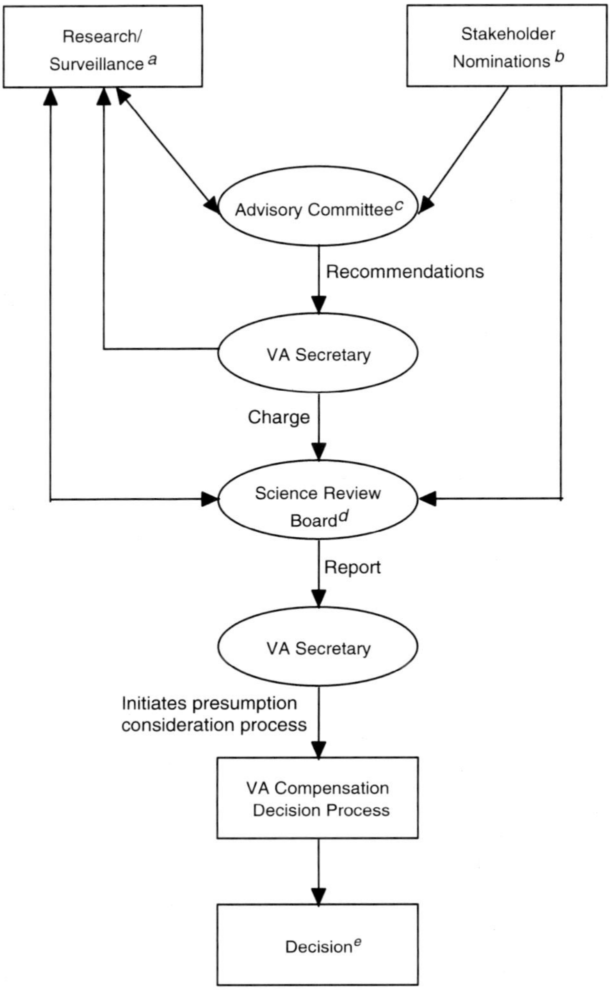

FIGURE S-2 Proposed framework for future presumptive disability decision-making process for veterans.

[a] Includes research for classified or secret activities, exposures, etc.

[b] Includes veterans, Veterans Service Organizations, federal agencies, scientists, general public, etc.

[c] This committee screens stakeholders' proposals and research in support of evaluating evidence for presumptions and makes recommendations to the VA Secretary when full evidence review or additional research is appropriate.

[d] The board conducts a two-step evidence review process (see report text for further detail).

[e] Final presumptive disability compensation decisions are made by the Secretary, Department of Veterans Affairs, unless legislated by Congress.

attributable to an exposure; a transparent decision-making process by VA; and an organizational structure to support the process. The Committee also calls for comprehensive tracking of exposures of military personnel and monitoring of their health while in service and subsequently.

Organizational Structure

The Committee recommends the creation by Congress of two new permanent boards: the Advisory Committee, serving in an advisory capacity to VA, and the Science Review Board (independent from VA). The Advisory Committee would consider the exposures and illnesses that might be a basis for presumptions and recommend to the VA Secretary exposures and illnesses needing further consideration. It would also consider research needs and assist VA with strategic research planning. The Science Review Board would evaluate the evidence for causation and, if warranted, estimate the service-attributable fraction of disease in veterans. One critical element in the deliberations of the Science Review Board would be evidence from monitoring the exposures and health of the veterans. The Science Review Board would provide VA with input for its presumptive decisions, including a summary report of the available scientific evidence in a standardized classification scheme.

Congress and VA may find alternative processes to achieve the overall objective of the Committee's recommendations: an evidence-based approach to making presumptive disability decisions. The Committee recognizes that specific elements of its proposal (e.g., the call for carrying out exposure assessments and making exposure estimates) are not yet fully practicable and would take time to develop and implement. However, future methodologic developments should enhance the feasibility of some of the challenging elements of this proposal. The Committee believes that this proposal can significantly improve the presumptive disability decision-making process for veterans and, therefore, the process for implementing it should begin without delay.

Underlying Principles

VA's decision to make a presumption may involve weighing difficult and incomplete scientific evidence, in the context of veterans' concerns and society's obligations to the affected veterans, and potential costs. Although the potential complexity of the decision-making process may make a complete codification difficult, the underlying principles can be clearly expressed. The Committee suggests the following six principles as a foundation for its proposed framework: (1) stakeholder inclusiveness; (2) evidence-based decisions; (3) transparent process; (4) flexibility; (5) consistency; and (6) using causation, not just association, as the basis for decision making. Flexibility and consistency are not contradictory constructs here. Flexibility refers to the ability to be adaptable through time in evaluating scientific evidence, and consistency refers to being consistent in the process of evaluating evidence and making consistent decisions based on a comparable level of certainty based on the scientific evidence.

Proposals to Review for Potential Presumption

In this process, conditions and causative agents or circumstances would be proposed for review based on evidence of a connection between the condition and military service and evidence that a sizable or well-defined group of veterans is likely to be affected. The possibility of a need for a presumption might arise from surveillance of veterans or active military personnel, laboratory research discoveries, or findings from studies of exposed workers. The process would be open, with proposals accepted from any source (e.g., veterans, veterans' families, VSOs, VA, DoD, other governmental bodies, researchers, the general public). Proposals accepted by the VA Secretary would be sent to the Science Review Board for full, comprehensive scientific evaluation.

Science Review Board

The Committee recommends a two-step process for scientific evaluation by the Science Review Board. The first step would involve a systematic review of all relevant data to decide the strength of evidence for causation, using one of four categories:

1. *Sufficient*: The evidence is sufficient to conclude that a causal relationship exists.
2. *Equipoise and Above*: The evidence is sufficient to conclude that a causal relationship is at least as likely as not, but not sufficient to conclude that a causal relationship exists.
3. *Below Equipoise*: The evidence is not sufficient to conclude that a causal relationship is at least as likely as not, or is not sufficient to make a scientifically informed judgment.
4. *Against*: The evidence suggests the lack of a causal relationship.

If the evidence for causation were categorized as *Sufficient* or at *Equipoise and Above*, then we anticipate that VA would consider a presumptive service connection based upon causal evidence categorization and its consideration of the service-attributable fraction if available (to be estimated in the second step of the process, described below). As is current VA policy, if the evidence is at *Equipoise*, the benefit of the doubt would be given to the veteran. If the evidence were categorized as *Against*, then we anticipate that VA would not consider a presumptive service-connection. If, however, the evidence were categorized as *Below Equipoise*, then we anticipate that VA would, after carefully considering the prospects and recommendations for future research, decide on an appropriate time frame for the subsequent scientific review of the evidence, with the expectation that the evidence would then be sufficient to resolve matters either for or against the causal claim at that time. Such information would be considered by the Advisory Committee serving in its capacity as overseer of the overall process and advisor to the VA Secretary.

If the VA Secretary were to decide that a presumption would not be established for evidence categorized as *Below Equipoise* or, for other reasons, for evidence categorized as *Equipoise and Above*, then during the period of further evidence development and gathering and prior to the subsequent scientific review of the evidence, VA should consider providing some support to potentially affected veterans, such as providing provisional access to medical care.

As evidence accumulates, the balance might move to strengthen or to weaken the case for causality. Importantly, the Science Review Board should be free to upgrade the level of evidence, to downgrade the level of evidence, or to leave it as the same categorization. For evidence that has reached the classification of *Sufficient*, we would not anticipate a potential lowering of the classification, if the original determination was correctly made and based on sound scientific evidence.

If the strength of the evidence reaches *Sufficient* or *Equipoise and Above*, then the evaluation would move to step two, the calculation of the service-attributable fraction of disease when required data and information are available. This calculation is independent of the classification of the strength of evidence for causation, and the magnitude of the service-attributable fraction is not considered in the application of the four-level schema for categorizing evidence. Rather, the service-attributable fraction would be of value for decision making, giving an understanding of the scope of the population to be covered by a presumption.

In step two, the Science Review Board would consider the extent of exposure among veterans and subgroups of veterans, as well as dose-response relationships. When such information is available, the board would estimate the service-attributable fraction and its related uncertainty. The purpose of step two is to convey the impact of the exposure on veterans as a whole for the purpose of decision making and planning, but not to serve inappropriately as an estimate of probability of causation for individuals. Some exposures may contribute greatly to the disease burden of veterans, while other exposure (even with a known causal effect) may have a small impact overall. This additional information would be useful to VA in its decision making as to whether a presumption should be made for the veteran population in general, for subgroups, or not at all. In the absence of service-attributable fraction data, as will likely occur for many exposures over the short term, we assume the VA would consider presumptions on the information contained in step one.

Expanding the Evidence Base

In the Committee's view, the best scientific decisions about presumptions can be made only with comprehensive exposure and health surveillance of military personnel. Data collection should begin on entry into the military and continue through discharge, and when harmful exposures are suspected surveillance should be extended indefinitely. Surveillance refers to the ongoing collection, analysis, and use of data relevant to the health of a population. Elements of a surveillance system are already in place, but fall short of what is required. A fully functioning surveillance system would track military exposures and health outcomes, during military service and after discharge, and maintain a repository of data and biological specimens so that emerging and unanticipated questions could be retrospectively addressed. The system needs to be seamless in following military personnel, including National Guard and reservists, from active duty as they transition and become civilians.

This surveillance system should also track job and deployment history for each Service member through the period of service, with exposure assessment and monitoring for a range of job categories. Information on disease risk factors more generally could also be tracked. Use of personal biological samples for individual monitoring also holds promise.

Assessing exposures relevant to the neuropsychiatric disorders that are frequent among veterans of recent and current combats is particularly problematic. Documentation of stress is requisite to the diagnosis of post-traumatic stress disorder (PTSD), but approaches for capturing exposures to such stressors and to the circumstances of combat have not yet been developed and put into place. Research is needed for this purpose that builds on existing approaches so that data become available over the long-term.

In addition to surveillance, the Committee recommends an effort to coordinate and focus research on the health effects of military exposures. Associations identified in the surveillance data might need follow-up through more focused epidemiologic studies or exposure assessments. Toxicological research might be indicated to explore the mechanistic basis for an association between an exposure and a health condition.

VA Procedures

Ultimately, the decision regarding which proposed topics for potential presumptions deserve full evaluation resides with VA. In the Committee's proposed process, VA also receives scientific input from the Science Review Board. We recommend that VA establish a uniform and transparent process for making decisions regarding presumptions following receipt of evidence reviews. VA should establish procedures with input from the many stakeholders, and a clear, evidence-based rationale should be offered for all decisions. The Committee's recommendations are aimed at providing a sound scientific framework for the presumptive disability decision-making process. The Committee clearly recognizes that there are social, economic, political, and legal factors beyond the scope of scientific evidence that may influence the presumptive disability decision-making process for veterans and the presumptive decisions that are established by Congress and VA.

Scientific evidence is not static, and it often is less than certain. Given that the scientific basis for presumptive decisions will change over time, the Committee recommends that VA should be able to adjust future decisions when such change is scientifically justified. This does not mean that the Committee recommends that benefits previously granted should be terminated. The Committee is aware that disabled veterans and their families are often dependent on such payments and that it could create a hardship to remove them, a matter that VA disability policy recognizes in other situations.

SPECIFIC RECOMMENDATIONS

Based on its evaluation of the current process for establishing presumptive disability decisions and its consideration of alternatives, the Committee has specific recommendations for an approach that would build stronger scientific evidence into the decision-making process and, at the same time, be even more responsive and open to veterans. We propose a transformation of the current presumptive disability decision-making process. We recognize that considerable time would be needed to implement some of these recommendations as would additional investment to create systems needed to track exposures and health status of currently serving military service personnel and veterans. Progress depends on greater research capacity and improvements in the evaluation and utilization of scientific evidence in making compensation decisions. We find that there are elements of the current process that could be changed quickly and we recommend that VA consider prompt action as it moves toward implementation of a new approach. The recommendations that follow are based around the Committee's proposed framework for making presumptive decisions. We list the recommendations in relation to the appropriate body.

Congress

Recommendation 1. Congress should create a formal advisory committee (Advisory Committee) to VA to consider and advise the VA Secretary on disability-related questions requiring scientific research and review to assist in the consideration of possible presumptions.

Recommendation 2. Congress should authorize a permanent independent review body (Science Review Board) operating with a well-defined process that will use evaluation criteria as outlined in this Committee's recommendations to evaluate scientific evidence for VA's use in considering future service-connected presumptions.

Department of Veterans Affairs

Recommendation 3. VA should develop and publish a formal process for consideration of disability presumptions that is uniform and transparent and clearly sets forth all evidence considered and the reasons for the decisions reached.

Science Review Board

The recommendations that follow are directed towards the proposed, future Science Review Board, the entity to be established in the Committee's proposed approach.

Recommendation 4. The Committee recommends that the goal of the presumptive disability decision-making process be to ensure compensation for veterans whose diseases are *caused by* military service and that this goal must serve as the foundation for the work of the Science Review Board. The Committee recommends that the Science Review Board implement its proposed two-step process.

Recommendation 5. The Committee recommends that the Science Review Board use the proposed four-level classification scheme, as follows, in the first step of its evaluation. The Committee recommends that a standard be adopted for "causal effect" such that if there is at least as much evidence in favor of the exposure having a causal effect on the frequency or severity of disease as there is evidence against, then a service-connected presumption will be considered.

1. *Sufficient*: The evidence is sufficient to conclude that a causal relationship exists.

2. *Equipoise and Above*: The evidence is sufficient to conclude that a causal relationship is at least as likely as not, but not sufficient to conclude that a causal relationship exists.
3. *Below Equipoise*: The evidence is not sufficient to conclude that a causal relationship is at least as likely as not, or is not sufficient to make a scientifically informed judgment.
4. *Against*: The evidence suggests the lack of a causal relationship.

Recommendation 6. The Committee recommends that a broad spectrum of evidence, including epidemiologic, animal, and mechanistic data, be considered when evaluating causation.

Recommendation 7. When the causal evidence is at Equipoise and Above or Sufficient, the Committee recommends that an estimate also be made of the size of the causal effect among those exposed.

Recommendation 8. The Committee recommends that, as the second part of the two-step evaluation, the relative risk and exposure prevalence be used to estimate an attributable fraction for the disease in the military setting (i.e., service-attributable fraction).

Department of Defense and Department of Veterans Affairs

The following recommendations are intended to improve the evidence on exposures and health status of veterans:

Recommendation 9. Inventory research related to the health of veterans, including research funded by DoD and VA, and research funded by the National Institutes of Health and other organizations.

Recommendation 10. Develop a strategic plan for research on the health of veterans, particularly those returning from conflicts in the Gulf and Afghanistan.

Recommendation 11. Develop a plan for augmenting research capability within DoD and VA to more systematically generate evidence on the health of veterans.

Recommendation 12. Assess the potential for enhancing research through record linkage using DoD and VA administrative and health record databases.

Recommendation 13. Conduct a critical evaluation of Gulf War troop tracking and environmental exposure monitoring data so that improvements can be made in this key DoD strategy for characterizing exposures during deployment.

Recommendation 14. Establish registries of Service members and veterans based on exposure, deployment, and disease histories.

Recommendation 15. Develop a plan for an overall integrated surveillance strategy for the health of Service members and veterans.

Recommendation 16. Improve the data linkage between the electronic health record data systems used by DoD and VA—including capabilities for handling individual Service member exposure information that is included as part of the individual's health record.

Recommendation 17. Ensure implementation of the DoD strategy for improved exposure assessment and exposure data collection.

Recommendation 18. Develop a data interface that allows VA to access the electronic exposure data systems used by DoD.

Recommendation 19. DoD and VA should establish and implement mechanisms to identify, monitor, track, and medically treat individuals involved in research and other activities that have been classified and are secret.

REFERENCES

IOM (Institute of Medicine). 1994. *Veterans and Agent Orange: Health effects of herbicides used in Vietnam*. Washington, DC: National Academy Press.

IOM. 1996. *Veterans and Agent Orange: Update 1996*. Washington, DC: National Academy Press.

IOM. 1999. *Veterans and Agent Orange: Update 1998*. Washington, DC: National Academy Press.

IOM. 2000a. *Gulf War and health, volume 1: Depleted uranium, pyridostigmine bromide, sarin, vaccines*. Washington, DC: National Academy Press.

IOM. 2000b. *Veterans and Agent Orange: Herbicide/dioxin exposure and type 2 diabetes*. Washington, DC: National Academy Press.

IOM. 2001. *Veterans and Agent Orange: Update 2000*. Washington, DC: National Academy Press.

IOM. 2003a. *Gulf War and health, volume 2: Insecticides and solvents*. Washington, DC: The National Academies Press.

IOM. 2003b. *Veterans and Agent Orange: Update 2002*. Washington, DC: The National Academies Press.

IOM. 2005a. *Gulf War and health, volume 3: Fuels, combustion products, and propellants*. Washington, DC: The National Academies Press.

IOM. 2005b. *Veterans and Agent Orange: Update 2004*. Washington, DC: The National Academies Press.

IOM. 2006. *Gulf War and health, volume 4: Health effects of serving in the Gulf War*. Washington, DC: The National Academies Press.

IOM. 2007. *Gulf War and health, volume 5: Infectious diseases*. Washington, DC: The National Academies Press.

Pamperin, T. J. 2006. *An overview of the Disability Benefits Program and presumptions affecting veterans' benefits*. Paper presented at the first meeting of the IOM's Committee on the Evaluation of the Presumptive Disability Decision-Making Process for Veterans, Washington, DC.

VBA (Veterans Benefits Administration). 2006. *Annual benefits report fiscal year 2005*. http://www.vba.va.gov/bln/dmo/reports/fy2005/2005_abr.pdf (accessed February 26, 2007).

VDBC (Veterans Disability Benefits Commission). 2006. *Statement of the Veterans' Disability Benefits Commission to the IOM's Committee on Presumptive Disability Decision-Making Process*. Washington, DC: VDBC.

Zeglin, D. E. 2006. *Presumptions of service connection*. Paper prepared for the Veterans' Disability Benefits Commission. https://www.1888932-2946.ws/vetscommission/e-documentmanager/gallery/Documents/Reference_Materials/Presumption-Paper_3-7-06.pdf (accessed March 8, 2007).

1

Introduction

Veterans and their families have served the American people and our country in ways that cannot easily be summarized or measured. Our nation has long recognized and honored military veterans' service and sacrifices. From the very beginning, benefits have been provided to those whose illnesses were incurred or aggravated by their military service. Ascertaining whether an illness is service connected is not unduly difficult when the illness emerges while the person is engaged in military service. But when an adverse health effect becomes manifest after military service, at times many years later, determining and proving a service connection may raise complex scientific and policy questions.

Presumptions enable veterans to be granted service connection who, through no fault of their own, are unable to establish that the injury was caused by their military service. Since 1921, Congress and the Department of Veterans Affairs (VA) have created numerous presumptions to assist veterans in establishing that they have a service-connected disease entitling them to disability payments (see Appendix D for an historical overview).

Much has happened since 1921 that has made the presumptive disability decision-making process more critical and complex. Fortunately, a far greater percentage of service men and women are surviving combat injuries, and the life expectancy of all veterans has greatly increased. As a result, disability payments are made for much longer periods, and recipients may develop medical complications that were much less frequent when presumptions were first employed. In addition, warfare has changed. Service personnel are subjected to numerous new types of exposures, about some of which we know very little. On the other hand, we understand a good deal more now about disease processes because of recent research based in epidemiology, toxicology, and genetics. This report proposes a framework for presumptive disability decision making that would employ our best scientific understanding while protecting the interests of veterans and other stakeholders by including them in the decision-making process. It provides findings from a committee convened to assess the current approach of the presumptive disability decision-making process for veterans and to provide a framework for a future approach. The committee was appointed by the Institute of Medicine (IOM) of the National Academies at the request of a special congressional commission (see below).

VETERANS' DISABILITY BENEFITS COMMISSION

The Veterans' Disability Benefits Commission (Commission) was created by the National Defense Authorization Act of 2004 (Public Law 108-136. 108th Cong., 1st Sess.). The Commission is charged with "studying the benefits provided to compensate and assist veterans for disabilities attributable to military service. The Commission was mandated to consult with the Institute of Medicine (IOM) of the National Academy of Sciences with respect to the medical aspects of contemporary disability compensation policies" (VDBC, 2006, p. 1; as found in Appendix A). The Commission was asked to evaluate and assess the following:

- The appropriateness of benefits
- The appropriateness of the level of those benefits
- The appropriate standard(s) for determining whether the disability should be compensated (VDBC, 2006, p. 1; as found in Appendix A)

To meet its goals, "the Commission produced a list of 31 research questions to be answered during its investigation" (VDBC, 2006, p. 1; as found in Appendix A). The Commission requested two studies from IOM. This report will address the issue of presumptions. Another committee, the Committee on Medical Evaluation of Veterans for Disability Compensation, issued a report entitled *A 21st Century System for Evaluating Veterans for Disability Benefits*, in June 2007. That report made recommendations to the Commission on how several components of VA's medical evaluation and disability rating process for veterans could be updated and improved.

The independent Commission "consists of 13 members who were appointed by the President and the leaders of Congress" (VDBC, 2006, p. 1; as found in Appendix A) and is funded by VA. Twelve of the commissioners have served in the military. Nine members have combat experience. "The Commission is charged to submit its report by October 1, 2007, to the President and Congress" (VDBC, 2006, p. 1; as found in Appendix A). The Commission's website is www.vetscommission.org.

IOM COMMITTEE CHARGE AND APPROACH

In response to a request from the Veterans' Disability Benefits Commission, IOM constituted the Committee on Evaluation of the Presumptive Disability Decision-Making Process for Veterans (Committee). To address the charge from the Commission, IOM assembled 14 full committee members, 1 volunteer scientific consultant, and 1 paid consultant—all with diverse backgrounds and expertise. The Committee's website is www.iom.edu/pddm.

As the independent Commission does not have its own funding source, this study was funded by VA. The task order description provided by VA is to (1) describe and evaluate the current model used to recognize diseases that are subject to service connection on a presumptive basis; and (2) if appropriate, propose a scientific framework that would justify recognizing or not recognizing conditions as presumptive.

The Committee gained many insights from a four-page statement clarifying the task order that was presented to the Committee at its first meeting by Commissioner John Grady (Grady, 2006; VDBC, 2006; as found in Appendix A). The statement emphasized that the granting of a presumptive service connection be "based on the best scientific evidence available" (VDBC, 2006, p. 4; as found in Appendix A). The Commission asked the Committee to "evaluate the current model used to determine diseases that qualify for service connection on a presumptive basis, and if appropriate, propose improvements in the model" (VDBC, 2006, p. 1; as found in Appendix A). The Commission emphasized that "having a method of granting service connection quickly and fairly based on a presumption is of critical importance to our disabled veterans and their surviving spouses," and asked the Committee to consider process improvements to address the long periods of elapsed time before presumptions are established (VDBC, 2006, pp. 3-4; as found in Appendix A).

During the first meeting, the Committee asked questions of the commissioners to further clarify the charge. In responding, the Commission indicated that it did not expect a full, exhaustive review of all presumptions established since 1921 and that a review of case studies would facilitate the Committee's understanding of the current process. The Commission also clarified the scope of the evaluation, indicating that it would like the Committee to evaluate all participants in the current process—including Congress, VA, IOM, veterans stakeholders, and any others—and to thoroughly assess the processes currently used to make presumptions, as well as in the past, since an understanding of past processes would be instructive in considering possible future processes (as stated during Commission Panel discussion on May 31, 2006; VDBC, 2006, as found in Appendix A). The Committee approached the review of present and past processes and practice, including the roles and responsibilities of the different parties involved, through a series of case studies (see Appendix I). The Commission asked if there should "be a defined process in place at VA to review and establish presumptions" and if "the same or a different process should be used periodically to review existing presumptions" (VDBC, 2006, p. 3; as found in Appendix A). The Committee deliberated the case studies to learn the past processes of presumptive decisions and to develop its proposed framework for the future of the presumptive disability decision-making process.

At the heart of such processes are the principles used by participants for evaluating evidence on whether or not an effect was caused by military service. The Commission therefore asked about the "amount of increase in occurrence rate . . . to warrant compensation" and for "advice, from an epidemiologic and statistical standpoint, on what strength of evidence would be the appropriate requirement when the Secretary of Veterans Affairs considers whether to establish a presumption" (VDBC, 2006, p. 3; as found in Appendix A). These requests address considerations of magnitude of risk and strength of evidence in making presumptive decisions, and the methodology used in determining causal relationships. These issues became a cornerstone for future Committee discussions regarding the use of causation versus association, interpretation of population versus individual risks, and use of attributable fraction or probability of causation for compensation purposes.

An important legal definition the Committee discussed throughout the study process was that "an association is considered 'positive' if the credible evidence for the association is equal to or outweighs the credible evidence against the association" (VA, 1996, p. 41368). This legal definition was an important part of deliberations for the Committee and became the foundation for the Committee's proposed strength of evidence categories.

Finally, the Commission asked the Committee to address some specific issues. First, several presumptions have been established "because it was not possible to document exposure to biological, chemical, radiological, or other environmental agents by accurate information on the exact locations to which military [S]ervice members were assigned during precise periods of time" (VDBC, 2006, p. 2; as found in Appendix A). The Commission stated the Committee "may be able to provide substantive advice concerning how to ensure that this situation is not repeated in the future" (VDBC, 2006, p. 3; as found in Appendix A). Second, in its statement, the Commission asked if the case of Vietnam veterans with diabetes and prostate cancer was fully supported by medical evidence for these presumptions (VDBC, 2006; as found in Appendix A). When the Committee questioned the commissioners whether the intent was for the Committee to reevaluate the body of evidence for these presumptions, it was determined that this was beyond the charge of the Committee (as stated during Commission Panel discussion on May 31, 2006; VDBC, 2006; as found in Appendix A). However, the Committee did decide to include these two presumptions as part of the case study series to learn more about the processes that put these presumptions in place.

INFORMATION GATHERING BY THE COMMITTEE

The Committee engaged in extensive information gathering while conducting its inquiries. This enabled the Committee to develop the case study series, review the work and processes of VA and of the National Academies' (IOM and National Research Council [NRC]) committees, consider congressional mandates and intent, consider future possible approaches for making presumptions, and review the underlying current and planned Service member and veteran surveillance systems at the Department of Defense (DoD) and VA that could support the presumptive decision-making process. The Committee collected and reviewed hundreds of public laws, congressional committee reports, federal government reports, National Academies' (IOM and NRC) reports, as well as other documents.

The Committee also held three open session meetings—on May 31, July 27, and October 4, 2006—for information gathering purposes. The agendas for these meetings may be found in Appendix B. The Committee heard from the key participants in the presumptive disability decision-making process for veterans during these meetings—past and present congressional staff, VA representatives, IOM representatives, DoD representatives, veterans service organizations (VSOs), veterans, and the general public. Among the VSOs the Committee heard from were the American Legion, AMVETS, NAM-POWS Corporation, Non-Commissioned Officers Association, Texas Veterans Commission, United Spinal Association, Veterans for America, Veterans of Foreign Wars of the United States, and Vietnam Veterans of America. The individuals who participated are noted in the acknowledgments.

To better and more clearly understand VA's process and how it uses the National Academies' (IOM and NRC) reports, the Committee asked VA for task force reports, working group documents, and cost estimate documents that related to specific, past presumptive decisions. VA declined the request to release these documents on the basis of the predecisional nature of the documents (Mansfield, 2006). As an alternative, VA offered to respond to questions offered by the Committee. A list of questions was prepared in writing by the Committee. VA did not respond to all of the Committee's questions and cited similar reasons for not responding as were expressed previously with regard to release of VA's task force documents (Dunne, 2006).

Availability of VA Documents

The IOM Committee sought to review VA's decision-making documents to better understand the factors considered in making recommendations by the working group and task force. These were not made available because VA considered them to be predecisional and possibly sensitive. As an alternative, VA prepared a white paper (found in Appendix G) that provides a general description of VA's decision process following the receipt of an IOM report on Agent Orange or the Gulf War. VA also offered to respond to Committee questions regarding VA's presumptive decision-making procedures. The Committee submitted questions, and VA responded to several but not all of them (VA, 2006). In a letter to the Committee Chair, VA explained it was reluctant to respond to some of the questions for the following reasons:[1]

- The requested answers would cause VA to describe the contents of memoranda and notes of internal meetings that are pre-decisional, and reflective of internal deliberations of VA personnel who advise the Secretary of Veterans Affairs on matters of policy and law.
- In order to ensure that the Secretary receives the best possible advice, VA personnel must remain free to engage in vigorous discussion of important issues facing the Department without the constraints that necessarily would apply, if their deliberations were subject to external review.
- Statements made in the context of robust deliberations, if viewed apart from that context, may be misconstrued or misrepresented.
- The possibility of public disclosure may inhibit free discussion in future deliberations and needlessly limit the thorough and thoughtful consideration that must attend the formulation of policies affecting our Nation's veterans.
- Providing the requested answers to the Presumptions Committee may effectively waive any protections VA would have against broader public disclosure of this pre-decisional information.

It should be noted that the Committee offered to receive redacted documents in accordance with the provisions of the Freedom of Information Act, but that offer was not accepted by VA. Similar reasons were given for not providing working group and task force reports to the Committee. In a separate letter to IOM, the Deputy Secretary of Veterans Affairs, Gordon

[1]Personal communication, P. W. Dunne, Department of Veterans Affairs, December 2006.

H. Mansfield, indicated VA was "concerned that statements made in the context of robust deliberations, if viewed apart from that context, may be misconstrued or misrepresented for purposes of litigation or other ends."[2] The Committee believes that this report has been limited to some degree by lack of access to requested documents, to an extent we cannot assess without actually seeing the documents.

ORGANIZATION OF THE REPORT

This report is organized into 13 chapters with supporting appendixes. Chapters 2 through 5 address the historical and current presumptive disability decision-making process for veterans and describe how it is working. An overview of presumptive disability decisions established by Congress and VA since 1921 is found in Chapter 2. Chapter 3 describes the current presumptive disability decision-making process, and the roles of Congress, VA, and IOM. The legislative background pursuant to the more current presumptions of Radiation, Agent Orange, and Gulf War is included in Chapter 4. Chapter 5 summarizes the past and current practices found in the Committee's 10 case studies (see Appendix I):

- Mental Disorders' Presumptions
- Multiple Sclerosis Presumption
- Prisoners of War Presumptions
- Amputees and Cardiovascular Disease Presumption
- Radiation Presumptions
- Mustard Gas and Lewisite Presumptions
- Gulf War Presumptions
- Agent Orange and Prostate Cancer Presumption
- Agent Orange and Type 2 Diabetes Presumption
- Spina Bifida Program (VA program but not a presumption)

The lessons learned from these case studies provided valuable insights into past and current processes, as well as presenting opportunities for process improvements by all participants in the presumptive disability decision-making process.

The second part of the report (Chapters 6-13) focuses on methodological aspects of the process, laying the foundation for a path forward, and proposes a process for establishing presumptions in the future. Following an overview of an evidence-based framework for making presumptive decisions in Chapter 6, Chapters 7 and 8 lay the groundwork for developing

[2]Personal communication, G. H. Mansfield, Department of Veterans Affairs, December 2006.

methods to consider whether a substance or exposure may cause a specific health condition of concern. Chapter 9 then focuses on to what extent military service could be responsible for a specific health condition in veterans (in general or in a group of veterans)—taking as a given that an exposure during military service can cause the illness. Accurate evidence is critical for the process of conducting the assessments discussed in Chapters 7 through 9. Chapter 10 summarizes health and exposure data systems within DoD for collecting exposure, incidence, and health status information during service, and within VA and other organizations for following military personnel after they leave service and through the remainder of their lives. Chapter 10 offers suggestions for improved research and surveillance to better support the presumptive disability decision-making process. Secrecy leads to gaps in evidence, and Chapter 11 therefore addresses governmental classification and secrecy. These earlier chapters are preparatory to Chapter 12, which introduces "The Way Forward" with the Committee's proposed framework for the future of presumptive disability decision making for veterans. Chapter 13 presents the Committee's recommendations to Congress, VA, a Science Review Board, and DoD.

The appendixes contain information organized by the Committee and IOM staff that may assist the reader who wishes to further delve into the issues and historical background on presumptions. In addition to the appendix material introduced earlier (i.e., Commission statement, meeting agendas), the appendixes include acronyms, abbreviations, and a glossary (Appendix C), an overview of the current compensation system and its historical context (Appendix D), summary tables of the presumptive decisions established by Congress and VA since 1921 (Appendix F), VA's White Paper (Appendix G), IOM's Agent Orange and Gulf War Statements of Tasks and Conclusions (Appendix H), the complete series of case study chapters (Appendix I), additional background material on causation and statistical causal methods (Appendix J), additional background material on exposure and health data for veterans (Appendix K), and additional classification and secrecy information (Appendix L). Finally, Appendix M provides brief biographical information for Committee members, consultants, and selected staff responsible for this effort.

The Committee was not asked to and did not make judgments regarding specific cases in which individual veterans have claimed injuries and illnesses. This report neither supports nor criticizes the presumptive decisions Congress and VA have established since 1921. As well, the Committee did not make recommendations for any new, specific presumptions. These areas were beyond the Committee's charge. However, the Committee did review, analyze, and report on the available information regarding the presumptive disability decision-making process for veterans.

COMMITTEE MEMBERS' COMMITMENT TO VETERANS

All Committee members agreed to serve on this effort because of the importance of the issue and because of their deep gratitude and respect for those serving in the military and veterans who have served in the past. We submit this report with the hope that our effort will be to the benefit of those who have served in the past and who will serve in the future.

REFERENCES

Dunne, P. W. 2006. *Department of Veterans Affairs responses: Questions following from the Veteran's Disability Benefits Commission's charge.* Letter to Jonathan M. Samet.

Grady, J. 2006. *Statement presented at the first committee meeting of the IOM's Committee on the Evaluation of the Presumptive Disability Decision-Making Process for Veterans.* Washington, DC.

Mansfield, G. H. 2006. *Internal VA process for reviewing reports on the Institute of Medicine under the Agent Orange Act of 1991 and the Persian Gulf War Veterans Act of 1998.* Letter to Susanne A. Stoiber.

VA (Department of Veterans Affairs). 1996. Diseases associated with exposure to certain herbicide agents. Proposed Rule. *Federal Register* 61(154):41368-41371.

VA. 2006. *Department of Veterans Affairs responses: Questions following from the Veteran's Disability Benefits Commission's charge.* Washington, DC: Department of Veterans Affairs.

VDBC (Veterans Disability Benefits Commission). 2006. *Statement of the Veterans' Disability Benefits Commission to the IOM's Committee on Presumptive Disability Decision Making Process.* Washington, DC.

2

A Brief History of Presumptive Disability Decisions for Veterans

INTRODUCTION

Presumptions have played an important role in both the conceptual basis for service connection and the actual administration of the Department of Veterans Affairs (VA) compensation program. Presumptions are used to bridge gaps in scientific and medical knowledge, as well as to resolve complex policy questions and simplify determinations of service connection for VA (VA, 1993a). This chapter offers a brief history of the presumptive disability decisions established for veterans since 1921. It is not intended as a comprehensive or exhaustive account of all presumptive decisions; rather, it provides background on presumptions—it explains how they operate, why they are used, and their role in making disability compensation available to veterans. The chapter focuses on presumptions for health outcomes rather than administrative presumptions. For a comprehensive review of presumptive decisions, the reader is referred to *Analysis of Presumptions of Service Connection* (VA, 1993a), *Presumptions of Service Connection* (Zeglin, 2006), *VA Disability Compensation Program: Legislative History* (Economic Systems Inc., 2004a), and *VA Disability Compensation Program: Literature Review* (Economic Systems Inc., 2004b).

What Is a Presumption?

In the law, there is general agreement about what a presumption is, although there is considerable controversy about what a presumption does. A presumption is a procedural device that dictates that once basic fact A is established, the existence of fact B must be assumed unless the presumed fact is rebutted. A presumption therefore operates to relieve a party of the burden of establishing facts that it would otherwise be required to prove in order to prevail on its claim. A presumption that cannot be rebutted is a rule of substantive law; it does not satisfy the definition of a presumption because fact B must be assumed conclusively rather than conditionally. It does not allow for the possibility that fact B can be disproved.

A legislature has numerous choices when drafting a presumption; there is no uniform terminology that must be employed. To ensure passage, presumptions are often couched in somewhat ambiguous terms, particularly when they deal with sensitive and controversial policy issues. The result may be a deliberate fuzziness and ambiguity in the language that governs a particular presumption that will ultimately require recourse to the courts (Allen, 1980). Consequently, it is not always simple to determine precisely why a particular presumption was adopted or how it should be interpreted.

Why Are Presumptions Created?

Presumptions are created for a number of reasons. They promote fairness by simplifying proceedings and by making it less burdensome for claimants to gather evidence that is more accessible to the party against whom the claim is asserted. When the probability of the presumed fact's existence is high if the basic fact exists, presumptions eliminate the expense and time that would be required to establish the presumed fact by direct evidence. Sometimes presumptions are established for policy reasons because of a desire to make it easier for particular types of claimants to establish their claims. This may for instance be true for veterans' claims when information needed for an epidemiologic assessment, such as exposure data, is unavailable because it was not collected at the relevant time. Gratitude and sympathy for those who served their country obviously also play an important role (Reagan, 1988).

What Does a Presumption Do?

A true presumption affects the burden of proof. This can, however, mean different things as legislators, administrators, and judges do not always use consistent terminology to express their intentions. *Burden of proof* is a term used to label two different concepts: the burden of production and the burden of persuasion (*Director, Office of Workers' Compensation Programs, Department of Labor v. Greenwich Collieries et al.*, 1994. 512 U.S. Supreme Court 267, Case No. 93-744). See 512 U.S. Supreme Court 267, Case No. 93-744, for an extensive discussion of the evolution of the term *burden of proof*. A claimant or plaintiff ordinarily begins with both burdens. For instance, a veteran who relies on direct proof to show that he has a service-connected disability must generally both (1) produce evidence on that issue, and (2) persuade VA that the service connection exists.

Types and Categories of Presumptions

There are two major types of presumptions. Type 1 presumptions shift both the burden of production and the burden of persuasion. Type 2 presumptions have a lesser effect. For type 2 presumptions, establishment of the basic fact does not shift to the other party the burden of persuading the adjudicator that the presumed fact does not exist. The other party of the presumption only has to produce evidence that is contrary to, or meets the presumption. If the other party does so, the presumption vanishes, and the party with the original burden of persuasion—the party that had to establish the basic fact—continues to have the burden of proving the presumed fact.

The difference between type 1 and 2 presumptions can be illustrated by the presumption of death after an unexplained absence of 7 years. If the presumption is a type 2 presumption, as it would be under the Federal Rules of Evidence unless Congress provides otherwise (Federal Rules of Evidence: Rule 301: Presumptions in General Civil Actions and Proceedings. 1975. Public Law 93-595. 93rd Cong., 2nd Sess.), the plaintiff would prove an absence of 7 years, the basic facts needed for the presumption to apply. Under Rule 301 if the opponent of the presumption introduces a witness to testify that she saw the absentee 1 year after his disappearance, the presumption vanishes, and the plaintiff has the burden of proving death as though there had never been a presumption. If this is a type 1 presumption, as it is in presuming death for veterans after a 7-year absence (Seven-Year Absence Presumption of Death. 2006. 38 U.S.C. § 108), the basic facts establish death unless VA has sufficient evidence to show that the veteran is alive.

Presumptions for Veterans

There are several reasons justifying the widespread use of presumptions in the adjudication of VA benefit claims. Presumptions may simplify and streamline the adjudication process by eliminating the need to obtain evidence and decide complex issues. Presumptions also promote accuracy and consistency in adjudications by requiring similar treatment in similar cases. Presumptions may relieve claimants and VA of the necessity of producing direct evidence when it is impractical or unduly burdensome to do so.

"Finally, presumptions may implement policy judgments that the burdens arising in certain cases be borne by the government rather than the veteran claimants notwithstanding the uncertainty surrounding the issue of whether the claimants' disabilities were, in fact, incurred or aggravated by service" (Zeglin, 2006, p. 3).

To establish direct service connection for a VA disability compensation claim, a veteran must demonstrate the following: (1) that a disability currently exists, (2) that an event of disease or injury occurred or was aggravated in the military, and (3) that a medical connection can be shown between the service event and the existing disability (as stated in Barrans, 2006). Presumptions lighten the burden of proof when patterns of circumstances impair veterans' abilities to establish direct service connection. A presumption relieves the veteran of proving one or more of the requirements for direct service connection. The only difference between direct and presumptive service connection is the amount of proof required. All entitlements under presumptive service connection are identical to those under direct service connection (VA, 2006c).

There are both statutory and regulatory presumptions. Some presumptions relate to particular medical health outcomes, and others are administrative in nature (Pamperin, 2006). For example, there are several well-known presumptions of an administrative nature: presumption of death, presumption of sound condition, presumption of service connection due to aggravation, and presumption of total disability. The definitions of these presumptions are as follows:

- Presumption of death: Presumption of death upon 7 years of unexplained absence (Seven-Year Absence Presumption of Death. 38 U.S.C. § 108[b])
- Presumption of sound condition: "Every veteran shall be taken to have been in sound condition when examined, accepted, and enrolled for service except as to defects, infirmities, or disorders noted at the time of the examination, acceptance, and enrollment, or where clear and unmistakable evidence demonstrates that the injury or disease existed before acceptance and enrollment and was not aggravated by such service." (Presumption of Sound Condition. 38 U.S.C. § 1111)
- Presumption of service connection—Aggravation: "A preexisting injury or disease will be considered to have been aggravated by active military, naval, or air service, where there is an increase in disability during such [active] service, unless there is a specific finding that the increase in disability is due to the natural progress of the disease." (Compensation for Service-Connected Disability or Death. Aggravation. 38 U.S.C. § 1153)
- Presumption of total disability: "A person shall be considered to be permanently and totally disabled if such person is . . . suffering from any

disability which is sufficient to render it impossible for the average person to follow a substantially gainful occupation, but only if it is reasonably certain that such disability will continue throughout the life of the person." (Veterans' Benefits. Determination with Respect to Disability. 38 U.S.C. § 1502)

Medical health outcome presumptions have generally been adopted after periods of war and have been driven by the concerns of and for returning Service members. Military service is demanding, and those serving often do not know where they will be stationed and to which agents they will be exposed. In addition, military personnel are governed by the "line of duty" clause. VA will cover disability for a veteran "resulting from personal injury suffered or disease contracted in line of duty, or for aggravation of a pre-existing injury suffered or disease contracted in line of duty, in the active military, naval, or air service," unless such injury or disease was "a result of the veteran's own willful misconduct or abuse of alcohol or drugs" (Compensation for Service-Connected Disability or Death. Basic Entitlement. 38 U.S.C. § 1110).

Presumptions established by Congress and VA have generally been defined by or linked to a location (e.g., service in Persian Gulf, Vietnam) or an activity (e.g., detonation of a nuclear device). Presumptions have also been defined by categories of disease. In general, VA categorizes medical health outcome presumptive decisions into the following categories: Chronic Diseases, Tropical Diseases, Former Prisoners of War (POWs), Radiation, Herbicide Agents, Mustard Gas/Lewisite, and Persian Gulf War (Zeglin, 2006).

Veterans are entitled to compensation for certain medical conditions that become manifest to a degree of 10 percent or more disability after they leave the military service, if there is a relationship between service and the condition being claimed (Presumptions Relating to Certain Diseases and Disabilities. 38 U.S.C. § 1112). The health outcomes for presumptions must be rated at least at a 10 percent level in order for a veteran to receive compensation for a specific presumption (Presumptions Relating to Certain Diseases and Disabilities. 38 U.S.C. § 1112). In addition, a veteran must establish the presumptive relationship within the prescribed presumptive period set by Congress or VA. The presumptive period is the allowable period after active duty period in which a veteran must develop a disease in order to be eligible for compensation. In the past, most presumptive periods were set at 1 year. Recently, the presumptive periods associated with certain diseases have been greatly lengthened to accommodate the long latency periods associated with some health outcomes (e.g., cancers), the considerable time required to resolve disability, the problems caused by government-mandated secrecy about some exposures (e.g., mustard gas during WWII) (see Appendix F, Table 1). Personal habits (e.g., tobacco use, alcohol and substance abuse) can be used to rebut presumptions, but in practice this is infrequently done (as stated in Barrans, 2006). Only subsequent to the diagnosis of mental health disorders will VA cover a veteran's alcohol and substance abuse treatment (as stated in Pamperin, 2006).

The last extensive study of the use of presumptions was performed by the Bradley Commission in the 1950s. The Bradley Commission recommended that the existing presumptions for service connection should be withdrawn. They felt that "there is otherwise in the law sufficient protection for the veteran to establish service connection of any and all diseases" (President's Commission on Veterans' Pensions, 1956, p. 178). The Bradley Commission noted that several diseases that were presumptively service connected were probably caused by old age, not necessarily service. It also believed that some diseases that were presumptively service connected had little to do with service in the military and in fact would be developed regardless of active duty. In addition to this, the specialists believed that more thorough medical exams should be given to Service members after military service to better classify health status after active duty. Overall, they believed that the list of chronic diseases at the time needed to be completely resurveyed to more accurately reflect the most updated medical knowledge. They noted advancements in treatment and diagnosing methods to support their theory. One criticism was that the system for presumptive conditions was outdated and overly simplistic. The findings not only called for a change in methods but also demanded much stricter guidelines for rating presumptive conditions. In addition, the Bradley Commission stated that medical principles should allow direct service connection rather than having to resort to presumptions in many instances. The analysis cited changes in medical knowledge and improving technology as reasons for updating the rating system and urged VA to completely change its policy of expansive presumptive periods to reflect the current situation of the medical world (President's Commission on Veterans' Pensions, 1956). Congressional hearings on the report were held, but no favorable action was taken on these recommendations.

THE PUBLIC POLICY DEBATE SURROUNDING PRESUMPTIONS

Members of Congress, representatives of VA, veterans service organizations (VSOs), and individual veterans have long debated the basis for and application of presumptions of service connection (VA, 2006b). The general categories of arguments favoring and opposing presumptions can be found in Table 2-1. Appendix E provides quotations that support these categories of arguments favoring and opposing presumptions.

TABLE 2-1 Categories of Arguments Favoring and Opposing Presumptions

Categories of Arguments Favoring Presumptions	Categories of Arguments Opposing Presumptions
1. **Medical uncertainty.** Onset of illness vs. appearance of symptoms. Doctors disagree over relationship to service. 2. **Inadequacy of service records and examinations.** 3. **Excessive burden of proof on veteran.** Unfair to veteran to require medical proof when medical science is uncertain. Unreasonable to expect veterans afflicted with mental disability to prove SC. 4. **Incidence of disease** among veteran population. 5. **Difficult/delayed Diagnoses.** Only medical specialists are likely to diagnose disease (MS) in early stages. Average person is unlikely to consult for original symptoms. 6. **Social benefits.** Treatment of disease has broad social benefits. Treatment and compensation improve health of the nation generally. 7. **Enforce Congress's view.** Congress disagreed with findings of VA doctors. 8. **Association with risk factors.** A disease associated with a known military risk factor and not associated with other risk factors. 9. **Promote health.** Providing disability benefits relieves veterans of the need to perform work that could further compromise their health. 10. **Conditions of service.** Long-range harm can be caused by particularly harsh conditions of service, such as those experienced by POWs.	1. **Questions of fact.** Each case should be considered on its own merits. Service connection should be a question of fact rather than a question of law. 2. **Relationship to service.** Presumptive disabilities cannot be shown to be related to circumstances of military service. 3. **Administrative function.** Selecting diseases for inclusion as presumptive disabilities involves detailed medical and adjudicatory determinations best addressed administratively. 4. **Improved military procedures/records.** Modern facilities, procedures, and record keeping allow case-by-case determinations. 5. **Advances in medical science.** Advancements in medical science (since WWI) facilitate detection and diagnosis of diseases. Accepted medical principles can reasonably and accurately establish onset of disease. 6. **Philosophy of program.** Statutory presumptions for disabilities that cannot be shown to be related to service are inconsistent with the theory of compensation. 7. **Elevates cases without merit.** Puts cases without merit (from standpoint of service connection) on a par with those proven to be service connected. 8. **Provisions are adequate without presumptions.** Reasonable doubt to be resolved in favor of veteran eliminates need for presumption. 9. **Qualifying criteria excessively liberal.** In some cases, a bill's language is seen as overly inclusive.

SOURCE: VA (Veterans Administration). 2006b (unpublished). *Presumption of service connection: The public policy debate.* Washington, DC: VA.

BRIEF CHRONOLOGICAL HISTORY OF PRESUMPTIONS

This section summarizes presumptions that were established by Congress and VA from the 1920s to present. The health outcomes covered can generally be organized into the following presumptive categories: Chronic Diseases, Tropical Diseases, Former Prisoners of War, Radiation, Herbicide Agents, Mustard Gas/Lewisite, and Persian Gulf War. Table 2-2 summarizes all of the health outcomes that have been service connected for these presumptive categories to date. The information in this table was compiled from the health outcomes found in Tables F-1 and F-2 of Appendix F, which list all of the appropriate public laws and statutory citations. There are nearly 150 health outcomes that have been presumptively connected by Congress and VA since 1921.

TABLE 2-2 Presumptive Categories and Their Designated Health Outcomes

Presumptive Categories	Health Outcomes (in alphabetical order)
Chronic Diseases	Anemia; arteriosclerosis; arthritis; atrophy; brain hemorrhage; brain thrombosis; bronchiectasis; calculi of the kidney, bladder, or gallbladder; cardiovascular-renal disease including hypertension; cirrhosis of the liver; coccidioidomycosis; diabetes mellitus; encephalitis lethargica residuals; endocarditis; endocrinopathies; epilepsies; Hansen's disease; Hodgkin's disease; leukemia; lupus erythematosus, systemic; myasthenia gravis; myelitis; myocarditis; nephritis; other organic diseases of the nervous system; osteitis deformans; osteomalacia; palsy, bulbar; paralysis agitans; psychoses; purpura idiopathic, hemorrhagic; Raynaud's disease; sarcoidosis; scleroderma; sclerosis, amyotrophic lateral; sclerosis, multiple; syringomyelia; thromboangiitis obliterans (Buerger's disease); tuberculosis, active; tumors, malignant, or of the brain or spinal cord or peripheral nerves; ulcers
Tropical Diseases	Amebiasis; blackwater fever; cholera; dracontiasis; dysentery; filariasis; leishmaniasis, including kala-azar; loiasis; malaria; onchocerciasis; Oroya fever; pinta; plague; schistosomiasis; yaws; yellow fever
Former Prisoners of War	Atherosclerotic heart disease and hypertensive vascular disease, including hypertensive heart disease; avitaminosis; beriberi; chronic dysentery; cirrhosis of the liver; dysthymic disorder (or depressive neurosis); helminthiasis; irritable bowel syndrome; malnutrition; organic residuals of frostbite; pellagra; peptic ulcer disease; peripheral neuropathy; posttraumatic osteoarthritis; psychosis; stroke; any other nutritional deficiency; any of the anxiety states

continued

TABLE 2-2 Continued

Presumptive Categories	Health Outcomes (in alphabetical order)
Radiation	Bronchiolo-alveolar carcinoma; cancer of the bile ducts, bone, brain, breast, colon, esophagus, gall bladder, lung, ovary, pancreas, pharynx, salivary gland, small intestine, stomach, thyroid, and urinary tract; leukemia; lymphomas; multiple myeloma; primary liver cancer
Herbicide Agents	Acute and subacute peripheral neuropathy; chloracne; chronic lymphocytic leukemia; Hodgkin's disease; multiple myeloma; non-Hodgkin's lymphoma; porphyria cutanea tarda; prostate cancer; respiratory cancers; soft-tissue sarcoma, including: adult fibrosarcoma, dermatofibrosarcoma protuberans, malignant fibrous histiocytoma, liposarcoma, leiomyosarcoma, epithelioid leiomyosarcoma, rhabdomyosarcoma, ectomesenchymoma, angiosarcoma, proliferating angioendotheliomatosis, malignant glomus tumor, malignant hemangiopericytoma, synovial sarcoma, malignant giant cell tumor of tendon sheath, malignant schwannoma, malignant mesenchymoma, malignant granular cell tumor, alveolar soft part sarcoma, epithelioid sarcoma, clear cell sarcoma of tendons and aponeuroses, extraskeletal Ewing's sarcoma, congenital and infantile fibrosarcoma, malignant ganglioneuroma; type 2 diabetes
Mustard Gas and Lewisite	Acute nonlymphocytic leukemia; cancers (nasopharyngeal, laryngeal, lung [except mesothelioma], squamous cell carcinoma of the skin); chronic conjunctivitis; chronic form of laryngitis, bronchitis, emphysema, and asthma; chronic obstructive pulmonary disease; corneal opacities; keratitis; scar formation
Persian Gulf War	An undiagnosed illness, which may be associated with the following chronic symptoms: fatigue; symptoms involving skin, headache, muscle pain, joint pain, neurological symptoms, neuropsychological symptoms; symptoms involving the respiratory system, sleep disturbances, gastrointestinal symptoms, cardiovascular symptoms, abnormal weight loss, or menstrual symptoms. Also included are the following medically unexplained chronic multisymptom illnesses that are defined by a cluster of signs or symptoms: Chronic Fatigue Syndrome, Fibromyalgia, and Irritable Bowel Syndrome

SOURCE: Appendix F, Tables F-1 and F-2.

1920s

The first presumptions were established in 1921: "In my opinion, that provision of the law which places the burden upon the disabled veteran of connecting his disease with his service has been responsible for more complaints, dissatisfaction and disappointment . . . than any other single provision. . . . Consequently, I propose to offer an amendment to section 18 which will shift the burden of proof in the case of two classes of disease only—tubercular and neuropsychiatric. I propose that when it is proved by an incapacitated soldier that he has either of these two types of disease he shall immediately be entitled to compensation unless the Government proves—the burden thus being shifted to the Government—that he has contracted the disease since the time of his discharge and it is not traceable to service in line of duty" (Senator Walsh, 61 Cong. Rec. 4105, 1921, as referenced in VA, 1993a, p. 7, and as found in Appendix E).

Neuropsychiatric disease (later called *psychoses*) and active pulmonary tuberculosis were the first two presumptions established on August 9, 1921 (Veterans' Bureau. Public Law 67-47. 1921. 67th Cong., 1st Sess.). These health outcomes must have manifested to 10 percent or more within 2 years of separation from active military service and must have been contracted during military service. On November 12, 1921, the first list of chronic constitutional diseases (later referred to as Chronic Diseases) was established (VA, 1921). These must have manifested within 1 year after the date of separation from service. The list included anemia (primary), arteriosclerosis, beriberi, diabetes insipidus, diabetes mellitus, endocrinopathies, gout, hemochromatosis, hemoglobinuria (paroxysmal), hemophilia, Hodgkin's disease, leukemia (all types), ochronosis, pellagra, polycythemia (erythremia), purpura, rickets, and scurvy. The category of Chronic Diseases was expanded in 1924 (World War Veterans' Act, 1924. Public Law 68-242. 68th Cong., 1st Sess.), 1925 (VA, 1925), and 1928 (VA, 1928).

1930s

In 1933, epilepsies and organic diseases of the nervous system were added to the Chronic Diseases category, and requirements for the manifestation of tuberculosis were more specifically characterized (Executive Order 6089. Instruction No. 2, Implementing Vet. Reg. No. 1. April 12, 1933). Osteitis deformans (Paget's disease) was added in 1935 (Executive Order 6089. Instruction No. 2-A, Implementing Vet. Reg. No. 1. August 14, 1935).

1940s

The 1940s saw the growth in the number of presumptions and the addition of one new presumptive category—Tropical Diseases. The first tropical disease for which a presumption was made was malaria in 1945 (VA, 1945). Malaria must have been contracted during active service with a presumptive period of 1 year after separation from active military service. The Tropical Diseases category was greatly expanded in 1946 (VA, 1947) and 1948 (Act of June 24, 1948. Public Law 80-748. 80th Cong., 2d Sess.) with clarifications appearing in 1949 (VA, 1949a). As well, the number of presumptions in the category of Chronic Diseases increased greatly in 1948 (Act of June 24, 1948. Public Law 80-748. 80th Cong., 2d Sess.) and 1949 (VA, 1949a,b). The increase in the number of presumptions during this decade was related to the high incidence of such diseases observed in returning veterans from WWII.

1950s

The 1950s were not very active in establishing new presumptions. Sarcoidosis was added to the Chronic Diseases category, and amebiasis was added to the Tropical Diseases category in 1950 (VA, 1950). Clarifications on the dates of service, locations, and presumptive periods occurred in 1957 (Veterans' Benefits Act of 1957. Public Law 85-56. Sec. 301. 85th Cong., 1st Sess.). It should be noted that the Bradley Commission, which reviewed the presumptive process and decisions, issued its report in 1956 (President's Commission on Veterans' Pensions, 1956).

1960s

In 1961, criteria for the presumptions in the Chronic Diseases and Tropical Diseases categories appeared (VA, 1961). No new presumptions were created during this decade.

1970s

A new presumptive category was established in the 1970s—Former Prisoners of War (POWs). POWs from WWII, the Korean War, and the Vietnam era were specifically connected for various physical and mental health outcomes in 1970 (Public Law 91-376. Sec. 3. 91st Cong., 2d Sess., 1970). "Problems with nutrition, forced labor, and other inhumane treatment were deemed to be strong reasons to presume that the conditions were the direct result of captivity" (Economic Systems Inc., 2004a, p. 20). Clarification for the presumptive periods of Hansen's disease (leprosy) and tuberculosis to 3 years as well as multiple sclerosis to 7 years from date of separation occurred in 1970 (VA, 1970). In 1979, ischemic heart disease (or other cardiovascular disease) was presumptively associated with service amputation of one lower extremity at or above the knee or service-connected amputations of both lower extremities at or above the ankles (VA, 1979).

1980s

The decade demonstrated an expansion of presumptions with in the categories of POWs, Herbicide Agents, and Radiation. In 1981, the POW imprisonment requirement of 90 days or more was reduced to 30 days or more (Former Prisoner of War Benefits Act of 1981. Public Law 97-37. 97th Cong., 1st Sess.). In 1985, chloracne was presumptively connected with dioxin exposure (VA, 1985). In that same year, presumptions for exposure to ionizing radiation in Hiroshima or Nagasaki, Japan (September 1945 until July 1946) and all forms of leukemia (except chronic lymphatic leukemia), many cancers, and multiple myeloma were made (VA, 1985). For POWs, organic residuals of frostbite and posttraumatic osteoarthritis were added in 1986 (Veterans' Benefits Improvements and Health-Care Authorization Act of 1986. Public Law 99-576. 99th Cong., 2d Sess.). In 1988, the scope of presumptive service connection law expanded dramatically when Congress passed a law providing a 40-year presumptive period for a long list of cancers associated with nuclear testing during the 1940s (Veterans' Benefits and Services Act of 1988. Public Law 100-322. 100th Cong., 2d Sess.). This law introduced the phrases "radiation-exposed veteran" and "radiation-risk activity," and added to the list POWs who were being held in Japan at the time of the nuclear detonations.

1990s

The generation of presumptions accelerated in the decade of the 1990s. Each year of this decade new presumptions or clarifications of presumptive periods were established by Congress or VA. The Radiation Exposure Compensation Act of 1990 (Public Law 101-426. 101st Cong., 2d Sess.) added presumptions for downwinders to the Radiation category, but it did not cover veterans. Also in 1990, non-Hodgkin's lymphoma was presumptively connected for Vietnam service (VA, 1990). In 1991, Congress passed the Agent Orange Act (Public Law 102-4. 102d Cong., 1st Sess.). This act added non-Hodgkin's lymphoma, soft-tissue sarcomas, and chloracne (or other acneform disease) in the presumptive category of Herbicide Agents. Presumptions for the Mustard Gas/Lewisite category, stemming from WWII full-body, field, or chamber experiments, were established in 1992 (VA, 1992a). Also in 1992, peripheral neuropathy was presumptively connected to the Herbicide Agents category (VA, 1992b), and cancer of the salivary gland and urinary tract were added to the Radiation category (Veterans' Radiation Exposure Amendments of 1992. Public Law 102-578. 102d Cong., 2d Sess.). Both ovarian cancer and parathyroid cancer were presumptively connected to the Radiation category in 1993 (VA, 1993b). During that same year, posttraumatic stress disorder was presumptively connected for military service and former POWs (VA, 1993c). Finally, several additional diseases associated with service in Vietnam were added in 1993 (VA, 1993d).

In 1994, numerous additions occurred in the presumptive categories of Mustard Gas/Lewisite (VA, 1994a), Herbicide Agents (VA, 1994d,e;

Veterans' Benefits Improvements Act of 1994. Public Law 103-446. 103d Cong., 2d. Sess.), and Radiation (VA, 1994b). Also in 1994, the Persian Gulf War undiagnosed illnesses were proposed (VA, 1994c). The Persian Gulf War undiagnosed illnesses were finalized in the 1995 Compensation for Certain Undiagnosed Illnesses rule, the first time that Congress had made a presumption for a list of medical terms (VA, 1995b). Additional presumptions in the Radiation category were added for cancer of the rectum and lymphomas (other than Hodgkin's disease) later that year (VA, 1995a). In 1996, prostate cancer as well as acute and subacute peripheral neuropathy were presumptively connected under the category of Herbicide Agents (VA, 1996). The presumptive period for undiagnosed illnesses to manifest within 2 years after service was extended to December 31, 2001, in 1997 (VA, 1997). Prostate cancer and any other cancer were presumptively connected for the Radiation category in 1998 (VA, 1998). The Persian Gulf War Veterans Act of 1998 (Public Law 105-277. 105th Cong., 2d Sess.) established service connection for diseases associated with exposure to biological, chemical, or toxic agents; environmental or wartime hazards; or preventive medicines or vaccines associated with service in the southwest Asia theater of operations during the Persian Gulf War. Finally, the Veterans Millennium Health Care and Benefits Act of 1999 (Public Law 106-117. 106th Cong., 1st Sess.) established a presumption for bronchiolo-alveolar carcinoma and radiation exposure.

2000 to Present

The final Veterans Millennium Health Care and Benefits Act presumptively connected bronchiolo-alveolar carcinoma to radiation exposure in 2000 (VA, 2000). In April 2001, VA published a final rule stating that veterans' use of tobacco products and associated adverse health outcomes would not be considered service connected (VA, 2001a). In May 2001, VA presumptively connected type 2 diabetes with herbicide exposure (VA, 2001b). In the same year, additional presumptions for the Radiation category were established (VA, 2001c) and clarifications for presumptive periods relating to Persian Gulf War and Vietnam service were published (VA, 2001d; Veterans Education and Benefits Expansion Act of 2001. Public Law 107-103. 107th Cong., 1st Sess.). Additional cancer presumptions were added for radiation-risk activities in 2002 (VA, 2002). Cirrhosis of the liver was presumptively connected in 2003 for former POWs (VA, 2003b), and chronic lymphocytic leukemia was presumptively connected the same year for herbicide exposures (VA, 2003a). The list of diseases presumptively connected for POWs was expanded in 2003 (Veterans Benefits Act of 2003. Public Law 108-183. 108th Cong., 1st Sess.), and additional diseases were presumptively connected for POWs in 2004 (VA, 2004). The definition of radiation-risk activity was clarified in 2004 to include service in a capacity if performed as an employee of the Department of Energy (Veterans Benefits Improvement Act of 2004. Public Law 108-454. 108th Cong., 2d Sess.). Once again, additional health outcomes were presumptively connected for POWs in 2005 (VA, 2005). In early 2006, Congress codified all presumptions established to date (Veterans' Benefits. Title 38 U.S.C.). In 2006, VA published an interim final rule that the presumptive period for undiagnosed illnesses to manifest within 2 years after service would be extended to December 31, 2011 (VA, 2006a).

SUMMARY

Many presumptive decisions have been made since the first presumptions were established in 1921. These decisions reflect the complexity of exposures during service. The increased longevity of veterans means that there are many more diseases from which veterans may suffer and which may have originated in military service. In the 50 years since the Bradley Commission's report was released (President's Commission on Veterans' Pensions, 1956), there have been substantial changes in medical care and in the evidence relevant to making presumptions. However, a need for presumptions has persisted, and the creation of new presumptions has increased rapidly in the last two decades.

REFERENCES

Allen, R. 1980. Presumptions in civil actions reconsidered. *Iowa Law Review* 66:843-867.

Barrans, D. 2006. *History of presumptions of service connection.* Paper presented to the Institute of Medicine's Committee on Evaluation of the Presumptive Disability Decision-Making Process for Veterans, Washington, DC.

Economic Systems Inc. 2004a. *VA Disability Compensation Program: Legislative history.* Washington, DC: VA Office of Policy, Planning and Preparedness.

Economic Systems Inc. 2004b. *VA Disability Compensation Program: Literature review.* Washington, DC: VA Office of Policy, Planning and Preparedness.

Pamperin, T. J. 2006. *An overview of the Disability Benefits Program and presumptions affecting veterans' benefits.* Presented to the Institute of Medicine's Committee on Evaluation of the Presumptive Disability Decision-Making Process for Veterans, Washington, DC.

President's Commission on Veterans' Pensions. 1956. *A report to the president: Veterans benefits in the United States: Findings and recommendations.* Vol. 1, Parts I and II. Washington, DC: Government Printing Office.

Reagan, R. 1988. Statement on signing the Radiation-Exposed Veterans Compensation Act of 1988. *Weekly Compilation of Presidential Documents* 24(20):641-642.

VA (Veterans Administration). 1921. *Internal memorandum implementing Veteran's Bureau Regulation No. 11.* Washington, DC: VA.

VA. 1925. *Schedule for rating disabilities.* Washington, DC: VA. P. 75.

VA. 1928. *Schedule of disability ratings.* Extension 6. Washington, DC: VA.

VA. 1945. *Veterans Administration Circular No. 8*. Section I. Washington, DC: VA.

VA. 1947. Disability ratings for malaria and chronic diseases characteristically tropical in origin. *Veterans Administration Technical Bulletin* 8-6. Washington, DC: VA.

VA. 1949a. Pensions, bonuses, and veterans' relief: Veterans' claims; miscellaneous amendments. Part 3. *Federal Register* 14(26):568-578.

VA. 1949b. Pensions, bonuses, and veterans' relief: Veterans' claims; miscellaneous amendments. Part 3. *Federal Register* 14(197):6174-6180.

VA. 1950. Pensions, bonuses, and veterans' relief: Veterans' claims; miscellaneous amendments. Part 3. *Federal Register* 15(169):5902-5910.

VA. 1961. Disease subject to presumptive service connection. *Federal Register* 26(36):1581-1582.

VA. 1970. Pensions, bonuses, and veterans' relief. Part 3: Adjudication. Subpart A: Pension, compensation, and dependency and indemnity compensation. *Federal Register* 35(232):18280-18283.

VA. 1979. Pension, compensation, and dependency and indemnity compensation, proximate results, secondary conditions. *Federal Register* 44(168):50339-50340.

VA. 1985. Adjudication of claims based on exposure to dioxin or ionizing radiation. Final rules. *Federal Register* 50(165):34452-34461.

VA. 1990. Claims based on service in Vietnam. Final regulations. *Federal Register* 55(208):43123-43125.

VA. 1992a. Claims based on chronic effects of exposure to mustard gas. Final rule. *Federal Register* 57(148):33875-33877.

VA. 1992b. Claims based on exposure to herbicides containing dioxin (peripheral neuropathy/lung cancer). Proposed rule. *Federal Register* 57(13):2236-2238.

VA. 1993a. *Analysis of presumptions of service connection*. Washington, DC: VA.

VA. 1993b. Claims based on exposure to ionizing radiation. Final rule. *Federal Register* 58(57):16358-16359.

VA. 1993c. Direct service connection (post-traumatic stress disorder). Final rule. *Federal Register* 58(95):29109-29110.

VA. 1993d. Diseases associated with service in the Republic of Vietnam. Final rule. *Federal Register* 58(95):29107-29109.

VA. 1994a. Claims based on chronic effects of exposure to mustard gas or lewisite. Final rule. *Federal Register* 59(159):42497-42500.

VA. 1994b. Claims based on exposure to ionizing radiation. Final rule. *Federal Register* 59(171):45975.

VA. 1994c. Compensation for certain undiagnosed illnesses. Proposed rule. *Federal Register* 59(235):63283-63285.

VA. 1994d. Disease associated with exposure to certain herbicide agents. Final rule. *Federal Register* 59(23):5106-5107.

VA. 1994e. Disease associated with exposure to certain herbicide agents (multiple myeloma and respiratory cancers). Final rule. *Federal Register* 59(110):29723-29724.

VA. 1995a. Claims based on exposure to ionizing radiation (lymphomas other than Hodgkin's disease and cancer of the rectum). Final rule. *Federal Register* 60(198):53276-53277.

VA. 1995b. Compensation for certain undiagnosed illnesses. Final rule. *Federal Register* 60(23):6660-6666.

VA. 1996. Diseases associated with exposure to certain herbicide agents (prostate cancer and acute and subacute peripheral neuropathy). Final rule. *Federal Register* 61(217):57586-57589.

VA. 1997. Compensation for certain undiagnosed illnesses. Interim rule with request for comments. *Federal Register* 62(82):23138-23139.

VA. 1998. Claims based on exposure to ionizing radiation (prostate cancer and any other cancer). Final rule. *Federal Register* 63(185):50993-50995.

VA. 2000. Veterans Millennium Health Care and Benefits Act. Final rule. *Federal Register* 65(136):43699-43700.

VA. 2001a. Claims based on the effects of tobacco products. Final rule. *Federal Register* 66(67):18195-18198.

VA. 2001b. Disease associated with exposure to certain herbicide agents: Type 2 diabetes. Final rule. *Federal Register* 66(89):23166-23169.

VA. 2001c. Diseases specific to radiation-exposed veterans. Proposed rule. *Federal Register* 66(153):41483-41485.

VA. 2001d. Extension of the presumptive period for compensation for Gulf War veterans' undiagnosed illnesses. Interim final rule with request for comments. *Federal Register* 66(218):56614-56615.

VA. 2002. Diseases specific to radiation-exposed veterans. Final rule. *Federal Register* 67(17):3612-3616.

VA. 2003a. Disease associated with exposure to certain herbicide agents: Chronic lymphocytic leukemia. Final rule. *Federal Register* 68(200):59540-59542.

VA. 2003b. Presumption of service connection for cirrhosis of the liver in former prisoners of war. Final rule. *Federal Register* 68(138):42602-42603.

VA. 2004. Presumptions of service connection for diseases associated with service involving detention or internment as a prisoner of war. Interim final rule. *Federal Register* 69(194):60083-60090.

VA. 2005. Presumptions of service connection for diseases associated with service involving detention or internment as a prisoner of war. Affirmation of interim final rule as final rule. *Federal Register* 70(123):37040-37042.

VA. 2006a. Extension of the presumptive period for compensation for Gulf War veterans. Interim final rule. *Federal Register* 7(242):75669-75672.

VA. 2006b (unpublished). *Presumption of service connection: The public policy debate.* Washington, DC: VA.

VA. 2006c (unpublished). *Presumptions of service connection.* Washington, DC: VA.

Zeglin, D. E. 2006. *Presumptions of service connection.* Paper prepared for the Veterans' Disability Benefits Commission. https://www.1888932-2946.ws/vetscommission/e-documentmanager/gallery/Documents/Reference_Materials/Presumption-Paper_3-7-06.pdf (accessed March 8, 2007).

3

The Presumptive Disability Decision-Making Process

This chapter describes the current presumptive disability decision-making process for veterans and outlines the roles of various participants in the process. The description is based on presentations at the Committee's open sessions, public documents, documents provided by the Department of Veterans Affairs (VA), the Institute of Medicine (IOM) reports, and other relevant materials.

SUMMARY OF THE PROCESS

The current presumptive disability decision-making process for veterans involves multiple parties and is not controlled by any single entity or organization. The process involves input from Congress, VA, the National Academies (IOM and National Research Council [NRC]) and the veteran community. Decisions made in the courts have also influenced the current presumptive process. Figure 3-1 depicts roles of participants in the current process. Although the number and extent of presumptions have varied over the last 80 years, it appears that the presumptive decisions established since the early 1990s have led to growing concerns and questions about the presumptive process itself.

When Congress enacted the Agent Orange Act of 1991 (Public Law 102-4. 102d Cong., 1st Sess.), it started a model for a decision-making process that is still in place today. Congress asked VA to contract with an independent organization—VA contracted with IOM—to review the scientific evidence related to Agent Orange and disease. The process begins with VA supplying a study charge to the IOM committee carrying out the review,

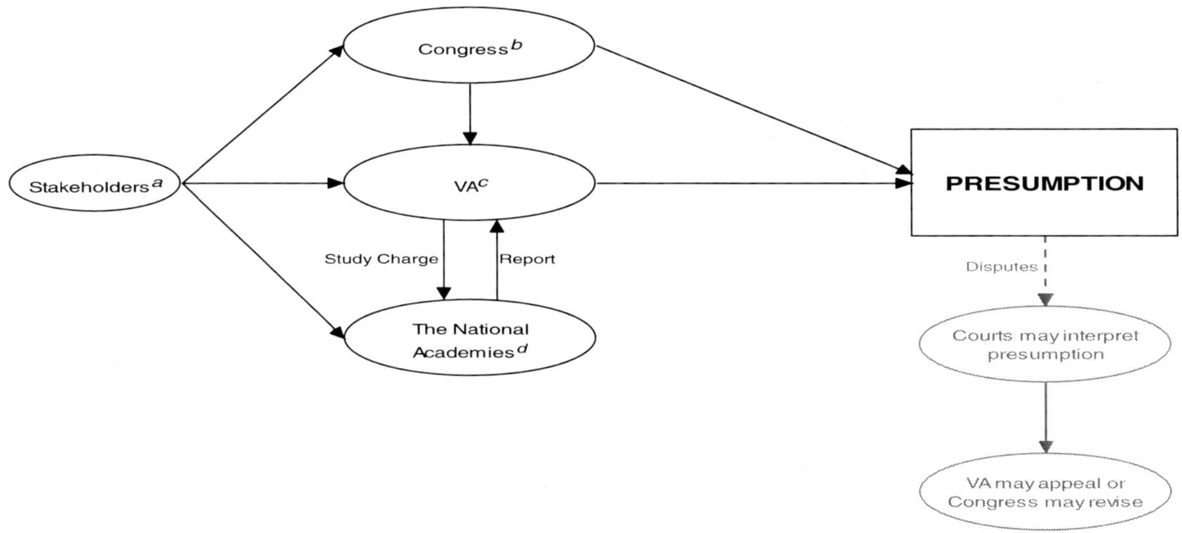

FIGURE 3-1 Roles of the participants involved in the presumptive disability decision-making process for veterans.
[a] Stakeholders include (but are not limited to) veterans service organizations (VSOs), veterans, advisory groups, federal agencies, and the general public; these stakeholders provide input into the presumptive process by communicating with Congress, VA, and independent organizations (e.g., the National Academies).
[b] Congress has created many presumptions itself; in 1921, Congress also empowered the VA Secretary to create regulatory presumptions; on several occasions in the past, Congress has directed VA to contract with an independent organization (e.g., the National Academies) to conduct studies and then use the organization's report in its deliberations of granting or not granting regulatory presumptions.
[c] VA can establish regulatory presumptions; VA sometimes contracts with the National Academies to conduct studies and uses the organization's report in its deliberations of granting or not granting regulatory presumptions.
[d] The National Academies (Institute of Medicine and National Research Council) submit reports to VA based on requests and study charges from VA.

and it ends with the IOM committee responding with a report, based on a comprehensive review, that addresses the charge. Since 1994, IOM has produced six biennial reports on Agent Orange (IOM, 1994, 1996, 1999, 2001, 2003b, 2005b) and five volumes on the Gulf War (IOM, 2000a, 2003a, 2005a, 2006b, 2007a) for VA to use in its deliberations when making presumptive decisions.

Through this process, health outcomes, such as prostate cancer and type 2 diabetes, have been presumptively service connected to Agent Orange exposure in Vietnam. The process for establishing presumptions continued to evolve in recent years to respond to veterans who were deployed to the Persian Gulf during or shortly following the Gulf War in 1990. Although the focus for presumptions among Vietnam veterans centered on their exposure and health outcomes relating to the dioxin-contaminated herbicide Agent Orange, the Gulf War has added new challenges caused by the multiple and various agents to which Service members were exposed. The IOM report process has responded to the multiplicity of agents of concern by developing reports on large groups of similar agents, such as combustion products (IOM, 2000a, 2003a, 2005a).This chapter reviews the roles of each major participant in the presumptive disability decision-making process for veterans.

DESCRIPTION OF ROLES FOR SPECIFIC PARTICIPANTS (IN ALPHABETICAL ORDER)

Role of Congress

The power to compensate veterans for their service-connected adverse health effects resides in Congress. Consequently, Congress has the power to create presumptions that make it easier for a veteran to establish service connection (see Chapter 2). Congress has sometimes exercised its power through legislation; at other times Congress has delegated its authority to the VA Secretary to prescribe "all rules and regulations . . . with respect to *the nature and extent of proof and evidence* and the method of taking and furnishing them in order to establish the right to benefits under such laws" (Rules and Regulations. 2003. 38 U.S.C. § 501(a); emphasis added). This general authority has been used sparingly by VA over the years to establish presumptions.

The vast majority of presumptions have resulted from public laws that specifically identify a disability or disease and set forth the conditions under which a presumption of service connection attaches (see Appendix F). Subsequent legislative enactments often modify the conditions under which these specific presumptions apply. As a matter of law, most presumptions can be rebutted by competent evidence (see Chapter 2) although this rarely occurs in practice.

Beginning in the 1980s, Congress has also legislated procedures to be employed in responding to service-related claims initially concerning herbicide and radiation exposures and later with respect to various exposures encountered during the Gulf War (see Appendix F). The procedures that Congress has established essentially involve review by a committee from the National Academies (e.g., IOM and NRC) of medical and scientific evidence concerning the relationship of disabilities or diseases to certain exposure agents. On a periodic basis, IOM furnishes findings for Agent Orange and Gulf War to the VA Secretary who must then decide whether or not to grant a presumption within a specified number of days of receipt of a report (Agent Orange Act of 1991. Public Law 102-4. 102d Cong., 1st Sess.; Veterans Programs Enhancement Act of 1998. Public Law 105-368. 105th Cong., 2d Sess.).

The formal role of Congress in establishing these presumptions follows a comparatively transparent process. Issues are brought to the attention of Congress by individual constituents seeking assistance from members in securing veteran benefits for which they claim entitlement, and by veteran service organizations (VSOs) that represent their interests. Media attention concerning veteran issues can also engage the interest of Congress. Finally, legislation concerning presumptions can also be initiated at the request of the executive branch, although this has been a rare occurrence.

A bill to establish a presumption is introduced in one or both houses of Congress, and it is usually accompanied by the sponsors' floor statements setting forth the reasons why it should be enacted. Public hearings are held by one or both of the veterans affairs committees and testimony is received from a variety of witnesses including VSOs and individual veterans who are often constituents of various committee members. VA's position on the legislation along with cost estimates prepared by the Director of the Congressional Budget Office, where applicable, are also received and considered by Congress (Johnson, 2003).

The Veterans Affairs Committee considering the legislation next moves to consider the legislation and amendments thereto in executive session. At one time these meetings were closed to the public, but they have been conducted in open session for approximately the past 30 years. After consideration of any amendments, the measure, if approved by the committee, is ordered to the floor for consideration by the entire Senate or House. The bill as amended is accompanied by a report prepared by the committee's majority staff that sets forth the rationale for the legislation. The report also includes a summary of testimony received and information considered together with the administration's position and cost estimates (Johnson, 2003). The report may also include separate and minority views, although this has been infrequent with veterans legislation that is more often than not reported unanimously.

Floor debate on the pending bill is televised and transcribed in the *Congressional Record*. Procedures for considering legislation on the floor, however, differ substantially between the House and the Senate. The amount of debate and the ability to consider amendments to the measure on the floor of the House is for the most part limited, which enhances the authority of the House Committee on Veterans Affairs. In the Senate the ability to attach amendments and to have extensive debate is rarely constricted (Johnson, 2003). Because of the frequent need to keep the "trains moving on time," an individual Senator need not be a member of the Veterans Affairs Committee to exercise considerable influence in shaping veterans legislation.

It should be observed parenthetically that historically the House Veterans Affairs Committee has been the initiator of most veterans legislation. This resulted from the fact that until 1971 only the House had a full standing committee on veterans affairs. The Committee enjoyed a stable, "tenured" leadership and staff for long periods of time that enabled it to develop considerable expertise in veterans' matters. Given House floor procedures, committee views were rarely challenged and invariably prevailed (Carr, 2001). In the Senate, by contrast, veterans legislation—depending on its content—was handled either by the Committee on Finance or the Committee on Labor and Public Welfare (SOURCE: http://veterans.senate.gov/index.cfm?FuseAction=About.CommitteeHistory), both of which had numerous other issues that engaged the committee members' time and interest. As a result, the Senate frequently deferred to the position of the House in veterans' matters prior to 1971.

The creation of the Senate Committee on Veterans Affairs in 1971 amid concern generated about treatment of returning Vietnam veterans altered the status quo as the Senate developed a larger voice in veterans' matters (SOURCE: http://veterans.senate.gov/index.cfm?FuseAction=About.CommitteeHistory). This contributed to changes in how presumptions were created as the issue of Agent Orange exposure grew in intensity.

In situations where the two houses have not adopted identical measures, the differences need to be resolved often through a formal House-Senate conference committee. The veterans affairs committees, however, rarely resort to the formal conference committee process. Instead they negotiate their differences in informal, nonpublic meetings that frequently involve committee staff acting as surrogates for the members. Once agreement is reached, an amended version is reported to the floor of either the House or the Senate where it is passed and sent to the other body, which accepts the measure as amended causing it to be transmitted to the President for action. Both committees insert an identical joint explanatory statement in the *Congressional Record* that sets forth the changes made and the parties' understanding and rationale of the compromise measure (Johnson, 2003).

As this description of the congressional process indicates, an extensive public record is developed with respect to the consideration and adoption of presumptions. Whether this record is a complete and accurate description of why a presumption was or was not adopted or why processes or standards were crafted in the manner they were is another matter. The politics of an issue often are not openly acknowledged in the public record. The personal views of key individual members can often have enormous weight. "Horse trading" on other matters often affects the shape and outcome of a particular bill. Moreover, substantive differences are sometimes papered over with ambiguous language to gain approval of the legislation, which presents a variety of problems to those who are charged with implementing their provisions. All of this suggests that the science justifying a presumption is but one factor considered by Congress in the enactment of the legislation. For additional information and analysis of the role of Congress in the development of presumptions, the reader is directed to the case studies, in particular the discussion of Agent Orange and Gulf War presumptions, found in Appendix I.

Congressional Perspective

The Committee received views from a panel of former congressional staff members, most of whom had served on either the Senate or the House Veterans Affairs committees in the 1980s and 1990s at a time when there were intense concern and questions about the effect of service exposures on the subsequent health of veterans (presentations made to the Committee on October 5, 2006). Among the factors arguably affecting the enactment of presumption legislation were (1) increasing concern about federal budget problems, (2) the perceived strength of key members of Congress considering the legislation, and (3) the continuing reminder of American Service members who had been recently killed or wounded and the debt our society owed them (Petrou, 2006; Ryan, 2006; Scott, 2006; Yoder, 2006).

It was observed that "scientific integrity is critical" in the presumptive disability compensation process and that if it was "lacking, the quality of the decisions [would] suffer, and veterans and the American people [would] lose faith in the decision-making process" (Petrou, 2006, p. 8). At the same time, faced with the claims of veterans with many real disabilities and diseases, it was acknowledged that presumptive decisions were shaped by the perceived "need to make 'yes or no' decisions in the face of pervasive uncertainty" with regards to the level, if any, of exposure and the likely health effects resulting therefrom (Yoder, 2006, p. 1). Panel members were critical of insufficient efforts to monitor the health of Service members. They noted the absence of predeployment health assessments and inadequate surveillance of environmental exposures that troops may have encountered during the Gulf War notwithstanding lessons that should have been learned from Agent Orange and Vietnam (Petrou, 2006; Ryan, 2006; Scott, 2006; Yoder, 2006). Although there was disagreement as to its wisdom, there was uniform agreement that if a connection between exposure and disease were established, Congress has a strong bias in favor of compensating *all* veterans even if the attributable risk was small and large numbers of false positives would result (Petrou, 2006; Ryan, 2006; Scott, 2006; Yoder, 2006).

Role of Department of Veterans Affairs (VA)

The Committee's description of the VA process is based on presentations to the Committee as well as a general description provided by VA (see Appendix G). The Committee requested internal documents related to specific presumptions, but these were not provided (see Chapter 1). Based on the information available, the Committee found that VA has developed an ad hoc process for establishing presumptions that relies upon National Academies (e.g., IOM and NRC) reports, recommendations of advisory committees, and VA research findings (Barrans, 2006; Pamperin, 2006a). Currently, VA follows the process that began with the Agent Orange Act of 1991 (Public Law 102-4. 102d Cong., 1st Sess.). Upon receipt of an IOM Veterans and Agent Orange (VAO) or Gulf War (GW) report, the VA Secretary is required to determine whether a presumption of service connection is warranted for any diseases discussed in the report.

VA has not adopted formal procedures governing its internal review and utilization of findings of IOM reports. However, a general practice has developed that VA usually follows in conducting its internal review. The general practice involves a three-tiered review with a working group (tier 1), a task force group (tier 2), and the VA Secretary (tier 3). Working group members include internal VA staff and outside experts as needed, with the option of seeking input from VSOs, Congress, and veterans (Deyton, 2006). Representatives at each tier are shown in Box 3-1.

The Working Group convenes after receiving the briefing from the IOM VAO or GW committee. "Prior to the meeting, VHA personnel usually will seek to identify, based on the IOM report and the committee briefing, the diseases that may warrant special consideration because IOM's findings with respect to those diseases appear to be potentially significant. The . . . VHA generally provides the working group members with additional information concerning those diseases, including copies of any significant scientific studies identified in the IOM report and other information. . ." (VA, 2006, p. 3; as found in Appendix G).

"At the initial working group meeting, the OGC [Office of the General Counsel] representative briefs the working group on the legal standard governing the VA Secretary's decision. . . . The working group will try to

BOX 3-1
Representatives at Each Tier of VA's Internal Review of NAS Reports

Tier 1: Working Group Representatives*

- Veterans Health Administration (VHA) Office of Public Health and Environmental Hazards (OPHEH)
- Veterans Benefits Administration (VBA)—Compensation and Pension Service (C&P Service)
- Office of the General Counsel (OGC)—Professional Staff Group II
- VHA personnel with specialized medical training or experience
- Outside technical experts such as National Institutes of Health (NIH), Centers for Disease Control and Prevention (CDC), and Environmental Protection Agency (EPA), as needed

Tier 2: Task Force Representatives**

- Under Secretary for Health
- Under Secretary for Benefits
- General Counsel
- Assistant Secretary for Policy and Planning
- Other experts (CDC, EPA, as appropriate)

Tier 3: The VA Secretary

SOURCE: Deyton, 2006; VA, 2006; as found in Appendix G.
*The members generally are assigned to the working group by supervisory personnel within VHA, VBA, and OGC. The working group may receive input from outside content experts as well as veterans, VSOs, and Congress.
**Appointed by the VA Secretary.

reach consensus as to whether the scientific evidence appears to warrant a presumption of service connection for any diseases under the applicable legal standard" (VA, 2006, p. 3; as found in Appendix G).

"If the Working Group concludes that the scientific evidence and legal standard do not provide a clear basis for recommending for or against establishing a presumption . . . the Working Group generally will agree to set forth a range of options for a decision by VA policy-making officials. In those circumstances, the Working Group will discuss the factors that preclude a clear recommendation, which may include ambiguity in the governing statutory standard as applied to certain IOM findings. . . . The Working Group will discuss the options available to the VA Secretary and may also discuss the factors that may be relevant to the VA Secretary's decision among those options" (VA, 2006, pp. 3-4; as found in Appendix G). The Working Group prepares a written report that typically includes the following:

- A summary of the issues to be decided under applicable law and the IOM report
- A summary of the findings contained in the IOM report
- A summary of the legal standard governing VA's decision
- A summary of the Working Group's analysis of the medical evidence in relation to the legal standard, particularly with respect to any potentially significant findings in the IOM report
- A statement of the Working Group's recommendations or of the options identified by the Working Group

In arriving at such recommendations, the Working Group generally does not prepare or obtain a cost estimate for the options. However, it may provide general information, for example, the prevalence rates of certain diseases under consideration. If the Working Group report lists a range of options available to the VA Secretary, it ordinarily would identify the scientific and legal considerations relevant to the VA Secretary's choice among those options, and may also identify policy implications associated with various options" (VA, 2006, p. 4; as found in Appendix G).

The VA task force receives this report and reviews its recommendations. "The Task Force often, though not always, provides a separate report to the VA Secretary that is . . . usually similar to the Working Group's report in format and content. . . . [O]nce the report is drafted, it is circulated to the Task Force members for signature and is then transmitted to the VA Secretary" (VA, 2006, p. 4; as found in Appendix G).

"Based on the Task Force's report, the VA Secretary determines whether to establish presumptions for any diseases discussed in the IOM report and directs appropriate action to implement the decision. . . . [I]f the VA Secretary determines that a presumption of service connection is warranted for any disease, VBA (through the C&P Service staff) will prepare proposed rules to establish such presumptions" and "an estimate of the costs associated with the rule. . . . VA will transmit the proposed rule and cost estimate to OMB [Office of Management and Budget] for review. If OMB approves the proposed rule, it will be transmitted to the VA Secretary for signature. VA will then transmit the rule to the *Federal Register* for publication. Once the period for providing public comments on the rule has ended, VBA will prepare a final rule. VA will submit the final rule to the *Federal Register* for publication" (VA, 2006, p. 5; as found in Appendix G).

"If the VA Secretary determines that a presumption of service connection is not warranted for certain diseases, VBA will prepare a notice explaining the scientific basis for that decision with respect to each such disease prior to publication" (VA, 2006, p. 5; as found in Appendix G). VA then publishes this notice in the *Federal Register*.

Presentations made at Committee open session meetings brought out several issues of importance to VA. The scientific, independent review process, as well as the breadth and thoroughness of IOM reports, provide credibility to the presumptive disability decision-making process. However, interpretation of the IOM reports can be problematic for VA. The difficulty lies not only in determining the effects of exposure but in separating the effects of a specific exposure of concern from the effects of other potential exposures. Past IOM committees have not been charged to provide guidance on this issue. VA is also hindered by not having exposure data for individuals. VA noted that some exposures known to contribute to conditions of concern are common in nonmilitary settings, complicating interpretation of studies of risks of military exposures for these outcomes.

VA, under statutes outlining the presumptive process for Agent Orange and Gulf War (Agent Orange Act of 1991. Public Law 102-4. 102d Cong., 1st Sess.; Veterans Programs Enhancement Act of 1998. Public Law 105-368. 105th Cong., 2d Sess.), is not required to consider any evidence on exposure magnitude that would be necessary for a direct service connection. It can offer little or no guidance for making decisions based on exposure magnitude or duration. VA is left to treat all exposures as equally likely to lead to an associated long-term health effect (Brown, 2006; Deyton, 2006).

The Impact of Presumptions

VA does not track the number of presumptive service-connected disability claims granted and/or denied for each condition, nor are health outcomes within the VBA data systems coded in a manner that would permit VA to easily determine how many veterans are presumptively service connected (as stated in Pamperin, 2006b). For various categories of health conditions, some information regarding the number of presumptions may be determined. That is, if it is clear that the only or most readily anticipated method for connection is via presumption (and not direct service connection), then one may conclude that the number of cases for various categories of health conditions are presumptively service connected (Pamperin, 2006b). The Committee was unable to obtain additional data on the number of presumptive cases or their impact to the overall VA system. Table 3-1 provides data that were provided to the Committee during its first open session meeting (Pamperin, 2006b).

Because disability cases adjudicated on the bases of presumptive decisions are not routinely counted, the costs are not known with certainty.

TABLE 3-1 Presumptions in VA's Disability Program

Condition	Number of Veterans	Disability Severity Rating
Chronic Diseases		
Arteriosclerosis	Unknown	Not differentiated
Arthritis	Unknown	Same
Leukemia	Unknown	Same
Raynaud's disease	Unknown	Same
Tropical Diseases		
Malaria	30,000	0%
Leishmaniasis	283	0%
Dysentery	872	0%
Plague	10	0%
Prisoners of War		
Any anxiety	Unknown	Most rated 100%
Stroke and its complications	Unknown	100%
Cirrhosis of the liver	Unknown	100%
Peripheral neuropathy	Unknown	100%
Radiation		
Lung cancer	Unknown	Not differentiated
Colon cancer	Unknown	Same
Lymphomas	Unknown	Same
Stomach cancer	Unknown	Same
Herbicide Agents		
Type II diabetes	197,000	Most are 10% and 20%
Prostate cancer	30,000	1/3 at 100%, average 40%
Respiratory cancer	5,000	Half at 100%
Non-Hodgkin's and Hodgkin's	5,000	Half at 100%, balance 50%
Gulf War		
Undiagnosed illness	3,259	Typically a 10% evaluation

SOURCE: Pamperin, 2006b.

However, estimates are made. VA estimated administrative costs for presumptive radiation decisions (bone, brain, colon, lung, and ovarian cancers) as $33,934,297 over 10 years with benefit costs of $768,601,698 over that same time period (McLenachen, 2005, slide 8). Estimated administrative costs for type 2 diabetes from 2001 through 2005 were $62 million with estimated benefit costs of $3.3 billion during that same time period. VA estimated that there would be 20,399 new type 2 diabetes awards in the first year and 179,000 over the next 5 years. The estimates did not include retroactive payments (McLenachen, 2005, slide 12). Today, the most frequent disability for which Vietnam veterans are receiving service-connected compensation is type 2 diabetes (VBA, 2006, p. 34). "At end of fiscal year

2006, nearly 248,000 veterans were service-connected for diabetes. More than 215,000 of these awards were based upon herbicide exposure in Vietnam" (VA, 2007, pp. 6B-13).

Role of Institute of Medicine (IOM)

The National Academies is a private, nonprofit, and independent entity that advises the nation on science, engineering, and health matters (NAS, 2007a). The IOM is one of four entities within the National Academies. The other entities are the National Academy of Sciences, which was created by Congress during Abraham Lincoln's presidency, the National Academy of Engineering, and the National Research Council.

The National Academies convenes committees of its own members and "other experts to address the scientific and technical aspects of society's most pressing problems" (NAS, 2007b, p. 2). All committee members serve without pay. Committee members are screened to ensure that they do not have conflicts of interest. The committees include "experts with the specific expertise and experience needed to address the study's statement of task" (NAS, 2007b, p. 3).

The National Academies use a systematic study process. Study committees typically gather information through "(1) meetings that are open to the public and that are announced in advance through the National Academies' Web site; (2) the submission of information by outside parties; (3) reviews of scientific literature; and (4) the investigations of the committee members and staff" (NAS, 2007b, pp. 5-6).

Committee deliberations are closed to the public and sponsors in order to "develop draft findings and recommendations free from outside influence. . . . All analyses and drafts of the report remain confidential" (NAS, 2007b, p. 6). A rigorous external peer review by a separate group of volunteer experts is undertaken prior to completion of the study. The National Academies are responsible for the final products and their public release. For additional information on the National Academies and the committee process, see http://nationalacademies.org/.

IOM Perspective

The Committee heard from IOM staff about how studies requested by VA were conducted over several decades (Martinez, 2006). On each occasion that VA has asked IOM to conduct a new study for Agent Orange or the Gulf War in support of a possible presumption, a new committee was selected and convened. Each committee had access to the publically available information regarding the work of previous IOM committees but interpreted their statement of task independent of prior committees.

As a result, each committee's operating assumptions and study plans were similar but not fully identical to those of prior committees. They were free to construct their own evidence criteria and ways to weigh the individual research studies that they considered (see Appendixes H-1 and H-2 for IOM Agent Orange and Gulf War committee study charges).

IOM has completed six full, biennial Veterans and Agent Orange (VAO) reviews (IOM, 1994, 1996, 1999, 2001, 2003b, 2005b) and three focused (IOM, 2000b, 2004b, 2006a) Agent Orange reviews (see Appendix H-1). A new VAO update report was recently published (IOM, 2007b); this VAO report was being drafted simultaneously and independently of this report. Each of the VAO committees was composed of experts with diverse backgrounds to address their charge. Because of the unique nature of the Agent Orange biennial reviews, some consistency of membership for subsequent reviews across committees has been sustained. As a result, approximately one-third of each VAO committee's members had served on a previous committee and were familiar with the past literature on Agent Orange. This overlap of membership helped to provide historical perspective and some consistency throughout the review process.

The IOM committees have been faced with significant challenges, including

- few directly applicable epidemiologic studies;
- no contemporaneous exposure measurements;
- uncertainty about which veterans were exposed to which agents;
- multiple, possibly synergistic exposures;
- possible long latency for health effects from some agents; and
- significant confounders. (Martinez, 2006, slides 7-8)

Source reference material includes epidemiologic studies (e.g., occupational, environmental, veterans) and toxicologic studies (e.g., animal health effects, cellular-level mechanistic).

The first IOM VAO committee categorized the strength of the evidence available into the following four categories: "(1) sufficient evidence of an association, (2) limited/suggestive evidence of an association, (3) inadequate/insufficient evidence to determine whether an association exists, and (4) limited/suggestive evidence of *no* association" (IOM, 1994, pp. 6-7). Although there have been minor changes to the characterization of these categories over the past 15 years, each of the committees has continued to categorize evidence in this manner (IOM, 1996, 1999, 2001, 2003b, 2005b; see also Appendix H-3).

The committees carrying out the Gulf War (GW) studies requested by VA have approached their task somewhat differently. Similar to the process outlined for Agent Orange, VA requested IOM to "conduct a study to evaluate the published scientific literature concerning the association between the agents to which the Gulf War veterans may have been exposed and adverse health effects" (IOM, 2000a, p. 2). The first IOM Gulf War committee began its work in January 1999 and identified an initial list of compounds of greatest concern to veterans. Two public laws (Veterans Programs Enhancement Act of 1998. Public Law 105-368. 105th Cong., 2d Sess.; Making Omnibus Consolidated and Emergency Appropriations for the Fiscal Year Ending September 30, 1999, and for other Purposes. 1998. Public Law 105-277. 105th Cong., 2d Sess.) mandated further studies.

The first IOM Gulf War and Health Study committee decided to categorize strength of evidence into the following five categories: (1) sufficient evidence of a causal relationship, (2) sufficient evidence of an association, (3) limited/suggestive evidence of an association, (4) inadequate/insufficient evidence to determine whether an association does or does not exist, and (5) limited/suggestive evidence of no association (IOM, 2000a, pp. 4-5). Although there have been minor language changes to these categories or description of these categories, the individual, stand-alone committees have continued to categorize evidence in this manner (IOM, 2003a, 2004a, 2005a, 2006b, 2007a; see also Appendix H-4). As in the case of the Agent Orange committees, there has been some overlap of committee membership in the Gulf War series. However, the nature of the individual Gulf War reports and specific statements of task have required less overlap of membership and increased the need for more specific scientific expertise and background in the various areas of biological, chemical, and infectious agents depending upon the specific charge to the committee.

These Agent Orange and Gulf War examples show important similarities and differences relevant to the overall presumptive process. Of note, Agent Orange reports by IOM did not explicitly include a causal category in the evaluation, whereas Gulf War reports did include a category of evidence sufficient to infer causation when characterizing the strength of evidence available for all agents evaluated. Consideration of the actual exposure potential for veterans was beyond the charges to the committees.

The statements of task and conclusions from each of the Agent Orange and Gulf War reports may be found in Appendix H.

Role of Veterans Service Organizations (VSOs)

There are numerous VSOs that voice their members' concerns. VSOs and their advisory committees have played an important role in the evaluations and actions of Congress, VA, and the National Academies (e.g., IOM and NRC). There are also special veteran advisory groups, such as the Advisory Committee on Former POWs, with direct access to the VA Secretary. The impact and voices of the veteran community can be very powerful. A review of the "Agent Orange Update," which describes some of the actions and influence VSOs and other organizations had in moving the Agent Orange Act forward (Cranston, 1990), provides insight into the role VSOs played in that specific congressional action.

The Committee received extremely helpful and diverse input from representatives of VSOs and individual veterans who attended open session committee meetings or who prepared written material to provide to the Committee for its consideration.

Veterans Perspective

The Committee heard that VSOs struggle with how scientific evidence that is uncertain and sometimes limited is used in evaluating cause and effect relationships. The VSO representatives wanted to make certain not only that the Committee considered past conflicts and practices but also that the Committee took into account what is occurring in today's environment and what future veterans may be facing, including emerging problems such as traumatic brain injuries, a signature wound of the current Gulf conflict (Sullivan, 2006).

Other issues raised included better data collection on exposures and health status during military service, the use of International Classification of Diseases codes for illness and injuries, and seamless transition to VA after discharge. The importance of collecting data for reservists and National Guard members identical to those serving active duty was emphasized (Sullivan, 2006).

The Committee repeatedly heard from representatives of VSOs and individual veterans that they expect a fair, equitable, and scientifically based system for establishing presumptions (Kinderman, 2006; Overstreet, 2006; Selfon, 2006). However, the Committee was also cautioned that more rigorous application of tests for cause and effect may not serve the process well (Violante, 2006).

Each of the VSOs reaffirmed the responsibility and commitment to care for all men and women who have served in our stead—past, present, and future. Each stakeholder brings an important perspective to the presumptive disability decision-making process for veterans. There are clearly factors other than science that are considered in these decisions especially when the science base is weak or absent. The future framework will seek to identify ways to improve information and the methods needed to make the best possible presumptive decisions.

REFERENCES

Barrans, D. 2006. *History of presumptions of service connection.* Paper presented at the first meeting of the IOM's Committee on the Evaluation of the Presumptive Disability Decision-Making Process for Veterans, Washington, DC.

Brown, M. 2006. *The role of science in Department of Veterans Affairs disability compensation policies for environmental and occupational illness and injuries.* Paper presented at the first meeting of the IOM's Committee on the Evaluation of the Presumptive Disability Decision-Making Process for Veterans, Washington, DC.

Carr, T. P. 2001. *CRS report for Congress. Parliamentary reference sources: House of Representatives.* CRS report RL30787. Washington, DC: Congressional Research Service. http://lugar.senate.gov/CRS%20reports/Parliamentary_Reference_Sources_House.pdf (accessed April 30, 2007).

Cranston, A. 1990. Agent Orange update. *Senate Congressional Record* 101st Cong., 2nd Sess. November 2. Presented by Scott, E. P., at the third meeting of the IOM's Committee on the Evaluation of the Presumptive Disability Decision-Making Process for Veterans, San Antonio, TX.

Deyton, L. 2006. *Introduction to VA health care system and assessing environmental/occupational exposures.* Paper presented at the second meeting of the IOM's Committee on the Evaluation of the Presumptive Disability Decision-Making Process for Veterans, Washington, DC.

IOM (Institute of Medicine). 1994. *Veterans and Agent Orange: Health effects of herbicides used in Vietnam.* Washington, DC: National Academy Press.

IOM. 1996. *Veterans and Agent Orange: Update 1996.* Washington, DC: National Academy Press.

IOM. 1999. *Veterans and Agent Orange: Update 1998.* Washington, DC: National Academy Press.

IOM. 2000a. *Gulf War and health, volume 1: Depleted uranium, pyridostigmine bromide, sarin, and vaccines.* Washington, DC: National Academy Press.

IOM. 2000b. *Veterans and Agent Orange: Herbicide/dioxin exposure and type 2 diabetes.* Washington, DC: National Academy Press.

IOM. 2001. *Veterans and Agent Orange: Update 2000.* Washington, DC: National Academy Press.

IOM. 2003a. *Gulf War and health, volume 2: Insecticides and solvents.* Washington, DC: The National Academies Press.

IOM. 2003b. *Veterans and Agent Orange: Update 2002.* Washington, DC: The National Academies Press.

IOM. 2004a. *Gulf War and health: Updated literature review of sarin.* Washington, DC: The National Academies Press.

IOM. 2004b. *Veterans and Agent Orange: Length of presumptive period for association between exposure and respiratory cancer.* Washington, DC: The National Academies Press.

IOM. 2005a. *Gulf War and health, volume 3: Fuels, combustion products, and propellants.* Washington, DC: The National Academies Press.

IOM. 2005b. *Veterans and Agent Orange: Update 2004.* Washington, DC: The National Academies Press.

IOM. 2006a. *Disposition of the Air Force Health Study.* Washington, DC: The National Academies Press.

IOM. 2006b. *Gulf War and health, volume 4: Health effects of serving in the Gulf War.* Washington, DC: The National Academies Press.

IOM. 2007a. *Gulf War and health, volume 5: Infectious diseases.* Washington, DC: The National Academies Press.

IOM. 2007b. *Veterans and Agent Orange: Update 2006.* Washington, DC: The National Academies Press

Johnson, C. W. 2003. *How our laws are made, revised and updated.* Washington, DC: Government Printing Office. http://www.senate.gov/reference/resources/ pdf/howourlawsaremade.pdf (accessed May 7, 2007).

Kinderman, Q. 2006. *Statement presented at the second meeting of the IOM's Committee on the Evaluation of the Presumptive Disability Decision-Making Process for Veterans.* Washington, DC.

Martinez, R. 2006. *Institute of Medicine: Agent Orange and Gulf War studies.* Presented at the second meeting of the IOM's Committee on the Evaluation of the Presumptive Disability Decision-Making Process for Veterans, Washington, DC.

McLenachen, D. 2005. *Presumptive service connection in VBA.* Presented to Veterans' Disability Benefits Commission, Washington, DC.

NAS (The National Academies). 2007a. *The National Academies: Advisors to the nation on science, engineering, and medicine.* http://www.nationalacademies.org/ (accessed May 9, 2007).

NAS. 2007b. *The National Academies study process: Ensuring independent, objective advice.* http://www.nationalacademies.org/studycommitteprocess.pdf (accessed May 9, 2007).

Overstreet, H. G. 2006. *Statement presented at the third meeting of the IOM's Committee on the Evaluation of the Presumptive Disability Decision-Making Process for Veterans.* San Antonio, TX.

Pamperin, T. J. 2006a. *An overview of the disability benefits program and presumptions affecting veterans' benefits.* Paper presented at the first meeting of the IOM's Committee on the Evaluation of the Presumptive Disability Decision-Making Process for Veterans, Washington, DC.

Pamperin, T. J. 2006b. *Presumptions in VA's disability program—The effect.* Paper presented at the first meeting of the IOM's Committee on the Evaluation of the Presumptive Disability Decision-Making Process for Veterans, Washington, DC.

Petrou, L. 2006. *Statement presented at the third meeting of the IOM's Committee on the Evaluation of the Presumptive Disability Decision-Making Process for Veterans.* San Antonio, TX.

Ryan, P. 2006. *Perspectives on veterans' legislative disability presumptions.* Paper presented at the third meeting of the IOM's Committee on the Evaluation of the Presumptive Disability Decision-Making Process for Veterans, San Antonio, TX.

Scott, E. P. 2006. Statement presented at the third meeting of the IOM's Committee on the Evaluation of the Presumptive Disability Decision-Making Process for Veterans, San Antonio, TX.

Selfon, L. J. 2006. Statement from the United Spinal Association presented at the second meeting of the IOM's Committee on the Evaluation of the Presumptive Disability Decision-Making Process for Veterans, Washington, DC.

Sullivan, P. 2006. Testimony presented at the third meeting of the IOM's Committee on the Evaluation of the Presumptive Disability Decision-Making Process for Veterans, San Antonio, TX.

VA (Department of Veterans Affairs). 2006. *Internal VA process for reviewing reports of the IOM under the Agent Orange Act of 1991 and the Persian Gulf War Veterans Acts of 1998.* Presented to the IOM's Committee on the Evaluation of the Presumptive Disability Decision-Making Process for Veterans, Washington, DC.

VA. 2007. *Fiscal year 2008 budget submission. National cemetery administration, benefits program, and departmental administration.* Vol. 2. Washington, DC: Department of Veterans Affairs. http://www.va.gov/budget/summary/ (accessed May 9, 2007).

VBA (Veterans Benefits Administration). 2006. *Annual benefits report fiscal year 2005.* Washington, DC: Department of Veterans Affairs.

Violante, J. A. 2006. *Public comments for the IOM's Committee on the Evaluation of the Presumptive Disability Decision-Making Process for Veterans.* San Antonio, TX.

Yoder, C. 2006. *Thoughts on presumptions of service-connection for veterans presumed to have been exposed to environmental hazards.* Paper presented at the third meeting of the IOM's Committee on the Evaluation of the Presumptive Disability Decision-Making Process for Veterans, San Antonio, TX.

4

Legislative Background on Presumptions

In previous chapters, the Committee has described the historical background for presumptions and the current approach as it has evolved to include Congress, the Department of Veterans Affairs (VA), the National Academies (Institute of Medicine [IOM] and National Research Council [NRC]) and stakeholders. This chapter addresses the legislative background, in greater depth, for three more recent issues that have been a focus for the National Academies (NRC and IOM) and VA: radiation exposure, Agent Orange, and the Gulf War. The same issues are also a focus for case studies that are summarized in the next chapter and provided in their entirety in Appendix I. The legislative materials covered in this chapter provide a picture of the concerns of veteran stakeholders and congressional responses and intent, as set out in specific legislation.

The complexities and perplexities that encumber the presumptive disability decision-making process are evident if we look at the evolution of presumptions governing radiation exposures, the Gulf War, and Agent Orange. We see a variety of approaches, not always consistent, a diverse group of participants—Congress, VA, the National Academies (NRC and IOM), stakeholders, and the courts—and somewhat opaque standards for making decisions. It should be noted that VA proposes to reorganize and rewrite all of its compensation and pension regulations (see 71 Fed. Reg. 16464 [March 31, 2006]) (VA, 2006b). Notices of Proposed Rulemaking have been published and will continue to be published. The discussion that follows does not take these new rules into account.

PRESUMPTIONS FOR VETERANS, IN GENERAL

VA clearly assumes that all congressional presumptions governing veterans' benefits are type 1 presumptions (see Chapter 2 for an explanation of the difference between type 1 and type 2 presumptions) (Zeglin, 2006). Consequently, the veteran is relieved both of producing sufficient evidence of an exposure that is service connected and of persuading VA that his or her adverse health effect was incurred through a service-connected exposure (Basic Entitlement. 2006. 38 U.S.C. § 1110 provides for disability payments for illnesses that were "aggravated" or "incurred" during service). Once a medical condition is service connected through presumptions, and the veteran can document military service consistent with the given exposure or risk, the veteran only has to show the basic fact that he or she suffers from the condition in order to receive the specified disability payment.

The discussion below will focus on the link between disease and service—the question to which scientific reviews are directed. Equally important to the compensation decision, however, is the creation of a presumption that relieves the veteran of having to provide evidence of a military exposure of sufficient magnitude to account for his or her illness or injury (Brown, 2005). See, for instance, 38 U.S.C.A. § 1116(f) (a veteran who served in Vietnam during a specified period is presumed to have been exposed to herbicide containing dioxin); 38 U.S.C. § 1116(f) (Presumptions of Service Connection for Diseases Associated with Exposure to Certain Herbicide Agents; Presumptions of Exposure for Veterans Who Served in the Republic of Vietnam. 2006. 38 U.S.C. § 1116(f); and *Haas v. Nicholson* (2006). United States Court of Appeals for Veterans Claims, Case Number 04-0491 § 1116[f]) is ambiguous as to whether it required veterans to have set foot in Vietnam, and the court extended the presumption to veterans serving in the waters near the shore of Vietnam. Often, as is evident in the case studies, exposure data are lacking, making it impossible to conduct epidemiologic studies of the veterans. In such cases, the medical evidence for the presumption that links the disease to the exposure will relate to a surrogate group, such as workers exposed to the substances at issue. For a discussion of this problem in connection with the Vietnam War presumptions, see Stellman and Stellman (2005).

In theory, all presumptions, including those that govern a veteran's ability to show exposure, prove health outcomes, establish that a disability did not predate service (*Wagner v. Principi*. 2004. United States Court of Appeals for the Federal Circuit, Case Number 02-7347), or establish some other element of a claim, are rebuttable as provided in 38 U.S.C.S. § 1113 (Presumptions Rebuttable. 2005. 38 U.S.C. § 1113). VA assumes that an individual was medically sound when entering military service. However, that presumption of soundness is sometimes challenged if evidence shows a preexisting condition. See examples in the *Veterans Benefits Manual* (VA, 2005). Federal circuit court has held that evidence rebutting a presumption must only meet a "preponderance of the evidence" standard unless Congress specifies a higher standard (*Thomas v. Nicholson*, 2005. United States Court of Appeals for the Federal Circuit, Case Number 05-7019).

In practice, presumptions establishing that a veteran's adverse health effects are service connected are rarely rebutted. David Barrans of the VA Office of the General Counsel acknowledged in response to a question after his oral presentation at the July 2005 Veterans' Disability Benefits Commission meeting that VA claims adjusters (veterans service representatives) generally do not seek to develop information to rebut presumptions. Accordingly, one does not see many claims rejected because of evidence that the disease predated the veteran's military service or because the presumptive condition is found to stem from an intercurrent cause. VA does have provisions for developing evidence of "willful misconduct" if it may affect these claims (Basic Entitlement. 2006. 38 U.S.C. § 1110; Basic Entitlement. 2007. 38 U.S.C. § 1131), but the limited provisions are rarely relevant to presumptive claims (see Presumptions Rebuttable. 2005. 38 U.S.C. § 1113; Line of Duty and Misconduct. 2005. 38 C.F.R. § 3.301). Accordingly, in practice the presumptions governing service connection are not rebutted and operate more as rules of law than procedural devices; they mandate finding a nexus between the veteran's service and a specified disability or disease.

If Congress wished, it could specify evidence that may or may not be used to rebut a presumption. It has done so in other statutes, unrelated to veterans' benefits that rely on presumptions to establish benefits under a compensation scheme. For instance, the Back Lung Benefits Act (Congressional Findings and Declaration of purpose. 2007. 30 U.S.C. § 901, et seq.) contains a number of rebuttable type 2 presumptions that operate to prove that a miner was disabled due to pneumoconiosis and that this disability arose out of his employment in coal mines. The regulation accompanying this legislation specifically provides that certain items of evidence shall not suffice to rebut the presumption of disability (Presumption of Entitlement Applicable to Certain Death Claims. 2003. 20 C.F.R. § 718.306[d]). The courts have taken this to mean that a combination of items can be used to rebut the presumption. Similarly, the National Childhood Vaccine Act (Establishment. 2007. 42 U.S.C. § 300aa-1) contains a vaccine injury table (Vaccine Injury Table. 2007. 42 U.S.C. § 300aa-14) setting out presumptions that particular adverse health effects occurring within a specified period after a child was vaccinated were caused by the vaccination. The act also requires showing that "there is not a preponderance of the evidence" that the claimed injury "is due to factors unrelated to the administration of the vaccine" (Determination of Eligibility and Compensation. 1999. 42 U.S.C.S. § 300aa-13[a][1][B]). These factors may, as shown by the claimant's evidence or other material in the record, "include infection, toxins, trauma (including birth trauma and related anoxia), or metabolic disturbances which have no known relation to the vaccine involved, but which in the particular case are shown to have been the agent or agents principally responsible for causing" the claimed injury (Determination of Eligibility and Compensation. 1999. 42 U.S.C. § 300aa-13[a][2][B]).

The claims process becomes more complicated, less certain, and more expensive if evidence has to be scrutinized by a claims adjuster. The current system of creating presumptions that permit "automatic" awarding of benefits when a veteran suffers from a named presumptive disease promotes administrative efficiency. It means, however, that scientific input into decisions about a veteran's entitlement to disability payments occurs only at the front end of the process when a decision is made whether or not to service connect.

PRESUMPTIONS GOVERNING RADIATION, AGENT ORANGE, AND GULF WAR EXPOSURES, IN GENERAL

Many veterans exposed to radiation or Agent Orange in Vietnam or who served in the Persian Gulf War[1] alleged they suffered from adverse health effects incurred through military service. Eventually, as discussed below, Congress legislated with regard to all three situations. Some of this legislation lists specific illnesses and adverse health effects and authorizes VA to adopt presumptions through rule making that would relieve a veteran from having to prove a service connection. Although the statutes resemble each other in some respects, and may have influenced each other, the case studies indicate that the data, decisions, and decision makers underlying the presumptions are quite dissimilar. For example, both Congress and VA have established presumptions for radiation. Only VA has established presumptions for Agent Orange. And although VA was given the authority by Congress to do so, VA has not made presumptions of service connection to date for diseases incurred by Persian Gulf War veterans; however, VA administers compensation for Persian Gulf War veterans who are service connected by the congressionally established presumption of "undiagnosed illnesses" that may become manifest within a presumptive period after service in the Gulf.

Although most radiation exposures occurred considerably earlier than the Agent Orange exposures during the Vietnam War, Congress started to pay attention to both problems at approximately the same time.

[1]As defined in 38 U.S.C. § 101 (33), the term "*Persian Gulf War*" means "the period beginning on August 2, 1990, and ending on the date thereafter prescribed by presidential proclamation or by law."

The Radiation Presumptions

In 1984, Congress passed the Agent Orange and Atomic Veterans Relief Act (Public Law No. 98-592, 98 Stat. 2725 [1984] eventually became Veterans' Dioxin and Radiation Exposure Compensation Standards Act. 1984. Public Law 98-542. 98th Cong., 2d Sess.), which provided benefits for veterans who had participated either in atomic bomb testing or in the postwar occupation of Hiroshima or Nagasaki if they developed leukemia, polycythemia vera, or carcinoma of the thyroid. This was intended to be a temporary measure until further studies were completed (see HR, Report 98-592, 98th Cong. 2d session, U.S. Congress, House of Representatives, 1984). This act does not contain presumptions but directed VA to adopt regulations that would assist veterans who had been exposed to radiation.

In 1988, Congress passed the Radiation Exposed Veterans Compensation Act (1988. Public Law 100-321. 100th Cong., 2d Sess.). The act created a presumption that a veteran who suffered from one of 13 specified cancers, and who had participated in atomic bomb testing or the postwar Japanese occupation or was a Japanese prisoner of war during the specified time period, was entitled to disability benefits and free medical treatment. In 2002, an additional 5 cancers were added to the presumptive list (VA, 2002).

Regulations adopted pursuant to the Veterans' Dioxin and Radiation Exposure Compensation Standards Act (Claims Based on Exposure to Ionizing Radiation. 2006. 38 C.F.R. § 3.311) were designed to assist veterans who are not suffering from one of the presumptive cancers. If the veteran is suffering from a "radiogenic" disease listed in the regulation, VA is required to assess the "size and nature of the radiation dose" that the veteran may have received. When VA receives dose information and the report reflects a range of possible exposure levels, then VA must presume exposure at the highest end of the reported exposure range in making its determination (Claims Based on Exposure to Ionizing Radiation. 2006. 38 C.F.R. § 3.311[a]). Even if the disease is not listed as a "radiogenic" disease, VA is nevertheless required to "consider the claim under the provisions of this section provided that the claimant has cited or submitted competent scientific or medical evidence" of the disease's being "radiogenic" (Claims Based on Exposure to Ionizing Radiation. 2006. 38 C.F.R. § 3.111[b][4]). Claims are referred to the Under Secretary for Benefits who must determine whether "sound scientific and medical evidence supports the conclusion" that "it is at least as likely as not the veteran's disease resulted from exposure to radiation in service. 'Sound scientific evidence' means observations, findings, or conclusions that are statistically and epidemiologically valid, are statistically significant, are capable of replication, and able to withstand peer review, and 'sound medical evidence' means observations, findings, or conclusions that are consistent with current medical knowledge and are so reasonable and logical as to serve as the basis of management of a medical condition" (Claims Based on Exposure to Ionizing Radiation. 2006. 38 C.F.R. § 3.111c).

Of all the presumptions, those governing exposure to radiation probably rest on the firmest scientific evidentiary basis. As the case study indicates (see Appendix I), a great deal is known about the effects of radiation. Groups other than veterans who were exposed to radiation, such as downwinders, had exposures similar to the veterans, unlike the very different exposures experienced by workers who were treated as surrogates for veterans in studying the effects of dioxin exposures in factory accidents.

Nevertheless, despite the presumptive diseases that have been established, many veterans have difficulty in establishing a service connection; they may be unable to furnish the required evidence of their exposure at a specified location and time, in part because such information may be classified as secret (Podgor, 2005). They may then seek compensation under the nonpresumptive regulations because those provide that if the veteran claims to have been in a specified location on a particular date and the government cannot prove otherwise, it must be assumed that the veteran participated in activities that would have given rise to a presumptive decision. However, because this is a nonpresumptive claim, the veteran will have to show adequate exposure (Podgor, 2005). In 2003, an NRC committee concluded that only about 50 nonpresumptive claims had been successful although thousands had been filed (NRC, 2003, p. 252).

The Agent Orange Presumptions

The historical background that led to the Agent Orange presumptions is set out in Chapter 2. By 1984, the courts had rejected the veterans' claims that their illnesses were caused by exposure to Agent Orange, and VA was not providing disability benefits except for cases of chloracne. The veterans had fared better with Congress, which in 1981 authorized VA to provide hospital and outpatient care for veterans whose health problems allegedly stemmed from Agent Orange exposures (Veterans' Health Care, Training, and Small Business Loan Act. 1981. Public Law 97-72. 97th Cong., 1st Sess.). When in 1984 Congress acted again and passed the Veterans' Dioxin and Radiation Exposure Compensation Standards Act (1984. Public Law 98-542. 98th Cong., 2d Sess.), President Reagan observed in his signing statement that VA had already furnished medical care to over one million Vietnam veterans (Reagan, 1984).

The 1984 act took three steps toward creating service-connection presumptions for diseases suffered by Vietnam veterans (Murphy, 1986). First, the act created some interim presumptions by directing VA to grant temporary disability benefits, lasting until September 30, 1986, to any veteran who contracted chloracne (a skin condition) or porphyria cutanea tarda (a liver disease) within one year of leaving Vietnam (Murphy, 1986). Second, the act required the Administrator of Veteran Affairs to promulgate guidelines and standards for determining whether claims based on exposure to Agent Orange were service connected (Murphy, 1986). Congress thereby authorized VA to handle dioxin claims via new procedures that it was to devise and promulgate through formal rule making rather than by adjudications in individual proceedings. Third, the act directed the formation of an advisory committee to collect and evaluate scientific studies relating to the possible health effects of exposure to Agent Orange (Veterans' Dioxin and Radiation Exposure Compensation Standards Act. 1984. Public Law 98-542. 98th Cong., 2d Sess.).

In August 1985, after receiving input from the Veterans' Advisory Committee on Environmental Hazards, VA issued final regulations relating to the 1984 act that set out a process for adjudicating claims based on Agent Orange exposure (VA, 1985). The regulations concluded that "sound medical and scientific evidence does not establish a cause-and-effect relationship between dioxin exposure" and any disease other than chloracne (Claims based on exposure to ionizing radiation. 1985. 38 C.F.R. § 3.311a[d]).

In 1987, a number of veterans instituted a lawsuit challenging VA's regulations as violating the 1984 act by adopting too high a standard for finding a connection between exposure to Agent Orange and manifestation of a particular disease (*Nehmer v. United States*, 1989, United States District Court for the Northern District of California, Case Number 86-6160). The plaintiffs contended that "Congress intended only that there be a significant 'statistical association' between dioxin and a particular disease in order to grant service connection for that disease." VA conceded that its regulation required "proof of a causal relationship to grant service connection." The court, after explaining that the issue to be decided was legal—what was Congress' intent—and not the scientific question of which test was scientifically valid, turned to the language of the 1984 act in order to determine congressional intentions (*Nehmer v. United States*, 1989, United States District Court for the Northern District of California, Case Number 86-6160, pp. 4-6).

The court first pieced together a number of different statements in the act because the applicable standard of proof was not directly addressed. The court found that "the language of the act is at best ambiguous, at worst silent" because Congress spoke in terms of both association and cause. Because the text was inconclusive, the court next looked at the legislative history to ascertain Congress' purpose. After reviewing comments by members of House and Senate committees that had jurisdiction over the act, the court concluded "that Congress did not intend VA to use a causal relationship," but suggested that "service connection to be granted on the basis of 'an increased risk of incidence,' or a 'significant correlation' between dioxin and various diseases." According to the court, this standard was consistent with previous practices that had established presumptions of service connectedness for amputees and prisoners of war (*Nehmer v. United States*, 1989, United States District Court for the Northern District of California, Case Number 86-6160, pp. 7-9).

VA announced that it would not appeal the *Nehmer* decision and that it would abide by the court's ruling and issue new Agent Orange regulations. The litigation has continued as to whether veterans denied benefits pre-*Nehmer* are entitled to receive benefits retroactively even for conditions that were service-connected after the date of *Nehmer*. The 9th Circuit Court of Appeals so held on July 19, 2007. Congress also took further steps. In 1991, after numerous hearings and committee reports, it enacted the Agent Orange Act (Agent Orange Act of 1991. Public Law 102-4. 102d Cong., 1st Sess.; codified, as amended, Presumptions of Service Connection for Diseases Associated with Exposure to Certain Herbicide Agents. 2006. 38 U.S.C. § 1116).

The Agent Orange Act continued to use both association and causation language, albeit in a somewhat different form. It gave the VA Secretary authority to prescribe regulations providing for a presumption "[w]henever the Secretary determines, on the basis of sound medical and scientific evidence, that a positive association exists between" the Agent Orange exposure and a disease. The act states that

> An association between the occurrence of a disease in humans and exposure to an herbicide agent shall be considered to be positive for the purposes of this section if the credible evidence for the association is equal to or outweighs the credible evidence against the association. (Agent Orange Act of 1991. Public Law 102-4. 102d Cong., 1st Sess.)

Rather than relying on an advisory committee to furnish scientific input, the act directed VA to contract with the National Academy of Sciences (NAS) "to review and evaluate the available scientific evidence regarding associations between diseases and exposure to dioxin and other chemical compounds in herbicides" (Agent Orange Act of 1991. Public Law 102-4. 102d Cong., 1st Sess.). In making an association determination, the VA Secretary was instructed to consider the NAS reports and "all other sound medical and scientific information and analyses available to the Secretary," and in evaluating any study, the VA Secretary is to "take into consideration whether the results are statistically significant, are capable of replication, and withstand peer review" (Agent Orange Act of 1991. Public Law 102-4. 102d Cong., 1st Sess.).

Congress directed the committee to answer "to the extent that available scientific data permit meaningful determinations" (Scientific Determinations Concerning Disease. 2006. 38 U.S.C. § 1116.3[d][1]) about

1. whether a statistical association with herbicide exposure exists, taking into account the strength of the scientific evidence and the appropriateness of the statistical and epidemiologic methods used to detect the association;
2. the increased risk of disease among those exposed to herbicides during service in the Republic of Vietnam during the Vietnam era; and
3. whether there exists a plausible biological mechanism or other evidence of a causal relationship between herbicide exposure and disease.

The first IOM Veterans and Agent Orange (VAO) committee that was convened to respond to these questions (IOM, 1994, p. 15) concluded that a lack of exposure data made it impossible to answer the second question. The other two questions required the committee to examine the cause of the particular health effect at issue. This is explicit in question 3, which mandates inquiry into a "causal relationship." Question 1 also requires a causal inquiry, though it makes this request implicitly. As Dr. Hertz-Picciotto, the chair of the 2000 and 2002 IOM committees explained: "[A]ny determination about the existence of 'statistical association' that takes into account 'strength' of the evidence and 'appropriateness' of the methods examines the same concerns that enter into a consideration of evidence for causation" (Hertz-Picciotto, 2005, p. 556).

The first IOM VAO committee began meeting in 1992 and issued its first review in 1994 (IOM, 1994). It decided to place the data it found and reviewed into one of four categories: sufficient evidence of an association; limited/suggestive evidence of an association; inadequate/insufficient evidence to determine whether an association exists; limited/suggestive evidence of no association. It was required to update its reports every 2 years or sooner.

The IOM VAO committees at times changed the category for several particular health outcomes, as successive reviews considered additional evidence. VA's response and establishment of a presumption to the IOM categorization of the particular health outcome was not necessarily consistent. For example, the VAO committees in 1994 and 1996 characterized the evidence linking Agent Orange to prostate cancer as limited/suggestive of an association (IOM, 1994, 1996). VA did not establish a presumption for prostate cancer in 1994. It was not until 1996 that VA decided that prostate cancer should be presumptively service-connected (VA, 1996). In another example, the 1994 IOM VAO committee characterized the evidence linking herbicides to type 2 diabetes to be inadequate/insufficient to determine if an association existed (IOM, 1994). In 2000, a special Agent Orange committee was constituted at the request of VA to evaluate type 2 diabetes independent of the IOM VAO biennial reviews (IOM, 2000b). The committee characterized the evidence as limited/suggestive of an association (IOM, 2000b). VA then decided that type 2 diabetes should be presumptively service-connected (VA, 2001). It was not clear from the *Federal Register* notice why VA concluded that the existence of limited/suggestive evidence was equivalent to the requirement of "credible evidence for the association is equal to or outweighs the credible evidence against the association" or a "positive association" as required by the Agent Orange Act of 1991 (Public Law 102-4. 102d Cong., 1st Sess.). The statement in the *Federal Register* reporting the VA Secretary's decision to presumptively service-connect (VA, 2001) did not explicitly explain how these conclusions were reached.

The Persian Gulf War Presumptions

The Persian Gulf War was fought during a very short period in 1991. Almost immediately, veterans began to complain of numerous adverse health effects that they attributed to service in the Gulf. It immediately became evident to Congress and VA that the Persian Gulf veterans' health complaints differed significantly from those voiced by the Vietnam veterans. The Vietnam veterans ascribed their medical woes to herbicides and Agent Orange, and they claimed that the numerous well-defined diseases from which they suffered, ranging from skin and liver diseases to a variety of cancers, could be attributed to exposure to herbicides and Agent Orange. The Persian Gulf War veterans, on the other hand, claimed to be suffering from syndromes and symptoms rather than established diseases, and they blamed these on exposures to a host of toxic environmental substances that were present in the Persian Gulf. Many of the exposures are no different than those experienced by civilians in the United States, and for the great majority of veterans, the magnitude of the exposures was small, and limited to a short period of time (Brown, 2005).

Congress began by authorizing VA to provide health-care services on a priority basis to Persian Gulf veterans (Priority VA Health Care for Persian Gulf Veterans. 1993. Public Law 103-210. 103d Cong., 1st Sess.). An effort was also undertaken to gather data about the nature of the illnesses and symptoms that veterans claimed to have, as well as to conduct research on environmental exposures that occurred during the war. In 1994, Congress passed the Veterans' Benefits Improvements Act (Public Law 103-446. 103rd Cong., 2d Sess., codified as Compensation for Disabilities Occurring in Persian Gulf War Veterans. 2006. 38 U.S.C. § 1117), which authorized VA to compensate veterans for certain chronic disabilities and illnesses that could not be attributed to any known clinical diagnosis. Originally, these adverse health effects had to manifest within 2 years of service in the Persian Gulf in order for a veteran to receive compensation. This presumptive time period has, however, been extended a number of times. Most recently in December 2006, compensation is now available provided the disability of "undiagnosed illness" becomes manifest by December 31, 2011 (VA, 2006a, p. 75672).

In 1998, Congress passed the Persian Gulf War Veterans Act of 1998 (Public Law 105-277. 105th Cong., 2d Sess., codified, in part, as Presumptions of Service Connection for Illnesses Associated with Service in the Persian Gulf During the Persian Gulf War. 2006. 38 U.S.C. § 1118) and the Veterans Programs Enhancement Act of 1998 (Public Law 105-368. 105th Cong., 2d Sess.). These acts, which are similar to the Vietnam War Agent Orange legislation, set up procedures for establishing presumptions of service connection for diseases incurred by Gulf War veterans. As in the Agent Orange legislation, "a positive association" is required between an environmental exposure associated with service in the Persian Gulf War and "the occurrence of a diagnosed or undiagnosed illness in humans or animals" (Presumptions of Service Connection for Illnesses Associated with Service in the Persian Gulf During the Persian Gulf War. 2006. 38 U.S.C. § 1118[b][1][B][ii]). In addition, the Gulf War Act stated that an association "shall be considered to be positive . . . if the credible evidence for the association is equal to or outweighs the credible evidence against the association" (Presumptions of Service Connection for Illnesses Associated with Service in the Persian Gulf During the Persian Gulf War. 2006. 38 U.S.C. § 1118[b][3]). The same review process as was set up for Agent Orange was established for Gulf War. An agreement was entered into with NAS to establish committees that were charged with answering similar questions as asked of the IOM VAO committees (Persian Gulf War Veterans Act of 1998. Public Law 105-277. 105th Cong., 2d Sess.). As with Agent Orange, the IOM committee provides its Gulf War reports to VA, and the VA Secretary must then determine whether a presumption should be established and announce the decision in the *Federal Register*. IOM has issued several volumes of Gulf War reports (IOM, 2000a, 2003, 2005, 2006, 2007).

Although VA was given the authority by Congress to do so, VA has not made presumptions of service connection to date for diseases incurred by Persian Gulf War veterans pursuant to 38 U.S.C. § 1118 (Presumptions of Service Connection for Illnesses Associated with Service in the Persian Gulf During the Persian Gulf War. 2006. 38 U.S.C. § 1118). However, VA administers compensation for Persian Gulf War veterans who are service connected by the congressionally established presumption of "undiagnosed illnesses" that may become manifest within a presumptive period after service in the Gulf. In February 2006, the VA Secretary wrote to leaders of the House and Senate Veterans Affairs Committees advising them that the evidence currently available did not warrant the establishment of Persian Gulf presumptions and that VA would publish notices of its decision in the *Federal Register* "explaining the basis for that determination" (Nicholson letters on file with committee, 2006a,b,c,d). As of the time of report publication, no statement appears in the *Federal Register*, although such statements are required to be filed within 60 days of the receipt of an IOM report (Presumptions of Service Connection for Illnesses Associated with Service in the Persian Gulf During the Persian Gulf War. 2006. 38 U.S.C. § 1118). Although the presumptive service-connection mechanism has not been a major factor for Persian Gulf veterans, a comparatively large percentage of Persian Gulf veterans have, nonetheless, been able to collect compensation through the direct service-connection route (Brown, 2006).

As of now, the Persian Gulf statutes would govern any presumptions dealing with current service in Iraq or any other area in the Gulf.

REFERENCES

Brown, M. 2005. The role of science in Department of Veterans Affairs disability compensation policies for environmental and occupational illness and injuries. *Journal of Law and Policy* 13(2):593-612.

Brown, M. 2006. *The role of science in Department of Veterans Affairs disability compensation policies for environmental and occupational illness and injuries.* Paper presented to the IOM's Committee on Evaluation of the Presumptive Disability Decision-Making Process for Veterans, Washington, DC.

Hertz-Picciotto, I. 2005. How scientists view causality and assess evidence: A study of the Institute of Medicine's evaluation of health effects in Vietnam veterans and Agent Orange. *Journal of Law and Policy (Brooklyn Law School)* 13(2):553-591.

IOM (Institute of Medicine). 1994. *Veterans and Agent Orange: Health effects of herbicides used in Vietnam.* Washington, DC: National Academy Press.

IOM. 1996. *Veterans and Agent Orange: Update 1996.* Washington, DC: National Academy Press.

IOM. 2000a. *Gulf War and health, volume 1: Depleted uranium, pyridostigmine bromide, sarin, vaccines.* Washington, DC: National Academy Press.

IOM. 2000b. *Veterans and Agent Orange: Herbicide/dioxin exposure and type 2 diabetes.* Washington, DC: National Academy Press.

IOM. 2003. *Gulf War and health, volume 2: Insecticides and solvents.* Washington, DC: The National Academies Press.

IOM. 2005. *Gulf War and health, volume 3: Fuels, combustion products, and propellants.* Washington, DC: The National Academies Press.

IOM. 2006. *Gulf War and health, volume 4: Health effects of serving in the Gulf War.* Washington, DC: The National Academies Press.

IOM. 2007. *Gulf War and health, volume 5: Infectious diseases.* Washington, DC: The National Academies Press.

Murphy, S. 1986. A critique of the Veterans Administration claims process. *Brooklyn Law Review* 52:533-569.

NRC (National Research Council). 2003. *A review of the dose reconstruction program of the Defense Threat Reduction Agency.* Washington, DC: The National Academies Press.

Podgor, M. F. 2005. The inability of World War II atomic veterans to obtain disability benefits: Time is running out on our chance to fix the system. *Elder Law Journal* 13(2):519-523.

Reagan, R. 1984. *Statement on signing the Veterans' Dioxin and Radiation Exposure Compensation Standards Act.* http://www.presidency.ucsb.edu/ws/ index.php?pid=39308&st=&st1= (accessed May 15, 2007).

Stellman, J. M., and S. D. Stellman. 2005. Characterization of exposure to Agent Orange in Vietnam veterans as a basis for epidemiological studies. *Journal of Law and Policy (Brooklyn Law School)* 13(2):505-525.

U.S. Congress, House of Representatives. 1984. *Agent Orange and Atomic Veterans Relief Act.* House Report 98-592. 98th Cong., 2nd Sess. January 25.

VA (Department of Veterans Affairs). 1985. Adjudication of claims based on exposure to dioxin or ionizing radiation. Final rules. *Federal Register* 50(165):34452-34461.

VA. 1996. Diseases associated with exposure to certain herbicide agents (prostate cancer and acute and subacute peripheral neuropathy). Final rule. *Federal Register* 61(217):57586-57589.

VA. 2001. Diseases associated with exposure to certain herbicide agents: Type 2 diabetes. *Federal Register* 66(89):23166-23169.

VA. 2002. Diseases specific to radiation-exposed veterans. Final rule. *Federal Register* 67(17):3612-3616.

VA. 2005. *VA M21-1MR Adjudication Procedures Manual Rewrite.* Washington, DC: Department of Veterans Affairs. http://www.warms.vba.va.gov/M21_1MR.html (accessed May 14, 2007).

VA. 2006a. Extension of the presumptive period for compensation for Gulf War veterans. *Federal Register* 71(242):75669-75672.

VA. 2006b. General provisions. Proposed rule. *Federal Register* 71(62):16464-16475.

Zeglin, D. E. 2006. *Presumptions of service connection.* Paper prepared for the Veterans' Disability Benefits Commission. https://www.1888932-2946.ws/vetscommission/e-documentmanager/gallery/Documents/Reference_Materials/Presumption-Paper_3-7-06.pdf (accessed March 8, 2007).

5

Case Studies Summary Chapter

INTRODUCTION

In addressing its charge with regard to characterizing Congress' and the Department of Veterans Affairs' (VA's) presumptive disability decision-making process for veterans, the Committee completed the set of case studies around specific exposures and illnesses listed in Table 5-1. The Committee determined that a thorough evaluation of selected case studies would capture past practices of all participants involved in the presumptive disability decision-making process for veterans—Congress, VA, the National Academies' (Institute of Medicine [IOM] and National Research Council [NRC]), stakeholders, and the courts—and provide a basis for making sound and practical recommendations for the future of this process. The complete, specific case studies are found in Appendix I.

The case studies were selected to reflect the range of presumptive decisions established by Congress and VA, as they made decisions using evidence ranging from abundant and quite conclusive in the case of radiation to much more limited in cases such as Agent Orange and prostate cancer. The examples were also chosen to illustrate approaches taken by IOM and NRC committees in evaluating evidence related to presumptions. In the case studies, the Committee focused on examining the evidence foundation available for evaluation by Congress, the IOM or NRC, and VA; the approaches taken for reviewing the evidence; the schema used to classify the level of evidence for causation; and the translation of the scientific evidence through the conclusions of the IOM and NRC committees into a decision by VA. The case studies also provided insights into principles embedded in the presumptive disability decision-making process.

TABLE 5-1 List of Case Studies (in chronological order of when presumptions were established by Congress or VA)

Mental Disorders' Presumptions
Multiple Sclerosis Presumption
Prisoners of War (POWs) Presumptions
Amputees and Cardiovascular Disease Presumption
Radiation Presumptions
Mustard Gas and Lewisite Presumptions
Gulf War Presumptions
Agent Orange and Prostate Cancer Presumption
Agent Orange and Type 2 Diabetes Presumption
Spina Bifida Program*

*Because spina bifida is a condition that affects the children of veterans, it is not a presumptive decision for veterans; however, the children of Vietnam and Korean War veterans are covered by a VA program.

The case studies were based on detailed review of public laws, legislative background, research reports, National Academies' IOM and NRC committees' reports, and VA materials. However, as described in Chapter 1, the case studies were limited by VA's response to the Committee's request for information, documents, and responses to the Committee's written questions. The case studies synthesize a large body of information. This body of information is summarized in Annex 5-1 at the end of this chapter, and the full case study series is in Appendix I. Additional materials on individual case studies and cost estimates are also referenced at the end of this chapter in Annexes 5-2 and 5-3. This chapter synthesizes the "lessons learned" from each of the case studies. We begin by summarizing each of the case studies and the particular lessons learned and then look across the case studies as a group for more general conclusions. The case studies are presented in chronological order as to when presumptions were established by Congress or VA. In drawing out these lessons as a basis for moving forward, the Committee's commentary should not be construed as a critique of past activities and processes of Congress, VA, and National Academies' IOM and NRC committees. This Committee recognizes that these activities took place over decades during which scientific research and evidence review processes were evolving and that tremendous efforts from all participants in the process went into producing all of the work that we summarize as follows.

MENTAL DISORDERS' PRESUMPTIONS

Description

There have been two major types of presumptive disabilities for mental disorders among U.S. veterans: those presumed to be chronic and those among POWs. The diversity of these disorders has posed a challenge. The presumptive disabilities assigned to posttraumatic stress disorder (PTSD), depression, and any anxiety state for POWs are well grounded in the scientific literature (Beebe, 1975; CDC, 1988; Cohen and Cooper, 1954; Engdahl and Page, 1991; Keehn, 1980; Nefgzer, 1970; Page et al., 1997). The presumptive disability category for psychosis among veterans has a more limited base of evidence (Beebe, 1975; Keehn, 1980) and appears a consequence of its initial inclusion as a presumptive disability when presumptions first began in 1921. At that time, the disorder (then called neuropsychiatric disease) had no treatment and was considered to be chronic.

Lessons Learned

Presumptive decisions for mental disorders have been made for veterans who are former POWs and veterans who developed chronic mental problems during or shortly after military service. Although legislation has been informed by the scientific evidence available at the time, the scientific evidence in some instances has been limited and with inconsistency around the disorders included. For example, if the strength of evidence classification of limited/suggestive evidence led to presumptive decisions for PTSD, dysthymia, and any anxiety state among former POWs, then there does not appear to be a clear basis for excluding other mental disorders with equal or stronger evidence of connection to being a POW, such as major depression. The presumptive decisions established with regard to the previously mentioned mental disorders make clear that these decisions have been influenced by not only scientific evidence but by political and social considerations that apply to these veterans (e.g., POWs) and the specific mental disorders they may manifest. The need to develop a stronger evidence base and consistent evaluation of the evidence base with regard to these mental disorders is great, particularly in light of the anticipated high rates of mental disorders among military personnel assigned to and returning from Iraq and Afghanistan. This case study also illustrates the need for a process to continually carry out research and update the scientific evidence base for presumptions.

MULTIPLE SCLEROSIS PRESUMPTION

Description

This case study examines the 1962 decision to grant compensation for service-connected disability to veterans diagnosed with multiple sclerosis (MS) within 7 years of their separation from the military. This presumption stems from the VA's interest in compensating disease and disability that has its onset *during* military service. Veterans with one of a defined list of chronic diseases may also be compensated if these are diagnosed within 1 year of separation from the military. The rationale here is that these diseases are sufficiently insidious and the diagnosis sufficiently challenging so as to make it impossible to conclude with certainty that the true disease onset *did not* occur during the period of military service.

Multiple sclerosis was eventually singled out from the other chronic illnesses and the period of diagnosis extended from 1 year (Veterans' Chronic and Tropical Diseases Act of 1948. Public Law 80-748. 80th Cong., 2d Sess.; VA, 1949), to 2 (Act of October 12, 1951. ch. 499, 65 Stat. 421 as cited in VA, 1993), to 3 years (Act of August 25, 1959. Public Law 86-187. 86th Cong., 1st. Sess. as cited in VA, 1993), and eventually to 7 years (Veterans' Disability Compensation Increase Act of 1962. Public Law 87-645. 87th Cong., 2d Sess. as cited in VA, 1993) following separation from military service. The rationale for this extension was the growing scientific evidence (much of it generated by VA researchers studying veterans) of the long delay between the onset of MS symptoms and eventual diagnosis, as well as the possibility that environmental factors may play a role in the etiology of MS. However, these studies also failed to find evidence that military service contributes to MS risk, and veterans do not appear to have higher rates of MS than the general population (Berkowitz and Santangelo, 1999; Kurtzke and Page, 1997; Kurtzke et al., 1979, 1985, 1992; Norman et al., 1983; Page et al., 1993, 1995; VA Multiple Sclerosis Study Group, 1956, 1957; Wallin et al., 2000).

Lessons Learned

The rationale for the MS presumption reflects two lines of reasoning used in making presumptions. The first reflects the possibility that MS diagnosed after separation from the military may, in fact, have been present during military service, and therefore subject to the same compensation rules as other direct service-connection disabilities. The second acknowledges that the etiology of MS is unclear and may be related to an environmental exposure received during military service. Understanding that both of these arguments have been used in the MS case is important, because the evidence required to support each is very different. In the first case, timing is the standard (specifically the possibility of disease onset during military service), and evidence for association between an exposure and outcome is not required. By contrast, in the second case, evidence from some association between exposure during service and future disease is necessary.

Congress did not call for a systematic review of the scientific literature on this topic; such a review might have allowed for more evidentiary discussion of the premise behind this presumption and the type of evidence that might be necessary to support it.

PRISONERS OF WAR PRESUMPTIONS

Description

Disability presumptions concerning American veterans who were captured and interned as POWs almost uniformly developed as a result of congressional initiatives prompted by concerns over the harsh treatment that POWs had endured and practical difficulties that they might encounter in establishing entitlement to benefits. Concerned that World War II POWs might lack official medical records and have difficulties establishing the conditions of their internment, Congress first instructed VA to give special consideration and apply liberal evidentiary standards to POWs' claims. As details of the harsh nature of the POW experience became more widely known, and as members received complaints from some former POWs having difficulties establishing disability benefit claims, Congress began to enact statutory presumptions for certain nutritionally related conditions and mental illness. Studies of mortality and morbidity among POWs suggesting connections of the POW experience with certain diseases and conditions also served as impetus for additional legislation, notwithstanding scientific limitations noted in those studies (Keehn, 1980; Nefzger, 1970; Page and Miller, 2000; Page and Ostfeld, 1994; Page and Tanner, 2000; VA, 1993). Over the course of more than 50 years, certain preconditions that had to be met before a presumption could attach, such as length or internment or the time period in which a condition must first be manifested, were progressively liberalized or eliminated by statute. In 2004 VA established administrative standards for any new POW presumptions based on "limited/suggestive evidence" of an association of the disease with internment provided that it was "biologically plausible" (VA, 2004).

Lessons Learned

Americans and their elected representatives have long been concerned with the welfare of those who protected, defended, and sacrificed for their country. The extensive system of veteran benefits and their liberalized rules for qualification are a manifestation of this concern. This concern is intensified when those veterans seeking assistance are viewed as having been subjected to extraordinary stresses and sacrifices, as have POWs. As VA declared in its 1980 study, the POW experience was an "extremely harsh and brutal experience," ". . . characterized by starvation, diet, poor quality or nonexistent medical care, 'death marches,' executions, and torture" (VA, 1980, p. 4).

Given this context, the creation of certain presumptions with respect to disabilities claimed to be connected with a veteran's experience as a POW reflects long established concern for their welfare. These presumptions simplify adjudication for otherwise difficult cases because of the lack of specific evidence on exposures and the complexity of the health consequences of having been a POW. A difficult burden of proof for the veteran and VA is removed by a presumption. Presumptions have been particularly helpful in assessing POW claims for which information about individual conditions of internment and complete medical records were frequently unavailable. Presumptions have enabled greater consistency in decision making for POWs; a previous lack of consistency generated much discontent by veterans who strongly communicated their concerns to elected representatives.

Research has been carried out on the health of former POWs (Beebe, 1975; Brass and Page, 1996; Cohen and Cooper, 1954; IOM, 1992; Keehn, 1980; Nefzger, 1970; Page and Brass, 2001; Page et al., 1991, 1997; VA, 1980). The studies, which date back to the early 1950s, have slowly provided evidence on the POW experience, particularly about malnutrition, stress, and the psychological consequences.

At the same time, evidence relevant to particular presumptions was sometimes limited by coming from a single study with a small sample size. Consequently, interpretations of most studies acknowledged the uncertainties of findings and urged caution at drawing unwarranted inferences. As described by one author, the mixture and interdependence of various factors of the POW experience and the variation of their relative intensities "from time to time, from place to place, and from man to man," have "limit[ed] the scope and specificity of the inferences that may be drawn statistically" (Nefzger, 1970, p. 124).

Given the suggestive but scientifically uncertain results of many studies, not surprisingly policy makers frequently decided to create service-connected presumptions when faced with the pressing claims of genuinely sick and disabled former POWs. As one author observed of his 1992 study of POWs, the "descriptive" data obtained had "uses beyond the scientific," specifically in the "discussion of military service-connected disabilities." He added, "[d]espite the fact that sound inferences about the group of all former POWs cannot be drawn from the exam data in this report, policymakers *who must deal with such issues* should be able to review this descriptive information" (IOM, 1992, p. 5; emphasis added). VA in its 2004 *Guidelines for POW Presumptions* responds to uncertainty; while expressing an intent to base its determinations on "sound scientific and medical evidence," it adopts a standard of "limited/suggestive evidence" of an association for former POWs and adds the additional caveat that "fairness to former POWs requires that VA fully evaluate the available data and not accord undue significance to the fact that such data are comparatively limited by the small size of the affected population" (VA, 2004, p. 60085).

The POW case study illustrates how uncertainties of the available scientific information have been relatively weighted against other driving factors for compensating POWs. Over time, the requirement that a presumptive decision be "based on sound scientific and medical evidence" has increasing been overshadowed by these other considerations, reflecting the determination to assure that compensation for former POWs has maximum sensitivity.

AMPUTEES AND CARDIOVASCULAR DISEASE PRESUMPTION

Description

This case study examines the 1979 presumption of service connection for cardiovascular disease that develops in veterans with certain types of service-related amputations. This case study was chosen to illustrate several important features. First, in contrast to many presumptions that exist because of the difficulty establishing exposure status among veterans, this presumption applies to a defined group of veterans for whom exposure (i.e., amputation) is not in question. Controversy regarding whether amputation was linked to cardiovascular disease prevented this complication from being compensated through standard individual claims and therefore necessitated the presumption. Second, this presumption was put in place through legislative action on the part of Congress, not administratively by VA, as is the case with many of the other presumptions. Third, the scientific basis for this presumption is a single Medical Follow-Up Agency (MFUA) study of World War II amputees and their mortality from cardiovascular disease (Hrubec and Ryder, 1980). During the more than 30 years of follow-up of the study population, 922 proximal amputees died; 714.1 deaths were expected based on the general U.S. male death rate. Compared with distal amputees and those with disfigurement, proximal amputees had a higher risk of all-cause mortality, diabetes, and cardiovascular disease, particularly atherosclerotic (ischemic) heart disease.

Lessons Learned

The lessons from this case study center around the type of evidence necessary to put a presumption in place, specifically what level of evidence should be required for a presumption; how the scientific base of evidence is updated based on new studies; how to evaluate evidence regarding exposures, outcomes, and potential mediators; and what types of evidence might make the scientific basis for a presumption more robust. This presumption was put into place largely on the basis of one study and further studies on cardiovascular disease in amputees have not been carried out, even though the occurrence, management, and natural history of cardiovascular diseases have changed substantially in the subsequent three decades. In the decades since the presumption was implemented, many aspects of cardiovascular disease have changed; incidence rates have dropped, as has mortality; new preventive approaches are available, and treatments are increasingly effective. However, further studies have not been carried out on cardiovascular disease in subsequent cohorts of amputees, nor were data systems put in place to carry out surveillance for changing disease risks in the amputees. Special populations, such as the amputees, could be closely tracked through registries (i.e., specific cohort studies) to make certain that previous scientific observations hold and to assess if the establishment of additional presumptions is needed.

RADIATION PRESUMPTIONS

Description

The radiation case study is concerned with the experience of the "atomic veterans" who were exposed to ionizing radiation, mainly through participation in nuclear weapons tests. In this case study, unlike most of the others, there is an abundant literature—some relating to dose-response relationships in general populations, some specific to veterans—upon which to base compensation policy (CIRRPC, 1988; IARC, 2000; IOM, 1996a, 2002; Lagakos and Mosteller, 1986; Lubin and Steindorf, 1995; NRC, 1980, 1984, 2003, 2005, 2006; Podgor, 2007; Prentice et al., 1983; RECAC, 1996; UNSCEAR, 2000). In general, most veterans for whom exposure estimates are available appear to have had relatively low doses, and a summary of the epidemiologic evidence suggests that the majority of cancers in this group were not caused by radiation. Despite this, there remain numerous uncertainties, particularly with respect to estimation of an individual's exposures and with respect to the risk for specific rare cancers. These uncertainties in large part are responsible for the shift in emphasis from individual dose-based criteria for compensation in the

Veterans' Dioxin and Radiation Exposure Compensation Standards Act of 1984 (Public Law 98-542. 98th Cong., 2d Sess.) to the establishment of presumptions in the Radiation-Exposed Veterans Compensation Act of 1988 (Public Law 100-321. 100th Cong., 2d Sess.), illustrating the need for presumptions even in this relatively data-rich situation. It also illustrates that epidemiologic studies of veterans themselves can be less informative than other nonmilitary populations because of such issues as limited sample size, inadequate length of follow-up, low doses, poor dosimetry, other potential biases, and difficulties in teasing out the effects of modifiers such as smoking. Finally, the radiation story illustrates the practical difficulties posed by the secrecy under which these nuclear weapons test operations were conducted, posing difficulties both for researchers and for individual veterans seeking to document their claims.

Lessons Learned

For radiation exposure, in contrast to the factors considered in the other case studies, epidemiological evidence on risks is abundant and the dose-response relationships for cancer have been described with reasonable precision from such major studies as that of the atomic bomb survivors. Epidemiological studies have been carried out on radiation-exposed veterans specifically. General models have been developed for quantifying the probability of causation, given the level of exposure. Additionally, there is a substantial body of research on mechanisms by which radiation causes cancer.

Nonetheless, uncertainties remain in extending this evidence to compensating particular veterans as their exposures are poorly estimated, disease outcomes lack specificity of cause, and for some rare cancers causation remains to be established. These uncertainties in large part appear responsible for the shift in emphasis from individual probability of causation (PC)-based criteria for compensation in the Veterans' Dioxin and Radiation Exposure Compensation Standards Act of 1984 (Public Law 98-542. 98th Cong., 2d Sess.) to the establishment of presumptions in the Radiation-Exposed Veterans Compensation Act of 1988 (Public Law 100-321. 100th Cong., 2d Sess.). Still unresolved is whether, in light of the uncertainties about site-specific risk, perhaps *all* cancers in radiation-exposed veterans should be treated as presumptively caused by radiation, at least absent very convincing evidence that the specific cancer is not caused by radiation. Arguably, the only site that might be excluded on this basis would be chronic lymphatic leukemia.

While the Committee has called for research and surveillance on the health of veterans, the studies of radiation effects in veteran populations have proven of limited utility, in part because of the relatively small number of excess cancers expected in the available cohorts and, importantly, because individual exposures were not tracked in a systematic manner. As a result an opportunity to carefully characterize radiation-related cancer risks among veterans may have been missed. Fortunately, there has long been a strong body of evidence from other populations, so that the weak evidence provided by the studies of veterans has not been construed as a basis for holding back on presumptions for radiation. The availability of strong epidemiologic data has made possible the construction of quantitative models to guide compensation policy for radiation-exposed veterans, which has often not been possible for other exposures. These models have not been used to quantify the burden of radiation-caused cancer among veterans.

Specificity is an issue in compensation of cancers in radiation-exposed individuals. Many cancers caused by radiation also have many other responsible risk factors, and cases caused by radiation cannot be distinguished from those caused by other factors. Additionally, for most radiation exposures received during military service, the probability of causation is low. In the example of smoking, which interacts with radiation for lung cancer, evidence-based policies can be developed based on an understanding of the joint effects of radiation and smoking. Potentially, if data are available, similar models could be developed for the interaction of radiation with other agents.

Ultimately, much of the force behind the movement for compensation for the atomic veterans came from the fact that the government deliberately exposed them to harm, while having at least some knowledge of the risks involved at the time. Furthermore, the risks were often denied by government officials, both at the time of exposure when military personnel were not properly informed and later when diseases were manifest and attempts at redress were dismissed. On this basis, veterans consider that the case for their claims for compensation is enhanced by the culpability of the government.

MUSTARD GAS AND LEWISITE PRESUMPTIONS

Description

This case study examines the 1992 and 1994 decisions by VA to establish presumptive service connection for health outcomes related to mustard gas and lewisite exposures among World War II veterans. This case study, the first involving a congressional request for the IOM to develop a report, raises a series of still persistent issues. With the recognition that some World War II veterans had been exposed to mustard gas during laboratory studies, VA in 1992 proposed a presumptive service-connection decision covering this exposure (VA, 1992a). The presumption was based on four primary factors: (1) the studies were classified, (2) participants were directed not to discuss their participation in the studies, (3) their medical records were sparse, and (4) no long term follow-up was conducted or provided for the participants (VA, 1992a). VA issued a final rule in July 1992 (VA, 1992b).

As a result of public comment to the proposed rule as found in the final rule (VA, 1992a,b), VA contracted with IOM to write a report on the health effects of exposure to mustard gas and lewisite. In early 1994, VA revised the presumption based on the IOM study, *Veterans at Risk: The Health Effects of Mustard Gas and Lewisite* (IOM, 1993), and issued a proposed rule (VA, 1994a). The second presumptive service-connection rule was issued in August 1994. This rule amended the original proposal by (1) adding more diseases to the original list of diseases, (2) adding the compound lewisite to the rule, (3) adding veterans who might have been exposed during World War I and in studies after the end of World War II, and (4) clarifying the extent of exposure (VA, 1994b).

Lessons Learned

A number of concerns are raised by this presumptive decision. Foremost is the unresolved problem raised by secrecy surrounding military/governmental studies involving exposure of military personnel to warfare agents that may have immediate or delayed effects on their health (IOM, 1993). Classifying warfare studies based on national security is necessary in many cases. However, this classification can lead to concerns about health that might not be resolved for decades.

In the case of mustard and lewisite agents, national security took precedence over the long-term health risks to the study participants. Participants in these studies maintained their secrecy oaths for decades even though they developed health problems consequent to their exposures. As health consequences emerged there were problems in finding information about exposure to mustard gas or lewisite in their medical records. Consequently, health-care providers could not provide appropriately targeted screening and care and long-term medical follow-up was not provided to the study participants. A third area of concern is that this classification precluded health-care providers from being aware that symptoms of mustard gas or lewisite exposure might be exhibited by patients. As a result, the health-care providers did not look for these occupationally related symptoms (IOM, 1993).

The consequences of secreting information were partially recognized in several Information Letters from the VA Under Secretary for Health (VA, 2002, 2005, 2006). As indicated in the Presidential Task Force 2003 report (President's Task Force to Improve Health Care Delivery for Our Nation's Veterans, 2003) and a recent Government Accountability Office (GAO) report (GAO, 2006a), the health of our veterans must be considered in relation to all aspects of military service. The presidential task force specifically cited the lack of exposure data to a known environmental hazard as a root cause for not being able to determine compensatory issues for our veterans (GAO, 2006a,b). While it appears that DoD is addressing the tracking and recording of the Service members' movements to link with exposure data that have been collected, both of these issues remain concerns for the veteran. Inadequate exposure data are collected, and the ability to vector these data to location and troop movement has limited attribution of disease to exposure agents for individual veterans. Exposure assessment is the key to disability benefits for veterans. A recent report (GAO, 2004) indicates that force health protection and surveillance policy are not as good as they could be, but are improving, especially with more current deployments.

The final rule for mustard gas and lewisite (VA, 1994b), based upon the 1993 IOM report, outlined three categories of casual relationships for health consequences of exposure: indicated, suggested, and insufficient evidence of a relationship. VA acknowledged in the final rule that certain health consequences could be linked directly to mustard gas or lewisite exposure and that a second grouping of health consequences had a suggestive linkage based upon the 1993 IOM report. Although the IOM report recommended many diseases that could be associated with exposure to these agents, VA specifically eliminated several of the diseases as not being related to mustard gas or lewisite exposure. Consequently, a precedent was established by VA for causal health consequences associated with specific chemical agents as recommended by IOM. Lastly, this case study indicates an apparent lack of communication and coordination between DoD and VA regarding individual Service members and government workers involved in studies, chemical agents used in these studies, and any actual or potential exposure data for the individuals involved. This lack of coordination was emphatically pointed out in the 1993 report *Veterans at Risk* (IOM, 1993).

GULF WAR PRESUMPTIONS

Description

While the Gulf War presumption process was heavily influenced by the Agent Orange presumptive history, the course of the Gulf War process was different from that of its predecessor. The lengthy Agent Orange process was a culmination of interactions between veterans and their advocates, Congress, the scientific community, the work of the IOM committees, and VA. However, when Congress established the initial Gulf War presumption termed "undiagnosed illnesses," two of the aforementioned four groups—

the scientific community and VA—were not involved in the decision-making process. This initial presumptive provision for "undiagnosed illnesses" by Congress was based on symptom complaints of returning Gulf War veterans and was not related to single organ systems or easily explained by a unifying exposure or mechanism. Rather, nonspecific signs and symptoms were grouped under the "undiagnosed illnesses" category for disability compensation. VA was directed by Congress to administer the program.

After the first two provisions of the Gulf War presumptions had been enacted (unexplained illnesses and chronic multisymptom illness) by Congress, Congress instructed VA to commission a scientific review examining the candidate exposures in the Gulf theater that may have contributed to the health effects experienced by veterans. These reviews were performed by IOM committees and reported in a five-volume series titled *Gulf War and Health* (IOM, 2000a, 2003a, 2005a, 2006, 2007). The reviews found limited evidence of linkages between veterans' health and specific environmental exposures during deployment. The majority of the scientific findings from the IOM Gulf War committees and subsequent decisions by the VA Secretary to presumptively service connect or not service connect have not yet appeared in the *Federal Register* as required by statute, and VA has not yet presumptively connected any health conditions with Gulf War service.

Lessons Learned

Compensation presumptions mandated by Congress in the absence of certain scientific evidence that link Gulf War service to adverse health outcomes, while well intentioned, may have contributed to confusion and suspicion around the presumptive process. In addressing health problems in Gulf War veterans, Congress and VA faced the difficulty of providing compensation for a syndromic illness that had not been linked to specific exposures. Two approaches were followed. The earlier decision (1995), to make "presumptive" a list of conditions, signs, or symptoms clustered under the rubric of "undiagnosed illnesses" allowed medical care and other benefits to be provided to affected veterans by VA. The second approach departed from the initial symptom-based presumption model, and a 1998 act mandated as "presumptive" any additional conditions or symptoms that could be linked to "a biological, chemical, or other toxic agent, environmental or wartime hazard or preventive medicine or vaccine," extending the possible list of potential illnesses considered presumptively linked to service in the Gulf (Persian Gulf War Veterans Act of 1998. Public Law 105-277. 105th Cong., 2d Sess. § 1602). Thus, the presumptive process for Gulf War Illnesses may have been driven by public expectations and pressure on Congress and VA to act more quickly than either Congress or VA had acted with regard to Agent Orange decisions. It was clear that Congress did not want to wait very long to provide assistance to Gulf War veterans following the experience they had in establishing the Agent Orange Act.

In a politically charged and time-pressured context, decisions about qualification for the initial Gulf War presumption needed to be made, even though the base of scientific evidence was incomplete. Additionally, since Gulf War Illness comprised a symptom complex without any specific diagnostic features, a presumption was established largely in response to reports of numerous individual veterans with inexplicable symptomatology, whose health had deteriorated. Congress made a decision to accept the veteran's self-reported symptom complaints as sufficient evidence and validation of a Gulf War service-connected illness. Congress then directed VA, through legislation, to provide service-connected benefits to veterans with qualifying health complaints.

Little consideration has been given to estimating exposures received by individual veterans and the levels of exposures, or to the potential for using such estimates, based on specific locations in theater, job title, or specific duties, in determining eligibility for a service-connected Gulf War condition. There has been a broad assumption of exposure to harmful agents that are associated with Gulf War Illness, even though the responsible exposures were uncertain. In this example, Congress directed VA to choose to include all possible claims, permitting high sensitivity (including all possible cases), but poor specificity (high false positive claims). These initial policies came from Congress and were implemented by VA with little scientific review.

In subsequent decisions related to the Gulf War, VA has engaged IOM in producing reports that VA considers in the presumptive disability decision-making process. VA has asked IOM to examine adverse health effects rather than the existing "undiagnosed illness" or "chronic diseases" provisions established by Congress with relation to Gulf War service. These reviews have been the basis for subsequent decision making by VA, which has not yet established any presumptions for the Gulf War.

A lack of exposure information has hindered evidence-based decision making. Information for retrospectively estimating troop exposures during military service has been limited by gaps in exposure information, a limitation receiving comment by IOM committees and other groups addressing service-connected disability determinations (IOM, 2000a, 2003a, 2005a). There are obvious barriers to collecting such information, including the complexity of doing so during wartime deployments. On the other hand, there has been increasing understanding of the need for exposure assessment as an element of force health protection and readiness (DoD, 1997, 2006).

This case study also points to the potential for decision making without having a sufficient evidence base to lead to unintended, adverse consequences, including erosion of public trust and confidence in the decision-making process. The Committee viewed the legislated presumption for Gulf War Unexplained Illness as having some negative consequences. The decision was not evidence-based and it gave credence to the existence of a still poorly characterized and poorly investigated illness complex. Absent research, the presumption may have strengthened the belief that some candidate toxicants, or a mixture of environmental hazards known or unknown, existed in the Gulf War theater and were pervasively present at sufficient concentration to affect the thousands of veterans with symptoms of unexplained illness. Despite acknowledging preventable exposures to environmental chemicals in the Gulf War theater, after several IOM inquires into these hazards, none of the IOM committee reports (IOM, 2000a, 2003a, 2005a, 2006, 2007) has endorsed either a unifying candidate toxicant as a cause for unexplained Gulf War illness or a combination of causes as evidence for the presumptions established by Congress.

AGENT ORANGE AND PROSTATE CANCER PRESUMPTION

Description

Prostate cancer is the second most common cause of cancer deaths in U.S. men (SOURCE: http://seer.cancer.gov/csr/1975_2003/results_merged/topic_mor_trends.pdf). Although the focus of extensive research, few specific etiologic factors that explain the occurrence of the disease have been identified, other than a very strong association with age. The observational evidence available on Agent Orange and prostate cancer risk comes from epidemiological studies of herbicide and dioxin exposed groups in the general population and military personnel exposed to Agent Orange in Vietnam (see Table 6-34 in IOM, 2005b, pp. 277-280).

Beginning with the 1994 Agent Orange report, IOM committees consistently found "limited/suggestive" evidence associating prostate cancer with Agent Orange—with the results of one high-quality study indicating a positive and statistically significant association with phenoxy herbicide exposure, along with weaker evidence and less consistent findings from other studies (IOM, 1994, 1996b, 1999, 2001, 2003b, 2005b). In the populations that have been investigated with higher levels of exposure evidence, excess risk of prostate cancer has been found in some studies and not uniformly across these studies (IOM, 1994, 2005b). However, in addition to the dioxin contaminant, the chlorophenoxy herbicide is a potential causative agent. Based in part upon the IOM finding that there was "limited/suggestive" evidence for association, VA established a presumption in 1996 that provides benefits to Vietnam veterans with prostate cancer (VA, 1996).

Lessons Learned

In this case study, the Committee focused on the use of the scientific evidence on Agent Orange and prostate cancer in the decision to establish a presumption. The Committee assessed the relationship of the congressional language to the IOM's criteria for classifying evidence and the use of the IOM's evidence evaluation for prostate cancer by VA. The Agent Orange Act of 1991 (Public Law 102-4. 102nd Cong., 1st Sess. Section 2[b][3]) states that a positive association is one for which "the credible evidence of the association is equal to or outweighs the credible evidence against the association." This statement is not necessarily equivalent to the category of "limited/suggestive" evidence for association used by IOM committees. The IOM limited/suggestive category covers a broad range of epidemiological evidence from relatively weak to strongly suggestive. In the instance of Agent Orange and prostate cancer, VA made a presumption based on the IOM's conclusion of "limited/suggestive" evidence for association; the evidence at the time was relatively limited, but did include one study showing a statistically significant excess and a number of other studies showing positive, but weak and non-significant associations. Because the Committee did not have documentation of the rationale for VA's decision beyond the *Federal Register* notice (VA, 1996), the basis for making a presumption given the particular IOM conclusion and scope of evidence was unclear to the Committee.

In reviewing evidence on Agent Orange, the 2005 IOM review considered biological and toxicological evidence when evaluating the biological plausibility of the association between prostate cancer and exposure to Agent Orange but did not integrate these other lines of evidence with epidemiological findings to come up with an overall evaluation (IOM, 2005b). In seeking to classify the strength of evidence, prior IOM committees have relied mostly on epidemiological findings, potentially leaving the resulting presumptions open to criticism for having insufficient scientific justification when viewed in a broader context. Additionally, there has been a relatively limited body of relevant toxicological literature on prostate cancer.

The criterion for reaching "limited/suggestive" evidence for association of Agent Orange used by the IOM is that the "[e]vidence is suggestive of an association between herbicides and the outcome but is limited because chance, bias, and confounding could not be ruled out with confidence. For example, at least one high-quality study shows a positive association, but the results of other studies are inconsistent" (IOM, 2005b, p. 8) The Agent Orange Committee evaluations for prostate cancer considered the totality of epidemiological evidence, but there were limitations of the exposure data available to aid in the evaluation of the studies considered. Previous Agent Orange committees also reviewed and reported on toxicological and mechanistic information, but according to their interpretation of their charge, did not integrate this information with the epidemiological evidence to make conclusions about the overall weight of the evidence for causal association. Several studies were of worker groups and measures of exposure to either the chlorophenoxy compounds or dioxin were not available to enable comparisons across studies. Dose-response relationships could be considered for a few studies; for example, the relative risk "of prostate cancer in Ranch Hands correlated with putative exposure to Agent Orange (high 6.04 vs low 2.17 vs background 1.5; $p = 0.01$)" (IOM, 2005b, p. 282). The lack of accurate estimates of exposure from the military experience has limited the study of the association between prostate cancer and exposure to Agent Orange in veterans.

AGENT ORANGE AND TYPE 2 DIABETES PRESUMPTION

Description

This case study examines the 2001 decision to establish presumptive service connection for type 2 diabetes among Vietnam veterans under the Agent Orange Act (Agent Orange Act of 1991. Public Law 102-4. 102nd Cong., 1st Sess.). This case study was chosen because of several features in the events leading to the presumption and because of the implications of this presumption for VA. First, although most of the Agent Orange presumptions have been the result of the biennial IOM review of the scientific literature, the scientific evaluation that resulted in this presumption was conducted by a special IOM panel commissioned by VA specifically for this topic, out of sequence with the biennial IOM reports (IOM, 2000b). Second, after its review, this special IOM committee determined that the evidence linking Agent Orange and diabetes would justify a change from the previous category of "inadequate/insufficient" to "limited/suggestive." Third, VA issued a presumption for type 2 diabetes on the basis of this "limited/suggestive" category of evidence, rather than the using the "sufficient evidence" standard. Finally, as a consequence of this presumption, all veterans who served in Vietnam receive compensation for their type 2 diabetes, as well as the associated complications of this morbid, chronic condition. This presumption will continue to have important financial consequences for VA as type 2 diabetes incidence generally increases with advancing age and as national rates of type 2 diabetes continue to rise in all segments of the population, fueled primarily by the high rates of obesity and inactivity.

Lessons Learned

This case study has several features in common with some of the other case studies. As for radiation and cancer, type 2 diabetes has multiple risk factors, including age, family history, inactivity, and obesity. The extent to which Agent Orange contributes to causation of type 2 diabetes in veterans is uncertain, but likely to be relatively small compared with these other factors.

Some IOM Agent Orange reports have commented on the extent that Agent Orange exposure may contribute to diabetes rates observed among Vietnam veterans:

> It must be noted, however, that these studies indicate that the increased risk, if any, from herbicide or dioxin exposure appears to be small. The known predictors of diabetes risk—family history, physical inactivity, and obesity—continue to greatly outweigh any suggested increased risk from wartime exposure to herbicides. (IOM, 2000b, pp. 3, 37)

Recognition of the relative contributions of multiple factors could be important for the identifying and compensating service-attributable type 2 diabetes that develops among aging Vietnam veterans. The IOM Agent Orange committee reports have not attempted to quantify the attributable burden of disease, although such calculations would be useful for decision making, both to understand the potential burden of disease overall and to anticipate decisions about compensation for individual veterans. An additional explicit analysis of service-attributable risk that attempts to quantify the fraction of disease risk attributable to military service might be more useful to VA and Congress when making legislative and administrative decisions based on complex scientific evidence, although it is recognized that conducting such an analysis for this case would be a challenge given the lack of adequate research in this area and the limited data on exposures to herbicides.

Analyses of high-quality data for a representative cohort of veterans could have been informative for determining the existence of an association between exposures during military service and the risk of disease or disability. A well-designed cohort study might have contributed data for evaluating the link between Agent Orange and type 2 diabetes, particularly if the design had included accurate assessments of exposure during service, evaluation of other risk factors that may have been present during service or developed subsequently (e.g., obesity), and longitudinally assessed occurrence of this disease. In fact, the Vietnam Experience Study (VES) provided an opportunity to initiate a cohort study. Continuation of the study as a cohort might have proven informative for diabetes and other potential health consequences of service in Vietnam.

In evaluating the observational studies, specific and formal methodological protocols did not appear to be used for synthesizing findings of available studies and updating the classification of evidence as the findings of additional studies became available to successive committees. The type 2 diabetes presumption came after the 2000 IOM committee "upgraded" the assessment of the existing evidence from "inadequate/insufficient" to "limited/suggestive" category. Although new studies were considered in this reassessment, no particular study was considered as providing conclusive evidence of association between Agent Orange and type 2 diabetes. Rather, the reclassification reflected the committee's view of the cumulative weight of the evidence. Having a more detailed evidence review algorithm and classification approach, such as IARC (IARC, 2006), could enhance the consistency of assessment of evidence across different committees.

The case study also points to a lack of transparency in the VA's process where scientific evidence is applied to legislative and administrative decisions. The type 2 diabetes presumption signaled an important trend on the part of VA to assign presumption on the bases of "limited/suggestive" classification of the levels of evidence, rather than the highest standard of "sufficient" evidence. This decision may have been influenced by a variety of considerations beyond the scientific evidence, i.e., political, economic, and administrative factors. The interplay of these multiple factors and their relative weighting by VA were not described in any of the materials available to the Committee.

SPINA BIFIDA PROGRAM

Description

This case study examines the 1996 and 2003 decisions to grant monetary compensation and health benefits to children of Vietnam and Korean War veterans with spina bifida based on the scientific evidence suggesting an association between herbicide exposure in Vietnam and Korea and spina bifida in the children of exposed veterans. Reproductive health effects were considered by the first IOM veterans and Agent Orange report issued in 1994 (IOM, 1994). The committee concluded that male exposure to toxins could plausibly be linked to adverse developmental consequences in their offspring:

> Animal and human data indicate that the exposure of the male to various toxic agents may increase the risk of the full spectrum of adverse developmental endpoints from fetal loss to cancer. (IOM, 1994, p. 595)

But the committee found the evidence to support the link between Agent Orange and a range of birth defects to be "inadequate/insufficient"

(IOM, 1994, p. 6). In its response to the IOM report, VA noted that although reproductive effects were considered by the IOM committee, there was no mechanism within the existing VA compensation structure to award benefits to any party other than the veteran; providing compensation to children of veterans with developmental effects attributable to Agent Orange exposure would require additional legislative action (VA, 1994c, p. 346).

Based on new research findings, in the 1996 Agent Orange report, the IOM committee assessed the evidence for the association between Agent Orange and spina bifida as "limited/suggestive" (IOM, 1996b). This reclassification was based on a re-analysis of the Ranch Hand study, in response to a critique in the IOM's 1994 report. In addition the committee considered three other studies, each of which had potential biases that were different and therefore unlikely to be responsible for demonstrating a consistent pattern of results (IOM, 1996b).

Public Law 104-204 (Departments of Veterans Affairs and Housing and Urban Development, and Independent Agencies Appropriation Act, 1997. 104th Cong., 2d Sess.) was passed in 1996, authorizing benefits for children born to Vietnam veterans with spina bifida. Additional legislation in 2000 (Veterans Benefits and Health Care Improvement Act of 2000. Public Law 106-419 § 401. 106th Cong., 2d Sess.) established benefits to children of "women Vietnam veterans" with birth defects; this law provided benefits to children of female veterans with a broad range of defects that might be attributable to maternal exposure during Vietnam service (excluding defects that were the result of familial predisposition or the injury suffered at birth). In 2003, these benefits were extended to children of veterans of the Korean War (Veterans Benefits Act of 2003. Public Law 108-103. 108th Cong., 2d Sess.).

Lessons Learned

Apart from the programs established by legislative action described above, there continues to be no overall mechanism for compensating offspring for health consequences attributable to maternal or paternal military service. Toxic exposures that occur during military service have the potential to cause adverse developmental effects, and all of the Agent Orange reports have described the biologically plausible mechanisms for these effects in both exposed female and male veterans. Given VA's interest in compensating veterans for adverse health effects incurred as a result of military service and the possibility that such effects may extend to the health of veterans' offspring, the absence of a clear and consistent policy on compensating affected offspring is notable. The need for a clear policy statement will continue to grow as VA considers the health effects of military service in the large population of reproductive-aged veterans and the growing number of women in the armed services.

Although the public laws providing compensation for particular categories of offspring with birth defects may have been expedient for these affected individuals, the approach of addressing the more general policy gap described above with these programs runs counter to principles of consistency and equity that should inform the approach to presumptions. Any new adverse reproductive consequences of Agent Orange exposure identified in IOM reports would again require legislative action for these specific effects in order for compensation to be granted; the administrative route that has applied to all other Agent Orange presumptions is not available for reproductive consequences of exposure at present.

It should be noted that the evidence standard for the spina bifida presumption was "limited/suggestive," not the more rigorous "sufficient" standard (IOM, 1996b). The difficulty with using this lesser standard as the basis for presumptions has been described in other case studies related to Agent Orange and type 2 diabetes and prostate cancer.

SYNTHESIS

These case studies offer a diverse set of lessons learned and indicate elements of the current presumptive disability decision-making process for veterans that need to be addressed moving forward. The case studies show that the process has acted to serve the interests of veterans in many instances. Overall, Congress and VA have repeatedly acted to maximize the sensitivity of presumptive decisions so as to ensure that specific groups of veterans are compensated. The particular interest in caring for veterans who have experienced the hardship of being a POW, for example, has led to a range of presumptions that apply to POWs. However, in maximizing the sensitivity of presumptive decision making for particular groups of veterans, substantial numbers of false positives may have resulted, as in the examples of Agent Orange and the Gulf War. Additionally, because no systematic process for approaching presumptive decision making exists, important omissions in this coverage remain without a clear mechanism for expanding coverage, as with potential reproductive health consequences of military service for the offspring of those who serve.

The case studies illustrate the use of presumptions to cover gaps in evidence, gaps that exist in part because of lack of information on exposures received by military personnel and inadequate surveillance of veterans for the occurrence of service-related illnesses. Secrecy is a particularly troubling source of incomplete information, as illustrated by the veterans who participated in studies of mustard gas and lewisite. Research has been carried out on the health of veterans, leading to the decision, for example, on cardiovascular disease in amputees. But the research has not been systematic, and in the example of cardiovascular disease in amputees, further evidence relative to a presumption made in 1979 has not been collected. Research on radiation risks in veterans has been severely constrained by a lack of dose information, and the resulting studies have not been informative. A lack of exposure information has hindered research on other agents as well and led to a sweeping exposure presumption with regard to exposure to Agent Orange in Vietnam.

Across the case studies, the Committee believes that prior efforts did not optimally synthesize all of the evidence on the health consequences of military service. In some cases there has not been an independent body that reviews the scientific evidence and updates the medical knowledge and scientific evidence relevant for a specific presumptive decision over time. As a consequence, some presumptions appear inconsistent (as with the psychiatric illnesses) or even aberrant (as with multiple sclerosis) in the face of contemporary medical and scientific knowledge. In other cases where an independent body has reviewed the scientific evidence, the synthesis of the evidence has not always been optimally comprehensive and standardized. The inferential target in IOM reports has shifted between causation (e.g., mustard gas and lewisite, Gulf War) and association (e.g., Agent Orange), and the more recent IOM Agent Orange reports have emphasized findings of observational studies without full attention to other lines of evidence. In the Agent Orange case studies the category "limited/suggestive" for association has been used when the epidemiological evidence base was fairly weak, including only one study with statistically significant findings. In the case of type 2 diabetes, at the time of the Agent Orange and diabetes report, there were multiple studies that were all substantially limited by bias or confounding. The categorization of the evidence as "limited/suggestive" by IOM has led to presumptions on the part of VA that appear to be irreversible once made, even though scientific evidence is dynamic. Stated in another way, even if further scientific evidence were unsupportive of previous research findings and a future IOM committee were to change its classification for strength of evidence, VA may not change its presumption. The Committee notes that presumptive decisions have been made to compensate health outcomes (e.g., type 2 diabetes, prostate cancer), based on evidence characterized by IOM committees as limited/suggestive for association, well below the evidence level needed to establish causation, absent strong mechanistic understanding.

The case studies document the particular problem that arises with regard to presumptions related to common, chronic diseases with multiple causes, such as type 2 diabetes, prostate cancer, and cardiovascular disease. In seeking high sensitivity for presumptions in general, specificity is sacrificed, and the resulting number of false positives may be particularly large for common conditions with multiple etiologies. These false positives are associated with large attendant costs, both financial and non-financial. Determining the degree to which the onset of a common disease with multiple etiologies may be attributable to prior military service may be particularly useful for presumptions related to such conditions, but neither the IOM committees nor VA have given full consideration to whether the attributable fraction should be estimated for veterans. Later chapters of this report discuss how the attributable fraction might be estimated for veterans, and how such estimates would benefit VA in its presumptive disability decision-making process.

In the case studies, the Committee's analyses were based on the very general information provided by VA about its internal decision-making processes. The case studies did make clear, however, that these processes are neither fully transparent nor consistent. This was further implied by VA's decision to withhold task force documents from the Committee's review, considering them pre-decisional in nature. VA believes that access to pre-decisional documents by outside sources would stifle candid staff opinions on issues. Once IOM carries out its reviews and provides VA with reports documenting the extent of evidence available on associations, the internal processes that follow are not fully open to scrutiny. This practice could degrade the trust of veterans in the presumptive disability decision-making process and may hinder efforts to optimize the use of scientific evidence.

In its proposed approach for future decision making, the Committee offers recommendations that address the strengths and challenges highlighted by the case studies.

REFERENCES

Beebe, G. W. 1975. Follow-up studies of World War II and Korean War prisoners. *American Journal of Epidemiology* 101(5):400-422.

Berkowitz, E. D., and M. J. Santangelo. 1999. *The Medical Follow-up Agency: The first fifty years 1946-1996*. Washington, DC: National Academy Press.

Brass, L. M., and W. F. Page. 1996. Stroke in former prisoners of war. *Journal of Stroke and Cerebrovascular Diseases* 6(2):72-78.

CDC (Centers for Disease Control and Prevention). 1988. Vietnam experience study—Psychosocial characteristics. *Journal of the American Medical Association* 259(18):2701-2707.

CIRRPC (Committee on Interagency Radiation Research and Policy Coordination). 1988. *Use of probability of causation by the Veterans Administration in the adjudication of claims of injury due to exposure to ionizing radiation*. Washington, DC: Office of Science and Technology Policy, Executive Office of the President.

Cohen, B. M., and M. Z. Cooper. 1954. *A follow-up study of World War II prisoners of war*. Washington, DC: U.S. Government Printing Office.

DoD (Department of Defense). 1997. *Implementation and application of joint medical surveillance for deployments*. Instruction number 6490.3. Washington, DC: Department of Defense.

DoD. 2006. *Deployment health.* Instruction number 6490.03. Washington, DC: Department of Defense.

Engdahl, B. E., and W. F. Page. 1991. Psychological effects of military captivity. In *Epidemiology in military and veterans populations: Proceedings of the second biennial conference, March 7, 1990*, edited by W. F. Page. Washington, DC: National Academy Press. Pp. 49-66.

GAO (Government Accountability Office). 2004. *Report to congressional requesters. Defense health care: Force health protection and surveillance policy compliance was mixed, but appears better for recent deployments.* GAO-05-120. Washington, DC: Government Accountability Office. http://www.gao.gov/new.items/d05120.pdf (accessed March 19, 2007).

GAO. 2006a. *Military disability evaluation: ensuring consistent and timely outcomes for reserve and active duty members.* GAO-06-561T. Washington, DC: United States Government Accountability Office. http://www.gao.gov/new.items/d06561t.pdf (accessed February 28, 2007).

GAO. 2006b. *VA and DOD health care: Efforts to provide seamless transition of care for OEF and OIF servicemembers and veterans.* GAO-06-794R. Washington, DC: United States Government Accountability Office. http://www.gao.gov/htext/d06794r.html (accessed July 9, 2007).

Hrubec, Z., and R. Ryder. 1980. Traumatic limb amputation and subsequent mortality from cardiovascular disease and other causes. *Journal of Chronic Disease* 33(4):239-250.

IARC (International Agency for Research on Cancer). 2000. *Ionizing radiation, part 1: X- and gamma (γ)-radiation, and neutrons.* Lyon, France: International Agency for Research on Cancer.

IARC. 2006. *IARC monographs on the evaluation of carcinogenic risk to humans: Preamble.* Lyon, France: International Agency for Research on Cancer. http://monographs.iarc.fr/ENG/Preamble/CurrentPreamble.pdf (accessed March 1, 2007).

IOM (Institute of Medicine). 1992. *The health of former prisoners of war.* Washington, DC: National Academy Press.

IOM. 1993. *Veterans at risk: The health effects of mustard gas and lewisite.* Washington, DC: National Academy Press.

IOM. 1994. *Veterans and Agent Orange: Health effects of herbicides used in Vietnam.* Washington, DC: National Academy Press.

IOM. 1996a. *Mortality of veteran participants in the CROSSROADS nuclear test.* Washington, DC: National Academy Press.

IOM. 1996b. *Veterans and Agent Orange: Update 1996.* Washington, DC: National Academy Press.

IOM. 1999. *Veterans and Agent Orange: Update 1998.* Washington, DC: National Academy Press.

IOM. 2000a. *Gulf War and health, volume 1: Depleted uranium, pyridostigmine bromide, sarin, vaccines.* Washington, DC: National Academy Press.

IOM. 2000b. *Veterans and Agent Orange: Herbicide/dioxin exposure and type 2 diabetes.* Washington, DC: National Academy Press.

IOM. 2001. *Veterans and Agent Orange: Update 2000.* Washington, DC: National Academy Press.

IOM. 2002. *The Five Series Study: Mortality of military participants in U.S. nuclear weapons tests.* Washington, DC: The National Academies Press.

IOM. 2003a. *Gulf War and health, volume 2: Insecticides and solvents.* Washington, DC: The National Academies Press.

IOM. 2003b. *Veterans and Agent Orange: Update 2002.* Washington, DC: The National Academies Press.

IOM. 2005a. *Gulf War and health, volume 3: Fuels, combustion products, and propellants.* Washington, DC: The National Academies Press.

IOM. 2005b. *Veterans and Agent Orange: Update 2004.* Washington, DC: The National Academies Press.

IOM. 2006. *Gulf War and health, volume 4: Health effects of serving in the Gulf War.* Washington, DC: The National Academies Press.

IOM. 2007. *Gulf War and health, volume 5: Infectious diseases.* Washington, DC: The National Academies Press.

Keehn, R. J. 1980. Follow-up studies of World War II and Korean Conflict prisoners. III. Mortality to January 1, 1976. *American Journal of Epidemiology* 111(2):194-211.

Kurtzke, J. F., and W. F. Page. 1997. Epidemiology of multiple sclerosis in U.S. veterans: 7. Risk factors for MS. *Neurology* 48(1):204-213.

Kurtzke, J. F., G. W. Beebe, and J. E. Norman, Jr. 1979. Epidemiology of multiple sclerosis in U.S. veterans: 1. Race, sex, and geographic distribution. *Neurology* 29(9):1228-1235.

Kurtzke, J. F., G. W. Beebe, and J. E. Norman, Jr. 1985. Epidemiology of multiple sclerosis in U.S. veterans: 3. Migration and the risk of MS. *Neurology* 35(5):672-678.

Kurtzke, J. F., W. F. Page, F. M. Murphy, and J. E. Norman, Jr. 1992. Epidemiology of multiple sclerosis in U.S. veterans: 4. Age at onset. *Neuroepidemiology* 11(4-6):226-235.

Lagakos, S., and F. Mosteller. 1986. Assigned shares in compensation for radiation-related cancers. *Risk Analysis* 6(3):345-380.

Lubin, J. H., and K. Steindorf. 1995. Cigarette use and the estimation of lung cancer attributable to radon in the United States. *Radiation Research* 141(1):79-85.

Nefzger, M. D. 1970. Follow-up studies of World War II and Korean war prisoners. I. Study plan and mortality findings. *American Journal of Epidemiology* 91(2):123-138.

Norman, J. E., Jr., J. F. Kurtzke, and G. W. Beebe. 1983. Epidemiology of multiple sclerosis in U.S. veterans: 2. Latitude, climate and the risk of multiple sclerosis. *Journal of Chronic Diseases* 36(8):551-559.

NRC (National Research Council). 1980. *The effects on populations of exposure to low levels of ionizing radiation.* Washington, DC: National Academy Press.

NRC. 1984. *Assigned share for radiation as a cause of cancer: Review of radioepidemiological tables assigning probability of causation.* Washington, DC: National Academy Press.

NRC. 2003. *A review of the dose reconstruction program of the Defense Threat Reduction Agency.* Washington, DC: The National Academies Press.

NRC. 2005. *Assessment of the scientific information for the Radiation Exposure Screening and Education Program.* Washington, DC: The National Academies Press.

NRC. 2006. *Health risks from exposure to low levels of ionizing radiation: BEIR VII—Phase 2.* Washington, DC: The National Academies Press.

Page, W. F., and L. M. Brass. 2001. Long-term heart disease and stroke mortality among former American prisoners of war of World War II and the Korean Conflict: Results of a 50-year follow-up. *Military Medicine* 166(9):803-808.

Page, W. F., and R. N. Miller. 2000. Cirrhosis mortality among former American prisoners of war of World War II and the Korean Conflict: Results of a 50-year follow-up. *Military Medicine* 165(10):781-785.

Page, W. F., and A. M. Ostfeld. 1994. Malnutrition and subsequent ischemic heart disease in former prisoners of World War II and the Korean Conflict. *Journal of Clinical Epidemiology* 47(12):1437-1441.

Page, W. F., and C. M. Tanner. 2000. Parkinson's disease and motor-neuron disease in former prisoners of war. Letter. *Lancet* 355(9206):843.

Page, W. F., B. E. Engdahl, and R. E. Eberly. 1991. Prevalence and correlates of depressive symptoms among former prisoners of war. *Journal of Nervous and Mental Disease* 179(11):670-677.

Page, W. F., J. F. Kurtzke, F. M. Murphy, and J. E. Norman, Jr. 1993. Epidemiology of multiple sclerosis in U.S. veterans: 5. Ancestry and the risk of multiple sclerosis. *Annals of Neurology* 33(6):632-639.

Page, W. F., T. M. Mack, J. F. Kurtzke, F. M. Murphy, and J. E. Norman, Jr. 1995. Epidemiology of multiple sclerosis in U.S. veterans: 6. Population ancestry and surname ethnicity as risk factors for multiple sclerosis. *Neuroepidemiology* 14(6):286-296.

Page, W. F., B. E. Engdahl, R. E. Eberly, C. S. Fullerton, and R. J. Ursano. 1997. Persistence of PTSD in former prisoners of war. In *Posttraumatic stress disorder: Acute and long-term responses to trauma and disaster*, edited by C. S. Fullerton and R. J. Ursano. Washington, DC: American Psychiatric Press. Pp. 147-158.

Podgor, M. F. 2007. The inability of World War II atomic veterans to obtain disability benefits: Time is running out on our chance to fix the system. *Elder Law Journal* 13(2):519-552.

Prentice, R. L., Y. Yoshimoto, and M. W. Mason. 1983. Relationship of cigarette smoking and radiation exposure to cancer mortality in Hiroshima and Nagasaki. *Journal of the National Cancer Institute* 70(4):611-622.

President's Task Force to Improve Health Care Delivery for Our Nation's Veterans. 2003. *A brief guide to the final report.* Arlington, VA: President's Task Force to Improve Health Care Delivery for our Nation's Veterans. http://veterans.house.gov/spotlight/ShortTaskForceReport.pdf (accessed July 11, 2007).

RECAC (Radiation Exposure Compensation Act Committee). 1996. *Final report of the Radiation Exposure Compensation Act Committee.* Washington, DC: Human Radiation Interagency Working Group. http://www.hss.energy.gov/HealthSafety/ohre/roadmap/uranium/index.html (accessed June 24, 2007).

UNSCEAR (United Nations Scientific Committee on the Effects of Atomic Radiation). 2000. *Sources and effects of ionizing radiation.* UNSCEAR 2000 Report Vol. II. New York: United Nations.

VA (Department of Veterans Affairs). 1949. Veterans claims miscellaneous amendments. *Federal Register* 14(26):568-578.

VA. 1980. *Study of former prisoners of war.* Washington, DC: U.S. Government Printing Office.

VA. 1992a. Claims based on chronic effects of exposure to mustard gas. Proposed Rule. *Federal Register* 57(10):1699-1700.

VA. 1992b. Claims based on chronic effects of exposure to mustard gas. Final Rule. *Federal Register* 57(148):33875-33877.

VA. 1993. *Analysis of presumptions of service connection.* Washington, DC: Department of Veterans Affairs.

VA. 1994a. Claims based on chronic effects of exposure to vesicant agents. Proposed Rule. *Federal Register* 59(15):3532-3534.

VA. 1994b. Claims based on chronic effects of exposure to mustard gas or lewisite. Final Rule. *Federal Register* 59(159):42497-42500.

VA. 1994c. Disease not associated with exposure to certain herbicide agents. Notice. *Federal Register* 59(2):341-346.

VA. 1996. Diseases associated with exposure to certain herbicide agents (prostate cancer and acute and subacute peripheral neuropathy). Final rule. *Federal Register* 61(217):57586-57589.

VA. 2002. *Possible occupational health exposures of veterans involved in Project Shad tests.* Veterans Health Administration and Under Secretary for Health information letter IL10-2002-016. Washington, DC: Department of Veterans Affairs. http://www1.va.gov/shad/docs/IL_10-2002-016.pdf (accessed February 28, 2007).

VA. 2004. Presumptions of service connection for diseases associated with service involving detention or internment as a prisoner of war. Interim final rule. *Federal Register* 69(194):60083-60090.

VA. 2005. *Health effects among veterans exposed to mustard and lewisite chemical warfare agents*. Under Secretary for Health Information letter IL 10-2005-004. www.va.gov/environagents/docs/USHInfoLetterIL10-2005-004_March _14_2005.pfd (accessed February 27, 2007).

VA. 2006. *Potential health effects among veterans involved in military chemical warfare agent experiments conducted from 1955 to 1975*. Under Secretary for Health information letter IL 10-2006-010. Washington, DC: Department of Veterans Affairs. http://www1.va.gov/environagents/docs/USHInfoLetterIL10-2006-010.pdf (accessed February 28, 2007).

VA Multiple Sclerosis Study Group. 1956. Isoniazid in the treatment of multiple sclerosis: Report on VA Cooperative Study. *Transactions of the American Neurological Association* (81st meeting):128–131.

VA Multiple Sclerosis Study Group. 1957. Isoniazid in the treatment of multiple sclerosis: Report on Veterans Administration Cooperative Study. *Journal of the American Medical Association* 163(3):168-172.

Wallin, M. T., W. F. Page, and J. F. Kurtzke. 2000. Epidemiology of multiple sclerosis in U.S. veterans: 8. Long-term survival after onset of multiple sclerosis. *Brain* 123(Pt. 8):1677-1687.

ANNEX 5-1 Legislative Documents Referenced for Case Studies

	CONGRESS					EXECUTIVE BRANCH (DEPARTMENT OF VETERANS AFFAIRS)		
Case Study	Public Law Name	Public Law Statute	CIS Index	House Report	Senate Report	Rule Name	Federal Register	Code of Federal Regulations
Mental Health	Veterans' Bureau Act of 1921	PL 67-47 42 STAT. 147, 153				Pensions, Bonuses, and Veteran's Relief (1949)	14 FR 571	38 CFR Part 3 Former 39 CFR 3.80, 3.86
	World War Veterans' Act, 1924	PL 68-242 43 STAT. 607, 615						
	Veterans, disability compensation, increase (1970)	PL 91-376 84 STAT. 787, 788	PL 91-376	HR 91-1166	SR 91-784 SR 91-785	Pensions, Bonuses, and Veterans' Relief (1970)	35 FR 18280	38 CFR Part 3
						Veterans Benefits; Former Prisoners of War (1981)	46 FR 57571	
	Former Prisoner of War Benefits Act of 1981	PL 97-37 95 STAT. 935, 936	PL 97-37	HR 97-28	SR 97-88	Veterans Benefits; Former Prisoners of War (1982) (final regulations)	47 FR 11655	38 CFR Part 3
	Veterans' Compensation and Program Improvements Amendments of 1984	PL 98-223 98 STAT. 37, 40	PL 98-223	HR 98-228 HR 98-425	SR 98-249	Direct Service Connection (Post-traumatic stress disorder) (1992) (proposed rule)	57 FR 34536	
	Veterans Benefits Act of 2003	PL 108-183 117 STAT. 2651	PL 108-183	HR 108-211	SR 107-86 SR 108-169	Direct Service Connection (Post-traumatic stress disorder) (1993) (final rule)	58 FR 29109	38 CFR Part 3

		Compensation for Certain Undiagnosed Illnesses (1994) (proposed rule)	59 FR 63283	38 CFR Part 3
		Compensation for Certain Undiagnosed Illnesses (1995) (final rule)	60 FR 6660	38 CFR Part 3
Multiple Sclerosis		Pensions, Bonuses, and Veterans' Relief (1949)	14 FR 571	38 CFR 3.86
		Pensions, Bonuses, and Veterans' Relief (1970)	35 FR 18280	38 CFR 3.307, 3.309
		Compensation and Pension Provisions of the Veterans Education and Benefits Expansion Act of 2001 (2003) (final rule)	68 FR 34539	38 CFR Parts 3 and 13
		Presumptions relating to certain diseases and disabilities (2006) (38 USC § 1112)		

continued

ANNEX 5-1 Continued

	CONGRESS					EXECUTIVE BRANCH (DEPARTMENT OF VETERANS AFFAIRS)		
Case Study	Public Law Name	Public Law Statute	CIS Index	House Report	Senate Report	Rule Name	Federal Register	Code of Federal Regulations
Prisoners of War	Veterans, disability compensation, increase (1970)	PL 91-376 84 STAT. 787	PL 91-376	HR 91-1166	SR 91-784 SR 91-785			
	Former Prisoner of War Benefits Act of 1981	PL 97-37 95 STAT. 935	PL 97-37	HR 97-28	SR 97-88			
	Veterans' Compensation and Program Improvements Amendments of 1984	PL 98-223 98 STAT. 37	PL 98-223	HR 98-228 HR 98-425	SR 98-249			
	Veterans' Benefits Improvement and Health-Care Authorization Act of 1986	PL 99-576 100 STAT. 3248	PL 99-576	HR 99-728 HR 99-729	SR 99-494 SR 99-200 SR 99-444			
	Veterans' Benefits and Services Act of 1988	PL 100-322 102 STAT. 487	PL 100-322	HR 100-191 HR 100-236 HR 100-578	SR 100-15 SR 100-215			
	Veterans Benefits Act of 2003	PL 108-183 117 STAT. 2651	PL 108-183	HR 108-211	SR 107-86 SR 108-169			

Amputees and Cardio-vascular Disease	Veterans Disability Compensation and Survivor Benefit Act of 1976	PL 94-433 90 STAT. 1374	PL 94-433	HR 94-1270	SR 94-1226	Pension, Compensation, and Dependency and Indemnity Compensation, Proximate Results, Secondary Conditions (1979) (final regulations)	44 FR 50339	38 CFR Part 3
Radiation	Veterans' Dioxin and Radiation Exposure Compensation Standards Act of 1984	PL 98-542 98 STAT. 2725	PL 98-542	HR 98-592 HR 98-828	SR 97-89	Guidance for the Determination and Reporting of Nuclear Radiation Dose for DoD Participants in the Atmospheric Nuclear Test Program (1945-1962) (1982)	47 FR 21853	32 CFR Ch. 1
	Radiation-Exposed Veterans Compensation Act of 1988	PL 100-321 102 STAT. 485	PL 100-321	HR 98-592 HR 100-235	SR 100-215			
	Radiation Exposure Compensation Act of 1990	PL 101-426 104 STAT. 920	PL 101-426	HR 101-463	SR 101-264	Guidance for the Determination and Reporting of Nuclear Radiation Dose for DoD Participants in the Atmospheric Nuclear Test Program (1945-1962) (1983) (final rule)	48 FR 10645	32 CFR Part 218
	Veterans' Benefits Programs Improvement Act of 1991	PL 102-86 105 STAT. 414	PL 102-86	HR 101-857 HR 102-130	SR 101-379 SR 102-139			

continued

ANNEX 5-1 Continued

	CONGRESS					EXECUTIVE BRANCH (DEPARTMENT OF VETERANS AFFAIRS)		
Case Study	Public Law Name	Public Law Statute	CIS Index	House Report	Senate Report	Rule Name	Federal Register	Code of Federal Regulations
Radiation (continued)	Veterans' Radiation Exposure Amendments of 1992	PL 102-578 106 STAT. 4774	PL 102-578	HR 102-757	SR 101-379 SR 102-139	Guidance for the Determination and Reporting of Nuclear Radiation Dose for DoD Participants in the Atmospheric Nuclear Test Program (1945-1962) (1985) (proposed amendment of final rule)	50 FR 19538	32 CFR Part 218
	Veterans' Benefits Improvements Act of 1994	PL 103-446 108 STAT. 4645	PL 103-446	HR 103-538 HR 103-668 HR 103-669	SR 103-280 SR 103-385 SR 103-386	Adjudication of Claims Based on Exposure to Dioxin or Ionizing Radiation (1985) (final rules)	50 FR 34452	38 CFR Parts 1 and 2
	Radiation Exposure Compensation Act Amendments of 2000	PL 106-245 114 STAT. 501	PL 106-245	HR 106-697		Claims Based on Exposure to Ionizing Radiation (1989) (final regulations)	54 FR 42802	38 CFR Part 3
	Veterans Benefit Improvements Act of 2004	PL 108-454 118 STAT. 3598	PL 108-454	HR 108-211 HR 108-572	SR 106-397 SR 108-169			

Claims Based on Exposure to Ionizing Radiation (1992) (proposed rule)	57 FR 10449	38 CFR Part 3
Claims Based on Exposure to Ionizing Radiation (Parathyroid Adenoma) (1992) (proposed rule)	57 FR 10853	38 CFR Part 3
Radiation Exposure Compensation Act of 1990 (1992) (proposed rule)	57 FR 40424	38 CFR Part 3
Claims Based on Exposure to Ionizing Radiation (1993) (final rule)	58 FR 16358	38 CFR Part 3
Radiation Exposure Compensation Act of 1990 (1993) (final rule)	58 FR 25564	38 CFR Part 3
Claims Based on Exposure to Ionizing Radiation (1994) (proposed rule)	59 FR 6607	38 CFR Part 3

continued

ANNEX 5-1 Continued

Case Study	CONGRESS					EXECUTIVE BRANCH (DEPARTMENT OF VETERANS AFFAIRS)		
	Public Law Name	Public Law Statute	CIS Index	House Report	Senate Report	Rule Name	Federal Register	Code of Federal Regulations
Radiation (continued)						Claims Based on Exposure to Ionizing Radiation (1994) (final rule)	59 FR 45975	38 CFR Part 3
						Claims Based on Exposure to Ionizing Radiation (Radiogenic Diseases) (1995) (final rule)	60 FR 9627	38 CFR Part 3
						Claims Based on Exposure to Ionizing Radiation (Lymphomas other than Hodgkin's Disease and Cancer of the Rectum) (1995) (final rule)	60 FR 53276	38 CFR Part 3

Claims Based on Exposure to Ionizing Radiation (Prostate Cancer and Any Other Cancer) (1996) (proposed rule)	61 FR 50264	38 CFR Part 3
Claims Based on Exposure to Ionizing Radiation (Prostate Cancer and Any Other Cancer) (1998) (final rule)	63 FR 50993	38 CFR Part 3
The Veterans Millennium Health Care and Benefits Act (2000) (final rule)	65 FR 43699	38 CFR Part 3
Diseases Specific to Radiation-Exposed Veterans (2001) (proposed rule)	66 FR 41483	38 CFR Part 3
Diseases Specific to Radiation-Exposed Veterans (2002) (final rule)	67 FR 3612	38 CFR Part 3
Claims Based on Exposure to Ionizing Radiation (2002) (final rule)	67 FR 6870	38 CFR Part 3

continued

ANNEX 5-1 Continued

	CONGRESS					EXECUTIVE BRANCH (DEPARTMENT OF VETERANS AFFAIRS)		
Case Study	Public Law Name	Public Law Statute	CIS Index	House Report	Senate Report	Rule Name	Federal Register	Code of Federal Regulations
Mustard Gas/ Lewisite						Claims Based on Chronic Effects of Exposure to Mustard Gas (1992) (proposed rule)	57 FR 1699	38 CFR Part 3
						Claims Based on Chronic Effects of Exposure to Mustard Gas (1992) (final rule)	57 FR 33875	38 CFR Part 3
						Claims Based on Chronic Effects of Exposure to Vesicant Agents (1994) (proposed rule)	59 FR 3532	38 CFR 3.307(b)
						Claims Based on Chronic Effects of Exposure to Mustard Gas or Lewisite (1994) (final rule)	59 FR 42497	38 CFR Part 3

Gulf War	Omnibus Consolidated and Emergency Supplemental Appropriations Act, 1999	PL 105-277 112 STAT. 2681	PL 105-277	HR 105-626	SR 105-362	Compensation for Certain Undiagnosed Illnesses (1994) (proposed rule)	59 FR 63283	38 CFR Part 3
	Veterans Education and Benefits Expansion Act of 2001	PL 107-103 115 STAT. 976	PL 107-103	HR 107-156	SR 107-86 SR 106-122	Compensation for Certain Undiagnosed Illnesses (1995) (final rule)	60 FR 6660	38 CFR Part 3
						Compensation for Certain Undiagnosed Illnesses (1997) (interim rule)	62 FR 23138	38 CFR Part 3
						Compensation for Certain Undiagnosed Illnesses (1998) (final rule)	63 FR 11122	38 CFR Part 3
						Illnesses Not Associated with Service in the Gulf during the Gulf War (2001) (notice)	66 FR 35702	

continued

ANNEX 5-1 Continued

	CONGRESS					EXECUTIVE BRANCH (DEPARTMENT OF VETERANS AFFAIRS)		
Case Study	Public Law Name	Public Law Statute	CIS Index	House Report	Senate Report	Rule Name	Federal Register	Code of Federal Regulations
Gulf War (continued)						Extension of the Presumptive Period for Compensation for Gulf War Veterans' Undiagnosed Illnesses (2001) (interim final rule)	66 FR 56614	38 CFR Part 3
						Extension of the Presumptive Period for Compensation for Gulf War Veterans' Undiagnosed Illnesses (2002) (final rule)	67 FR 78979	38 CFR Part 3
						Compensation and Pension Provisions of the Veterans Education and Benefits Expansion Act of 2001 (2003) (final rule)	68 FR 34539	38 CFR Parts 3 and 13

Agent Orange and Prostate Cancer	Veterans' Dioxin and Radiation Exposure Compensation Standards Act of 1984	PL 98-542 98 STAT. 2725	PL 98-542	HR 98-592 HR 98-828	SR 97-89	Adjudication of Claims based on Exposure to Dioxin or Ionizing Radiation (1985) (final rules)	50 FR 34452	38 CFR Parts 1 and 3
	Agent Orange Act of 1991	PL 102-4 105 STAT. 11	PL 102-4	HR 101-672 HR 101-857	SR 100-215 SR 100-439 SR 101-82 SR 101-379	Claims Based on Service in Vietnam (1990) (proposed regulations)	55 FR 25339	38 CFR Parts 3 and 4
	Veterans' Benefits Improvements Act of 1994	PL 103-446 108 STAT. 4645	PL 103-446	HR 103-538 HR 103-668 HR 103-669	SR 103-280 SR 103-385 SR 103-386	Claims Based on Service in Vietnam (1990) (final regulations)	55 FR 43123	38 CFR Parts 3 and 4
	Veterans' Benefits Improvements Act of 1996	PL 104-275 110 STAT. 3322	PL 104-275	HR 104-649	SR 99-101 SR 100-439 SR 104-371	Claims Based on Exposure to Herbicides Containing Dioxin (Soft-Tissue Sarcomas) (1991) (proposed regulations)	56 FR 7632	38 CFR Parts 3 and 4
						Claims Based on Exposure to Herbicides Containing Dioxin (Soft-Tissue Sarcomas) (1991) (final regulation)	56 FR 51651	38 CFR Parts 3 and 4

continued

ANNEX 5-1 Continued

	CONGRESS					EXECUTIVE BRANCH (DEPARTMENT OF VETERANS AFFAIRS)		
Case Study	Public Law Name	Public Law Statute	CIS Index	House Report	Senate Report	Rule Name	Federal Register	Code of Federal Regulations
Agent Orange and Prostate Cancer (continued)						Claims Based on Exposure to Herbicides Containing Dioxin (Peripheral Neuropathy/Lung Cancer) (1992) (proposed rule)	57 FR 2236	38 CFR Part 3
						Diseases Associated with Service in the Republic of Vietnam (1992) (proposed rule)	57 FR 30707	38 CFR Part 3
						Diseases Associated with Service in the Republic of Vietnam (1993) (final rule)	58 FR 29107	38 CFR 3.309(e)
						Disease Associated with Exposure to Certain Herbicide Agents (1993) (proposed rule)	58 FR 50528	38 CFR Part 3

	Diseases Not Associated with Exposure to Certain Herbicide Agents (1994) (notice)	59 FR 341	
	Disease Associated with Exposure to Certain Herbicide Agents (1994) (final rule)	59 FR 5106	38 CFR Part 3
	Disease Associated with Exposure to Certain Herbicide Agents (Multiple Myeloma and Respiratory Cancers) (1994) (proposed rule)	59 FR 5161	38 CFR Part 3
	Disease Associated with Exposure to Certain Herbicide Agents (Multiple Myeloma and Respiratory cancers) (1994) (final rule)	59 FR 29723	38 CFR Part 3

continued

ANNEX 5-1 Continued

	CONGRESS					EXECUTIVE BRANCH (DEPARTMENT OF VETERANS AFFAIRS)		
Case Study	Public Law Name	Public Law Statute	CIS Index	House Report	Senate Report	Rule Name	Federal Register	Code of Federal Regulations
Agent Orange and Prostate Cancer (continued)						Diseases Associated with Exposure to Certain Herbicide Agents (Prostate Cancer and Acute and Subacute Peripheral Neuropathy) (1996) (proposed rule)	61 FR 41368	38 CFR Part 3
						Disease Not Associated with Exposure to Certain Herbicide Agents (1996) (notice)	61 FR 41442	

Diseases Associated with Exposure to Certain Herbicide Agents (Prostate Cancer and Acute and Subacute Peripheral Neuropathy) (1996) (final rule)	61 FR 57586	CFR Part 3
Veterans' Benefits Improvements Act of 1996 (1997) (final rule)	62 FR 35421	38 CFR Part 3
Diseases Not Associated with Exposure to Certain Herbicide Agents (1999) (notice)	64 FR 59232	
Diseases Not Associated with Exposure to Certain Herbicide Agents (2002) (notice)	67 FR 4 2600	

continued

ANNEX 5-1 Continued

	CONGRESS					EXECUTIVE BRANCH (DEPARTMENT OF VETERANS AFFAIRS)		
Case Study	Public Law Name	Public Law Statute	CIS Index	House Report	Senate Report	Rule Name	Federal Register	Code of Federal Regulations
Agent Orange and Prostate Cancer (continued)						Disease Associated with Exposure to Certain Herbicide Agents: Chronic Lymphocytic Leukemia (2003) (proposed rule)	68 FR 14567	38 CFR Part 3
						Compensation and Pension Provisions of the Veterans Education and Benefits Expansion Act of 2001 (2003) (final rule)	68 FR 34539	38 CFR Parts 3 and 13
						Disease Associated with Exposure to Certain Herbicide Agents: Chronic Lymphocytic Leukemia (2003) (final rule)	68 FR 59540	38 CFR Part 3

Agent Orange and Type 2 Diabetes	Veterans' Dioxin and Radiation Exposure Compensation Standards Act of 1984	PL 98-542 98 STAT. 2725	PL 98-542	HR 98-592 HR 98-828	SR 97-89	Adjudication of Claims based on Exposure to Dioxin or Ionizing Radiation (1985) (final rules)	50 FR 34452	38 CFR Parts 1 and 3
	Agent Orange Act of 1991	PL 102-4 105 STAT. 11	PL 102-4	HR 101-672 HR 101-857	SR 100-215 SR 100-439 SR 101-82 SR 101-379	Claims based on Service in Vietnam (1990) (proposed regulation)	55 FR 25339	38 Parts 3 and 4
	Veterans' Benefits Improvements Act of 1994	PL 103-446 108 STAT. 4645	PL 103-446	HR 103-538 HR 103-668 HR 103-669	SR 103-280 SR 103-385 SR 103-386	Claims based on Service in Vietnam (1990) (final regulation)	55 FR 43123	38 Parts 3 and 4
	Veterans' Benefits Improvements Act of 1996	PL 104-275 110 STAT. 3322	PL 104-275	HR 104-649	SR 99-101 SR 100-439 SR 104-371	Claims Based on Exposure to Herbicides Containing Dioxin (Soft Tissue Sarcomas) (1991) (proposed regulation)	56 FR 7632	38 Parts 3 and 4
	Veterans Education and Benefits Expansion Act of 2001	PL 107-103 115 STAT. 976	PL 107-103	HR 107-156	SR 107-86 SR 106-122			
						Claims Based on Exposure to Herbicides Containing Dioxin (Soft Tissue Sarcomas) (1991) (final regulation)	56 FR 51651	38 Parts 3 and 4

continued

ANNEX 5-1 Continued

	CONGRESS					EXECUTIVE BRANCH (DEPARTMENT OF VETERANS AFFAIRS)		
Case Study	Public Law Name	Public Law Statute	CIS Index	House Report	Senate Report	Rule Name	Federal Register	Code of Federal Regulations
Agent Orange and Type 2 Diabetes (continued)						Claims Based on Exposure to Herbicides containing Dioxin (Peripheral Neuropathy/Lung Cancer) (1992) (proposed rule)	57 FR 2236	38 CFR Part 3
						Diseases Associated with Service in the Republic of Vietnam (1992) (proposed rule)	57 FR 30707	38 CFR Part 3
						Diseases Associated with Service in the Republic of Vietnam (1993) (final rule)	58 FR 29107	38 CFR 3.309(e)
						Disease Associated with Exposure to Certain Herbicide Agents (1993) (proposed rule)	58 FR 50528	38 CFR Part 3

Disease Associated with Exposure to Certain Herbicide Agents (1994) (final rule)	59 FR 5106	38 CFR Part 3
Disease Associated with Exposure to Certain Herbicide Agents (Multiple Myeloma and Respiratory Cancers) (1994) (final rule)	59 FR 29723	38 CFR Part 3
Veterans' Benefits Improvements Act of 1996 (1997) (final rule)	62 FR 35421	38 CFR Part 3
Diseases Not Associated with Exposure to Certain Herbicide Agents (1999) (notice)	64 FR 59232	

continued

ANNEX 5-1 Continued

	CONGRESS					EXECUTIVE BRANCH (DEPARTMENT OF VETERANS AFFAIRS)		
Case Study	Public Law Name	Public Law Statute	CIS Index	House Report	Senate Report	Rule Name	Federal Register	Code of Federal Regulations
Agent Orange and Type 2 Diabetes (continued)						Disease Associated with Exposure to Certain Herbicide Agents: Type 2 Diabetes (2001) (proposed rule)	66 FR 2376	38 CFR Part 3
						Disease Associated with Exposure to Certain Herbicide Agents: Type 2 Diabetes (2001) (final rule)	66 FR 23166	38 CFR Part 3
						Disease Associated with Exposure to Certain Herbicide Agents: Chronic Lymphocytic Leukemia (2003) (proposed rule)	68 FR 14567	38 CFR Part 3

Compensation and Pension Provisions of the Veterans Education and Benefits Expansion Act of 2001 (2003) (final rule)	68 FR 34539	38 CFR Parts 3 and 13
Disease Associated with Exposure to Certain Herbicide Agents: Chronic Lymphocytic Leukemia (2003) (final rule)	68 FR 59540	38 CFR Part 3
Change of Effective Date of Rule Adding a Disease Associated with Exposure to Certain Herbicide Agents: Type 2 Diabetes (2004) (final rule)	69 FR 31882	38 CFR Part 3

continued

ANNEX 5-1 Continued

	CONGRESS					EXECUTIVE BRANCH (DEPARTMENT OF VETERANS AFFAIRS)		
Case Study	Public Law Name	Public Law Statute	CIS Index	House Report	Senate Report	Rule Name	Federal Register	Code of Federal Regulations
Spina Bifida						Disease Not Associated with Exposure to Certain Herbicide Agents (1994) (notice)	59 FR 341	
						Disease Not Associated with Exposure to Certain Herbicide Agents (1996) (notice)	61 FR 41442	

ANNEX 5-2

The following National Academies' reports were evaluated by committee members for inclusion in the individual case studies (see Appendix I). The reports appear below in chronological order:

NRC (National Research Council). 1982. *Possible long-term health effects of short-term exposure to chemical agents.* Vol. 1. Washington, DC: National Academy Press.

NRC. 1984. *Assigned share for radiation as a cause of cancer: Review of radioepidemiological tables, assigning probabilities of causation.* Washington, DC: National Academy Press.

NRC. 1984. *Possible long-term health effects of short-term exposure to chemical agents: Cholinesterase reactivators, psychochemicals and irritants and vesicants.* Vol. 2. Washington, DC: National Academy Press.

NRC. 1985. *Mortality of nuclear weapons test participants.* Washington, DC: National Academy Press.

NRC. 1985. *Possible long-term health effects of short-term exposure to chemical agents: Final report. Current health status of test subjects.* Vol. 3. Washington, DC: National Academy Press.

NRC. 1988. Overview. In *Health risks of radon and other alpha-emitters: BEIR IV.* Washington, DC: National Academy Press.

NRC. 1990. *Health effects of exposure to low levels of ionizing radiation: BEIR V.* Washington, DC: National Academy Press.

IOM (Institute of Medicine). 1991. *Epidemiology in military and veteran populations: Proceedings of the Second Biennial Conference, March 7, 1990.* Washington, DC: National Academy Press.

IOM. 1992. *The health of former prisoners of war.* Washington, DC: National Academy Press.

IOM. 1993. *Veterans at risk: The health effects of mustard gas and lewisite.* Washington, DC: National Academy Press.

IOM. 1994. *Health effects of herbicides used in Vietnam.* Washington, DC: National Academy Press.

IOM. 1994. *Veterans and Agent Orange: Health effects of herbicides used in Vietnam.* Washington, DC: National Academy Press.

IOM. 1995. *Health consequences of service during the Persian Gulf War: Initial findings and recommendations for immediate action.* Washington, DC: National Academy Press.

IOM. 1995. *Recommendations for research on the health of military women: Bibliographies.* Washington, DC: National Academy Press.

IOM. 1995. *A review of the dosimetry data available in the Nuclear Test Personnel Review (NTPR) Program.* Washington, DC: National Academy Press.

IOM. 1996. *Health consequences of service during the Persian Gulf War: Recommendations for research and information systems.* Washington, DC: National Academy Press.

IOM. 1996. *Interactions of drugs, biologics, and chemicals in U.S. military forces.* Washington, DC: National Academy Press.

IOM. 1996. *Mortality of veteran participants in the Crossroads nuclear test.* Washington, DC: National Academy Press.

IOM. 1996. *Veterans and Agent Orange: Update 1996.* Washington, DC: National Academy Press.

IOM. 1997. *Characterizing exposure of veterans to Agent Orange and other herbicides used in Vietnam: Scientific considerations regarding a request for proposals for research.* Washington, DC: National Academy Press.

IOM. 1997. *An evaluation of radiation exposure guidance for military operations: Interim Report*. Washington, DC: National Academy Press.

IOM. 1998. *Adequacy of the VA Persian Gulf registry and uniform case assessment protocol*. Washington, DC: National Academy Press.

IOM. 1998. *Assessing readiness in military women: The relationship of body, composition, nutrition, and health*. Washington, DC: National Academy Press.

IOM. 1998. *Measuring the health of Persian Gulf veterans: Workshop summary*. Washington, DC: National Academy Press.

IOM. 1999. *Gulf War veterans: Measuring health*. Washington, DC: National Academy Press.

NRC. 1999. *Health effects of exposure to radon: BEIR VI*. Washington, DC: National Academy Press.

IOM. 1999. *Potential radiation exposure in military operations: Protecting the soldier before, during, and after*. Washington, DC: National Academy Press.

IOM. 1999. *Veterans and Agent Orange: Update 1998*. Washington, DC: National Academy Press.

IOM. 2000. *The Five Series Study: Mortality of military participants in U.S. nuclear weapons tests*. Washington, DC: National Academy Press.

IOM. 2000. *Gulf War and health, volume 1: Depleted uranium, pyridostigmine bromide, sarin, vaccines*. Washington, DC: National Academy Press.

NRC. 2000. *A review of the draft report of the NCI-CDC working group to revise the 1985 radioepidemiological tables*. Washington, DC: National Academy Press.

IOM. 2000. *Veterans and Agent Orange: Herbicide/dioxin exposure and type 2 diabetes*. Washington, DC: National Academy Press.

IOM. 2001. *Gulf War veterans: Treating symptoms and syndromes*. Washington, DC: National Academy Press.

IOM. 2001. *Veterans and Agent Orange: Update 2000*. Washington, DC: National Academy Press.

IOM. 2002. *Veterans and Agent Orange: Herbicide/dioxin exposure and acute myelogenous leukemia in the children of Vietnam veterans*. Washington, DC: National Academy Press.

IOM. 2003. *Characterizing exposure of veterans to Agent Orange and other herbicides used in Vietnam: Interim findings and recommendations*. Washington, DC: The National Academies Press.

IOM. 2003. *Characterizing exposure of veterans to Agent Orange and other herbicides used in Vietnam: Final report*. Washington, DC: The National Academies Press.

IOM. 2003. *Gulf War and health, volume 2: Insecticide and solvents*. Washington, DC: The National Academies Press.

IOM. 2003. *Veterans and Agent Orange: Update 2002*. Washington, DC: The National Academies Press.

NRC. 2003. *A review of the dose reconstruction program of the Defense Threat Reduction Agency*. Washington, DC: The National Academies Press.

IOM. 2004. *Gulf War and health: Updated literature review of sarin*. Washington, DC: The National Academies Press

IOM. 2004. *Veterans and Agent Orange: Length of presumptive period for association between exposure and respiratory cancer*. Washington, DC: The National Academies Press.

NRC. 2004. *Review of the Army's technical guides on assessing and managing chemical hazards to deployed personnel*. Washington, DC: The National Academies Press.

IOM. 2005. *Gulf War and health, volume 3: Fuels, combustion products, and propellants*. Washington, DC: The National Academies Press.

IOM. 2005. *Veterans and Agent Orange: Update 2004*. Washington, DC: The National Academies Press.
NRC. 2005. *Assessment of the scientific information for the Radiation Exposure Screening and Education Program*. Washington, DC: The National Academies Press.
IOM. 2006. *Amyotrophic lateral sclerosis in veterans: Review of scientific literature*. Washington, DC: The National Academies Press.
IOM. 2006. *Disposition of the Air Force Health Study*. Washington, DC: The National Academies Press.
IOM. 2006. *Gulf War and health, volume 4: Health effects of serving in the Gulf War*. Washington: The National Academies Press.
IOM. 2006. *Gulf War and health, volume 5: Infectious diseases*. Washington, DC: The National Academies Press.
NRC. 2006. *Health risks from exposure to low levels of ionizing radiation: BEIR VII Phase 2*. Washington, DC: The National Academies Press.
IOM. 2006. *Posttraumatic stress disorder: Diagnosis and assessment*. Washington, DC: The National Academies Press.
NRC. 2006. *Toxicity testing for assessment of environmental agents interim report*. Washington, DC: The National Academies Press.

ANNEX 5-3

The VA provided the Committee with the following cost estimates (in chronological order):

VA (Department of Veterans Affairs). 1988. *Cost estimate of Agent Orange legislation: Non-Hodgkin's lymphoma*. Washington, DC: VA.
VA. 1996. *Cost estimate for regulation on claims based on exposure to herbicides: Estimated benefit and administrative costs. Adding prostate cancer and peripheral neuropathy to list of diseases for which VA will provide presumptive service connection based on herbicide exposure*. Washington, DC: VA.
VA. 1996. *Memorandum: Costing for regulation on claims based on exposure to herbicides*. Washington, DC: VA.
VA. 1999. *Costing of H.R. 690: Adding bronchiolo-alveolar carcinoma to list of diseases presumed service connected for certain radiation-exposed veterans*. Washington, DC: VA.
VA. 2000. *Costing of regulation RIN 2900-AK63: Disease associated with exposure to certain herbicide agents: Type 2 diabetes*. Washington, DC: VA.
VA. 2001. *Costing of regulation RIN 2900-AK83: Presumption of service connection for cirrhosis of the liver in former prisoners of war*. Washington, DC: VA.
VA. 2003. *Costing of RIN 2900-AL55: To establish a presumption of service connection for chronic lymphocytic leukemia (CLL)*. Washington, DC: VA.
VA. 2004. *Costing of RIN 2900-AM09: Additional presumptions for former POWs*. Washington, DC: VA.

6

Establishing an Evidence-Based Framework

OVERVIEW

The Committee's review of Congress' and the Department of Veterans Affairs' (VA's) approach to establishing presumptions has identified multiple elements of the process for reconsideration. In the next four chapters, the Committee develops a conceptual foundation for implementing an evidence-based system for compensation and offers recommendations for future approaches in Chapter 12. This chapter serves as an introduction to this section of the report, offering general considerations on the basis for making presumptions and their role in compensation by VA.

There are two ideas that underpin these four chapters:

- Decisions about presumptions should be grounded in a scientific evaluation of the full range of evidence that the exposure of interest *causes* the disease or disability.
- If there is sufficient evidence to infer a causal relationship, the amount of disease attributable to the exposure should be estimated.

Chapters 7 and 8 address the first question of whether a causal relationship exists. Chapter 7 makes explicit what is meant by *cause* in contrast to statistical *association* and details the sources of evidence necessary to reach a conclusion as to whether there is a causal relationship. Chapter 8 then discusses quantitative and qualitative approaches for integrating epidemiological, laboratory, and other kinds of evidence to reach conclusions about the strength of evidence for association and causation. This background provides a foundation for the Committee's specific recommendations in Chapter 12, which outlines a classification system for characterizing the strength of evidence in support of a general causal relationship. Assuming that such a causal relationship has been established, Chapter 9 discusses how to quantify the strength of the causal effect, using measures most relevant to compensation decisions under the presumptive process: the *attributable fraction* for the population of exposed veterans, and the *probability of causation* for an individual. Chapter 10 covers the various types of data necessary to assess the existence of a causal relationship and to quantify the size of the causal effect. It proposes future comprehensive exposure and health data collection strategies for military personnel and veterans.

Provision of compensation to a veteran, or to any other individual who has been injured, on a presumptive basis requires a *general* decision as to whether the agent or exposure of concern has the potential to *cause* the condition or disease for which compensation is to be provided, in at least some individuals, and a *specific* decision as to whether the agent or exposure has caused the condition or disease in the particular individual or group of individuals. The determination of causation for veterans is based on review and evaluation of all relevant evidence including (1) measurements and estimates of exposures of military personnel during their service, if available; (2) direct evidence on risks for disease in relation to exposure from epidemiologic studies of military personnel; (3) other relevant evidence, including findings from epidemiologic studies of nonmilitary populations who have had exposure to the agent of interest or to similar agents; and (4) findings relevant to plausibility from experimental and laboratory research. Scientists and scientific organizations, such as the Institute of Medicine (IOM), have developed approaches for reviewing evidence and determining if causation can be inferred. Typically, these approaches involve a comprehensive review and the judgment of a panel of experts as to whether the evidence supports causation and with what degree of strength. The determination of causation for a particular veteran is based first on the general determination as to whether the exposure causes disease, and then on information on the exposures and possibly on clinical features of the individual being evaluated for compensation.

Compensation decisions critically depend on determinations of cause, but the information available for determining general or specific causation may be incomplete or inconclusive. For a group, the evidence may be insufficient or still evolving, and for an individual, information on exposure may be lacking, or there may be uncertainty as to the role of service-related factors versus the roles of other factors in causation. In the Agent Orange example, information on cancer risk in exposed veterans was not available until they had been followed for a sufficient time, reflective of the latency between exposure and disease risk for carcinogens. For individual Vietnam veterans, exposure to Agent Orange cannot be estimated with any certainty, and VA has made a presumption with regard to exposure of Vietnam veterans to Agent Orange (VA, 2002). VA has also presumptively linked certain outcomes, such as prostate cancer and type 2 diabetes, based on evidence for association to Agent Orange exposure. By contrast, presumptions are not needed for combat-related casualties for which there is no uncertainty as to causation.

The role of presumptions becomes evident when the complete suite of information needed by VA for making compensation decisions for groups and for particular individuals is considered. Figure 6-1 describes information gathering and how information may be used for making general and specific judgments about causation and for making evidence-based decisions with regard to compensation. The schema in the figure assumes that the availability of information for making these determinations, as well as the roles of factors beyond the scientific evidence, such as costs and political considerations, are all figured into the process. Presumptions are made when there are gaps in the information related to exposure and causal classification. Factors other than the evidence relevant to the causal classification may affect the compensation decision.

If complete information were available, the process in the table could flow without presumptions, but the review of presumptions in Chapter 2 shows that this ideal has been infrequent and many presumptions have been made. The military workplace and particularly combat can lead to many exposures that may affect future health status and disease occurrence. Military personnel sustain a variety of exposures, some specific to the military and others not, that may increase risk for disease. If exposures of potential concern were tracked during military service and disease surveillance were in place and maintained, even for those who have left active duty, evidence could be generated directly relevant to the causation of disease in veterans. Disease rates could be compared in exposed and nonexposed veterans, for example. Lacking such evidence, reviewing groups turn to epidemiologic studies of other populations and gauge the relevance of the findings for the exposures of veterans. Such groups also give consideration to toxicological and other research information. For a specific individual, the determination of eligibility for compensation would be based ideally in full knowledge of that individual's risk and an estimation of his or her probability of causation, given exposure history and observational information on the associated risk from similarly exposed people. However, this level of information and scientific understanding has not yet been fully achieved for individual causation for any agent.

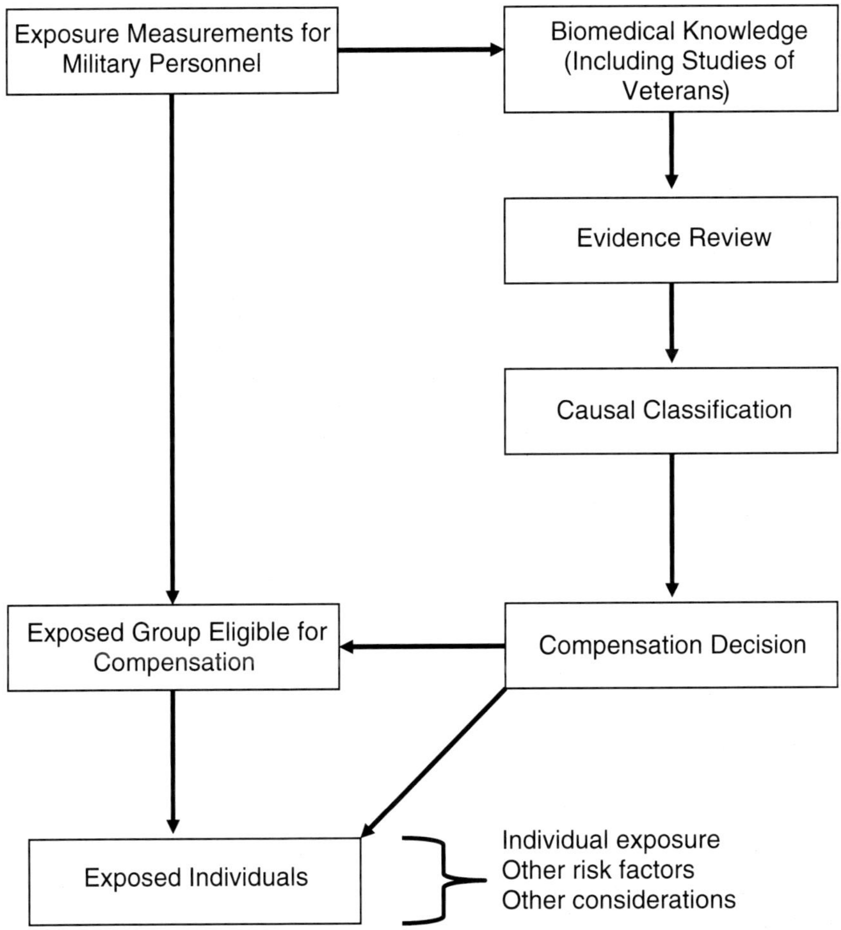

FIGURE 6-1 Information gathering and its use in making general and specific compensation decisions.

A FRAMEWORK FOR PRESUMPTIONS

For all veterans or a particular group of veterans, the evidence may be sufficient to identify a causal relationship between an exposure and a health outcome. However, certainty as to whether an individual veteran's service caused his or her disability or illness will vary depending on clinical characteristics and the availability of information on the veteran's exposures during service.

In decisions to award compensation, two types of errors may occur: giving compensation to a veteran whose illness was not caused by the service-related factor (false positive) and denying compensation to a veteran whose illness was caused by the factor (false negative). These two types of errors need consideration in the design of compensation schemes.

This section establishes a framework for reasoning about compensation for service-attributable disability and illness and for making presumptions, and discusses the concept of a disability or illness being *service attributable*—that is, *caused by* a veteran's service. (A more detailed discussion of models of causation is presented in Chapter 8 and Appendix J.) This section also describes the types of errors that can be made and the potential costs of each. It then addresses presumptions, viewed as one approach to completing gaps in the evidence needed for making decisions about compensation. The Committee emphasizes the need to address the false positive and false negative rates of particular decisions.

To simplify this chapter, the Committee considers the onset of a particular definable disease, a dichotomous outcome. Of course, some diseases are non-specific in their characteristics and the extent of disability associated with a particular disease may be a continuum from mild to very severe.

Service-Attributable Disease

In the circumstance that a veteran has a specific medical disease, the primary question for presumptive compensation is whether the disease is *attributable*, that is, caused by exposures during military service. We ask whether, absent service, the disease would have occurred at all or would have been less severe. The answer for any particular veteran can never be known exactly because it is not possible to observe the same person as exposed and non-exposed. The needed comparison for what would have happened to the exposed person, had they not been exposed, is referred to as the "counterfactual"—in other words, counter to the actual facts. We use information from unexposed but similar persons to describe the counterfactual. For example, the rate of posttraumatic stress disorder (PTSD) in former prisoners of war (POWs) could be compared to the rate in veterans with combat service who had not been POWs. There is an implicit assumption that the rate in non-POWs represents the rate in POWs, had they not been POWs. The excess in the POWs reflects the contribution of having been a POW.

The degree of certainty as to whether a disease is caused by service will vary substantially across different exposures and diseases. At one extreme, if the health problem is the direct result of an event during service, such as a battle wound, then full service attribution can be made with certainty. For chronic diseases with multiple causes there may be much less certainty. For example, consider a Vietnam veteran who develops diabetes. His service has been established as a potential risk factor based on findings of epidemiologic studies and knowledge that some Vietnam veterans were exposed to Agent Orange, leading to a presumption of exposure of all Vietnam veterans. However, other factors, such as obesity and age, also contribute to the development of diabetes. Service attribution for diabetes in this particular veteran is much more uncertain than for disability from the battle wound. The uncertainty comes both from gaps in the general evidence linking Agent Orange to diabetes and from limitations of the information available on exposure and other relevant characteristics for the particular veteran.

In deciding whether to compensate a group of veterans on a presumptive basis, review is needed of all relevant data to assess if the disease is service attributable, including information about wartime exposures and other risk factors (such as obesity, age, and gender, in the example of diabetes). This information would then be used to estimate the likelihood, that is, the chance that exposure during military service contributed to the disease in the group. Currently, with the exception of radiation for which quantitative risk approaches are available, VA takes a more qualitative approach to determining service attribution, while using information about the exposure and other factors, as available. For some diseases of current concern with several causes, the causal agents contributing in a particular individual cannot be known with certainty so that presumptions will lead to false positive and negative errors.

Errors

The two possible errors that can be made in deciding service attribution (assuming knowledge of whether or not a veteran's disease was caused by exposures during service) are summarized in Table 6-1. A false positive decision is made when the veteran's disease is not caused by his or her service, but VA decides that it was. A false negative decision is made when the disease is caused by service, but VA does not determine it to be service attributable.

The rates of correct decisions are called the *sensitivity* or true positive rate (TPR) and the *specificity* or the true negative rate (TNR). In other words, the proportion of all truly service caused cases that are correctly classified as service attributable is called *sensitivity*, whereas the proportion of all truly non-service caused cases that are correctly judged not to be service attributable is called *specificity*. Sensitivity is the probability of correctly deciding that a person's disease was caused by service. Specificity is the probability of correctly deciding that it was not.

The example above addresses the correct classification of veterans with regard to the causation of disease by exposures during military service. The

TABLE 6-1 Possible Decisions About Service-Attributable Diseases (SADs) with Associated Errors and Losses

Decision	Truth	Error	Rate of Error	Loss
Disease NOT caused by service	Disease NOT caused by service	No error	Specificity [True Negative Rate (TNR)]	0
Disease NOT caused by service	Disease IS caused by service	Failure to attribute disease to service	1-Specificity [False Negative Rate (FNR)]	Failure to cover veteran with SAD • Monetary loss to veteran • Injustice to veteran
Disease IS caused by service	Disease NOT caused by service	False attribution of disease to service	1-Sensitivity [False positive rate (FPR)]	• Monetary loss to society • Incorrect disease label and consequences
Disease IS caused by service	Disease IS caused by service	No error	Sensitivity [True positive rate (TPR)]	0

same concept and terminology is used with regard to classification of exposures and diseases. Exposure status is often classified on the basis of incomplete or imperfect information so that some persons designated as exposed were not (false positives) and some designated as non-exposed were (false negatives). The same considerations extend to disease classification. For some diseases, there are relatively specific and firm diagnostic criteria (e.g., type 2 diabetes), while for others, the diagnostic picture is more ambiguous, (e.g., some neuropsychiatric disorders), and both false positive and false negative errors of diagnostic classification may be made.

Losses

As is nearly always the case, errors of classification have associated costs or losses. False negative errors are readily understood: a veteran who should receive compensation does not. The consequences of false negative errors elicit strongly motivated responses from all parties: veterans, VA, Congress, and society in general. Because there is strong motivation to avoid false negative decisions, a compensation scheme may be constructed to minimize the risk of making them by maximizing sensitivity (the probability of deciding in favor of compensation when a service-attributable disease has occurred). In avoiding false negatives, however, there is usually a trade-off with the numbers of false positives, as increasing sensitivity will generally reduce specificity. In other words, planning for as few false negatives as possible increases the number of false positives. In balancing the risks of false negative decisions against numbers of false positives, VA presenters and past congressional staffers at public Committee meetings indicated a strong motivation to compensate veterans who may have been harmed by their military service, even if false positives are incurred (as stated during Pamperin, 2006; as stated during Petrou, 2006; as stated during Ryan, 2006; as stated during Scott, 2006; as stated during Yoder, 2006).

However, false positive errors may also come with losses. These include the injustice of inappropriately awarding compensation to veterans not actually harmed by their service and the unnecessary expenditure of public funds. A compensation system that tends to have a high false positive rate may become generally suspect, particularly if compensation costs escalate rapidly. Uncompensated veterans may be troubled by the seemingly high rate of compensation among fellow veterans. Balancing the losses of false negatives and false positives is difficult, as the loss from a false negative is the injustice done to deserving but uncompensated veterans and that from false positives includes economic costs along with non-economic consequences of having a non-specific system.

Service-Attributable Fraction of Disease

In public health, calculations have long been made on the amount of disease caused by a factor. One well-known example is the number of deaths each year in the United States attributable to cigarette smoking. Similarly, it is possible to estimate the amount of disease among veterans with a given exposure and given risk profile that exceeds what is observed in otherwise similar, but unexposed persons. That is, one can compare the rate of disease in exposed veterans to the rate in otherwise similar persons who were known not to be exposed. If there is a difference between these two rates, and the assumption is that the difference is due to a causal effect of the exposure on disease occurrence, then the fraction of disease *attributable* to the exposure can be quantified. If for a subgroup of veterans with a homogeneous risk profile, the rates of disease among exposed and unexposed are r_1 and r_0, respectively, then the fraction of disease *attributable to service* is the relative increase associated with exposure expressed as a fraction of the rate among the exposed. That is, assuming causation, the service-attributable fraction (SAF) can be calculated by the following equation:

$$\text{SAF} = (r_1 - r_0)/r_1 \text{ or } = 1 - r_0/r_1$$

As r_1—the additional risk from exposure—increases, the term r_1 becomes smaller and the SAF increases towards 1.0. Consider again the examples of battle wounds and diabetes. Because all battle wounds occur only among those in combat, $r_0 = 0$ so that the attributable fraction is 1.0 for battle wounds. For diabetes, however, the fraction of cases attributable to service in Vietnam is likely to be much smaller than 1.0, given the existence and strength of other factors (e.g., obesity) that contribute to its causation.

Rates of disease for exposed veterans and for otherwise similar veterans who were not exposed are required to estimate the SAF of disease for a population of exposed veterans. The rates are needed for each subgroup as defined by the exposure of interest, other risk factors, and perhaps other covariates. Of course, taking account of all the various subgroups defined by the resulting array of variables is likely to be difficult or even impossible in practice. If relevant data are available, an analytic approach using a statistical model can be used for taking the covariates into account so that the SAF can be calculated for each subgroup.

To illustrate the estimation of service-attributable disease, consider the hypothetical data in Table 6-2 showing diabetes occurrence in 5,000 veterans exposed to Agent Orange and 5,000 otherwise similar, but unexposed, persons in a particular stratum of demographic and other risk factors.

In this hypothetical example, 150 of the 10,000 veterans have diabetes. Again in this example, only 100 of the diabetics were exposed to the putative cause, and thus 100/150 = 67 percent of the total funds spent on diabetes are for exposed individuals. Even among the exposed veterans, not all cases of diabetes were caused by the exposure, as 50 would be expected absent exposure, based on the experience of the unexposed veterans of whom 50 of 5,000 developed diabetes. Therefore, we can assume, absent exposure (i.e., the counterfactual), that 50 of the 100 cases among the exposed veterans would have occurred, even if those veterans had not been exposed. Hence, only the remaining 50 or 50/100 = 50 percent are attributable to the exposure associated with service in Vietnam. In this example, providing compensation for all exposed veterans with diabetes means that the false positive rate is 50 percent.

TABLE 6-2 Hypothetical Example of the Estimation of Service-Attributable Disease

	Diabetes	No Diabetes	Total
Exposed veterans	100	4,900	5,000
Unexposed veterans	50	4,950	5,000
Total	150	9,850	10,000

In this example, the costs of compensation can be apportioned between the true positives and false positives. Assume funds of \$10,000 per person compensated and three scenarios: (1) knowledge of who is exposed and has disease caused by exposure, (2) knowledge of who is exposed and no knowledge of which cases were caused by exposure, and (3) no knowledge of who is exposed or which cases were caused by exposure. In the first situation, \$500,000 would be awarded, only to true positives. In the second, if the exposure status of specific individuals were known but individual causation not known, \$1,000,000 would be awarded. With a SAF of 50 percent, \$500,000 would be for true positives and \$500,000 for false positives. If exposure status were unknown for all individuals, then the compensation scheme would award \$1,500,000 including \$1,000,000 for false positives. Applying the SAF of 33 percent (67 × 50 percent) to the total disability costs (150 × \$10,000) again gives \$500,000 in costs attributable to the exposure. In the first situation, with known exposures and disease causation, only those exposed receive payment, while, in the third, all with disease receive payment.

This simple example shows that the attributable costs for a population with a given set of characteristics are determined by two fractions:

- Probability that a veteran was actually exposed to the putative cause given that he or she has the disease and given his or her estimated or measured exposure data and information on other relevant factors
- Probability that the disease in an exposed veteran was caused by his or her exposure given that the veteran has the disease, and given his or her estimated or measured exposure information and information on other relevant factors

These probabilities can be estimated, if the requisite data are available; otherwise, values must be assumed. Presumptions for exposure or causation, as currently implemented by VA, correspond to assuming that these probabilities are equal to 1.0. Service in a particular theater may lead to a presumption of exposure, an assumption meaning that the probability of exposure is 1.0; with regard to causation, there may be a further assumption that the disease is caused by the exposure, again acting as though the second probability is 1.0. If either of these two probabilities were assumed to be 0, then compensation would not be awarded.

In the illustration above, we calculated a single SAF from the rates of disease among exposed and otherwise similar unexposed veterans. This calculation is based upon the assumption that we are comparing like to like persons, except for the exposure. It can be difficult to form groups of exposed and unexposed veterans that are the same with respect to other factors affecting the disease process. Typically, statistical methods for adjustment are used to attempt to achieve this comparability.

Statistical methods, however, are only as good as the data to which they are applied. Accurate and precise estimates of SAFs depend on detailed data on exposure, key covariates, and disease outcomes. Chapter 10 provides a detailed discussion of approaches to compiling such data as an element of surveillance of veterans. To the extent that data are incomplete, a frequent situation, the estimates of the SAF will be subject to uncertainty to a degree that will depend on the extent of missing data.

Making Presumptions

To this point, we have described the concept of service-attributable disease for a population and for an individual. We have indicated that application of a presumption can be thought of as equivalent to acting as though the probability of exposure and/or the probability that an exposed veteran's disease is caused by his or her service are equal to 1.0. We show that any scheme may lead to two types of error and that avoiding false negatives, a desirable property of a compensation system, may increase the false positive rate. One key consideration is the basis for setting the sensitivity of the approach. We have set out the losses associated with each of the two types of error. When a veteran's illness is not attributed to a service-related exposure when it should be, he or she is denied benefits to which entitled, and an injustice is rendered. When a veteran's illness is attributed to a service-related exposure even when he or she was not exposed (or, if exposed, the disability was not caused by that exposure), compensation is provided that is not truly warranted.

Uncertainty

Uncertainty, lack of complete and perfect knowledge, inherently affects the presumptive disability decision-making process. Presumptions are needed because information is incomplete, in relation both to causation generally and to whether specific individuals have an illness caused by service in the military. Because uncertainty is inevitably present, a vocabulary to express its extent, including adjectives such as *unknown*, *improbable*, *possible*, *likely*, or *certain* is needed. In using uncertain scientific evidence for decision making, we depend upon quantification of uncertainty for guidance on how to weigh more and less certain evidence.

In attributing disease to military service, uncertainty may be unavoidable for some exposures, although obviously not for others, such as a wound and its consequences. As described in Chapters 7 and 8, one necessary step in the presumptive disability decision-making process is to determine whether a disease was caused by factors related to military service.

The counterfactual notion of cause compares disease occurrence in two worlds, one with and the other without the exposure. Because only one of these worlds is observable, the likelihood of an event in the other must be predicted, and the outcome of the prediction is inherently uncertain.

The determination of whether a particular military exposure has the potential to cause a disease or condition is often subject to substantial uncertainty. Experimental studies have the advantage of having an explicit comparison group selected at random so that the counterfactual state is experimentally established. However, data from controlled experiments in human populations are generally not available and would generally not be applicable to exposures that cause disease only after a substantial period of time, as is true for many chemicals and risk for cancer. Findings from observational or epidemiologic studies of risk in exposed compared to unexposed persons, while attempting to control for other factors, are often used instead. The effort to control for other factors and to thereby assure comparability of exposed and nonexposed persons may not be fully successful, and other sources of bias may also add to uncertainty in results of observational studies. Typically, results of in vitro and animal studies of biological mechanisms are also considered. However, in using the results of such research, uncertainty arises from the extrapolation of results from cells, animals, or other systems to humans. Approaches for quantifying these diverse sources of uncertainty about causation have been developed but do not fully reflect the scope of the uncertainty and its implications for decision making. Most often, judgment of expert panels to gauge the degree of uncertainty is used as a guide to decision making.

Even if general causation is established, assignment of causation in a particular veteran may still be subject to uncertainty. Limited or no information may be available on exposure. Exposures in a war theater may vary greatly over space and time, and without detailed information on the spatiotemporal profiles of exposure and on locations of individual Service members, exposure estimates will be imprecise and possibly invalid.

Uncertainty as to individual causation would not be eliminated by having "perfect" exposure data. Conditions and diseases often have multiple causes, each possibly causing some proportion of the observed cases. Absent some marker that indicates that a particular case of disease was attributable to a specific factor, uncertainty as to causation by military service, when other factors also contribute to etiology, is inherent. Variation in susceptibility to an exposure is a further source of uncertainty in considering causation in individuals.

Uncertainty also affects the SAF, a statistic recommended by the Committee as an index of the extent of disease that is attributable to an exposure. The *attributable fraction* is defined as the fraction of an exposed and diseased population whose disease was caused by the exposure, meaning it is the fraction of the population who, but for the exposure, would not have developed the disease. The value of the attributable fraction may depend on multiple factors, including the level and the timing of exposure, the dose-response curve, the time since exposure, and the baseline susceptibility of the population. The true function relating the attributable fraction to exposure is unknown in terms of both its general form and its specific values. We estimate the function describing the attributable fraction from finite data that are subject to variability. Hence, there is typically uncertainty in estimates of the attributable fraction used to describe the burden of disease attributable to an exposure and to assess whether disease in an individual veteran was caused by service.

Scientists have constructed mathematical systems to quantify uncertainty; the theory of probability is the most widely applied. There are two distinct notions of probability: frequentist and subjectivist. In the former, probability represents the long-run frequency of events. For example, the probability of a heads or tails represents the fraction of heads or tails out of a large number of coin tosses. Subjectivist probability is instead an expression of belief about the likelihood of an event. For example, we represent an individual's risk of disease as a probability between 0, indicating no chance, and 1, indicating certainty. For either notion, there is the same precise calculus for representing, combining, and manipulating probabilities as measures of uncertainty.

In subsequent chapters, the Committee sets out concepts related to general and specific causation that are critical for improving the current approach to making presumptions.

SUMMARY

This chapter introduces some of the key concepts involved in using scientific evidence as the basis for compensation of groups of exposed individuals. It sets out the need to determine general causation and to consider how much disease is attributable to exposure. These concepts are elaborated in subsequent chapters. Gaps in the scientific evidence on exposure and causation lead to a need for presumptions. Chapters 10 and 11 address how surveillance of exposures and disease among active duty personnel and veterans could reduce these gaps.

REFERENCES

Pamperin, T. J. 2006. *An overview of the disability benefits program and presumptions affecting veterans' benefits.* Paper presented at the first meeting of the IOM's Committee on the Evaluation of the Presumptive Disability Decision-Making Process for Veterans, Washington, DC.

Petrou, L. 2006. *Statement presented at the third meeting of the IOM's Committee on the Evaluation of the Presumptive Disability Decision-Making Process for Veterans*. San Antonio, TX.

Ryan, P. 2006. *Perspectives on veterans' legislative disability presumptions*. Paper presented at the third meeting of the IOM's Committee on the Evaluation of the Presumptive Disability Decision-Making Process for Veterans, San Antonio, TX.

Scott, E. P. 2006. *Statement presented at the third meeting of the IOM's Committee on the Evaluation of the Presumptive Disability Decision-Making Process for Veterans*. San Antonio, TX.

VA (Department of Veterans Affairs). 2002. *Veterans health initiative. Independent study course. Vietnam veterans and Agent Orange exposure*. Washington, DC: Department of Veterans Affairs. http://www1.va.gov/agentorange/docs/VHIagentorange.pdf (accessed May 12, 2007).

Yoder, C. 2006. *Thoughts on presumptions of service-connection for veterans presumed to have been exposed to environmental hazards*. Paper presented at the third meeting of the IOM's Committee on the Evaluation of the Presumptive Disability Decision-Making Process for Veterans, San Antonio, TX.

7

Scientific Evidence for Causation in the Population

INTRODUCTION

This chapter describes the kinds of scientific evidence used for establishing a general causal relationship between exposure and disease, an important input to presumptive service-connection decisions. Unlike individual service-connection claims, in which a particular veteran has to make a case that a particular condition affecting him or her was caused by or aggravated by military service, a presumptive service connection applies to a group, or population of veterans. Presumptive service connections remove the burden of proof from individual veterans, but establishing presumptions necessitates an assessment of the scientific evidence for *population causal claims* (i.e., was some group of veterans *exposed* to conditions or substances that *aggravated* existing or *caused* new health problems after service separation). More specifically, the goal is often to establish whether, in a *population* of individuals, exposures received by members of the population resulted in a change in the *frequency of occurrence or in the average severity* of a disease. For example, we might ask whether the frequency of non-Hodgkin's lymphoma (NHL) among Vietnam veterans who were exposed to benzene during service is higher than the frequency among those who were not. If so, then we might assert that exposure to benzene is capable of *causing* NHL. The causal claim about the population does not mean that every veteran exposed to benzene during service will develop NHL or that every case of NHL would not have happened but for benzene exposure. On the population level, causal claims typically involve how risk (the *probability* of disease) changes in *response* to exposure.

In this chapter we will focus on the scientific issues involved in establishing these sorts of causal claims. We will review the issues facing scientists or others who review evidence to collectively decide on population causal claims. The next chapter provides a framework for doing so. At the start of this chapter, we discuss the types of scientific information considered in evaluating the strength of evidence for inferring causation. Then we discuss how epidemiologists define and assess association and how association differs from causation. This distinction is essential to understanding prior approaches to presumptive disability decision making and also this Committee's proposed approach. In Appendix J, we offer an extended discussion of what we mean by causation and how it is modeled statistically. We have placed this material in an appendix, not as a reflection of its importance, but because the topic is too complicated to cover in a short section.

Next we discuss the scientific strategies used to establish association, and lastly we discuss the scientific strategies used to move beyond just determining the presence of an association to inferring causation. We conclude the chapter by discussing uncertainty—both with respect to association and with respect to causation. We leave to the next chapter a discussion of strategies for synthesizing potentially diverse sources of evidence into a single overall judgment of the strength of evidence for a causal claim.

SOURCES OF EVIDENCE

Evidence about population causal claims (hereafter just "causal claims") comes from a variety of sources. In some cases, we have extensive knowledge about the mechanism by which exposure causes disease. For example, we do not need a randomized clinical trial to establish that bullet or shrapnel wounds have a deleterious effect on health. In other cases, such as low levels of exposure to lead and cognitive deficits in children, we know much less about the mechanisms and turn to other types of scientific evidence including findings of epidemiologic studies. Any scientific assessment of a causal claim combines the mechanistic knowledge and statistical evidence from epidemiologic studies. In this section we briefly survey the types of statistical evidence used to establish causal claims, and then we sketch the types of toxicologic, biologic, and mechanistic knowledge used to support or reject causal claims. By statistical evidence we mean the quantitative relationships between a set of measured variables in a sample. Case reports about individual patients may be useful for suggesting etiologic hypotheses, particularly with exposures that are followed quickly by disease onset.

Randomized Clinical Trials

The most persuasive human evidence for establishing a causal relationship comes through experimental studies in which investigators control exposure. Randomized clinical trials (RCTs) are the counterpart in humans to the controlled laboratory experiment with animals. In clinical trials, the exposure (usually considered as potentially beneficial, such as a new medication) is allocated randomly to the study population in such a way that the treated and untreated groups are otherwise equivalent, at least in expectation. If the randomization process has been successful, then any differences between the treated and comparison groups should reflect a causal relationship between treatment and disease (or outcome) risk. Randomization assures comparability of the two groups on factors that may affect the occurrence of the outcome.

Although the RCT is simple in concept, proper execution in human populations is often quite challenging and complicated. Even if randomization is successful in assuring comparability of exposed and comparison groups, validity of results for causal inference is not assured. For example, there are powerful placebo effects that operate in humans, which can be eliminated, in some instances, by concealing treatment status from the study participants. More subtle problems can arise when the doctors or others administering the treatment and collecting the outcome data are aware of treatment status. This potential for bias has prompted the use of the "double-blind" design, in which neither the study personnel in contact with participants nor the participants themselves know the treatment status. A refinement of this design is the crossover study, in which treatment and nontreatment are given in random order to each participant, allowing each person in the study group to be his or her own control. This design illustrates the kind of evidence we would like to have to draw causal claims, since we directly observe the response of the same person when they are treated and not treated, so that the treatment can be reasonably inferred to be the "cause" of any differences in response under the two conditions. Unfortunately, crossover trials are a practical approach only for studying short-term responses to agents for non-fatal conditions, so that they cannot be used for assessing effects of environmental exposures on chronic diseases.

In most other designs, including RCTs of standard design and most observational studies, we have to base such conclusions on differences in rates between exposed and unexposed groups of *different* individuals, rather than on the responses of the same individual in exposed and unexposed states. Interpretation of differences in outcome frequency as a causal effect when comparisons are made between different groups requires a form of inference known as "counterfactual." Using the counterfactual (i.e., counter to the facts) we infer what would have happened in the exposed group had the exposure been some alternative by making a comparison with the outcomes of others who actually experienced the different exposure. The counterfactual approach needs comparability of the exposed and comparison groups.

RCTs and other experiments involving humans are ethically limited in the range of questions to which they can be applied. Many of the major questions of public health—for example, the effects of air pollution or pesticides on human health—cannot be addressed through RCTs because it is not ethical to expose humans experimentally to substances in quantities that are presumed harmful. For such questions, we are limited to passively observing the health of people "naturally" exposed—that is, to observational studies. Nonetheless, the model of the RCT remains useful as a framework for considering limitations of findings of observational studies. Randomized interventions can be ethically carried out to reduce exposure to harmful agents (e.g., tobacco use).

Observational Studies

In an observational study, the investigator does not control exposure of the people in the study and does not intervene in any way in the population under study. Although observational studies may lack the comparability of exposed and non-exposed characteristic of controlled experiments, they are nonetheless capable of providing evidence about the relationship between exposure and health and are generally the only option available to obtaining human evidence of the effect of potentially harmful exposures.

Broadly speaking, observational study designs fall into three categories: cross-sectional studies, cohort studies, and case-control studies. In cross-sectional studies, a variety of factors are recorded at a particular point in time. In cohort studies, persons exposed or unexposed to a given factor are observed over a period of time for health effects related to the exposure. The case-control study compares persons with a given disease (*cases*) to those without the disease (*controls*) with regard to their history of exposure. Each of these general designs has appropriate analytic strategies, and each design has its own strengths and weaknesses. There are variations of each of these approaches, and a few additional approaches as well (for example, case-crossover studies). These designs are well described in standard epidemiologic references.

One general difficulty of observational studies, regardless of design, is that exposure is not randomized. Rather, exposure status may be determined by where people live or work, what they eat, what social group they belong to, or by a host of other factors that can be associated with disease risk. As a consequence of these other factors, associations between exposures and disease risk may occur even if the exposure does not cause the disease. Conversely, no association may be measured when the exposure actually does cause disease because these factors act to reduce the effect.

Toxicologic, Mechanistic, and Biologic Knowledge

In addition to randomized clinical trials and observational studies, which provide statistical evidence of a relationship between exposure and disease, a wide variety of other types of scientific evidence may be crucial for inferring a causal relationship between exposure and disease (IOM, 2006a,b; IOM/NRC, 2005). Controlled laboratory experiments with animals and research in in vitro systems and other relevant biological, physical, or even social data can be used to assess the likelihood that a given substance or circumstance can cause a particular human health effect. Approaches to assessing the combined evidence from human and animal investigations, as well as from in vitro systems, have been formulated by a number of agencies including the International Agency for Research on Cancer (IARC, 2006b), the Institute of Medicine (IOM) (IOM, 2006b; IOM/NRC, 2005), and the Environmental Protection Agency (EPA, 2005). These formalized approaches offer guidance on assessment of evidence and relative weighting of various lines of evidence.

Even without statistical evidence from epidemiologic studies, the findings of animal studies and mechanistic investigations on how an agent causes a health effect can be sufficiently convincing to support a causal conclusion. For example, IARC identified benzo(a)pyrene as a human carcinogen primarily based on non-epidemiologic evidence (Straif et al., 2005). However, we infrequently amass this level of biological understanding for agents affecting human health. More typically, non-epidemiologic lines of research are considered to support the conclusion that a substance, or chemical, "probably" causes, or is "likely" or "reasonably anticipated" to cause an adverse effect such as cancer or other health endpoints (e.g., EPA, 2005; IARC, 2006b; NTP, 2005; NTP CERHR, 2003, 2005). When there are epidemiologic findings supporting an association between an agent and disease, however, experimental or other biological evidence may provide sufficient weight and understanding for scientists to conclude that the association is due to a causal relationship. For example, in several species the agent may produce the same effect as observed in human studies, and by a mechanism that is conserved and relevant across species with key features of the mechanism observed through experiments in human cell lines or other systems.

As a case in point, epidemiologic, animal, and mechanistic data were all considered in establishing that industrial exposure to butadiene can cause lymphohematopoietic cancers (IARC, 1999). Epidemiologists showed that styrene-butadiene exposed rubber workers had elevated lymphohematopoietic cancer rates. Toxicologists showed that potentially carcinogenic metabolites of butadiene in butadiene-exposed workers activated potential oncogenes, providing mechanistic knowledge on carcinogenesis, and biologists induced tumors in mice and rats, both with exposure to butadiene and to a known metabolite that occurs in humans and mice and rats, providing animal evidence.

Formaldehyde provides a contrasting example. IARC (2006a, sec. 5-2) noted that epidemiologic studies found "strong but not sufficient evidence for a causal association" between formaldehyde exposure and leukemia. Their interpretation of the finding as causal was guarded because of some limitations in the several positive studies (e.g., small numbers of deaths) and lack of finding of effect in a high-quality study. There was uncertainty with regard to possible underlying mechanisms. The IARC monograph noted lack of good rodent models for human acute myeloid leukemia. It also considered various possible mechanisms, "such as clastogenic damage to circulatory stem cells" (IARC, 2006a, sec. 5-4). Unable to identify a mechanism for the induction of leukemia in humans from formaldehyde and data to support it, IARC did not conclude that formaldehyde was a known cause of human leukemia. Golden et al. (2006) have advanced arguments that the relationship could not be causal. For example, they argued that inhaled formaldehyde is so reactive that it is unlikely to travel as formaldehyde from the upper airways to the bone marrow; also they argued that "there is no indication that formaldehyde is toxic to the bone marrow/hematopoietic system" as are other known leukemogens benzene, ionizing radiation, and chemotherapeutic agents (Golden et al., 2006, p. 146).

ASSOCIATION AND CAUSATION

Association

Absent strong mechanistic understanding, the first step towards establishing a causal relationship between exposure experienced by people and a disease is to establish a statistical *association* between exposure and the disease. Exposure and disease are positively associated in a group if the incidence of disease among those exposed is higher than the incidence among those not exposed. For example, in the early 1950s Doll and Hill demonstrated that tobacco smoking and lung cancer mortality were associated. In a cohort of British physicians, lung cancer mortality was much higher among people who smoked 25 g of tobacco daily compared with those who didn't smoke (Doll and Hill, 1954, p. 1530). Even though a detailed mechanism between inhaling smoke and contracting lung cancer was not evident, a vague but plausible mechanism based on the carcinogenic properties of tobacco tar allowed scientists to hypothesize that the association was produced by a causal relationship. Had there been no observed difference in lung cancer mortality between smokers and nonsmokers, they would have likely assumed that smoking had no causal influence on lung cancer.

The strength of association between exposure and disease is typically measured with a statistic called the *relative risk* (RR). RR is the ratio of the incidence of disease among the exposed over the incidence in the unexposed:

$$RR = \frac{incidence(\text{exposed})}{incidence(\text{unexposed})} = \frac{\text{\# exposed with disease / \# exposed}}{\text{\# not exposed with disease / \# not exposed}}$$

An RR of 1.0 means that the frequency of disease among the exposed is the same as among the unexposed. An RR of 10 means that the rate of disease among the exposed is 10 times as high as among the unexposed.

A high RR does not imply a high absolute risk in the population. If, for example, one in a million unexposed individuals and 10 in a million exposed individuals get the disease, then the RR is 10, even though the chances of getting the disease among those exposed is only 1 in 100,000.

Another measure of association, commonly used in case-control studies, is the *odds ratio* (OR):

$$\begin{aligned} OR &= \frac{\text{\# with disease \& exposed / \# with disease \& not exposed}}{\text{\# without disease \& exposed / \# without disease \& not exposed}} \\ &= \frac{\text{\# with disease \& exposed / \# without disease \& exposed}}{\text{\# with disease \& not exposed / \# without disease \& not exposed}} \end{aligned}$$

From this formula, it can readily be seen that the OR, expressed in the first line as the odds of exposure in cases divided by the odds of exposure in controls, is also (second line) the odds of disease in the exposed divided by the odds of disease in the unexposed. The OR has the desirable property of being approximately equal to the RR if the disease is rare (Greenland and Thomas, 1982). This is true even though the absolute risks in exposed and unexposed cannot be estimated from case-control studies.

Association Is Not Causation

Association is not the same as causation. It is prima facie evidence for causation, but not sufficient by itself for proving a causal relationship between exposure and disease. For example, although they did not record its presence, Doll and Hill would presumably have found a high positive association between having tar-stained fingers and lung cancer mortality in their study. Clearly having tar stains on one's fingers does not by itself *cause* lung cancer, but it could be associated with lung cancer risk because heavier smokers, at greater risk for lung cancer, would also be more likely to have tar-stained fingers.

Unlike associations, causal claims support making counterfactual claims, that is, claims about what the world would have been like had something been different, or changed. For example, what *would have* been the rate of lung cancer mortality among a group of smokers had they been prevented from smoking? For this, the counterfactual claim would be the rate of lung cancer mortality among never smokers. What would have been the rate of lung cancer mortality among those with tar-stained fingers had we eliminated their stains with special soap? Although tar stains and smoking are both associated with lung cancer, we can answer these questions because we know the causal mechanisms: smoking is a common cause of tar stains and lung cancer, but tar stains by themselves have no effect on lung cancer mortality. Service-connection claims require the same attention to counterfactual questions: what would have been the rate of adult-onset type 2 diabetes had Vietnam veterans not been exposed to Agent Orange, for example.

Claims about association alone do not support the sorts of claim that must underlie presumptive service connections, while causal claims do. We call an association that arises in a population from an exposure that causes disease a *causal association*. Associations are termed *spurious* if they arise for some other reason. For example, the association between tar-stained fingers and lung cancer is spurious.

Spurious associations can arise in many ways. One is from a common factor (confounder) that is associated with the exposure under study and also a cause of the disease of interest, and another is from reverse causality (the disease is a cause of exposure) as depicted in Figure 7-1.

In the context of presumptive service connections, exposure typically occurs prior to the medical condition under consideration. Thus, we can almost always rule out the possibility that a medical condition was a cause of exposure, but the development of disease may influence apparent exposure. For example, it has been speculated that early subclinical manifestations of diabetes could increase storage of polychlorinated biphenyls (PCBs) in the body, leading to apparent associations of PCBs with diabetes even when the exposure is measured years before the emergence of the disease. More intuitively, people developing asthma might choose to not have cats if the presence of a cat exacerbated their asthma. The inverse association that would be observed between asthma and cat ownership would represent reverse causation and not a causal, protective effect of cats on risk for asthma. Thus, reverse causation may produce a spurious association even with carefully collected prospective data.

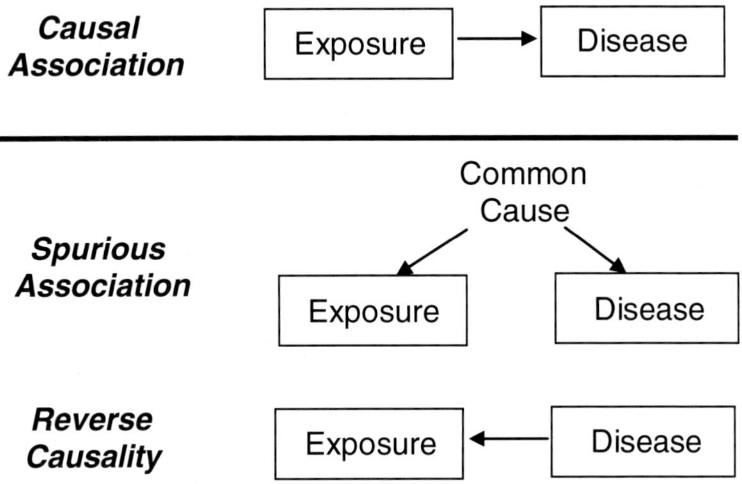

FIGURE 7-1 Causal and spurious associations.

If we can measure potential confounders (i.e., common causes) that might give rise to spurious association, then statistical adjustment can be used to remove the part of the observed association that arises spuriously from confounders. We discuss this strategy in a later section.

There is also the possibility that exposure causes disease, but that the two are *not* associated in the population under study. For example, if a confounder produces negative association between exposure and disease, but the true causal relationship produces positive association, and the two associations (true and confounded) are of roughly same magnitude, then the observed association will be small as represented in Figure 7-2. Note that dropouts are excluded from this example. Fortunately, because hiding a causal association requires a spurious association of similar magnitude but opposite sign as the causal association, this situation occurs infrequently.

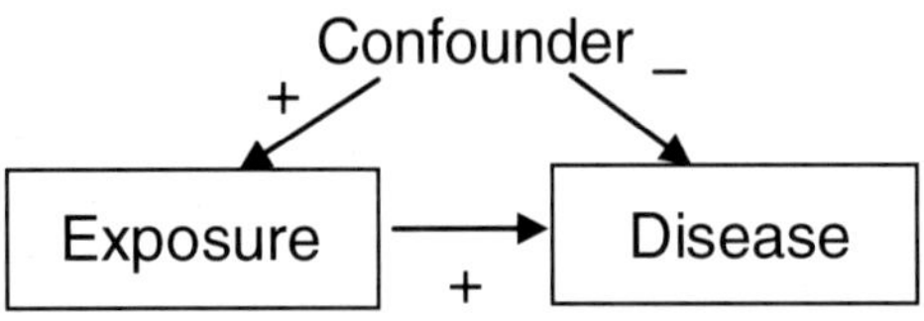

FIGURE 7-2 Scenario for causation without association.

The Problem of Bias

Even if confounding and reverse causation can be ruled out (or statistically controlled for, as we discuss below), observational studies might still be affected by other forms of bias, including information bias and selection bias. *Bias* in this context does not suggest prejudice on the part of the researcher, but rather denotes systematic error arising from the collection of information or the selection of participants that produces an observed association not attributable to an underlying causal relationship between exposure and disease. For example, systematic error might occur in a case-control study of patients with pancreatic cancer in which most of the cases have died before they could be interviewed. If the interviewer relies on family members for information about exposures of the dead person but on living controls themselves, then the quality of the exposure information is likely to differ for the cases and the controls. Differential quality of data for cases and controls can in turn easily distort the true association between an exposure and a disease. This would be an example of *information bias*, a broad class of bias that relates to the quality of data collected. Another kind of bias is *selection bias*, which occurs when the selection process by which the study sample is derived distorts the relationship between exposure and outcome. For example, suppose half of the patients in the treatment arm of an RCT drop out of the study from side effects, while no one from the control arm drops out, and suppose that the dropouts are the ones who began the study in worse health. Even if the treatment has no benefit whatsoever on the outcome, the treated group will appear to fare better than the untreated group. Once possible biases are identified, their possible impact on the results can be assessed through sensitivity analysis (discussed below).

EVIDENCE FOR ASSOCIATION

Although it is not sufficient for establishing causation, association is nevertheless prima facie evidence for causation, and the lack of association is prima facie evidence for lack of causation. Thus, if mechanistic knowledge is insufficient to settle the issue, a first stage in any evidence-based approach to presumptive service connection is to empirically establish and quantify the level of association in the service population under consideration, or in similarly exposed populations.

Epidemiologists (e.g., Rothman, 2002) use risk measures such as the RR and the OR to quantify the association between exposure and disease in a population. Other measures might also be of interest, such as the *attributable fraction (AF)*—the proportion of disease in either the total population or an exposed subgroup that is caused by exposure—which is particularly relevant for compensation policy (see next chapter). This report uses the terminology *service-attributable fraction (SAF)* when the subgroup of interest is a military population. More complex conceptual and statistical models are needed when there are several risk factors to be considered in combination, as will be discussed later in this chapter.

Risk measures are estimated by applying statistical techniques to data from a particular sample drawn from the population of interest (e.g., a study of 1,000 randomly selected veterans of a particular conflict). The result of this process is an estimate of the population risk measure (e.g., the RR), together with a measure of the uncertainty in those estimates (a standard error or confidence interval) caused by the inherent variability in a random sampling process. Note that these uncertainty estimates usually account only for random variation, not the consequences of any bias.

Statistical techniques are also used to test specific hypotheses, particularly the null hypothesis that there is no association between exposure and disease in the population. The null hypothesis is of particular interest—unless it can be rejected, there is insufficient empiric evidence to conclude the existence of an association in the population.

The statistical tests related to the null hypothesis are referred to as significance tests, and the test results are commonly expressed in the form of a *P* value, the probability of observing a sample result at least as extreme as that observed in the sample if the null hypothesis were true. Note that the *P* value does not provide the probability that the null hypothesis is true given the observed data. That would require specification of one's prior belief in the null hypothesis before seeing the data. Additionally, failing to find the *P* value needed to reject the null hypothesis at some level of probability does not exclude the possibility of an association. There should be enough precision to rule out a counter explanation that the study was inadequate to detect a meaningful effect size.

EVIDENCE FOR GOING BEYOND ASSOCIATION TO CAUSATION

If an association has been established, the next (and more difficult) task is to assess the evidence for causation by trying to eliminate alternative explanations to causality for the association. For example, tobacco companies and some academic researchers initially dismissed the association between smoking and lung cancer by proposing explanations other than causation. Arguments were advanced such as: perhaps a poor economic background would expose someone to conditions besides smoking that would lead to lung cancer and would also make them more likely to smoke or perhaps there are genes that dispose people to smoke and also to be more susceptible to lung cancer. Only after some years of epidemiologic research, animal studies, and scientific debate did the scientific community reject all alternative explanations and conclude that the association between smoking and cancer is causal. Postulating and eliminating alternatives are core skills in observational research. This process can use data from many sources, including the basic sciences and toxicology. If reasonable alternatives are possible, then we cannot move beyond association to a firm causal conclusion.

Experimental Control: Inferring Causation in RCTs

Randomized clinical trials remove two of the possible alternative explanations of an observed association: confounding and reverse causality. By assigning treatment (exposure) randomly, the design removes the influence of any confounder that might influence exposure (Figure 7-3a), and the influence of the outcome on exposure, if there is any (Figure 7-3b). Done properly, and setting aside the play of chance, only a causal relationship from exposure to health outcome should produce observed association in an RCT (Figure 7-3c). However, RCTs are generally not possible for the kinds of causal questions facing VA in presumptive disability decision making.

Statistical Control: Inferring Causation from Observational Studies

Adjusting for Confounding

When associations are found in observational studies, the first approach for removing spurious associations from confounders is statistical control of characteristics that may differ between exposed and unexposed persons (i.e., adjustment). Multiple regression models are one way to estimate the association between exposure and outcome after adjusting for charac-

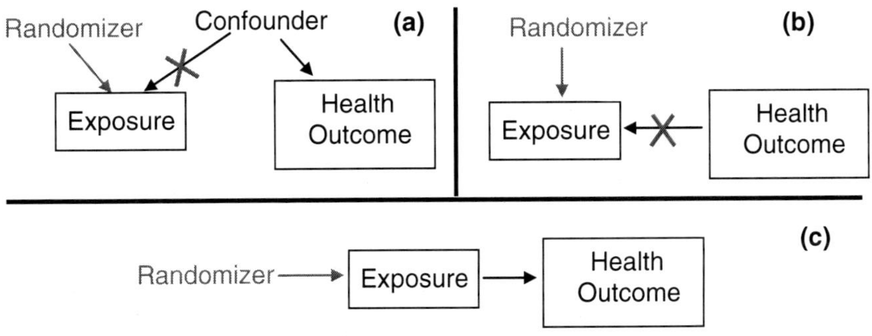

FIGURE 7-3 The power of randomization.

teristics of participants that might confound the results. If investigators have successfully measured characteristics that distort the results, then adjustment of these factors will help separate a spurious from a causal association.

For example, suppose we conduct an observational study of veterans, each exposed during service to some level of a toxin that can permanently degrade respiratory function. Suppose further that older veterans are more likely to have been exposed to more of the toxin, as it was used more frequently in the early segment of a war. Since age (after military service) also naturally degrades respiratory function, it is a confounder of the association between the exposure and respiratory function in this study (Figure 7-4) and must be included as a *covariate* in a multiple regression to adjust for its biasing effect. If age is the only such confounder in the study, and it is measured accurately, then we can indeed separate the spurious from the causal association statistically.[1]

Two problems are common in such an approach, however. First, unlike randomization, which can eliminate the influence of all confounders without having to identify and measure any of them, appropriate statistical adjustment for confounders requires identifying and measuring *all* of them. If, for example, age were not the only confounder of the association of exposure with respiratory function (Figure 7-5), then the association between exposure and respiratory function, statistically adjusted for age, would still combine both spurious and causal association, and thus present a misleading estimate of the effect of exposure on respiratory function.

Deciding which variables to control for in a statistical analysis of the association between exposure and disease depends upon knowledge about the possible mechanisms connecting them. For example, dozens of observational studies, some involving thousands of subjects, have shown an association between watching TV and childhood obesity (IOM, 2006a). Can we move beyond an association and say that watching TV causes childhood obesity?

These studies include a variety of statistical adjustments, depending on the mechanisms the researchers consider important. The primary mechanisms thought to connect TV and obesity are shown in Figure 7-6. Thus, several studies controlled for socioeconomic status (SES), as a child from a low socioeconomic status home might be allowed to watch more TV and also allowed to eat a higher proportion of high-calorie/low-nutrition foods

[1]Assuming all relations are linear, that is, Respiratory Function = β_1Exposure + β_2Age + an "error" term $\varepsilon \sim N(0,\sigma^2)$, and all boxed variates standard normal, then the expected observed covariance (association) between exposure and respiratory function is $\beta_1 + \beta_2\phi$. The expectation of the estimate of the association between exposure and respiratory function adjusting for age in fact equals β_1.

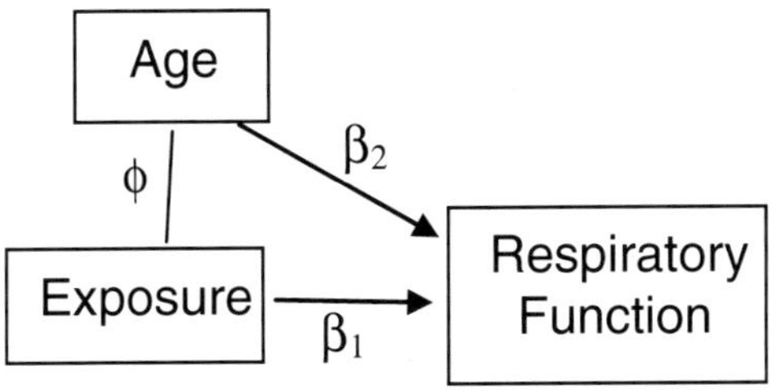

FIGURE 7-4 Age as a confounder.

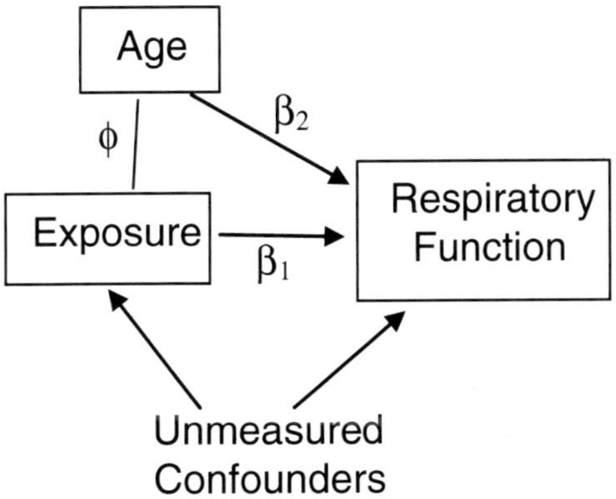

FIGURE 7-5 Unmeasured confounders.

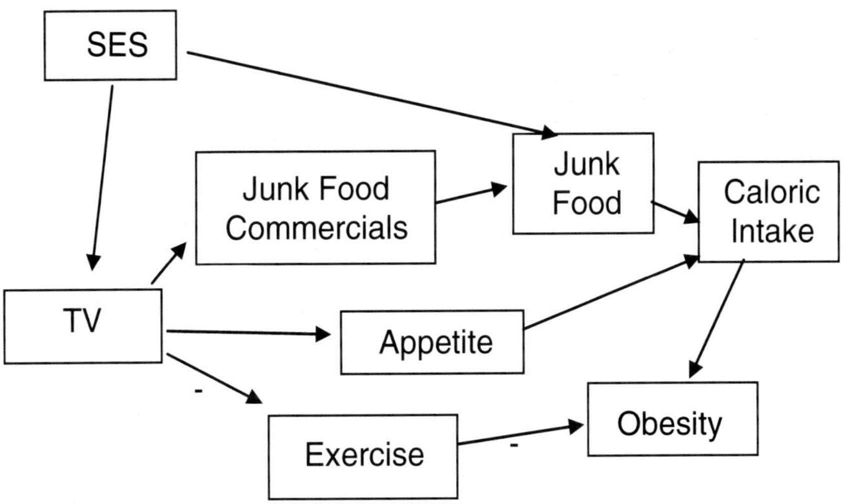

FIGURE 7-6 TV and obesity.

("junk" foods). Several studies attempted to separate out the potential contribution of TV to obesity through replacing or suppressing exercise, which in turn would lead to more obesity, or by increasing caloric intake, either through increasing exposure to food marketing, or by increasing appetite through other means (e.g., people like to snack when they are relaxing passively in front of a TV). Being able to identify these mechanisms allows us to identify and control for potential sources of spurious association and also to tease apart the importance of a variety of possible mechanisms.

Measurement Error

A further problem in adjusting for spurious associations involves measurement error. If a confounder has been included in the statistical analysis as a covariate but has been measured poorly, then the included variable is only a surrogate for the true variable. This is equivalent to partially omitting the variable and thus does not allow all confounding bias to be removed from the estimate of the causal association (Kennedy, 2003). The more measurement error in the confounding variables the greater the potential for incomplete control of bias.

Another problem similar to measurement error occurs when covariates are measured too coarsely. If, for example, TV was not measured in minutes per day, but rather as high, medium, and low, then differences in TV watching levels within these coarse categories could still affect the probabilities of exposure to junk food commercials. Statistically adjusting for this imprecise measure of TV would fail to remove all confounding.

To summarize, statistically adjusting for confounders can separate the causal from the spurious association between exposure and disease, but it can do so completely only if all confounders have been identified, measured accurately, and represented in a valid statistical model. Thus, in assessing a report on a study that claims that adjustment for confounding has been made, the adjusted association estimates the causal association if the study has

- included all reasonable confounders,
- measured them with reasonable precision and accuracy, and
- used them in a valid statistical model.

Instrumental Variables

An alternative to measuring and adjusting for confounders is *instrumental variable* estimation, a technique favored by econometricians (Kennedy, 2003) but not yet widely used in epidemiology (Greenland, 2000). An instrumental variable must be related directly to the putative cause but independent of all potential confounders. Under this condition, we can separate variation in the cause that might spuriously come from the confounders or from reverse causation from true variation in the cause that will translate to variation in the effect. By using the instrument to show how much of the variation is *not* from the confounders and *not* from reverse causation, we can then statistically adjust the observed association between cause and effect without even measuring the confounders or being concerned about reverse causation.

An example of an instrumental variable might be distance from the hypocenter for veterans of a nuclear weapons test. The true causal variable here would be their ionizing radiation exposure. For some participants this may have been measured by a film badge dosimeter, but these measurements are incomplete and inaccurate. However, one could use the mean of the measured doses for all participants located at the same distance from the hypocenter as an instrumental variable for assigning dose to all participants, and then examine the relationship between these assigned doses and subsequent cancer risk. Assuming a Service member's assignment to a particular location during the test was effectively at random with respect to potential confounders (Service members weren't assigned to locations based on their future cancer risks), this would be expected to yield an unbiased assessment of the exposure-response relationship (Figure 7-7).

Although instrumental variable estimation is a potentially powerful strategy for separating causal from spurious association, it depends heavily on the availability of an informative instrumental variable and on the untestable assumption that the *instrument* is independent of all the other potential confounders and not an independent risk factor for disease given radiation dose. Thus, its practical applications in epidemiologic research are limited.

Other Guides to Causal Knowledge

There have been several attempts to create sets of criteria to guide scientific judgments when moving beyond observed association to causa-

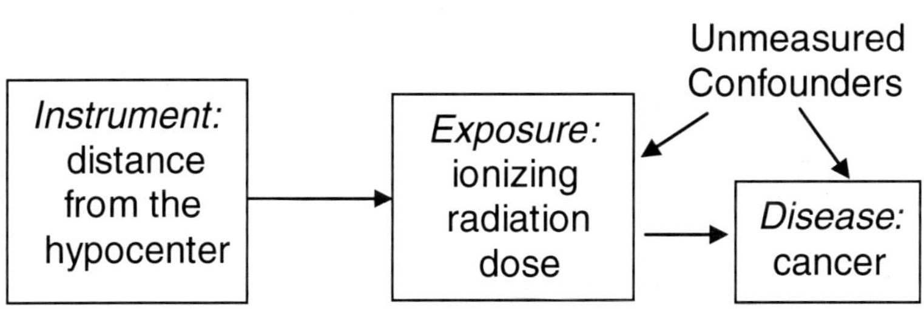

FIGURE 7-7 Instrumental variable.

tion. Some of these criteria can be traced to the "canons of inference" proposed by John Stuart Mill (1862). In the early days of microbiology, Koch developed his famous "postulates" as formal criteria for establishing a causal association of a clinical infectious disease with a microorganism. Koch's postulates include the identification of the suspect causal organism in people with the disease and the causation of the illness in an animal by infection with the organism (Koch, 1884). Unfortunately, such experimentally based criteria are of little help in establishing the causality of an environmental exposure with a chronic disease. The version of the criteria most familiar to epidemiologists and other public health researchers is the Bradford-Hill criteria, which are: the strength of the association, consistency, specificity, temporality (logical time sequence), dose-response (biologic gradient), plausibility, coherence, experimental evidence, and analogy (Hill, 1965). Although each of these criteria has limitations or exceptions, they can be useful guides to assessing the overall evidence. For example, see the introductory chapter in the 2004 Surgeon General's report on smoking (DHHS/CDC, 2004).

As we discussed above, background knowledge about the biologic mechanisms by which an exposure might or might not cause disease can prove crucial in establishing a causal claim or its negation. The tools of experimental biology have been extraordinarily valuable in developing insights into human physiology and pathology. Such laboratory tools have been extended to explore the effects of putative toxins on human health, especially through the study of model systems in other species. The field of toxicology has flourished in recent decades, allowing arguments of plausibility to be developed for a range of environmental toxicants. At the same time, species can differ in fundamental aspects of physiology (e.g., metabolism, hormonal regulation) that limit extrapolation from one species to another.

REALISTIC CAUSAL INFERENCE

Multifactorial Causation

Epidemiologists have long recognized that most chronic diseases, such as cancer or coronary heart disease, result from a complex "web of causation," whereby one or more external agents (exposures) taken into the body initiate a disease process, the outcome of which could depend upon many factors including age, genetic susceptibility, nutritional status, immune competence, social factors, and others. Exposures may occur over an extended period of time with some cumulative effect, and exposure to multiple agents together could result in synergistic or antagonistic effects different from what might result from each separately. These general notions were formalized by Rothman (1976) in a "sufficient component causes model," which postulates that disease can result from a number of different constellations of causal factors, each of which may comprise several components (e.g., exposure plus susceptibility plus timing) that are all necessary to make them a complete cause. This framework is useful in thinking about exposure to multiple causal factors. For example, consider the diagram in Figure 7-8.

Consider the data from a hypothetical epidemiologic study of veterans exposed to some particular exposure illustrated in Table 7-1. In this hypothetical example, smoking is a much larger contributor to risk than is the military exposure of the participants, but the two factors are not confounded, since among the population at risk, the proportion of smokers is the same in the exposed and unexposed. It is also evident that the two effects on risk are multiplicative, since individuals with both factors

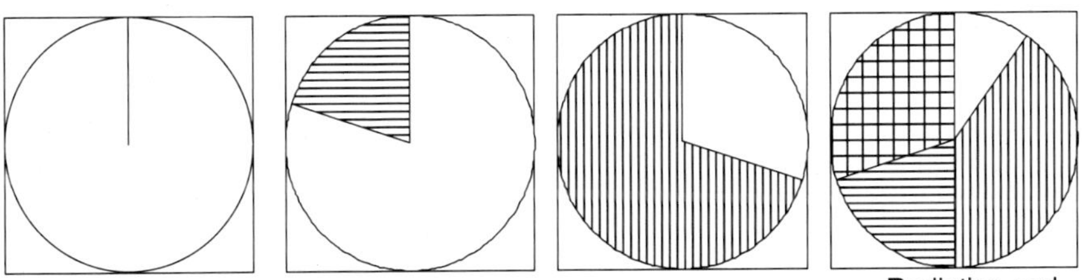

FIGURE 7-8 Rothman's sufficient component causes model.
NOTE: Each circle represents a different constellation of factors that is sufficient to produce disease; within any circle, the sectors represent specific factors that are all necessary to comprise a complete cause. Blank space represents host susceptibility plus background exposures; vertical bars, ionizing radiation; horizontal bars, tobacco smoking; cross-hatched, joint action of smoking and radiation. SOURCE: Rothman, 1976.

TABLE 7-1 Hypothetical Example of Military Radiation Exposure, Smoking, and Cancer

Military Radiation Exposure	Smoking Habit	Number at Risk	Cancer Cases	Relative Risk
No	Never	1,000	10	1
No	Current	1,000	100	10
Yes	Never	1,000	30	3
Yes	Current	1,000	300	30

have an RR of 30, the product of the RR for smoking (10) and for military exposure (3). In other exposure situations, the pattern of combined effects could be less than multiplicative, or greater. Two specific models have special relevance to compensation policy. The first is the multiplicative model just illustrated, which can be represented mathematically as

$$RR_{mult} = RR_E \times RR_S,$$

where RR_E is the RR for exposed nonsmokers relative to nonexposed nonsmokers, and RR_S is the RR for unexposed smokers relative to unexposed nonsmokers. Under this model, the effect of exposure is the same in both nonsmokers ($RR_{E|NS}$ = 3) and smokers ($RR_{E|S}$ = 30/10 = 3). The other important situation is an additive model of the form:

$$RR_{add} = 1 + (RR_E - 1) + (RR_S - 1)$$

$$= RR_E + RR_S - 1$$

In other words, the risk from exposure to both factors is the background risk plus the sum of the additional risks from each factor separately. Thus, in our hypothetical example, if the single-factor risks were as before, we would have expected an RR for exposed smokers of 1 + (10 – 1) + (3 – 1) = 12, rather than 30 as above. Under this model, the excess RR ($ERR = RR - 1$) for exposure is the same in nonsmokers ($ERR_{E|NS} = 3 - 1 = 2$) and smokers ($ERR_{E|S} = 12 - 10 = 2$). Of course, the actual joint effect could be different from either of these specific models. The effect when both exposures are present could be less than additive (e.g., a joint *RR* of 11), greater than multiplicative (e.g., 50), or in between (e.g., 20).

Models for Interaction

Epidemiologists use the term *interaction* (or *effect modification*) to denote the departure of the observed joint risk from what might be expected based on the separate effects of the factors. However, any estimate of interaction is model specific, meaning it depends on what model of interaction we expect (multiplicative, additive, or some other). In claiming interaction, one must therefore specify the model for the combined effect from which the observed data deviate. For example, one could define a multiplicative interaction RR as

$$RR_{Int(mult)} = \frac{RR_{joint}}{RR_E \times RR_S},$$

or an additive interaction RR as $RR_{Int(add)} = RR_{joint} - RR_E - RR_S + 1$. For the data illustrated in the table above, $RR_{Int(mult)} = 30/(3 \times 10) = 1$ and $RR_{Int(add)} = 30 - 3 - 10 + 1 = 18$, indicating no departure from a multiplicative model but a large positive deviation from an additive model. Likewise, if the joint *RR* were 12, the multiplicative interaction *RR* would have been 0.4 and the additive interaction would have been 0, indicating a less than multiplicative joint effect and no departure from an additive model. These concepts have natural extensions to more than two risk factors, such as the inclusion of main effects and interactions in the widely used logistic regression model (which assumes a multiplicative model). The following chapter will describe how these parameters can be used to estimate the proportion of disease among exposed individuals that is attributable to the separate or joint action of each factor or other unknown factors, and the relevance and limitations of such estimates for attributing causation in individuals.

The previous example presumes that there is no causal connection between the military exposure and smoking—that prior smoking did not cause the individual's exposure in the military or vice versa. If this assumption did not hold, a very different analysis would be required. For example, suppose a nonsmoking recruit received a serious battle wound leading to amputation, which subsequently caused him or her to take up smoking for self-medication, and he or she ultimately developed lung cancer. In this case, one might wish to estimate the direct effect of battle trauma on lung cancer risk and the indirect effect mediated through smoking. However, as a policy matter, one might conclude that both routes were ultimately the consequence of battle trauma and should not be distinguished for the purpose of deciding on compensation. In other words, an individual's smoking history would be irrelevant.

UNCERTAINTY

The science of estimating the causal influence of an exposure on disease, especially in cases where controlled experiments are not feasible, is fraught with uncertainty. Dealing with uncertainty in a principled way is one of the goals of statistics, however, and it need not stop us from rational analysis. In this section we provide a framework for dealing with the uncertainty inherent in assessing *population causal claims.*

There are three levels of uncertainty in making a case for a service connection:

1. Uncertainty as to the correct causal model
2. Uncertainty as to the statistical (parameter) estimates within each model
3. Uncertainty about the specifics of a given individual within a group

The uncertainty about the correct causal model involves uncertainty about whether exposure in fact causes disease at all, about the set of confounders that are associated with exposure and cause disease, about whether there is reverse causation, about what are the correct parametric forms of the relations of the exposure and confounders with outcome, and about whether there are other forms of bias affecting the evidence. One currently used method for making this uncertainty clear is to draw a set of causal graphs, each of which represents a particular causal hypothesis, and then consider evidence insofar as it favors one or more of these hypotheses and related graphs over the others. We explain this approach in more detail in Appendix J.

Uncertainty about the model is not just limited to the qualitative causal structure; however, it also involves uncertainty about the parametric form of the model specified, the variables included, whether or not measurement error is modeled, and so on. When mechanistic knowledge exists, this sort of uncertainty is mitigated. Nevertheless, model uncertainty is perhaps the most important level of uncertainty.

By comparison, uncertainty about the parameter estimates (regression coefficients) for a *given* model is a well-studied problem. When the newspaper reports that a political poll is accurate to "within 3 percentage points," it is attempting to report the uncertainty about the estimates reported by the poll. When a regression analysis produces an OR with a confidence interval (or a *P* value for the null hypothesis that the adjusted association is 0), it is quantifying the uncertainty caused by the random variation that we can expect from one sample to another. The important point is that these reports of uncertainty are *conditional on the model being a sufficiently adequate approximation to reality so that the inferences drawn are valid.* The overall scientific inference involves uncertainty about the model *and* uncertainty about the parameter estimates given each model. It would be misleading to neglect the uncertainty in the model, and act as if the *P* values and confidence intervals delimit and make precise our overall scientific uncertainty.

Beyond model uncertainty and parameter estimate uncertainty, we still face uncertainty in applying causal models to individuals. Typically, causal models will provide a prediction about the chances or severity of a disease, given a particular level of exposure and particular levels of the covariates, such as age or social class. For a given individual, we might be highly uncertain about the level and duration of exposure, as well as uncertain about the levels of covariates. This level of uncertainty is also important to presumptive service-connection claims, as will be discussed in the following chapter.

There are two systematic, quantitative approaches for including uncertainty about the model into an assessment of overall uncertainty about a causal inference. The first is sensitivity analysis, and the second is model averaging. In sensitivity analysis we attempt to quantify the sensitivity of the parameter estimate to assumptions about the model. In model averaging, we attempt to provide an overall uncertainty to our estimate by calculating the estimate of a common parameter or target and its uncertainty for each model we consider plausible, and then by weighting the estimates and the uncertainties by the likelihood of each model. It is essential that the target have the same interpretation in each model, or the combination of the estimates has no meaning.

Sensitivity Analysis

In general, sensitivity analysis is the attempt to systematically explore the sensitivity of a particular parameter estimate, such as the size of the causal effect of exposure on disease, to any assumption made in the model that itself can be parameterized. For example, in estimating the effect of cumulative exposure to lead on a child's IQ, cumulative lead exposure for a child can be estimated by measuring the concentration of lead in the child's shed baby teeth. Although this is an improvement over blood lead, it still involves error. The estimate of the effect of lead on IQ is sensitive to the amount of measurement error for lead, and the measurement error can be parameterized by the proportion of the variance of the measure thought to come from actual lead as opposed to error. A sensitivity analysis can then be performed by estimating the effect under a progression of levels of this proportion. This provides an assessment of how sensitive the causal estimate is to various possibilities of measurement error, and provides a more specific statement of what we must assume about measurement error in order to reach the causal conclusion.

Paul Rosenbaum (2002), along with Charles Manski (1995), has developed a formal technique for dealing with unmeasured confounding or bias called *sensitivity analysis*. The essential idea is to make reasonable guesses as to the range of distortion introduced by possible bias, or the extent of the associations underlying the possible confounding, and then to use those ranges to estimate the extent to which the outcome is changed under those assumptions. If the outcome turns out to be highly sensitive to such perturbations, one cannot rule out the possibility that the observed association is an artifact. Greenland (1996) has advocated a more quantitative approach to directly modeling multiple sources of bias.

Model Averaging

Given the inevitable uncertainty about the true model form, one might ask how one should estimate the RR (or any other epidemiologic effect parameter derived from it) and an "honest" confidence interval for it that allows for this possibility of model specification error. There is an extensive statistical literature on this question (see, for example, Leamer, 1978, for a review), but in practice the problem is frequently ignored. Frequently, an investigator conducts a number of different analyses and ends up reporting only a single best-fitting model, or the one model in which he or she holds the strongest belief, and reports confidence limits on the parameters of that model, as if it were the "true" model. Sometimes, an investigator may acknowledge this uncertainty about model form by reporting a range of alternative models in the spirit of sensitivity analyses. This can leave the reader uncertain as to which specific set of estimates to use, particularly if several models fit the data more or less equally well, yet yield different estimates and confidence intervals. There are, however, a number of formal approaches to this problem from both a frequentist and a Bayesian perspective.

Here we summarize briefly just one of them, known as Bayesian model averaging (Hoeting et al., 1999). Suppose we have a parameter of interest β (measuring the effect of interest) and a range of alternative models m = 1, . . . M, yielding estimates $\hat{\beta}_m$ and variances estimates $V_m = \text{var}\left(\hat{\beta} \middle| M = m\right)$ of this same parameter under different models (for this purpose, we must assume that the parameter β has the same interpretation under each of the different models, i.e., the effect of exposure, conditional on different choices of adjustment variables). Let $\pi_m = \Pr\left(M = m \middle| D\right)$ denote the posterior probability of model m, conditional on the observed data D. Then a natural estimator of β that takes account of model uncertainty might be a simple weighted average of the model-specific estimators, $\bar{\beta} = \sum_m \hat{\beta}_m \pi_m$ with variance $\text{var}\left(\bar{\beta}\right) = \sum_m \left(V_m + \left(\beta_m - \bar{\beta}\right)^2\right) \pi_m$. This formal approach has seldom been applied in practice, although there are some examples in the epidemiologic literature. It also has some potential for misuse, as when many highly correlated variables are considered in the same model. In model averaging, we attempt to deal with model uncertainty by calculating the estimate of a common parameter or target and its uncertainty for each model we consider plausible, and then by weighting the estimates and the uncertainties by the likelihood of each model.

SUMMARY

Presumptive service-connection decisions depend on population-level causal questions, such as "Were some cases of type 2 diabetes among Vietnam veterans caused by exposure to dioxin in Agent Orange during military service?" Assessing such claims scientifically involves review of statistical evidence from epidemiologic studies, evidence from experiments in other animals, and mechanistic evidence from basic biologic science.

Because a statistical association between exposure and disease does not prove causation, plausible alternative hypotheses must be eliminated by careful statistical adjustment and/or consideration of all relevant scientific knowledge. Epidemiologic studies that show an association after such adjustment, for example through multiple regression or instrumental variable estimation, and that are reasonably free of bias and further confounding, provide evidence but not proof of causation. Mechanistic knowledge about how particular agents might produce adverse health effects provides further evidence. For example, ionizing radiation is known to cause mutations in DNA that can result in cancer. Animal studies may provide further evidence by showing that an agent may induce in several different species the same effect observed in human studies, and by a mechanism that is conserved across species with key features of the mechanism observed.

Uncertainty about a causal claim can arise because of uncertainty about which among a set of plausible models is correct, or because of uncertainty about study design and execution, or it can arise because of uncertainty caused by simple sampling variability, or it can arise because of uncertainty in the basic science required to analyze other evidence. The overall uncertainty about the claim in question is some combination of all of these uncertainties.

Additional information on causation and statistical causal methods can be found in Appendix J.

REFERENCES

DHHS/CDC (Department of Health and Human Services/Centers for Disease Control and Prevention). 2004. *The health consequences of smoking: A report of the Surgeon General.* http://www.cdc.gov/tobacco/data_statistics/sgr/sgr_2004/index.htm (accessed July 27, 2007).

Doll, R., and A. B. Hill. 1954. The mortality of doctors in relation to their smoking habits; A preliminary report. *British Medical Journal* 1(4877):1451-1455.

EPA (Environmental Protection Agency). 2005. *Guidelines for carcinogen risk assessment.* EPA/630/P-03/001B. Washington, DC: Environmental Protection Agency. http://www.epa.gov/IRIS/cancer032505.pdf (accessed March 1, 2007).

Golden, R., D. Pyatt, and P. G. Shields. 2006. Formaldehyde as a potential human leukemogen: An assessment of biological plausibility. *Critical Reviews in Toxicology* 36(2):135-153.

Greenland, S. 1996. Basic methods for sensitivity analysis of biases. *International Journal of Epidemiology* 25(6):1107-1116

Greenland, S. 2000. An introduction to instrumental variables for epidemiologists. *International Journal of Epidemiology* 29(4):722-729; Erratum 29(6):1102.

Greenland, S., and D. Thomas. 1982. On the need for the rare disease assumption in case-control studies. *American Journal of Epidemiology* 116(3):547-553.

Hill, A. B. 1965. The environment and disease: Association or causation? *Proceedings of the Royal Society of Medicine* 58:295-300.

Hoeting, J., D. Madigan, A. Raftery, and C. Volinsky. 1999. Bayesian model averaging. *Statistical Science* 14:382-401.

IARC (International Agency for Research on Cancer). 1999. *IARC monographs on the evaluation of carcinogenic risk to humans: Re-evaluation of some organic chemicals, hydrazine and hydrogen peroxide.* Vol. 71. http://monographs.iarc.fr/ENG/Monographs/vol71/volume71.pdf (accessed March 1, 2007).

IARC. 2006a. *IARC monographs on the evaluation of carcinogenic risk to humans: Formaldehyde, 2-butoxyethanol and 1-tert-butoxypropan-2-ol.* Lyon, France: International Agency for Research on Cancer. http://monographs.iarc.fr/ENG/Monographs/vol88/volume88.pdf (accessed August 22, 2007).

IARC. 2006b. *IARC monographs on the evaluation of carcinogenic risk to humans: Preamble.* Lyon, France: International Agency for Research on Cancer. http://monographs.iarc.fr/ENG/Preamble/CurrentPreamble.pdf (accessed March 1, 2007).

IOM (Institute of Medicine). 2006a. *Food marketing to children and youth: Threat or opportunity.* Washington, DC: The National Academies Press.

IOM. 2006b. *Asbestos: Selected cancers.* Washington, DC: The National Academies Press.

IOM/NRC (National Research Council). 2005. *Dietary supplements: A framework for evaluating safety.* Washington, DC: The National Academies Press.

Kennedy, P. 2003. *A guide to econometrics.* 5th ed. Cambridge, MA: MIT Press.

Koch, R. 1884. Die aetiologie der tuberkulose. *Mittheilungen aus dem Kaiserlichen Gesundheitsamte* 2:1-88.

Leamer, E. E. 1978. *Specification searches: Ad hoc inference with nonexperimental data.* New York: John Wiley & Sons.

Manski, C. 1995. *Identification problems in the social sciences.* Cambridge, MA: Harvard University Press.

Mill, J. S. 1862. *A system of logic: Ratiocinative and inductive, being a connected view of the principle of evidence, and the methods of scientific investigation.* 5th ed. London, UK: Parker, Son and Bowin.

NTP (National Toxicology Program). 2005. *Report on carcinogens.* 11th ed. Washington, DC: National Toxicology Program. http://ntp.niehs.nih.gov/index.cfm?objectid=32BA9724-F1F6-975E-7FCE50709CB4C932 (accessed March 1, 2007).

NTP CERHR (NTP Center for the Evaluation of Risks to Human Reproduction). 2003. *NTP-CERHR Monograph on the Potential Human Reproductive and Developmental Effects of Di-n-Butyl Phthalate (DBP).* Research Triangle Park, NC: NTP CERHR, U.S. Department of Health and Human Services.

NTP CERHR. 2005. *Guidelines for CERHR Expert Panel Members.* Research Triangle Park, NC: NTP CERHR, U.S. Department of Health and Human Services.

Rosenbaum, P. R. 2002. *Observational studies.* 2nd ed. New York: Springer-Verlag.

Rothman, K. J. 1976. Causes. *American Journal of Epidemiology* 104(6):587-592.

Rothman, K. J. 2002. *Epidemiology: An introduction.* Oxford, UK: Oxford University Press.

Straif, K., R. Baan, Y. Grosse, B. Secretan, F. E. Ghissassi, and V. Cogliano. 2005. Carcinogenicity of polycyclic aromatic hydrocarbons. *Lancet Oncology* 6(12):931-932.

8

Synthesizing the Evidence for Causation

In Chapter 7 we discussed the challenges of inferring a causal relationship between an exposure and a health outcome, and the range of evidence typically considered in making such inferences. In this chapter we discuss the problem of combining potentially diverse types of evidence in making a single, overall judgment about whether an exposure causes a health outcome. We begin by discussing the problem of integrating the evidence from multiple epidemiologic studies. We then describe a framework for combining epidemiologic and other evidence into a single *quantitative* judgment about the strength of causation. Next we discuss *qualitative* frameworks that have been used by expert committees for categorizing the overall strength of evidence for or against a causal claim. And lastly we propose a qualitative framework for causal reference to be used in the presumptive disability decision-making process.

We include this material because the scientific group that we propose in our new approach will review evidence on the health of veterans and will have the task of integrating an accumulating stream of results and interpreting new findings in the context set by previous findings and prior reviews. The successive Institute of Medicine (IOM) Agent Orange committees are illustrative. While the methods are presented in a theoretical fashion, they would be key components of the approach recommended by this Committee and, in reality, they are already inherent to the approaches used by the IOM committees.

META-ANALYSIS: COMBINING EVIDENCE FROM MULTIPLE STUDIES

Scientific evidence relevant to causal relationships between exposure and disease comes from different types of investigation, including randomized clinical trials (RCTs) on humans, epidemiologic studies, animal experiments, and cell studies, and also from fundamental biological knowledge. We use the term *human studies* to refer to RCTs or observational studies involving people. Although an evidence-based approach must combine all forms of scientific evidence, in this section we limit our discussion to the problem of synthesizing the information from multiple human studies.

The idea of pooling information from multiple studies has a long tradition in statistics that goes back at least to Karl Pearson in 1904. A meta-analysis involves gathering all studies with evidence related to a particular question, and statistically combining the results of these studies. In many contexts, health researchers have mathematically combined the results from multiple, yet comparable RCTs to derive a summary estimate of the effect of some substance on health; the estimate appropriately combines the results of all the individual studies. Such summaries are often carried out, for example, to determine if there is a benefit of a drug or perhaps an excess occurrence of an unwanted side effect. One approach for combining evidence, random effects meta-analysis, allows for heterogeneity between studies; with this technique, a meta-analysis is not strictly limited to studies involving similar populations.

In observational studies, there may be more variability in findings from study to study because study variables are not under the investigator's control. The populations studied may vary considerably in their characteristics, and the variables measured as covariates for statistical adjustment may also differ. Nevertheless, meta-analysis is applied to observational study results as well as to RCT data. Meta-regression (Greenland and O'Rourke, 2001) allows pooling of data across observational studies with some unexplained heterogeneity, and recent work by E. Kaizar (2005) improves on meta-regression for situations with data available from both RCTs and observational studies.

Although the development of meta-analytic methods has generated extensive methodological discussion (see, for example, Berlin and Antman, 1994; Berlin and Chalmers, 1988; Dickersin and Berlin, 1992; Greenland, 1994a,b; Stram, 1996; Stroup et al., 2000), it is a technique that can be quite useful when there are multiple studies on the same question. For example, for each of a number of different cancers, the 2006 IOM Committee on Asbestos and Selected Cancers (IOM, 2006a) did a quantitative meta-analysis on studies that combined the effect of asbestos exposure on risk based on multiple studies for each of a set of cancers. The report presented the results of individual studies as well as an overall estimate that came from the combination of the estimates from the individual studies.

THE BAYESIAN APPROACH

No matter how sophisticated the meta-analytic technique, it is still limited to combining statistical evidence from different studies into a single statistical estimate of the effect size. As we discussed in Chapter 7, the scientific evidence germane to causal claims also includes mechanistic knowledge, findings of animal or cell and molecular studies, and other knowledge relevant to biological plausibility. A technique for combining all the available evidence into a single judgment needs to accommodate these other types of information. One approach for combining all the evidence available into a single quantitative judgment uses a *Bayesian* approach.

Bayesian methodology conceives of probability as degrees of belief. Any proposition can be given a degree of belief. For example, one person might have a personal degree of belief of 0.30 (30 percent) in the proposition that garlic prevents colds, while another might give the proposition 0.80. The Bayesian approach provides a rule for updating the existing degree of belief in response to additional evidence (Bayes' rule, see below). Provided that no experts are inflexible in their belief,[1] a group of experts who update their beliefs by Bayes' rule will almost certainly converge to the same degree of belief after considering enough of the same relevant evidence.[2] Thus, a group of scientists considering the overall evidence for a causal claim such as "formaldehyde causes leukemia" might begin with a *prior* degree of belief about the claim and then update their belief in the light of accumulating evidence, regardless of the type of evidence. In more detail, if we consider each separate causal model relating formaldehyde (exposure) and leukemia as a separate hypothesis, H_i, then we can begin by using background knowledge or the results of previous studies, to assign a *prior probability* to each such hypothesis.

The Bayesian approach then seeks to compute the *posterior probability* $\Pr(H_i \mid D)$, namely the probability of (i.e., degree of belief in) hypothesis H_i given the new observed data D. The computation of these posterior probabilities is given by the famous rule first described by the Rev. Thomas Bayes, known as Bayes' theorem or rule, which in simple form is

$$P(H_i|D) = \frac{P(H_i)P(D|H_i)}{P(D)}.$$

[1]That is, assigns degree of belief 0 to what turns out to be the "true" proposition.

[2]And a raft of other assumptions—see Howson and Urbach, 1989.

Loosely translated, this formula reflects the prior probability for the hypothesis $P(H_i)$, the *likelihood*, meaning the probability of the data D given the hypothesis H_i is true, and $P(D)$, the probability of the data before any hypothesis.

The Bayesian framework provides a useful perspective on how weak additional evidence may have little impact on a strong prior probability or strong additional evidence may have substantial impact on a weak prior probability. For example, assume that we have very strong prior radiobiological and epidemiologic evidence that ionizing radiation can cause cancer, but a study of veterans who participated in nuclear weapons testing maneuvers fails to provide strong evidence of an association. In this example, assume that the data from the study do not lead to rejection of the null hypothesis of no association in a study of veterans exposed to radiation. This null finding might arise because the available sample size or length of follow-up was too small to yield an adequate number of cancers in the study group or because of inherent biases in the study design, such as inaccuracy of the available radiation dose information. If the veterans' data are highly uncertain, then a null result might change the prior estimate of population radiation risk (e.g., the synthesis of the world literature by expert committees such as the National Research Council's [NRC] Biological Effects of Ionizing Radiation [BEIR] committee) downward for this group, but by only a very modest amount. The posterior probability would still strongly favor a presumption (Figure 8-1a).

On the other hand, assume that there was very little prior knowledge about the effect of dioxins on cancer risk and a large, well-designed study of Vietnam veterans yielded a large and highly significant positive relative risk for non-Hodgkin's lymphoma (NHL) (Figure 8-1b). In this case the absence of prior knowledge would have little influence on the degree of judgment given to the estimates from the veterans' study.

A further example is provided by the National Research Council's Biological Effects of Ionizing Radiation (BEIR) IV Committee (NAS, 1988), which addressed the cancer risk of plutonium in humans. The available human data were very limited: no bone cancers were observed among 18 patients injected with plutonium for experimental purposes or among a small number of others occupationally exposed in the Manhattan Project. The BEIR IV committee adopted an empirical Bayes approach that assumed that the ratio of carcinogenic potencies of plutonium to various other radionuclides would be roughly constant across species. As there are substantially more human data about the carcinogenicity of various isotopes of radium and extensive animal data about plutonium, radium, and other radionuclides, it was possible to estimate the risk of plutonium in humans from a combined analysis that incorporated animal and human data. The committee carried out an uncertainty analysis that incorporated the variability in the ratios

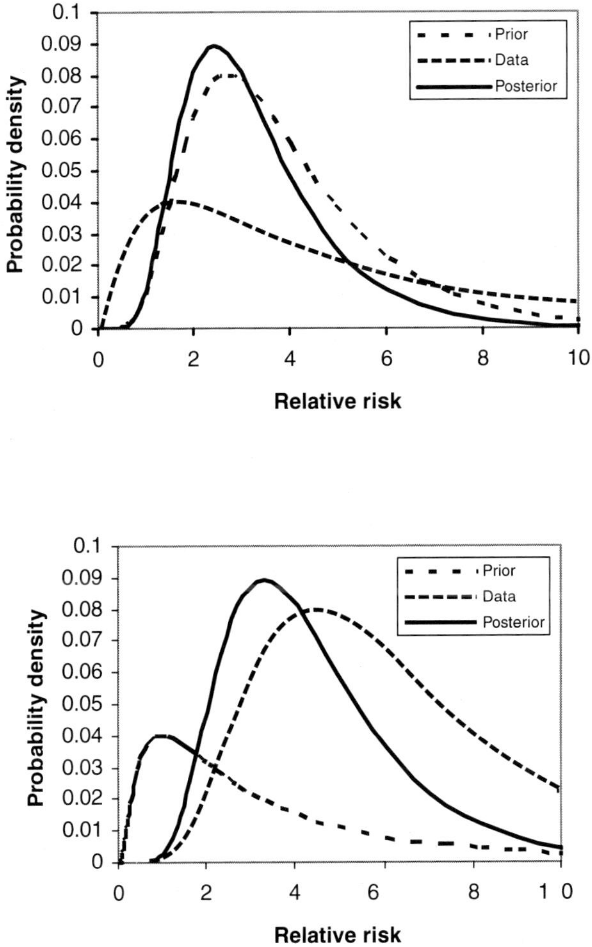

FIGURE 8-1 Hypothetical illustrations.
NOTE: Hypothetical illustrations of the combination of prior knowledge or judgment with study data to yield posterior estimates of a causal parameter, here the relative risk: (a) strong prior probability for a nonnull effect combined with weak data showing little or no effect in the study sample, and (b) weak prior probability combined with strong data showing a major effect.

of the relative carcinogenicities of the radionuclides across species. In this analysis, the limited human data for plutonium shifted the posterior probability distribution of the carcinogenicity estimates only slightly downward relative to the prediction resulting from the animal data.

The Bayesian approach can also focus scientific attention as new evidence becomes available. For example, as discussed in Chapter 7, there are many ways to generate an observed association between an exposure and a health outcome. The association might be the result of the exposure causing the health outcome, confounding, other forms of bias or of chance. In carrying out an observational study, epidemiologists try to measure and adjust for confounders and eliminate bias with good study design and appropriate data analysis. Scientific opinion about how much of the adjusted association might still be from unmeasured confounding or bias is useful in judging the degree of confidence about the estimate of an association.

To illustrate, consider the diagram in Figure 8-2, which graphically depicts the epidemiologists' concerns. Assuming a simple linear model, for illustration, the parameter β represents the *causal association*, that is, the amount of observed association between exposure and health due to the causal influence of exposure on health. The parameter α represents the amount of association from confounding that we *can* statistically adjust for,

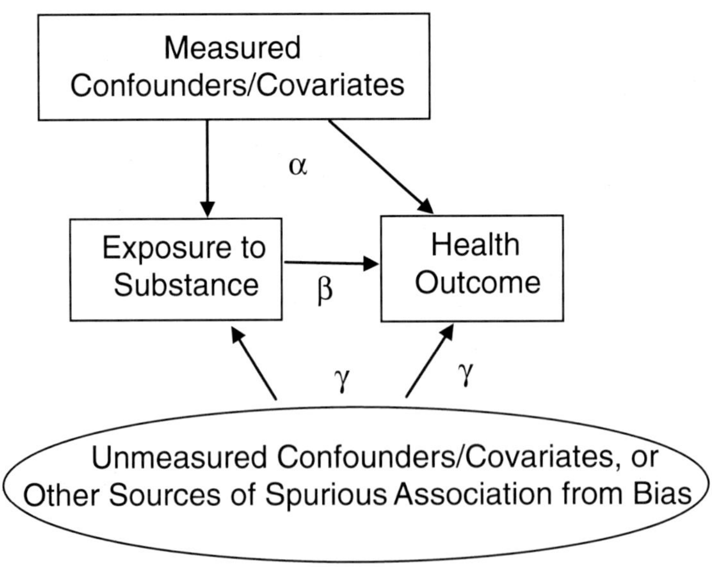

FIGURE 8-2 Focusing on unmeasured confounders/covariates, or other sources of spurious association from bias.

given the right model, and the parameter γ represents the amount of spurious association that we *cannot* statistically adjust for. Because the estimate of the causal association β will be biased in proportion to the size of γ, scientific attention should be focused on γ. In a Bayesian approach, we can encode scientific opinion about the size of γ into a prior probability, and then compute a posterior probability over β that appropriately takes into account uncertainty over γ.

In principle, then, the Bayesian approach provides an entirely quantitative framework for combining theoretical beliefs and evidence from previous studies along with the data at hand to update estimates of model parameters or of the probability that a particular hypothesis is true. In principle, each researcher undertaking a new study would apply the procedure to interpret the new evidence from the study in the context of already existing evidence, arriving at a posterior probability that is a methodologically appropriate combination of prior beliefs and accumulated evidence.

In practice, however, the Bayesian approach is *far* from a panacea for the complex task of combining diverse types of evidence. In typical scientific contexts, it may be difficult to move from fairly inchoate and diverse sorts of background knowledge to a communal "prior." By their nature, these prior odds are a matter of judgment, about which consensus amongst scientists can be difficult to obtain.

Further, although "updating" a posterior probability from certain kinds of evidence is reasonably straightforward, updating from other kinds of evidence is not. For example, consider estimating the relative risk of leukemia as a function of benzene exposure. After specifying a prior probability over this function, updating from a new sample of 400 veterans who were exposed to twice the usual level of benzene and who have a relative risk of 1.8 for leukemia is fairly straightforward mathematically. How are we to update based on experimental evidence showing that rats exposed to 50 times the background level of benzene develop leukemia at 3 times the rate of those exposed to background levels? What is the likelihood of this evidence, assuming any particular hypothesis about humans? Here we move beyond mathematics and statistics and into opinion about the comparability of leukemia and its causation in rats and humans.

QUALITATIVE FRAMEWORKS USED BY EXPERT COMMITTEES

Faced with diverse mechanistic and biological evidence that cannot be incorporated into a single statistical meta-analysis, and with opinions and judgments too varied and vague to employ a formal Bayesian approach, expert committees have resorted to qualitative categorizations of the strength of evidence for causation. There is a lengthy history of doing so, dating back to the 1950s as evidence began to develop on disease causation by radiation and tobacco smoking (Bayne-Jones et al., 1964). Judgments as to the level of evidence for causation can have substantial impact and often have regulatory implications. For example, the International Agency for Research on Cancer (IARC) (2006b), the U.S. Environmental Protection Agency (EPA) (2005), and the National Toxicology Program (NTP) (NTP, 2005) have developed systems for classifying the level of evidence in support of a causal relationship between chemicals and cancer. Similar classification systems have been developed for causal relationships for other health-specific effects such as reproductive outcomes (see e.g., NTP CERHR, 2003, 2005; Shelby, 2005), or between agents and health outcomes in general (IOM/NRC, 2005), or between smoking and disease (DHHS/CDC, 2004).

Each of these classification systems relies on evidence from a variety of research sources: epidemiologic, toxicological, and biological. The approach of combining diverse sources into an overall judgment on the strength of evidence for general causation, at least in a public health context, can be traced back to the 1964 *Report of the Advisory Committee to the Surgeon General on Smoking and Health* (Bayne-Jones et al., 1964), as well as other early summary reports on smoking and health. In the introductory chapters to the 1964 report, the committee described the different sorts of evidence to be considered. They specifically listed animal experiments, clinical and autopsy studies, and population studies, but were expansive in the evidence considered. They described the importance of expert evaluations of the quality of published reports, wrote two pages on their working definition of causation, and codified a subset of Sir Bradford Hill's criteria for establishing causation in epidemiology and public health contexts: consistency of the association, strength of the association, specificity of the association, temporality of the association, and the coherence of the association. The report that followed was an extended attempt to review all the evidence then available and synthesize it into an overall judgment: smoking causes lung cancer, bronchitis, emphysema, and is a "health hazard of sufficient importance in the United States to warrant appropriate remedial action" (Bayne-Jones et al., 1964, p. 33).

Although the Surgeon General's 1964 report did not explicitly categorize the *level* of evidential support for any of its conclusions, the 2004 Surgeon General's report does, as do recent reports from IARC (2006b) and IOM (2006a). A variety of categorizations exist. For example, the 2004 Surgeon General's report on smoking (DHHS/CDC, 2004), as well as the 2006 IOM Committee on Asbestos (IOM, 2006a, p. 20), employed a four-level categorization of the strength of evidence of causation (the latter was based on the 2004 Surgeon General's Report on Smoking [DHHS/CDC, 2004]):

1. Sufficient to infer a causal relationship
2. Suggestive but not sufficient to infer a causal relationship
3. Inadequate to infer the presence or absence of a causal relationship
4. Suggestive of no causal relationship

IARC forms expert committees and instructs them to first categorize the level of evidence within three subcategories—human, animal, and mechanistic—and then to synthesize the subcategories of evidence into an overall evaluation on a five-category scale ranging from carcinogenic to probably not carcinogenic. Figure 8-3 depicts the IARC evaluation scheme.

Several groups, including some IOM committees on Agent Orange (IOM, 1994, 1996, 1999, 2001, 2003b, 2005b) and other veterans' health issues, have based their approaches on the IARC (2006b) system for classifying the evidence in the *subcategory* pertaining only to human evidence. Within this subcategory, IARC systematically reviews available epidemiologic studies, considering study quality, relevance, and strength of findings. It then classifies the overall epidemiologic evidence as *sufficient evidence* if there is a finding that "a positive relationship has been observed between the exposure and cancer in studies in which chance, bias, and confounding could be ruled out with reasonable confidence" (IARC, 2006b, p. 19). For *limited evidence*, a "positive association has been observed between exposure to the agent and cancer for which a causal interpretation is considered by the working group to be credible, but chance, bias, or confounding could not be ruled out with reasonable confidence" (IARC, 2006b, pp. 19-20). With *inadequate evidence*, either there are no epidemiologic data or study quality, or power, or consistency across studies precludes a conclusion regarding causal association.

The IOM committees assessing the impact of Agent Orange have published biennial reports since 1994. Table 8-1 contains the four-level categorization for the strength of epidemiologic evidence used in the 1994 report (IOM, 1994), which is quite similar to IARC's subcategory scheme for human evidence (IARC, 2006b). Subsequent reports have used a similar classification scheme.

IOM committees (IOM, 2000, 2003a, 2004, 2005a, 2006b, 2007) examining Gulf War and health have added a causal category to those used by the IOM Agent Orange committees (IOM, 1994, 1996, 1999, 2001, 2003b, 2005b). Table 8-2 shows the classification scheme from Volume 1 of the Gulf War and Health series (IOM, 2000). The additional category makes causation explicit and includes evidence beyond that found in just epidemiologic studies.

The IOM Agent Orange categorization (IOM, 1994, 1996, 1999, 2001, 2003b, 2005b) relies less on mechanistic and animal evidence and more

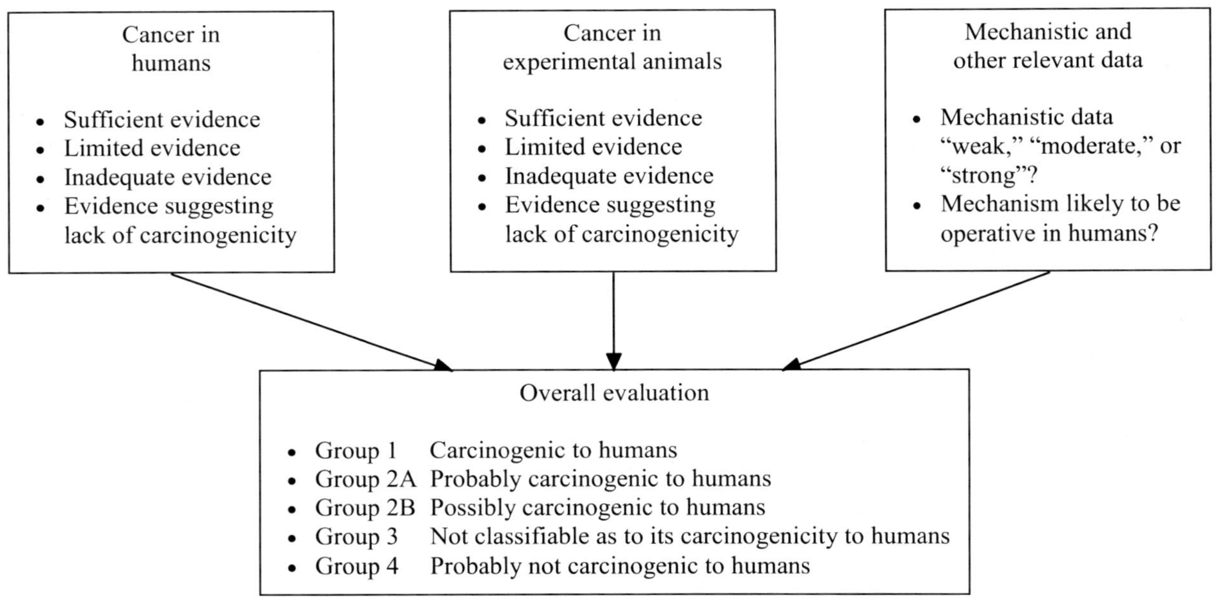

FIGURE 8-3 IARC evaluation scheme.
SOURCE: Adapted from Cogliano, 2006.

TABLE 8-1 IOM Categorization from the Executive Summary of *Veterans and Agent Orange: Health Effects of Herbicides Used in Vietnam*

Sufficient Evidence of an Association	Evidence is sufficient to conclude that there is a positive association. That is, a positive association has been observed between herbicides and the outcome in studies in which chance, bias, and confounding could be ruled out with reasonable confidence. For example, if several small studies that are free from bias and confounding show an association that is consistent in magnitude and direction, there may be sufficient evidence of an association.
Limited/Suggestive Evidence of an Association	Evidence is suggestive of an association between herbicides and the outcome but is limited because chance, bias, and confounding could not be ruled out with confidence. For example, at least one high-quality study shows a positive association, but the results of other studies are inconsistent.
Inadequate/Insufficient Evidence to Determine Whether an Association Exists	The available studies are of insufficient quality, consistency, or statistical power to permit a conclusion regarding the presence or absence of an association. For example, studies fail to control for confounding, have inadequate exposure assessment, or fail to address latency.
Limited/Suggestive Evidence of No Association	Several adequate studies, covering the full range of levels of exposure that human beings are known to encounter, are mutually consistent in not showing a positive association between exposure to herbicides and the outcome at any level of exposure. A conclusion of "no association" is inevitably limited to the conditions, level of exposure, and length of observation covered by the available studies. *In addition, the possibility of a very small elevation in risk at the levels of exposure studied can never be excluded.*

SOURCE: IOM, 1994.

on epidemiologic data than do the IARC, NTP, or EPA models. As there may be many cases relevant to presumptive service connection in which the epidemiologic evidence on veterans specifically is extremely thin or even non-existent, giving animal and mechanistic evidence a more prominent and systematic role in the overall evaluation scheme is warranted. The causal category added by the Gulf War committees is a step in this direction. Previous IOM Agent Orange committees also reviewed and reported on toxicological and mechanistic information, but according to their interpretation of their charge, did not figure this information into the conclusions about the strength of evidence for association and causation.

TABLE 8-2 IOM Categorization from the Executive Summary of *Gulf War and Health, Volume 1: Depleted Uranium, Pyridostigmine Bromide, Sarin, Vaccines*

Sufficient Evidence of a Causal Relationship	Evidence is sufficient to conclude that a causal relationship exists between the exposure to a specific agent and a health outcome in humans. The evidence fulfills the criteria for sufficient evidence of an association (below) and satisfies several of the criteria used to assess causality: strength of association, dose-response relationship, consistency of association, temporal relationship, specificity of association, and biological plausibility.
Sufficient Evidence of an Association	Evidence is sufficient to conclude that there is a positive association. That is, a positive association has been observed between an exposure to a specific agent and a health outcome in human studies in which chance, bias, and confounding could be ruled out with reasonable confidence.
Limited/Suggestive Evidence of an Association	Evidence is suggestive of an association between exposure to a specific agent and a health outcome in humans, but is limited because chance, bias, and confounding could not be ruled out with confidence.
Inadequate/Insufficient Evidence to Determine Whether an Association Does or Does Not Exist	The available studies are of insufficient quality, consistency, or statistical power to permit a conclusion regarding the presence or absence of an association between an exposure to a specific agent and a health outcome in humans.
Limited/Suggestive Evidence of No Association	There are several adequate studies covering the full range of levels of exposure that humans are known to encounter, that are mutually consistent in not showing a positive association between exposure to a specific agent and a health outcome at any level of exposure. A conclusion of no association is inevitably limited to the conditions, levels of exposure, and length of observation covered by the available studies. In addition, the possibility of a very small elevation in risk at the levels of exposure studied can never be excluded.

SOURCE: IOM, 2000.

A PROPOSED QUALITATIVE FRAMEWORK FOR EVALUATING CAUSAL CLAIMS

Incorporating the Full Range of Evidence

The new process recommended by this Committee involves a categorization of the strength of evidence in support of a causal claim that incorporates the full weight of all evidence, including expert opinion, findings from epidemiologic and animal studies, and mechanistic knowledge. Reliance on the broad range of pertinent scientific data is also in keeping with the original congressional language that specifies consideration by NAS of the biological plausibility of any association. Before describing our proposed classification scheme, we briefly consider the consequences of extending the range of evidence considered. One issue is whether a seemingly more rigorous bar of evidence would reduce the likelihood of reaching a classification level at which compensation is made.

We approach this issue through case studies. Incorporating information derived from mechanistic studies and animal toxicology can lead to an upgrading or downgrading of a classification based on the weight of evidence classification. Some examples are described below.

Particulate Air Matter

Deployed personnel in the first Gulf conflict were exposed to airborne particles from the oil fires in Kuwait, exhaust from military vehicles and other combustion sources, and dust stirred by troop movements. The health effects of airborne particles are of general concern and the scientific evidence is subject to periodic review in the setting of the National Ambient Air Quality Standard (NAAQS) by the U.S. Environmental Protection Agency (SOURCE: http://epa.gov/pm/naaqsrev2006.html). The standard is evidence-based and the process of setting a new NAAQS involves a comprehensive review of all relevant scientific evidence, including epidemiologic and toxicological data as well as information on exposure patterns. For the last two reviews of the NAAQS, 1996 and 2006, the epidemiological evidence has been extensive, showing significant associations of airborne particles with increased risk for premature mortality and morbidity. The effects are relatively small, however, and biological plausibility has been a major consideration in evaluating the evidence and determining if the associations can be judged as causal. Information relevant to the plausibility of the associations comes from studies of the chemical and physical properties of particles and from toxicological studies that have addressed responses to particles in in vitro and in vivo models. Using a "weight of evidence" approach, the Environmental Protection Agency has judged the associations of airborne particles with adverse effects to be causal (SOURCE: http://epa.gov/pm/naaqsrev2006.html).

2,3,7,8-Tetrachlorodibenzo-para-dioxin (TCDD)

TCDD, a potent dioxin, was listed in 1997 as a Group 1 carcinogen by IARC based on limited evidence in humans, sufficient evidence in experimental animals, and abundant mechanistic information including data demonstrating that TCDD acts through the aryl hydrocarbon receptor (AhR), which is present in both humans and animals (IARC, 1997).

Formaldehyde

IARC has recently concluded that formaldehyde should be added to that group of agents that are carcinogenic to humans (Group 1 carcinogen) (IARC, 2004, p. 1). This upgrade was based upon new epidemiologic evidence of an association with nasopharyngeal cancer. "[T]here is now sufficient evidence that formaldehyde causes nasopharyngeal cancer in humans, a rare cancer in developed countries" (IARC, 2004, p. 1). Previous laboratory, animal, and mechanistic evidence supported this association. The IARC found "strong but not sufficient evidence for a causal association between leukemia and occupational exposure to formaldehyde," falling "slightly short of being fully persuasive because" of limitations in the cohort and conflict with nonpositive findings in another cohort (IARC, 2006a, p. 5). IARC noted findings of lymphomas and leukemias in one study in male rats, and several possible mechanisms for the induction of human leukemia, such as clastogenic damage to circulatory stem cells. However IARC also noted the lack of good rodent models that simulate the occurrence of acute myeloid leukemia in humans, and did not identify a mechanism for its induction in humans (IARC, 2006a).

Saccharin

Saccharin was originally classified as "reasonably anticipated to be a human carcinogen" by NTP (NIH, 2000, p. 1) and "possibly carcinogenic to humans" by IARC (IARC, 1987, p. 334) based on data clearly showing bladder cancer in rats. Although there was some limited epidemiologic evidence associating bladder cancer with saccharin sweeteners, the epidemiologic evidence was classified by IARC as inadequate. Subsequent mechanistic studies attributed the animal cancer findings as being due to a mechanism that would only occur at high doses in rats. "Saccharin produces urothelial bladder tumours in rats by a non-DNA-reactive mechanism that involves the formation of a urinary calcium phosphate-containing precipitate, cytotoxicity and enhanced cell proliferation. This mechanism is not relevant to humans because of critical interspecies differences in urine composition" (IARC, 1999, p. 50). Saccharin has since been delisted as a reasonably anticipated carcinogen by NTP and deemed "not classifiable as to its carcinogenicity to humans" by IARC (IARC, 1999, p. 50; NIH, 2000).

These case studies illustrate the potential contributions of mechanistic information as evidence relevant to causation is evaluated. A certain understanding of mechanism of action may have substantial impact in considering the overall weight of evidence.

Committee Recommended Categories for the Level of Evidence for Causation

In light of the categorizations used by other health organizations and agencies as well as considering the particular challenges of the presumptive disability decision-making process, we propose a four-level categorization of the strength of the *overall evidence* for or against a *causal relationship* from exposure to disease:

1. *Sufficient*: The evidence is sufficient to conclude that a causal relationship exists.
2. *Equipoise and Above*: The evidence is sufficient to conclude that a causal relationship is at least as likely as not, but not sufficient to conclude that a causal relationship exists.
3. *Below Equipoise*: The evidence is not sufficient to conclude that a causal relationship is at least as likely as not, or is not sufficient to make a scientifically informed judgment.
4. *Against*: The evidence suggests the lack of a causal relationship.

We use the term "equipoise" to refer to the point at which the evidence is in balance between favoring and not favoring causation. The term "equipoise" is widely used in the biomedical literature, is a concept familiar to those concerned with evidence-based decision making, and is used in VA processes for rating purposes as well as being a familiar term in the veterans' community.

Below we elaborate on the four-level categorization that the Committee recommends.

Sufficient

If the overall evidence for a causal relationship is categorized as Sufficient, then it should be scientifically compelling. It might include

- replicated and consistent evidence of a causal association: that is, evidence of an association from several high-quality epidemiologic studies that cannot be explained by plausible noncausal alternatives (e.g., chance, bias, or confounding), or
- evidence of causation from animal studies and mechanistic knowledge, or
- compelling evidence from animal studies and strong mechanistic

evidence from studies in exposed humans, consistent with (i.e., not contradicted by) the epidemiologic evidence.

Using the Bayesian framework to illustrate the evidential support and the resulting state of communal scientific opinion needed for reaching the Sufficient category (and the lower categories that follow), consider again the causal diagram in Figure 8-2. In this model, used to help clarify matters conceptually, the observed association between exposure and health is the result of (1) measured confounding, parameterized by α; (2) the causal relation, parameterized by β; and (3) other, unmeasured sources such as bias or unmeasured confounding, parameterized by γ. The belief of interest, after all the evidence has been weighed, is in the size of the causal parameter β. Thus, for decision making, what matters is how strongly the evidence supports the proposition that β is above 0. As it is extremely unlikely that the types of exposures considered for presumptions reduce the risk of developing disease, we exclude values of β below 0. If we consider the evidence as supporting degrees of belief about the size of β, and we have a posterior distribution over the possible size of β, then a posterior like Figure 8-4 illustrates a belief state that might result when the evidence for causation is considered Sufficient.

As the "mass" over a positive effect (the area under the curve to the right of the zero) vastly "outweighs" the small mass over no effect (zero), the evidence is considered sufficient to conclude that the association is causal. Put another way, even though the scientific community might be uncertain as to the size of β, after weighing all the evidence, it is highly confident that the probability that β is greater than zero is substantial; that is, that exposure causes disease.

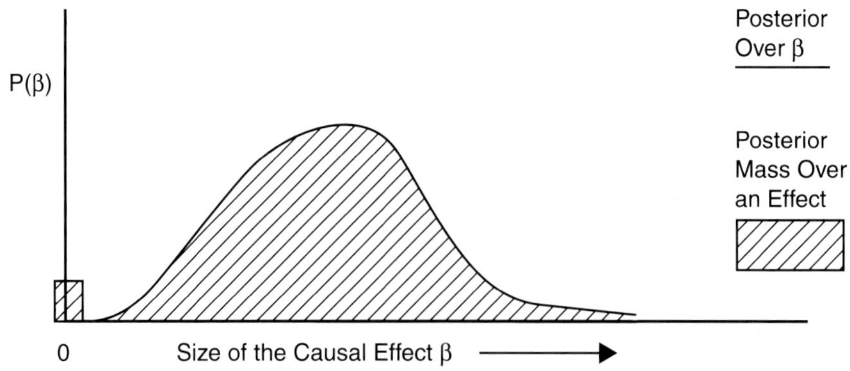

FIGURE 8-4 Example posterior for *Sufficient*.

Equipoise and Above

To be categorized as Equipoise and Above, the scientific community should categorize the overall evidence as making it more confident in the existence of a causal relationship than in the non-existence of a causal relationship, but not sufficient to conclude causation.

For example, if there are several high-quality epidemiologic studies, the preponderance of which show evidence of an association that cannot readily be explained by plausible noncausal alternatives (e.g., chance, bias, or confounding), and the causal relationship is consistent with the animal evidence and biological knowledge, then the overall evidence might be categorized as Equipoise and Above. Alternatively, if there is strong evidence from animal studies or mechanistic evidence, not contradicted by human or other evidence, then the overall evidence might be categorized as Equipoise and Above. Equipoise is a common term employed by VA and the courts in deciding disability claims (see Appendix D).

Again, using the Bayesian model to illustrate the idea of Equipoise and Above, Figure 8-5 shows a posterior probability distribution that is an example of belief compatible with the category Equipoise and Above.

In this figure, unlike the one for evidence classified as Sufficient, there is considerable mass over zero, which means that the scientific community has considerable uncertainty as to whether exposure causes disease at all; that is, whether β is greater than zero. At *least* half of the mass is to the right of the zero, however, so the community judges causation to be at least as likely as not, after they have seen and combined all the evidence available.

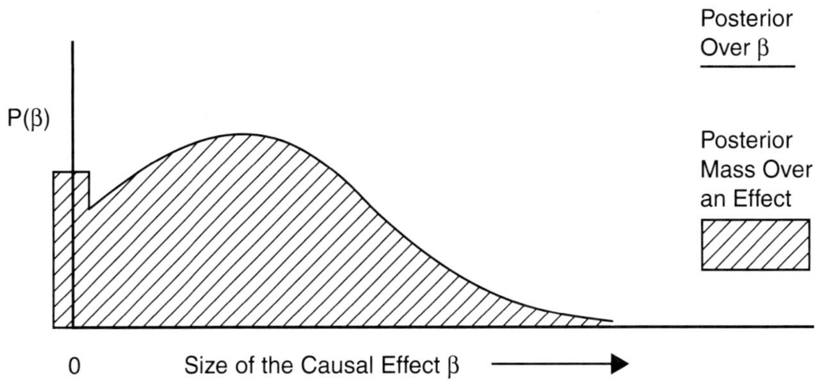

FIGURE 8-5 Example posterior for *Equipoise and Above*.

Below Equipoise

To be categorized as Below Equipoise, the overall evidence for a causal relationship should either be judged not to make causation at least as likely as not, or not sufficient to make a scientifically informed judgment.

This might occur

1. when the human evidence is consistent in showing an association, but the evidence is limited by the inability to rule out chance, bias, or confounding with confidence, and animal or mechanistic evidence is weak, or
2. when animal evidence suggests a causal relationship, but human and mechanistic evidence is weak or inconsistent, or
3. when mechanistic evidence is suggestive but animal and human evidence is weak or inconsistent, or
4. when the evidence base is very thin.

Figure 8-6 shows a posterior probability distribution that is an example of belief compatible with the category Below Equipoise.

Against

To be categorized as Against, the overall evidence should favor belief that there is no causal relationship from exposure to disease. For example, if there is human evidence from multiple studies covering the full range of exposures encountered by humans that are consistent in showing no causal association, or there is animal or mechanistic evidence supporting the lack of a causal relationship, and combining all of the evidence results

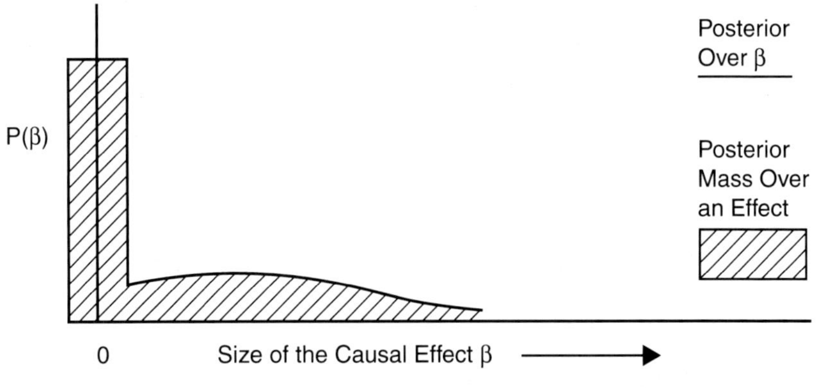

FIGURE 8-6 Example posterior for *Below Equipoise*.

in a posterior resembling Figure 8-7, then the scientific community should categorize the evidence as *Against* causation.

Comparison of the Committee's Proposed and Previous Frameworks

The Committee's proposed framework departs from that used by previous IOM committees in assessing Agent Orange (Table 8-1) in at least three respects. First, as noted, previous IOM committees evaluating Agent Orange (IOM, 1994, 1996, 1999, 2001, 2003b, 2005b) relied primarily on epidemiologic studies to classify strength of evidence for association and did not systematically incorporate evidence from animal toxicology and mechanistic studies.

Second, the Agent Orange categorization differentiated between levels of evidence for *association* instead of *causation* (IOM, 1994, 1996, 1999, 2001, 2003b, 2005b). As we have proposed in the previous chapter, the claims at issue related to compensation of veterans are causal claims, not associational claims. Association, especially association adjusted for potential confounders, is *evidence* for the causal claim, but it is *not identical to* the causal claim. In fact, making a presumptive decision to compensate on the basis of "limited/suggestive" evidence of an association presents the possibility that there is no causal link at all, and all of those receiving compensation because of such a presumption could be false positives. A causal category was added by previous IOM committees on Gulf War and Health, but the categories below "Sufficient evidence of a causal relationship" retain the language of association (IOM 2000, 2003, 2004, 2005a, 2006b, 2007). This Committee recommends, therefore, a categorization

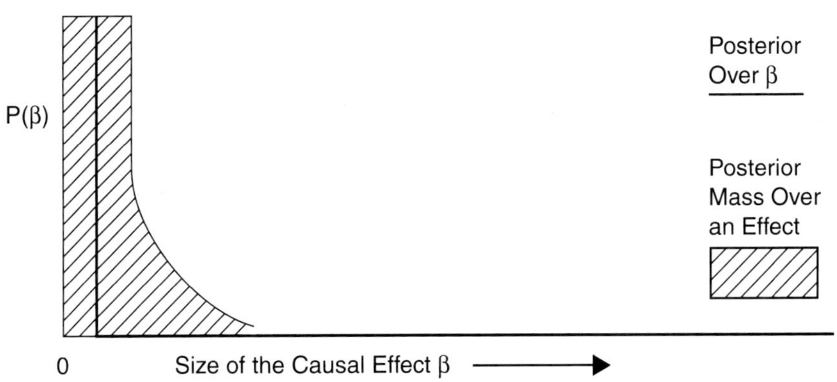

FIGURE 8-7 Example posterior for *Against*.

that makes explicit the evidential role of association, but that keeps the clear and explicit overall goal of assessing causation.

Third, we created the category of Equipoise and Above to capture the spirit of presumption: the tie goes to the veteran, and to stay true and scientifically consistent to the evidential standard suggested by Congress in the Agent Orange Act of 1991 (Public Law Number 102-4, 102d Cong., 1st Sess.), which gave the VA Secretary authority to prescribe regulations providing for a presumption "[w]henever the Secretary determines, on the basis of sound medical and scientific evidence, that a positive association exists between" herbicide exposure and a disease. Section (4)(b)(3) states the following:

> An association between the occurrence of a disease in humans and exposure to an herbicide agent shall be considered to be positive for the purposes of this section if the credible evidence for the association is equal to or outweighs the credible evidence against the association.

In our categorization, Equipoise and Above represents a state in which there *is* credible evidence, and the credible evidence *for* causation is equal to or greater than the credible evidence *against* causation. We also intend this categorization to be flexible over time. We expect that, as the evidence base grows, evaluations about the state of evidence for a causal claim may be upgraded *or* downgraded over time. The descriptive categorization language used by previous IOM Agent Orange committees for "limited/suggestive" evidence of an association implies that a single high-quality epidemiologic study can in some circumstances be sufficient for the "limited/suggestive" category:

> Evidence is suggestive of an association between herbicides and the outcome but is limited because chance, bias, and confounding could not be ruled out with confidence. For example, at least one high-quality study shows a positive association, but the results of other studies are inconsistent. (IOM, 1994, p. 97; IOM, 1996, 1999, 2001, 2003b, 2005b)

If a scientific committee's conclusion were based on a single study and later studies were to show more definitive evidence of an association, a subsequent committee could upgrade the "limited/suggestive" classification of this association to Sufficient. On the other hand, if definitive studies were reported that supported an overall weight of the evidence of below "limited/suggestive," a subsequent committee could downgrade the classification. Under the current approach, however, it is unclear if any reclassifications of evidence may lead to a change in a presumptive decision that VA has established based upon the classification of "limited/suggestive" evidence of an association.

SUMMARY

Combining human evidence with meta-analysis is very useful when several reasonably exchangeable studies are to be combined. However, the technique cannot be used to combine the full range of evidence relevant to classifying the level of evidence for causation. A very general technique for combining diverse evidence into a single, quantitative description of belief about the causal claim at stake is the Bayesian approach, but its usefulness in a presumptive disability decision-making context may be limited. As a result, other organizations such as IARC have resorted to a qualitative categorization of the strength of evidence for causation. These agencies base the overall categorization on separate judgments about the strength of evidence from epidemiologic studies, animal studies, or other mechanistic, toxicological, or biological sources.

For the presumptive disability decision-making process, this Committee recommends categorizing the level of overall evidence for a causal relationship between exposure and health outcome in one of the following categories:

1. *Sufficient*: The evidence is sufficient to conclude that a causal relationship exists.
2. *Equipoise and Above*: The evidence is sufficient to conclude that a causal relationship is at least as likely as not, but not sufficient to conclude that a causal relationship exists.
3. *Below Equipoise*: The evidence is not sufficient to conclude that a causal relationship is at least as likely as not, or is not sufficient to make a scientifically informed judgment.
4. *Against*: The evidence suggests the lack of a causal relationship.

REFERENCES

Bayne-Jones, S., W. J. Burdette, W. G. Cochran, E. Farber, L. F. Fieser, J. Furth, J. B. Hickam, C. LeMaistre, L. M. Schuman, and M. H. Seevers. 1964. *Smoking and health. Report of the Advisory Committee to the Surgeon General of the Public Health Service*. Public Health Services Publication No. 1103. Washington, DC: Public Health Service. http://www.cdc.gov/tobacco/sgr/sgr_1964/sgr64.htm (accessed February 13, 2007).

Berlin, J. A., and E. M. Antman. 1994. Advantages and limitations of metaanalytic regressions of clinical trials data. *Online Journal of Current Clinical Trials*. Doc. No. 134.

Berlin, J., and T. C. Chalmers. 1988. Commentary on meta-analysis in clinical trials. *Hepatology* 8:690-691.

Cogliano, V. J. 2006. *IARC monographs on the evaluation of carcinogenic risks to humans*. Slideshow. http://www.oehha.ca.gov/prop65/public_meetings/pdf/IARCVJCogliano121206.pdf. (accessed May 14, 2007).

DHHS/CDC (Department of Health and Human Services/Centers for Disease Control and Prevention). 2004. The health consequences of smoking: A report of the Surgeon General. http://www.cdc.gov/tobacco/data_statistics/sgr/sgr_2004/index.htm (accessed July 27, 2007).

Dickersin, K., and J. A. Berlin. 1992. Meta-analysis: State-of-the-science. *Epidemiology Review* 14:154-176.

EPA (Environmental Protection Agency). 2005. *Guidelines for carcinogen risk assessment.* EPA/630/P-03/001F. Washington, DC: EPA Risk Assessment Forum.

Greenland, S. 1994a. Can meta-analysis be salvaged? *American Journal of Epidemiology* 140:783-787.

Greenland, S. 1994b. Invited commentary: A critical look at some popular meta-analytic methods. *American Journal of Epidemiology* 140:290-296.

Greenland, S., and K. O'Rourke. 2001. On the bias produced by quality scores in meta-analysis, and a hierarchical view of proposed solutions. *Biostatistics* 2:463-471.

Howson, C., and P. Urbach. 1989. *Scientific reasoning: The Bayesian approach.* Peru, IL: Open Court Publishing Company.

IARC (International Agency for Research on Cancer). 1987. *IARC monographs on the evaluation of carcinogenic risks to humans overall evaluations of carcinogenicity: An updating of IARC Monographs.* Vol. 1 to 42. Supplement 7. http://monographs.iarc.fr/ENG/Monographs/suppl7/suppl7.pdf (accessed May 4, 2007).

IARC. 1997. *Polychlorinated dibenzo-para-dioxins and polychlorinated dibenzofurans. IARC monographs on the evaluations of carcinogenic risks to humans.* Vol. 69. http://monographs.iarc.fr/ENG/Monographs/vol69/volume69.pdf (accessed May 4, 2007).

IARC. 1999. IARC *Monographs on the evaluation of carcinogenic risks to humans. Some chemicals that cause tumours of the kidney or urinary bladder in rodents and some other substances. Summary of data reported and evaluation.* Vol. 73. http://monographs.iarc.fr/ENG/Monographs/vol73/volume73.pdf (accessed May 4, 2007).

IARC. 2004. *IARC classifies formaldehyde as carcinogenic to humans.* Press Release No. 153. http://www.iarc.fr/ENG/Press_Releases/archives/pr153a.html (accessed February 13, 2007).

IARC. 2006a. *Formaldehyde, 2-butoxyethanol and 1-tert-butoxypropan-2-ol.* IARC monograph. Vol. 88. http://monographs.iarc.fr/ENG/Monographs/vol88/volume88.pdf (accessed February 13, 2007).

IARC. 2006b. *IARC monographs on the evaluation of carcinogenic risks to humans: Preamble.* Lyon, France: World Health Organization/International Agency for Research on Cancer. http://monographs.iarc.fr/ENG/Preamble/CurrentPreamble.pdf (accessed February 13, 2007).

IOM (Institute of Medicine). 1994. *Veterans and Agent Orange: Health effects of herbicides used in Vietnam.* Washington, DC: National Academy Press.

IOM. 1996. *Veterans and Agent Orange: Update 1996.* Washington, DC: National Academy Press.

IOM. 1999. *Veterans and Agent Orange: Update 1998.* Washington, DC: National Academy Press.

IOM. 2000. *Gulf War and health, volume 1: Depleted uranium, pyridostigmine bromide, sarin, vaccines.* Washington, DC: National Academy Press.

IOM. 2001. *Veterans and Agent Orange: Update 2000.* Washington, DC: National Academy Press.

IOM. 2003a. *Gulf War and health, volume 2: Insecticides and solvents.* Washington, DC: The National Academies Press.

IOM. 2003b. *Veterans and Agent Orange: Update 2002.* Washington, DC: The National Academies Press.

IOM. 2004. *Gulf War and health: Updated literature review of sarin.* Washington, DC: The National Academies Press.

IOM. 2005a. *Gulf War and health, volume 3: Fuels, combustion products, and propellants.* Washington, DC: The National Academies Press.

IOM. 2005b. *Veterans and Agent Orange: Update 2004*. Washington, DC: The National Academies Press.

IOM. 2006a. *Asbestos: Selected cancers*. Washington, DC: The National Academies Press.

IOM. 2006b. *Gulf War and health, volume 4: Health effects of serving in the Gulf War*. Washington, DC: The National Academies Press.

IOM. 2007. *Gulf War and health, volume 5: Infectious diseases*. Washington, DC: The National Academies Press.

IOM/NRC (National Research Council). 2005. *Dietary supplements: A framework for evaluating safety*. Washington, DC: The National Academies Press.

Kaizar, E. E. 2005. Meta-analyses are observational studies: How lack of randomization impacts analysis. *American Journal of Gastroenterology* 100:1233-1236.

NAS (National Academy of Sciences). 1988. *Health risks of radon and other internally deposited alpha-emitters (Beir IV)*. Washington, DC: National Academy Press.

NIH (National Institutes of Health). 2000. *Fact sheet: The report on carcinogens*. 9th ed. http://www.nih.gov/news/pr/may2000/niehs-15.htm (accessed June 3, 2007).

NTP (National Toxicology Program). 2005. *Report on carcinogens. 11th report on Carcinogens*. Research Triangle Park, NC: NTP.

NTP CERHR (NTP Center for the Evaluation of Risks to Human Reproduction). 2003. *NTP-CERHR Monograph on the Potential Human Reproductive and Developmental Effects of Di-n-Butyl Phthalate (DBP)*. Research Triangle Park, NC: NTP CERHR, U.S. Department of Health and Human Services.

NTP CERHR. 2005. *Guidelines for CERHR Expert Panel Members*. Research Triangle Park, NC: NTP CERHR, U.S. Department of Health and Human Services.

Shelby, M.D. 2005. National Toxicology Program Center for the Evaluation of Risks to Human Reproduction: Guidelines for CERHR Expert Panel Members. *Birth Defects Research (Part B)* 74:9-16.

Stram, D. O. 1996. Meta-analysis of published data using a linear mixed-effects model. *Biometrics* 52:536-544.

Stroup, D. F., J. A. Berlin, S. C. Morton, I. I. Olkin, G. D. Williamson, D. Rennie, D. Moher, B. J. Becker, T. A. Sipe, and S. B. Thacker. 2000. Meta-analysis of observational studies in epidemiology: A proposal for reporting. Meta-analysis of Observational Studies in Epidemiology (MOOSE) group. *Journal of the American Medical Association* 283: 2008-2012.

9

Applying Population-Based Results to Individuals: From Observational Studies to Personal Compensation

The previous chapters address problems of inferring causation from observational studies in the context set by other types of evidence. We also provide a classification scheme for the level of evidence in support of causation in general. Having determined that the level of evidence is sufficient to infer causation, two additional matters are of interest: (1) What is the burden of disease among those exposed that is caused by the exposure? and (2) What is the likelihood that the disease was caused by exposure in a particular individual? Information pertinent to the first question is relevant to forecasting the administrative and financial implications of the causal determination. Information relevant to the second question may be of value in handling individual cases.

In the present chapter we address these topics, beginning with the simplifying assumption that a causal association has been established in the population, and that we have an accurate estimate of relative risk (RR) among exposed people. We turn to an epidemiologic measure, the attributable fraction (AF), to answer these questions. This chapter also addresses the complexities of using the AF in devising compensation approaches. It provides a conceptual foundation that should prove useful in the further elaboration of the Committee's framework and its implementation.

ATTRIBUTABLE FRACTION

Definitions and Assumptions

The *attributable fraction* (AF) is used several ways in the literature (Rothman and Greenland, 1998). We use the term in a way most relevant to compensation by the Department of Veterans Affairs (VA), namely as the proportion of disease *in an exposed group* that can be attributed to the exposure. This report uses the terminology *service-attributable fraction* (SAF) when the exposed group is a military population. We begin with two simplifying assumptions: (1) exposure produces new cases of the disease that would not have occurred otherwise, and (2) the additional RR from exposure is stable over age and across subgroups within the population of exposed veterans. Later we discuss complications that might occur when these assumptions do not hold. Under these two assumptions, the AF is interpreted as the probability that among the exposed people with the disease, their disease has actually been caused by the exposure.

Crucial Properties of the AF

In applying the AF, there are two key properties. First, it is *not* a statement about whether the exposure is *able* to cause the disease. In calculating the AF, we take as given that the exposure does, in fact, cause the disease. However, even among exposed persons, the exposure does not necessarily cause *all cases of* the disease—most diseases have many possible causes. When an exposed person gets the disease, the chance that the disease is caused by the exposure is almost certainly less than one. The AF represents this probability.

The second important aspect of the AF is that it cannot specifically tell us which exposed people have their disease because of the exposure. All the AF can provide is an estimate of the average probability for all exposed persons. We can refine this estimate in various ways (e.g., by age or levels of exposure), but even with perfect information it is seldom, if ever, possible with current methods to identify which particular cases of a disease with multiple causes were caused by the exposure and which were not.

Estimating the AF

An AF is based on an estimation of RR, which is the ratio of disease risk among exposed persons compared to the risk among otherwise similar, but unexposed persons. RR is the most common expression of disease risk in epidemiologic studies. As discussed in Chapter 7, odds ratios from case-control studies approximate the RR.

The AF is calculated by the following formula:

$$AF = \frac{[Risk\ (exposed) - Risk\ (unexposed)]}{Risk\ (exposed)}$$

This may also be expressed as: $AF = (RR - 1)/RR$.

Consider the example of smoking and lung cancer. The RR for lung cancer among smokers is around 20. Applying the formula above, a RR of 20 yields an attributable risk of 95 percent, $AR = (20 - 1)/20$. In other words, 95 percent of all lung cancers among smokers can be attributed to their smoking, possibly acting in combination with other factors, while the remaining 5 percent of the lung cancers of smokers come from other causes. For another example, smoking and cardiovascular disease, the RR is close to 2. Thus, only half of the cases of cardiovascular disease among smokers, 50 percent = (2 – 1)/2, can be attributed to smoking. The lower the RR, the less likely it is that the disease in an exposed person is caused by the exposure, and the more likely that other factors are the cause.

Factors That Can Distort the AF

Broadly speaking, there are two problems that can bias an estimate of disease burden due to an exposure when using the AF. One is *portability*—that is, the degree to which the RR estimated from one population can be properly applied to another population. The second problem is error in the measurement of exposure. We consider each of these limitations below.

Problems in Portability

Chapter 7 discusses the biases and confounding that can distort estimates of RR. Even if these problems have been carefully handled in the original estimation of RR, the application of a valid RR to a new group introduces a fresh set of opportunities for distortions. This problem goes under the general rubric of portability, that is, the ability of a valid RR in one population to be applied to a new population. The portability of RRs and hence of AFs is often uncertain because of differing characteristics of the population in which the AF was estimated compared to those in which it is to be applied.

A simple example of a problem with portability is effect modification by gender. Suppose that, at a given level of exposure, the RR of disease differs by gender of the exposed person (a common observation). If the distribution of men and women in the study group is different from the exposure group to which the RR is being applied, and gender is ignored, the resulting AF will be incorrect. This particular problem can be handled by applying gender-specific RRs to gender strata of the exposed population. However, more complicated scenarios of confounding or effect modification can be readily anticipated; methods to handle these have been proposed by Bruzzi et al. (1985) and Benichou (2001). Although such methods work in principle, they may require detailed data for subgroup-specific RRs that are difficult to obtain.

A similar problem can arise when the RR is estimated in a population with high exposure (as in an occupational setting) and then applied to a population with lower levels of exposure. The RR will tend to overestimate the AF for the lower-exposed population. With enough information from epidemiologic studies on exposure-specific risk and information on levels of exposure in the population of interest, the appropriate adjustments of the AF can be made to account for exposure.

In summary, problems of portability do not call into question the validity of the original RR, but rather its generalizability—that is, the validity of its application to a new population and the estimate of the AF. Even when the causal association is certain (as we assume here), the problems of portability raise questions about the strength of the disease risk in the population of interest—and thus the size of the AF.

Problems in Exposure Classification

The second distortion that can occur with the AF is when the RR is applied to a population in which some persons classified as exposed were not in fact exposed. (This problem is especially relevant in the context of the charge of this Committee, in that VA is frequently unable to establish actual exposure during military service, and therefore must infer it—with inevitable error.) Usually the decision is to err in the direction of assuming people are exposed when they may not be exposed.

When an "exposed" group includes some people who are not actually exposed, the AF for the whole "exposed" group would be

$$AF_{\text{``}exp\text{''}} = \frac{\left(P_{exp}\right) \times \left(RR_{exp} - 1\right)}{\left[P_{exp} \times \left(RR_{exp} - 1\right)\right] + 1},$$

where $AF_{\text{``}exp\text{''}}$ = the AF for an "exposed" group containing some unexposed people, P_{exp} = the proportion of the supposedly "exposed" group who are truly exposed, and RR_{exp} = the RR for the truly exposed group.

Typically, we do not know what proportion of those reported as exposed were actually exposed. However, we can make reasonable assumptions and see how much difference such errors might make. In our previous smoking example, if only half of the "exposed" group had truly been exposed, then the true AF for the "exposed" group would be 90 percent instead of 95 percent. Thus, exposure misclassification introduces a trivial difference between the true AF and the calculated AF when the RR is high.

This is not true when the RR is lower (as is often the case). Taking the example of $RR = 2$ (for smoking and cardiovascular disease), the true AF is 50 percent when every person in the "exposed" group was truly exposed, but only 33 percent, if half of the "exposed" group had actually been unexposed. Thus, when the RR is low, misclassification of exposure results in an estimated AF that is an overestimate of the true AF.

Reconsidering the Assumptions of the AF and Alternatives

A basic assumption in calculating the AF is that the RR is known. In the real world, RRs are only estimates and typically include some measure of the statistical imprecision of that estimate. The implications of such uncertainty can be explored by calculating a range of AFs under different assumptions for the RR.

What if other assumptions about the AF are untrue? For example, what if the exposure accelerates disease among persons who were going to get the disease anyway, instead of causing disease in persons who would not otherwise have gotten the disease? In this more complex scenario, the AF may not adequately capture the total burden of disease caused by the exposure. Alternatives to the AF that attempt to capture the total impact of exposure on disease include "years of life lost" (YLL) (Robins and Greenland, 1989a; Steenland and Armstrong, 2006) and "years of life lived with disability" (YLD).

Methods for the calculation of YLL, YLD, and disability-adjusted life years (DALYs) have been recently reviewed (Steenland and Armstrong, 2006). YLL is the total number of deaths caused by the disease of interest multiplied by the average number of years of survival expected beyond the age of death from that disease. YLD is the product of the number of incident cases, a disability weight, and mean duration of disease; in the absence of incidence data an estimate can be based on mortality data and case-fatality rates. The total burden of disease can be estimated as the sum of YLL and YLD and is known as disability-adjusted life years, or DALYs. YLL, YLD, and DALYs caused specifically by military service exposure can be calculated by multiplying them by the AF (Steenland and Armstrong, 2006). In the case of military service, we refer to this as the service-attributable fraction (SAF). Because the AF is a fundamental element of these alternatives to the AF, they are subject to the same caveats about portability and misclassification of exposure as the AF itself. In the section

"Promoting the Use of AFs in Determining Compensation for Veterans" we return to this discussion with regard to the AF and the SAF.

Further Refinements of the AF

Once we have estimated the *total* disease burden caused by the exposure using the AF, it may be possible to refine this estimate further by considering characteristics of persons, including features of their exposure, that make their individual risk of disease higher or lower than in the exposed population as a whole. In other words, we can move from an estimate of overall AF, applied equally to all, to estimates for subgroups or even individuals, based on additional information regarding their risk factors. This refined expression of the AF as estimated for individuals has usually been designated as the *probability of causation*, or PC, although in actuality it is simply the AF estimated for subgroups of those exposed.

PROBABILITY OF CAUSATION FOR AN INDIVIDUAL

The AF attempts to apportion the disease burden in a population between the exposure and other factors causing the disease. In contrast, the PC attempts to address the question of whether the exposure could have caused a particular disease in an individual, given that individual's particular characteristics of genetic makeup, lifestyle, and personal history—that is, the characteristics that determine individual susceptibility. For the past two decades, estimates of the PC have been available to guide the compensation of atomic veterans and others exposed to ionizing radiation (DHHS, 2002; NIH, 1985; Thomas, 2000). These estimates have been possible because of the extensive information on cancer risk in relation to radiation exposure.

PC Definition

A precise definition of PC will help illustrate the challenges in estimating it. Following the National Institutes of Health (NIH) Working Group (1985), the PC_i is the probability that individual *i*'s disease was caused by the exposure, given *i*'s unique set of characteristics (call them X_i). Symbolically, PC_i, is defined using two terms—the probability that the individual would have developed the disease given no exposure, $(\bar{E}),\left[P\left(D,\bar{E}|X_i\right)\right]$, and the probability that the individual developed the disease given the exposure, $\left[P\left(D,E|X_i\right)\right]$:

$$PC_i = \frac{\left[P\left(D,E|X_i\right) - P\left(D,\bar{E}|X_i\right)\right]}{P\left(D,E|X_i\right)}$$

PC_i = probability of causation for an individual P = probability D = disease E = exposure $\bar{E}$ = no exposure X_i = an individual's unique set of characteristics

Notice the equation represents an allocation of the probability of disease between the exposed and unexposed. The probability that the background caused the disease in individual *i* is simply $1 - PC_i$. If everyone in the population is identical in susceptibility to the disease and in the extent of exposure, and if the exposure-induced cases are completely independent of other cases (i.e., cases that were caused by something else), then the PC for every individual in the population is given by the population AF. Implications of not meeting these assumptions are discussed below in "Promoting the Use of AFs in Determining Compensation for Veterans." Still, additional information on the levels of exposure, age at exposure, time since exposure, mechanism of disease causation, and other factors can be used to define subgroups within populations, and then to estimate AFs for these subgroups. As described below, these subgroup measures provide the basis for better estimates of PCs for individuals within these classes.

Because individuals may vary in susceptibility to a particular exposure because of genetics, lifestyle, and other factors, estimates of PCs are not necessarily expected to resemble the true probability that an individual's disease was caused by the exposure. The term *assigned share* (AS) has been used in place of *PC*, especially as it pertains to issues of compensation (Lagakos and Mosteller, 1986). The NIH Ad Hoc Working Group to Develop Radioepidemiological Tables (NIH, 1985) (for use in compensating cancer victims exposed to ionizing radiation) found itself constrained by legislative mandate to use the term *probability of causation* rather than *assigned share.* Reflecting on the history of the use of the terms, a more recent National Research Council (NRC) committee decided to use the terms synonymously (NRC, 2000).

Refining Estimates by Differences in Exposure Levels

Exposures to any given chemical or other disease-causing factor would be expected to vary substantially among veterans in any theater of war or duty, with corresponding large differences in individual risk and hence PCs. Also, the pattern of exposure can be important. For the same cumulative dose, the dose rate, timing, and duration may play a significant role in determining those who get the disease and those who do not. Route and exposure pathways are also to be considered. Although obtaining accurate estimates of exposure among veterans will typically be challenging, in some cases exposures may differ by orders of magnitude, and it may be possible to develop at least crude exposure estimates.

If exposure can be quantified and the relationship between risk and exposure is understood, the AF can be expressed as a function of exposure. For example, dose-response relationships can be derived from occupational epidemiologic data for various carcinogens. As the example below shows, it can be important to stratify by the degree of exposure if this information is available, because the AF can vary substantially with exposure level.

Consider the following simple relationship between the lifetime probability of cancer P, or risk, and the air concentration, D, and the duration of exposure t, $P(D) = 1 - \exp(-a - bDt)$, which at P less than 10 percent is closely approximated by a simple linear relationship $P(D) = a + bDt$, where a, the intercept, is the risk in the absence of exposure, and b, the slope, describes the incremental increase in risk with increasing air concentration and time. Here RR is given by

$$RR = \frac{(a + bDt)}{a} = 1 + \frac{bD}{a},$$

and the AF is given by

$$AF = \frac{(RR - 1)}{RR},$$

which, substituting in the above, reduces to

$$AF = \frac{\left(\frac{bD}{a}\right)}{\left(1 + \frac{bDt}{a}\right)} = \frac{bDt}{(a + bDt)}.$$

P = lifetime probability (or risk) of cancer
D = air concentration
t = duration of exposure
a = risk in the absence of exposure
b = incremental increase in risk with increasing air concentration and time
RR = relative risk
AF = attributable fraction

Benzene provides an example of how very different AFs can result from differently exposed subgroups. We show how when exposure is taken into account PC estimates can be made for individuals with different levels of exposure. Benzene is an established cause of acute myelogenous leukemia (AML) in humans (Austin et al., 1988). Benzene exposures are ubiquitous; for example, benzene is a constituent of gasoline and also cigarette smoke. The general population in the United States is exposed to levels averaging from 1 to 5 ppb in indoor and outdoor air, and it would be anticipated that Service members would be similarly exposed. In addition, some in the service may have duties that result in exposures to considerably higher levels of benzene (e.g., those servicing airplanes or working in garage facilities). We might assume that some service jobs result in exposures as high as 10 ppm.

AML is relatively uncommon, with a lifetime risk of diagnosis (an estimate for parameter a in the equation above) of about 0.3 percent. A lifetime exposure to 1 ppm causes AML in roughly 5 percent of those so exposed, corresponding to an estimate of b in the above equation of 0.00062/ppm-years (= 0.05/ppm/78 years). Applying these parameter estimates, AFs can be derived, while acknowledging the caveats and limitations noted above, including the issue of portability since the b was estimated from occupational cohorts in China and the United States (OEHHA, 2001). Service members who contract AML after being exposed during a tour of duty of 3 years to general background levels (e.g., 5 ppb) have a 0.2 percent chance that their leukemia arose because of their military exposure ($AF = [0.00062 \times 0.005 \times 3]/[0.003 + 0.00062 \times 0.005 \times 3]$). Thus, any case of AML among the exposed Service members would be highly unlikely to have resulted from military exposure. The AF associated with military service lasting 30 years is higher, at 3 percent. In contrast, Service members with a 3-year tour of duty who were exposed to 10 ppm during work hours, or a daily average of approximately 5 ppm, have an

AF of 76 percent: $AF = (0.00062 \times 5 \times 3)/(0.003 + 0.00062 \times 5 \times 3)$. This simple example illustrates the importance of segregating groups in terms of the magnitude and duration of exposure when those data are available. It also illustrates the importance of identifying those most heavily exposed in determining whether disease caused by an exposure to a given factor deserves compensation.

As illustrated below, it is occasionally possible to classify or otherwise identify individuals or groups of individuals in terms of their exposure duration, age at exposure, exposure intensity, as well as other factors to derive exposure group-specific AFs and hence more refined estimates of PCs for individuals.

Refining Estimates in the Presence of Multiple Known Causes of Disease

Many illnesses considered for compensation have multiple causes. For example, lung cancer has many known causes in addition to smoking, including asbestos, arsenic, radiation, and environmental tobacco smoke (NCI, 2006). Some lung cancers occur in individuals without significant exposures to any known cause. The proportion of disease that is attributable to military service exposure can be estimated when there are valid RR estimates for (1) the military service-related exposure in the absence of the other known causes (RR_E), (2) other known causes that individuals in the group were subjected to (such as smoking—RR_S), and (3) the joint exposure of both military service and other specific known causes (RR_{both}).

As an illustration, the proportion of disease attributable to military exposure and smoking, separately and jointly, is estimated for the hypothetical case described in Chapter 7. This is derived for two cases below, with smoking and military exposure interacting either additively or multiplicatively. In the additive model, smoking adds a constant RR over background ($RR_S - 1$) regardless of whether there is military exposure. Thus, in the presence of both exposures, the RR is $RR_{both} = RR_E + RR_S - 1$. In the multiplicative model, $RR_{both} = RR_E \times RR_S$.

We introduce new terminology to aid in the derivation of AFs for the joint and separate effects of these multiple known causal exposures. The population attributable fraction (PAF) is the proportion of disease in the entire population attributable to an exposure or any other factor. (The relation of the PAF to the AF will be discussed below.)

Assume that all disease in the population is attributed either to the background or to the two identified causes. PAF_0 is the proportion of disease attributable to background factors unrelated to smoking or military exposure. PAF_{both} is the proportion of disease attributable to smoking and military exposures. The two sum to unity $1 = PAF_0 + PAF_{both}$. Analogous to the AF, the PAF_{both} is given by

$$PAF_{both} = \frac{(RR_{both} - 1)}{RR_{both}}.$$

Thus PAF_0 is given by

$$PAF_0 = 1 - PAF_{both} = 1 - \frac{(RR_{both} - 1)}{RR_{both}},$$

which reduces to

$$PAF_0 = \frac{1}{RR_{both}}.$$

PAF_E, the proportion attributable to military exposure alone, is simply the proportion of disease attributable to background factors multiplied by the excess RR above the background (RR_E – 1):

$$PAF_E = (RR_E - 1) \times PAF_0,$$

which reduces to

$$PAF_E = \frac{(RR_E - 1)}{RR_{both}}.$$

Similarly PAF_S, the proportion attributable to smoking acting alone, is

$$PAF_S = \frac{(RR_S - 1)}{RR_{both}}.$$

The additional proportion attributable to the two factors acting in combination (i.e., interacting), PAF_{Int} is

$$PAF_{Int} = \frac{(RR_{both} - RR_E - RR_S + 1)}{RR_{both}}.$$

PAF_0 = proportion of disease attributable to background factors unrelated to smoking or military exposure
PAF_{both} = proportion of disease attributable to smoking and military exposures
PAF_E = proportion of disease attributable to military exposure alone
PAF_S = proportion of disease attributable to smoking acting alone
PAF_{Int} = the additional proportion of disease attributable to the two factors acting in combination
RR_E = RR estimates for military service-related exposure in the absence of the other known causes
RR_S = RR estimate for other known causes that individuals in the group were subjected to (e.g., smoking)
RR_{both} = RR for the joint exposure of both military service and other specific known causes

Table 9-1 provides the parameter values for the hypothetical case described in Chapter 7 for the two different cases—when smoking and military exposure interact multiplicatively and when they interact additively.

The calculations of AFs to the separate and joint exposures for this hypothetical example are laid out in Table 9-2. For the multiplicative example, one might be tempted to conclude that the contribution of military exposure was very small, since in the absence of the smoking interaction, the AF is only 6.7 percent. However, due to its interaction with smoking, the total contribution of military exposure is 66.7 percent (Table 9-2). (Note that this is the same PAF_E as for nonsmokers, [3 – 1]/3 = 67 percent [Table 9-1], revealing that under a multiplicative model, the total PAF_E

TABLE 9-1 Hypothetical Example of Risks from Multiple Causal Exposures

Military Exposure	Smoking Habit	Number at Risk	Cancer Cases		Relative Risk
No	Never	1,000	10		1
No	Current	1,000	100		10
Yes	Never	1,000	30		3
Yes	Current	1,000	Multiplicative	300	30
			Additive	120	12

TABLE 9-2 Hypothetical PAFs Due to Smoking and Military Exposure

PAF Due to	Multiplicative Model	Additive Model
Background only, PAF_0	1/30 = 3.3%	1/12 = 8.3%
Military exposure only, PAF_E	2/30 = 6.7%	2/12 = 16.7%
Smoking only, PAF_S	9/30 = 30%	9/12 = 75%
Military exposure and smoking interaction, PAF_{Int}	(30 – 3 – 10 + 1)/30 = 60%	(12 – 3 – 10 + 1)/12 = 0%
Total: $PAF_0 + PAF_E + PAF_S + PAF_{Int}$	3.3 + 6.7 + 30 + 60 = 100%	8.3 + 16.7 + 75 = 100%
SAF: Disease preventable by eliminating military exposure, $PAF_E + PAF_{Int}$	6.7 + 60 = 66.7%	16.7 + 0 = 16.7%

does not depend upon smoking.) Of course, the same calculation applied to smoking would yield an estimate of 90 percent for the total fraction attributable to that factor. If one were naively to add these two figures, it would appear that more than 100 percent of the risk would be accounted for, but of course, this is simply because the interaction contribution has been counted twice. In terms of prevention, 66.7 percent of the cancer cases in this group could have been prevented had the military exposure not occurred (or 90 percent [30 percent + 60 percent] if they had not smoked or 96.7 percent [30 percent + 60 percent + 6.7 percent] if both causes were eliminated [Table 9-2]).

Under a purely additive model, there is no interaction, no proportion of disease is attributable to the interaction, and the term PAF_{Int} becomes zero (Table 9-2). Among smokers, then, the proportion attributable to military exposure is 16.7 percent, considerably lower than in the multiplicative case. Among nonsmokers, however, military exposure accounts for 67 percent of the cases (PAF_E = [3 – 1]/3 = 67 percent [Table 9-1]), revealing that under an additive model (or any less-than-multiplicative model), the PAF_E will be larger for nonsmokers than for smokers. This holds even if the relative effect of smoking is much larger than exposure.

Chapter 7 also considered a scenario where one of the two factors was an intermediate variable on a causal pathway from exposure to disease (the example was smoking resulting from an amputation and leading to lung cancer). In this case, one would not want to partition the AF in this manner, because the direct effect of smoking on lung cancer was itself a consequence of the exposure (battle trauma) and is therefore part of the total lung cancer burden attributable to that trauma.

Turning to the concept of the AF that was introduced at the beginning of this chapter, as the fraction of disease in the population that would not have occurred had the exposure not occurred, the AF can be derived from PAFs computed in this manner. It is simply

$$AF = PAF_E + PAF_{Int}.$$

As before, the AF can be refined to provide estimates for individuals in specific subgroups, with the same caveats and cautions discussed earlier. For the multiplicative case in the hypothetical illustration above, the SAF is thus estimated to be 66.7 percent (Table 9-2). The elimination of exposure would have eliminated the excess cases due to exposure acting alone and those due to its joint action with smoking. Hence, both components are counted in deriving the SAF. For the additive case, with the interaction term (PAF_{Int}) equal to zero, the SAF estimate is 16.7 percent. This underscores the importance of understanding the potential for interaction among multiple causal factors when evaluating the SAF for specific subgroups to be applied to individuals.

Using Data on Susceptibility and Exposure to Refine an AF Estimate

People differ in their susceptibility to disease and predispositions toward certain disabilities. Some of these differences are within an individual's control (e.g., food choices and eating habits), while other differences (e.g., genetics, age, and gender) are not. Differences in susceptibility remain to a great extent unquantifiable for most diseases, and thus are a source of uncertainty that in turn cannot be quantified in estimating the PC for individuals. When the background risk (in the absence of the exposure in question) varies substantially among individuals in the group, or there are strong interactions between background factors and exposure, the PCs among individuals can vary substantially, even for the same exposure level, and these will be misestimated by the AFs calculated for specific subgroups that cannot incorporate information on background risk.

Epidemiologic data may provide the basis for refining estimates of the AF for subgroups to be applied to individuals. As illustrated above, data on smoking or other causes of a disease not related to military service may allow refinement of the SAF. A variety of susceptibility and other factors have been used to refine estimates of the AF for radiation-induced cancers. In 1985, a set of radioepidemiological tables was released that provided probability of causation estimates for radiation exposures in terms of a person's gender, age at exposure, age of cancer diagnosis, dose, and other factors (DHHS, 2002; NIH, 1985) (see the case study on radiation in Appendix I for details). These tables have since been updated using mathematical models of risk incorporating the characteristics of the individual claimant. In addition to gender, age at exposure and diagnosis, and smoking status, the dose, type, and energy intensity of the radiation are addressed. These estimates can now be obtained using an interactive computer program. The program also explicitly accounts for uncertainty in model inputs to "help minimize the possibility of denying compensation to claimants under the Energy Employees Occupational Illness Compensation Program (EEOICPA) for those employees with cancers likely to have been caused by occupational radiation exposures" (NIOSH, 2007, p. 3). Few if any other exposures lend themselves to such precise adjustments of risk.

Other Complexities of the AF

Most of the above discussion treats RR of exposure as fixed. A typical assumption for cancers is that, following a latency period after exposure, d, there is an age-specific incidence $p(t,d)$ that is a fixed multiplicative factor above the nonexposed

$$p(t,d) = RR(d) \times p(t,0).$$

In other words, there is a constant RR at any age t. An alternative assumption—constant excess risk—is that a given exposure d increases the absolute risk in the exposed by a fixed amount $g(d)$, so that $p(t,d) = g(d) + p(t,0)$. Because background incidence of every type of cancer changes with age, the constant excess risk model is incompatible with the assumption of constant RR. Another aspect of this problem is that for some diseases there are ages at which an individual is more susceptible to certain diseases. For radiation carcinogenesis there are considerable data for evaluating dose-response relationships that account for exposure level and duration, and age at exposure, and still uncertainty remains regarding how best to model these relationships for the purpose of calculating AFs for individuals (DHHS, 2002). For other cancer causes and other diseases there is usually much greater uncertainty about these relationships.

AF AND COMPENSATION

Earlier in this chapter, the concepts of the AF and the SAF were further developed after being initially introduced in Chapter 6. The extension of these concepts to attempt to estimate refined AFs that could be applied to individuals was then introduced and discussed. We now bring these concepts to bear on the issue of compensation.

Considerations in Assessing Alternative Compensation Schemes

Exposure-Based Schemes

Compensation can theoretically be based on any number of considerations, not all of which make use of the notion of causation. For example, compensation could simply be based on a determination that certain types of exposure are so hazardous or extreme that they merit compensation regardless of whether they cause a disease. The Prisoner of War (POW) experience could reasonably be a candidate for an experience worthy of compensation on the basis of exposure alone, regardless of whether any illnesses resulted from this "exposure," and with perhaps some consideration of the severity of the experience. Similarly, when an exposure strongly increases the risk of a specific disease or condition, compensation could be granted regardless of whether the disease actually occurs. This approach was considered by the Presidential Commission on Catastrophic Nuclear Accidents and discarded (Presidential Commission, 1990). These approaches to compensation will not be considered further here, as they are matters of policy. We restrict our discussion to the compensation of persons whose exposure was causally linked to a health outcome and who were actually diagnosed with the outcome of interest.

A Traditional Approach Using the PC

For most questions of compensation, the decision rests on whether a specific exposure has been established as the cause of a disease or condition. It is usually not possible to establish the fact of causation for individuals (also referred to as *causation in fact* or *individual causation*) because the exposed cases caused by the exposure cannot be distinguished from the exposed cases caused by something else (Presidential Commission, 1990, pp. 107, 110). Furthermore, it is often difficult, if not impossible, to reconstruct the past doses, or even the exposures, when the latency period is very long. One approach to establishing the fact of causation in these circumstances has been to use an estimate of the *probability of causation* (PC) to determine whether compensation should be provided (OSTP, 1988). This estimate of PC (which is itself sometimes also referred to as *PC*), as discussed above, is the AF refined to be applicable to subgroups of individuals and is used to assign group risk to exposed individuals with the condition. A minimum threshold value of this estimated PC is then selected to determine whether one is eligible for compensation. This PC can also then be used to determine, in those below this threshold, what lesser degrees of compensation might be provided.

The Presidential Commission on Catastrophic Nuclear Accidents used this approach when it recommended, in the context of radiation exposure, that someone for whom PC was determined to be more likely than not (i.e., $PC > 0.50$) would merit full compensation (Presidential Commission, 1990). At the other end of the spectrum, those in which it was determined that "it is extremely unlikely that an illness results from" an exposure would receive no compensation. For those who fell in between those two extremes, a "proportional recovery" approach was recommended in which compensation was awarded in relation to the PC (Presidential Compensation, 1990, p. 10). This approach, then, uses PC at a threshold of 0.5 to determine full compensability, with PC being determined by estimated exposure dose. Information on dose is then again brought to bear in determining the amount of compensation for those who do not meet the threshold PC, but who have received a dose that could possibly have caused the disease. Some of these issues are developed in more detail below (see "Possible Applications of the AF in Determining Individual Compensation").

A cogent critique has been developed that argues against the use of PC for the purpose of determining compensation (Cox, 1984, 1987; Greenland, 1999; Greenland and Robins, 1988, 2000; Robins, 2004; Robins and Greenland, 1989a,b, 1991). This critique has important implications as to whether the AF itself should be used in compensation. We later summarize the relevant aspects of this critique in the context of promoting use of AFs for this purpose as it relates to veterans (see "Promoting the Use of AFs in Determining Compensation for Veterans").

Use of YLL, YLD, and DALYs in Compensation

As an alternative to the use of PC or AF, Greenland and Robins proposed an approach to compensation based on expected years of life lost (YLL) (Greenland and Robins, 2000) (see above, "Reconsidering the Assumptions of the AF and Alternatives," where YLL, YLD, and DALYs are defined). Compensation would then be based on some reasonably assessed amount per year of life lost. An important feature of such a scheme is that it takes into account *when* an exposure caused death rather than merely *whether* it caused death. A compensation scheme based on YLL, it is argued, is economically rational because the total compensation payable under such a scheme corresponds to the total health burden caused by an exposure (at least as reflected by mortality), a quantity that can be estimated from epidemiologic data. However, because YLL cannot be estimated for any individual from epidemiologic data, it is not possible to determine the correct apportionment of the total YLL among those exposed (Robins and Greenland, 1991).

Apportioning compensation among exposed individuals would still require a policy decision based on unverifiable, but—one hopes—realistic, assumptions. Because mortality is not as relevant for veterans' compensation as illness and disability, the above scenario can use YLD and DALYs instead.

Applying Concepts of Sensitivity and Specificity to Compensation Schemes

Criteria for determining compensation make both explicit and implicit assumptions. One set of assumptions involves sensitivity and specificity (see Chapter 6). Sensitivity in this context is the probability that someone whose condition (or disease) was caused by a specific exposure is identified as such. Specificity is the probability that someone whose condition (or disease) was caused by something other than the specific exposure is identified as such. Typically when one improves sensitivity, specificity deteriorates, and vice versa. By trying to provide compensation for everyone whose condition was caused by the exposure, we typically increase the likelihood of mistakenly compensating some whose condition was not caused by the exposure. Conversely, in trying to exclude from compensation those who do not warrant it, we increase the chance of excluding those whose disease was in fact caused by exposure.

It is difficult to maximize both sensitivity *and* specificity. Optimizing one or the other means making some kind of mistake: either we optimize sensitivity by compensating some whose disease was not caused by exposure or we optimize specificity by failing to compensate some whose disease was caused by exposure.

The closely related concepts of true positive (TP) and false positive (FP), and true negative (TN) and false negative (FN), describe making the right and the wrong decisions (Table 9-3). True positives are those correctly identified by some criteria. False positives are those mistakenly identified by the criteria. False negatives are those not identified by the criteria, but who should have been. True negatives are those who were correctly not identified by the criteria.

Sensitivity is $TP/(TP + FN)$—the proportion of those whose condition was in fact caused by the exposure $(TP + FN)$ who are correctly identified

TABLE 9-3 True and False Positive and Negative Rates

		Disease Caused by Exposure	
		Yes	No
Compensation criteria	Met	TP	FP
	Not met	FN	TN

as such (*TP*). Specificity is *TN*/(*TN* + *FP*)—the proportion of those whose condition was in fact not caused by the exposure (*TN* + *FP*) who are correctly identified as such (*TN*).

The positive predictive value (PPV) and negative predictive value (NPV) are important related concepts that are also defined from Table 9-3. The PPV is the proportion of those who meet the criteria whose condition was caused by the exposure, namely, $PPV = TP/(TP + FP)$. The NPV is the proportion of those who do not meet the criteria whose condition was not caused by the exposure, namely, $NPV = TN/(TN + FN)$.

A hypothetical example using two alternative criteria for compensation will be used to help clarify these concepts. Consider a disease, *D*, caused by an exposure, *E*, and service in a theater, *T*, the only theater in which exposure to *E* was known to have occurred. First, criteria that would provide compensation to all veterans who are eventually diagnosed with *D* and who served in *T*, and who would therefore have potentially been exposed to *E*, are very sensitive criteria (Criteria A in Table 9-4). No veteran whose disease *D* was caused by exposure to *E* would be missed by using these criteria (i.e., sensitivity is excellent). However, because we have elected to make sure that all veterans whose disease *D* was caused by exposure to *E* are compensated, we likely mistakenly also compensate those individuals whose disease *D* had another cause (i.e., specificity is poor). The use of criteria in this case to make certain that everyone in whom the disease was caused by exposure to *E* is compensated results in compensating many with the disease in whom it was not caused by *E*.

In contrast, criteria that would provide compensation only to veterans with the disease *D* who, for example, also had documented exposure to *E* for a specified period of time and of a specified intensity, and who also were diagnosed with *D* within a specified number of years of their first exposure, would be very "specific" criteria (Criteria B in Table 9-4). One can be more certain that if any group of veterans got *D* from exposure to *E*, those who were provided compensation by these criteria would be most likely to

TABLE 9-4 Comparing Sensitivity and Specificity of Two Hypothetical Sets of Compensation Criteria

		Specificity			
		excellent	good	some	poor
Sensitivity	excellent				Criteria A
	good				
	some	Criteria B			
	poor				

belong to that group (i.e., specificity is excellent). However, these specific criteria could potentially result in not providing compensation to some of those in whom *D* was in fact caused by *E* (i.e., sensitivity is compromised). The use of *specific* criteria increases the likelihood of denying compensation to some whose disease was in fact caused by *E*.

Sensitivity and specificity are not affected by the AF (the proportion of those with the condition whose condition was caused by the exposure). However, PPV and NPV are strongly influenced by the AF. Because the PPV indicates what fraction (or percentage) of veterans compensated for a condition actually had their disease caused by the exposure, varying the AF will change the likelihood that those compensated will have had their disease caused by the exposure. The following tables illustrate how this works. It is assumed that the compensation criteria have fixed excellent sensitivity (0.90) and relatively poor specificity (0.20)—a realistic scenario. What happens when the AF is allowed to vary? In Table 9-5, we begin with a hypothetical scenario in which half of the veterans with the disease will have gotten it as a result of the exposure ($AF = 0.50$). Here the PPV is 9,000/17,000 = 0.53, or 53 percent of those who are compensated will have had the disease caused by the exposure.

In Table 9-6, a lower and in some instances a more realistic AF of 0.09 is assumed, produced here by decreasing the number of those whose disease was caused by the exposure 10-fold. Here the PPV is 900/8,900 = 0.10, which means only 10 percent of those compensated will have it caused

TABLE 9-5 Hypothetical Scenario 1: PPV When AF = 50 Percent

		Disease Caused by Exposure		
		Yes	No	Total
Compensation criteria	Met	9,000	8,000	17,000
	Not met	1,000	2,000	3,000
Total		10,000	10,000	20,000

TABLE 9-6 Hypothetical Scenario 2: PPV When AF = 9 Percent

		Disease Caused by Exposure		
		Yes	No	Total
Compensation criteria	Met	900	8,000	8,900
	Not met	100	2,000	2,100
Total		1,000	10,000	11,000

by the exposure, but 90 percent will have been compensated without the exposure having played a role. If the AF is even lower, say 0.02 (2 percent), then PPV falls to 0.02 and only 2 percent of those compensated will actually have had it caused by exposure while 98 percent will have been compensated without the exposure having contributed (Table 9-7).

The definition of *exposure* as used in these calculations plays a large role in determining whether the AF is large or small. For example, if exposure is defined precisely based on documented exposure to a specific agent, then a larger AF may be realistic. However, if a nonspecific exposure is used, such as presence in a given theater where relevant exposure to the agent is relatively uncommon, then the AF might be expected to be very small, meaning that the proportion of disease caused merely by being in a given theater would often most likely be small. As discussed above, while the AF can clearly vary depending on level of exposure, in this case, it is the definition of exposure that strongly influences the AF.

The Receiver Operator Characteristics Curve

A more flexible and informative way of displaying these concepts is by the use of the receiver operator characteristics (ROC) curve (Obuchowski, 2003). An ROC curve (Figure 9-1) can display similar features as Table 9-4, but allows sensitivity (the proportion of true positives) and specificity (in this case reflected by the proportion of false positives [1 – specificity]) to be expressed on a continuous scale. The straight line of identity indicates combinations of sensitivity and specificity for criteria that do no better than chance in distinguishing those with disease caused by the exposure from those with disease not caused by exposure; the ability of criteria along this line to distinguish the two is no greater than that of tossing a coin.

Points on curved lines that are displaced upwards and to the left of the line of identity indicate combinations of sensitivity and specificity corresponding to specific criteria (cut points) that perform better than chance. Points on a line are generated using different criteria and produce an empirical ROC curve. The resulting curve illustrates how sensitivity and the

TABLE 9-7 Hypothetical Scenario 3: PPV When AF = 2 Percent

		Disease Caused by Exposure		
		Yes	No	Total
Compensation criteria	Met	180	8,000	8,180
	Not met	20	2,000	2,020
Total		200	10,000	10,200

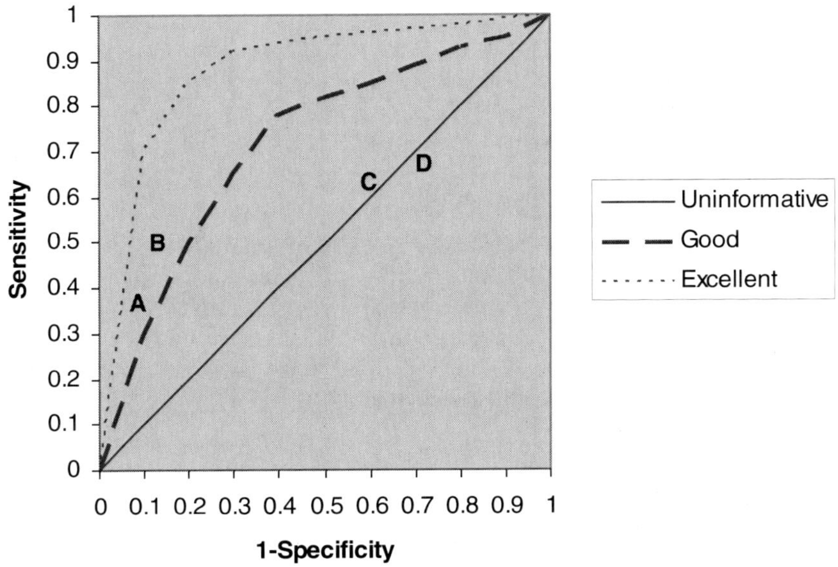

FIGURE 9-1 Example of ROC curves.
NOTE: Example of ROC curves. Different individual compensation criteria (A and B, and C and D) are displayed for different sets of criteria (dashed and dotted lines).

specificity vary together for different criteria. Each curved line corresponds to a different set of criteria for which varying the criteria within each set corresponds to different points along the line. Those curves displaced further upwards to the left than curves with lesser degrees of displacement generally perform better in distinguishing those with disease caused by exposure from those in which it was not caused by exposure. The point at the extreme upper left corner indicates largely unachievable criteria in which there is both perfect sensitivity and specificity—all those whose disease was caused by exposure receive compensation and none of those whose disease was not caused by the exposure receive compensation. The relevant advantages of an ROC curve over the table presented above are that the ROC curve (1) displays all possible criteria, (2) displays the relationship between sensitivity and specificity for different criteria, and (3) allows the performance of different sets of criteria (curves) to be directly compared.

The hypothetical example of disease *D* and exposure *E* can also serve to attempt to make ROC curve concepts clearer. A set of criteria were presented above in which compensation was provided only to veterans who developed *D* with documented exposure to *E* for a specified period of time and of a specified intensity, and who also were diagnosed with *D* within a specified number of years of their first exposure. Using this set of criteria, alternative specific criteria can be considered. Criteria that favor specificity (A, Figure 9-1) might require cumulative exposure to *E* of at least 3 months of direct dermal or inhalational exposure and diagnosis of *D* within 10 years of first exposure (i.e., a latency of diagnosis of less than 10 years). Alternative criteria (B) that favored sensitivity might only require 1 week of direct dermal or inhalational exposure to *E*, with the same latency requirement. Each of these criteria would correspond to a specific point on an ROC curve, with corresponding sensitivity and specificity.

Another set of criteria could be considered that only uses information on exposure *E*, for example, but did not incorporate information on latency of diagnosis of *D*; this set of criteria would generate a new curve, with points corresponding only to different criteria for exposure. Another curve could be generated that only used information on time in theater *T*, for example 6 months (C) or 3 months (D), without any attempt to incorporate information either on exposure *E* or on latency. These criteria would be less specific, but probably more sensitive, than criteria A or B.

A feature shared by the ROC curve, and sensitivity and specificity, since the ROC curve simply displays sensitivity and specificity, is that there is no allowance for graded decisions. Compensation does not necessarily need to be an either-or decision, but instead could incorporate a mechanism (see below) that allows degrees of compensation. Sensitivity and specificity, and therefore the ROC curve, cannot accommodate such decisions.

In the earlier discussion pertaining to the AF and compensation ("A Traditional Approach Using the PC" in which PC terminology was used in place of AF terminology) it was noted that the level of the AF can be used to determine compensation. Note that selection of a specific AF for this purpose necessarily implies some sensitivity and specificity. Selection of a large AF would be less sensitive but more specific (i.e., with the more stringent criteria entailed by a larger AF, more people whose disease was caused by the exposure would not be compensated, but those compensated would be less likely to have had their disease caused by something besides the exposure), while a small AF would be more sensitive, but less specific.

Valuing Sensitivity or Specificity

Another feature of ROC curves, as was also noted above in discussing sensitivity and specificity, is that they are not affected by the proportion of a disease caused by the exposure (i.e., the AF) and therefore do not directly incorporate information on PPV and NPV. However, consideration of the AF can inform deliberations as to which criteria along an ROC curve are better than others. Specifically, the ROC curve does not tell us whether we should place more value on improving sensitivity at the expense of specificity, or vice versa. The AF, by identifying the proportion of those with the disease that is caused by the exposure and thereby allowing us to calculate PPV, provides information that allows us to quantify the mistakes entailed in using different criteria.

The value (or cost) placed on these mistakes will play an important part in determining which mistake is least (or more) tolerable, and therefore whether it is better to optimize sensitivity or specificity. One could argue, using an analogy from the battlefield, that it is intolerable to think of leaving any wounded behind on the battlefield. In the compensation context, this sentiment might translate into optimizing sensitivity to make sure that no one whose disease was in fact caused by the exposure was denied compensation, even at the expense of mistakenly providing compensation to many whose disease was not caused by the exposure. Alternatively, if economic concerns were paramount (for example, if there were severe budgetary constraints on the total amount of money available to a compensation program), then it might be better to optimize specificity, making sure that only those whose disease was caused by exposure received compensation, even at the expense of mistakenly not providing compensation to some whose disease was in fact caused by the exposure.

Options for compensation criteria lie on the spectrum that ranges from complete sensitivity (top right corner of the ROC curve) to complete specificity (bottom left corner). Obviously, there is no universally correct choice from among the options along this spectrum. However, whether this is done explicitly, or whether this is merely implicit in the decisions (which is normally the case), a compensation policy chooses some combination of sensitivity and specificity. Typically such decisions favor one over the other. In the case of a common disease or illness, if there is a fixed budget available for compensation, then use of very sensitive criteria, such as motivated by the battlefield analogy, might result in many receiving only a small amount of compensation. If the budget is not fixed, use of very sensitive criteria would result in the total amount of compensation paid out becoming exceedingly large. These issues are further developed in the following section.

Developing a Basis for Compensation Based on AF

In earlier sections of this chapter, we discussed the properties of the AF, its underlying assumptions, and its inherent limitations. Here we discuss a critique of AF as a tool for determining compensation and propose justifications for its continued use in the context of veterans' compensation. We also explore options for the application of AF for this purpose.

Promoting the Use of AFs in Determining Compensation for Veterans

In the 1980s, Cox published an important critique of using epidemiologic data based on groups (and therefore the AF that is derived from these data) to draw conclusions about individuals, as is done in compensation settings (Cox, 1984, 1987). This theme was extended in a series of papers published from 1988 to 2004 by Robins and Greenland in which they developed their own critique of using probability of causation, and by implication, AF, as a basis for compensation or liability (Greenland, 1999; Greenland and Robins, 1988, 2000; Robins, 2004; Robins and Greenland, 1989a,b, 1991). There are at least three points in their critique that are relevant to the issue of AF and compensation.

First, compensation schemes based on AF alone allow consideration only of *whether* a disease occurs, not *when* the disease occurs. Although RRs, and the AFs derived from them, can vary by time in the sense that they can be estimated for different ages and for varying times since exposure, they do not reflect time lost due to disability or death. Those who live with a disease for a longer period of time, or had their life shortened by a longer period of time, presumably deserve more compensation. Approaches that use YLD or YLL (or DALYs) reflect when disease occurs and therefore provide an attractive alternative. (It should be recalled that the AF is a component of any calculation of YLD or YLL that tries to estimate the portion due to exposure [Steenland and Armstrong, 2006], and so any limitations inherent to the estimation of the AF itself will also apply to these extensions of the AF.)

Second, with an RR we cannot distinguish a situation where an exposure causes new disease *in a few* that would otherwise not have occurred from the extreme case where an exposure accelerates the onset of disease that would have occurred anyway *in all* of the exposed (Robins, 2004). In fact any RR, no matter how little elevated above a no-effect RR of 1.0, is as consistent with the exposure accelerating the onset of disease in all exposed as it is with the exposure causing the disease in the fraction of the exposed represented by the AF. One important implication is that an RR of 2.0 (and hence an AF of 0.5) does not equate to a 50 percent probability that exposure contributed to the disease in either the population or in an individual. That is, an RR of 2.0 does not make it *as likely as not* that the exposure caused the disease. It is important to understand that the distinction between accelerating the onset of a disease and causing disease that would not have occurred without the exposure is a blurry one. For example, because most men have latent prostate cancer by age 80 (Oh et al., 2003), it is often assumed that all men, if they were to live long enough, will get prostate cancer. Yet we have no hesitation in referring to exposures as potential *causes* of prostate cancer even though any exposure would in reality have accelerated the onset in all who got it as a result of the exposure.

Third, when there is heterogeneity in baseline disease risks (i.e., when the risk of disease in the absence of exposure is different for different people, which is the usual situation), the AF does not necessarily equal the average of the probabilities that exposure caused the disease in each individual. This follows from the general principle that a nonlinear function (in this case a ratio) of averages does not in general equal the average of individual nonlinear functions (i.e., individual ratios). In the case here, the ratio of averages is the AF, and the average of ratios is the average of individual probabilities that exposure caused the disease. The greater the individual differences in the baseline probabilities, the greater the disparity between the AF and the average of individual probabilities.

In light of these compelling arguments, why would the AF continue to be recommended in compensation plans? Part of the answer relates to the features of a given compensation plan. A compensation plan that pays a lump sum to a veteran (or spouse/survivor) in direct proportion to the AF would be open to the criticisms of Robins and Greenland. VA compensation does not work in this way. VA compensation has many features of a compensation plan based on YLD or YLL. For diseases associated with disability only (which is common), monthly VA disability benefits begin when a case is approved for compensation and continue until death. VA compensation therefore accounts for the period of time a veteran lives with a disability.

Further, the amount of each monthly payment is intended to reflect the amount of disability, another feature incorporated in YLD (Steenland and Armstrong, 2006). Even though VA compensation does not directly account for YLL, spouse/survivor benefits for diseases that result in early mortality continue for the lifetime of the spouse/survivor. Thus, if the spouse/survivor outlives the veteran by many years because the veteran's life was shortened by many years due to the disease, the total payment would reflect this degree of life shortening. Although this might not be true in any individual case (if the spouse/survivor also dies early, for example) VA compensation nonetheless accounts for YLL at least indirectly.

Although we acknowledge the limitations, we also recognize the simplicity and transparency of the AF as a measure of disease burden. As others have deliberated similar issues of AF and assigned shares (NRC, 2000), we accept the utility of the AF as an input to compensation. In the following section we explore ways in which the AF might be applied for VA compensation.

Possible Applications of the AF in Determining Individual Compensation

There are several possible criteria for choosing among compensation plans. We focus here on two: economic rationality and fairness.

An economically rational basis for compensation is one in which the total compensation provided to the population is equal to the total burden of disease caused by exposure in the exposed group (as defined by the AF). Thus, the total compensation given to the exposed group is determined by the total disease burden caused by their exposure. For example, if the AF is 50 percent (and we make the simplifying assumption that half of the cases of disease among the exposed are due to the exposure), then the total economically rational compensation is the amount needed to compensate half of the afflicted persons. Unless the AF were 100 percent (a rare occurrence), the total economically rational compensation is always less than full compensation to every person with the disease.

One problem with the economically rational approach is that it says nothing about how to divide the total fairly among the eligible persons. The "correct" way would be to compensate each person according to his or her particular burden of disease caused by the exposure. We have discussed ways in which better information on exposure or individual susceptibility might improve estimates of individual PC. Ultimately, however, it is almost always impossible to determine which person's disease was caused by military exposure. This is because most disabilities and diseases have multiple causes, and each exposed person is also exposed to other causes of the condition. *Even with perfect research*, it is not usually possible to determine which case of the disease was caused by the military exposure and which was not. This is a central feature and problem of compensation for military exposure.

Given this problem, one approach would be to spread the total compensation evenly among all exposed persons who have the disease. For example, if half of the disease cases among the exposed were caused by the exposure (*AF* = 50 percent), then half compensation could be given to everyone. More generally, under this plan every exposed person with the disease would get a percent of compensation equal to the AF for their disease. This plan is illustrated in Figure 9-2. This approach has been used in class-action suits, but to our knowledge has not been used for military compensation.

A criticism of this approach is that even if we cannot identify them, we know there are probably some people whose disease was actually caused by their military exposure. Such people get only partial compensation, which can be construed as unfair. The only way to guarantee this never happens is to compensate everyone 100 percent, regardless of the likelihood that their disease was caused by their exposure (Figure 9-3). Such an approach achieves

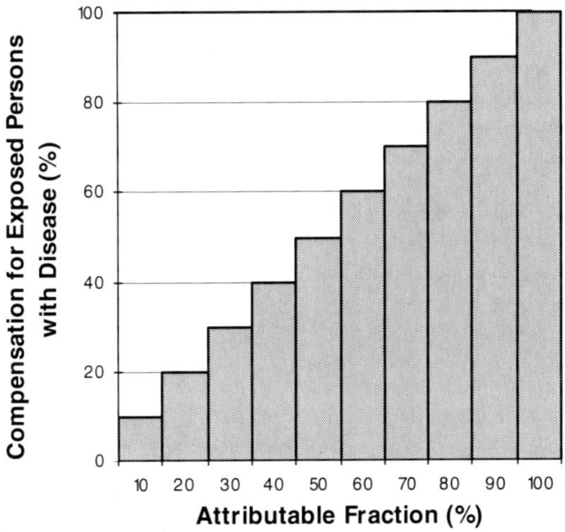

FIGURE 9-2 "Economically rational" compensation plan, based on the attributable fraction.

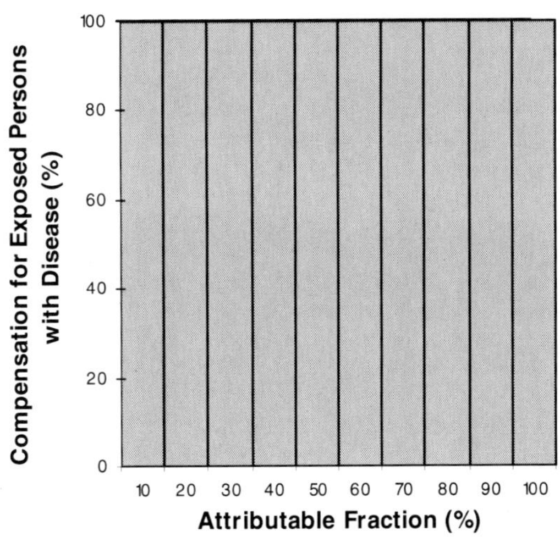

FIGURE 9-3 Complete compensation (100 percent) for all exposed persons with disease, regardless of attributable fraction.

extremely high sensitivity, but at high cost. This plan is not economically rational, in that it provides more compensation to the exposed population (in some cases, far more compensation) than the total disease burden would justify. It is worth noting that other criteria may legitimately be regarded by policy makers as more important than economic rationality.

The two plans described in Figures 9-2 and 9-3 define the boundaries of practical plans for compensation. The economically rational model provides the minimum rational compensation (Figure 9-2) and the compensation-to-all model provides the maximum possible compensation (Figure 9-3). All remaining plans discussed here fall somewhere between.

One in-between approach would be to establish a level of AF necessary for 100 percent compensation. The usual criterion is 50 percent—that is, the chance that the disease in an exposed person was caused by their exposure is at least 50:50. This approach is shown in Figure 9-4.

A criticism of the "50 percent criterion" is its all-or-none property. Because of uncertainty in the estimate of RR, there is little real difference between an RR of 2.1 and 1.8 (producing AFs of 52 percent and 44 percent), and yet a disease with the first AF might get 100 percent compensation, and a disease with the other might get none. By the criterion of economic rationality, the plan in Figure 9-4 undercompensates persons when the AF is less than 50 percent, and overcompensates them when it is 50 percent or greater.

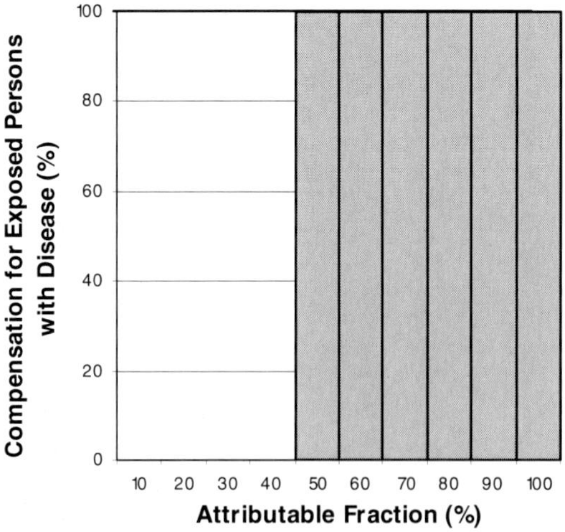

FIGURE 9-4 Complete compensation for all exposed persons only when attributable fraction is 50 percent or more.

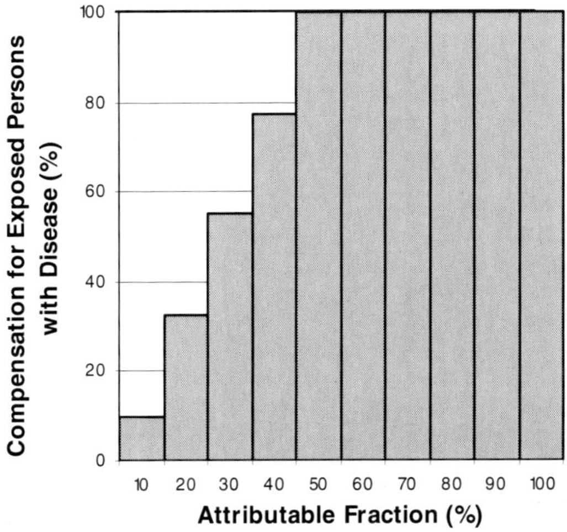

FIGURE 9-5 Complete compensation for an AF of 50 percent or more, plus graduated compensation below 50 percent.

This problem of all or none has been addressed in an alternative compensation scheme. The 1984 NRC Oversight Committee (NRC, 1984) suggested that when the AF was 50 percent or greater, compensation should be 100 percent, and when it is less than 50 percent, it should be linearly scaled down to 10 percent. This is shown in Figure 9-5.

A graded strategy of compensation (such as Figure 9-5), is more fair than an arbitrary cutoff of 50 percent and comes closer to achieving economic rationality—although at any given AF, it still provides total payouts much larger than the total burden of disease.

In the past, there has been a policy not to compensate individuals at levels less than 10 percent. Such a threshold would be relevant if any these models generated estimated compensations under 10 percent.

INTEGRATIVE SYNTHESIS: ROLES FOR PRESUMPTIONS

In this chapter the factors that can serve as information inputs to the decision-making process underlying the determination of veterans' compensation have been identified and discussed. These factors and the point(s) in the process at which they come into play are displayed in Figure 9-6. Additional inputs to the compensation process that are not strictly informational in nature are also displayed. These consist of ethical, political, and economic considerations that in practice can be critical determinants of the

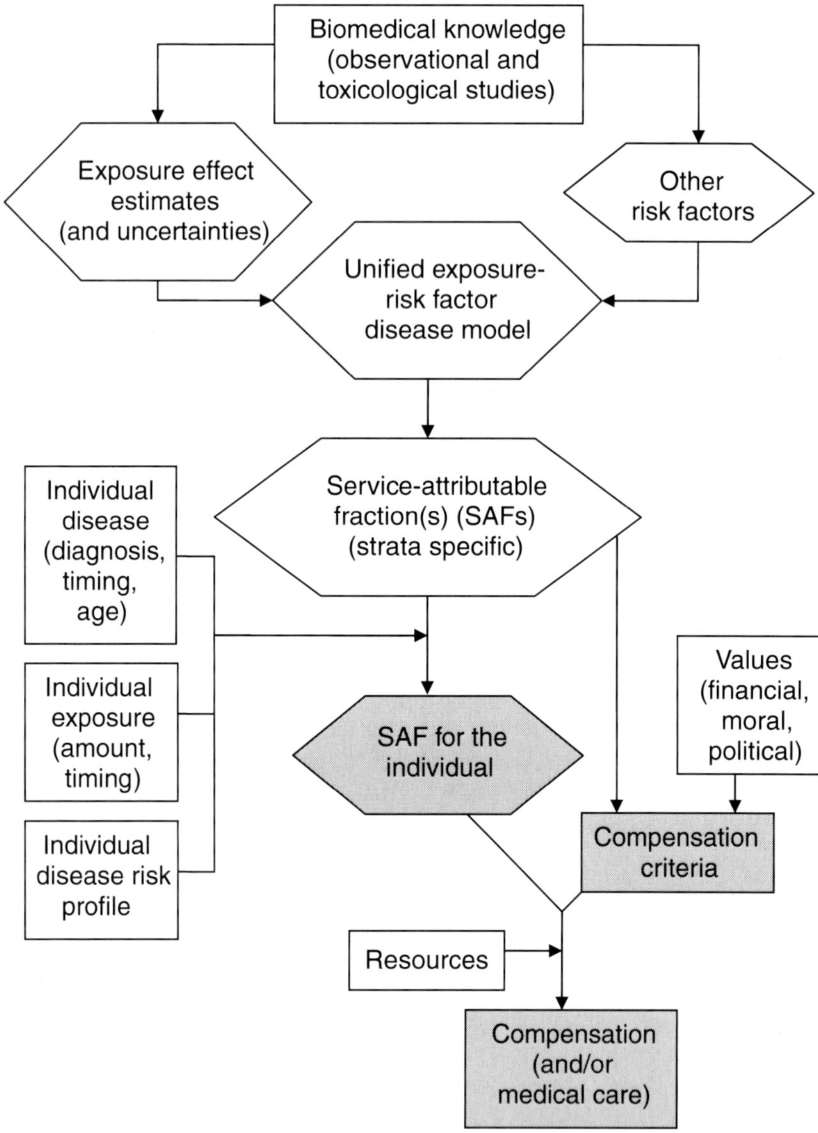

FIGURE 9-6 A rational process for determining veterans' compensation.

outcome of the process, but do not lend themselves to the type of exploration that has been undertaken in this chapter.

A Rational Compensation Determination Process

The compensation determination process for veterans displayed in Figure 9-6 is, we argue, a scientifically based and rational scheme, albeit necessarily somewhat idealized for most situations. Scientific findings here form the foundation for compensation. These scientific findings are more typically observational in nature, although toxicological or other experimental findings, depending on the specific exposure or disease, can either complement the observational findings or occasionally comprise the bulk of the findings. However, to be useful in this scheme, science must provide estimates of exposure effect that can be used to derive estimated AFs, and such effect estimates are best derived from observational data. Measures of uncertainty in the effect estimates could potentially play a role in some compensation schemes, although we have not here presented applications of how this might work. Toxicological findings, or the lack of them, could be reflected in the measures of uncertainty.

The size of effect estimates are affected by the extent of exposure and, by definition, effect modifiers. These, then, also affect the SAFs. Moreover, as we have seen, the SAF can be affected by how other risk factors interact with the exposure in causing disease, being affected not at all if they interact multiplicatively, but potentially dramatically if they interact additively (see Table 9-2 and corresponding discussion). To make use of these influences on the AF in the compensation process, science must not only provide information on how exposure and effect modifiers influence effect estimates, but also provide information on the form of interactive effects of other disease risk factors.

Armed with a host of exposure SAFs that correspond to levels (strata) of exposure, to states (strata) of the modifying factors, and to states of other risk factors if their interactions with the exposure are other than additive, individual SAFs can be estimated. Assuming that this information on exposure and these factors are also available for a given veteran seeking compensation, a corresponding SAF can be assigned to the veteran in lieu of our ability to know any individual's PC.

A compensation scheme for a specific exposure-disease combination that is economically rational (i.e., one that provides a total award reflecting the total disease burden of the exposed group) is formulated. A compensation scheme can potentially incorporate features relating to the certainty of the scientific information that is used in estimating the SAF, although we have not provided examples as to how this might be done. Criteria that define who is eligible for some form of compensation implicitly assume some sensitivity and specificity, and for the population of concern, corresponding false positive and false negative rates. The AF, as shown above (Tables 9-5 to 9-7), has a great impact on both of these rates for a fixed sensitivity and specificity, and therefore could influence the selection of compensation criteria apart from its role in determining the individual SAF. Because of the trade-offs involved in choosing one set of criteria over another, the choice will always entail invoking values of some sort, for example, ethical, political, or financial (i.e., resource) values.

For many cases, including those involving veterans, this version of a compensation process may seem farfetched. It is unlikely that any single instance involving determination of compensation for veterans has features that look exactly like this. Nevertheless, it is instructive to consider how individual processes differ from this version. First, by identifying how actual cases differ from this framework, insight can be gained into some not so obvious assumptions that have been made in these cases. Second, this framework might help pinpoint or clarify the critical influences on any given compensation process. Finally, this framework can serve to identify information needs that, if met, would improve the specific presumptive disability decision-making process.

One way of viewing presumptions is as compromises necessitated by either poor or absent information on one or several of the inputs to the veterans' compensation determination process. For example, absent information on exposures of Service members in a specific theater, a presumption could be used to make the determination that any Service member who served in that theater was exposed. As another example, epidemiologic and other evidence about the association between a specific exposure and disease may be inadequate for estimating the AF. A presumption could be used to determine that any veteran with the disease who had been exposed most likely had the disease caused by the exposure. Or, there may be no information on how risk factors other than the exposure of interest influence the risk of disease, or how timing of disease occurrence influences the likelihood that the exposure was relevant. Even if this information existed, there may be no reliable way of obtaining this information for a veteran. A presumption might be used to determine that all exposed veterans, regardless of gender, age, the time since exposure, or exposure to other suspected disease risk factors, have the same AF.

Some Case Studies Revisited

It is instructive to again examine some of the case studies in light of this view of presumptions, and to assess characteristics of presumptions pertaining to sensitivity and specificity, and positive and negative predictive value. The contrasting cases of Agent Orange and type 2 diabetes and of radiation and lung cancer will be used for this purpose.

With Agent Orange and type 2 diabetes, much of the information needed to apply our proposed process is unavailable or of poor quality (see Agent Orange and type 2 diabetes case study in Appendix I). First, scientific information that can be used to estimate an SAF indicates that the SAF is small, at best, and uncertain. Consequently, it is difficult based on this information to provide meaningful SAFs that correspond to different levels of exposure, or SAFs that correspond to different strata of possible modifying factors. There is information on the effect of several diabetes risk factors, but none is available on how any of these interact with Agent Orange exposure to influence diabetes risk.

Assuming that meaningful SAFs could be estimated, information about the veteran to make use of the SAFs is needed. First, information on exposure to Agent Orange is needed, including first and foremost whether exposure occurred, and the intensity and duration of exposure. Although there has been little attempt to make use of possible sources of exposure information for Agent Orange in Vietnam veterans for the purpose of compensation, attempting to characterize exposure based on current information will nevertheless be difficult. Information on the time of onset of diabetes, the certainty of diagnosis, and diabetes risk factors, while not perfect, is comparatively good.

Compensation schemes for Agent Orange and type 2 diabetes could take several forms, any of which might require some type of presumptions. We assume that the scientific findings indicate that exposure to constituents of Agent Orange causes type 2 diabetes, with some degree of certainty. With the SAF being small, even among those with well-documented exposure, the total disease burden is relatively small. This is true whether total disease burden is estimated directly from the SAF or using the SAF to modify a YLD or DALY. For compensation to be economically rational, the total compensation award to the veterans affected would then also be relatively small. Alternatively, if the overall cost of compensation for Agent Orange and type 2 diabetes is not relevant, then economic rationality is also not pertinent. With a small SAF, it is also likely that the proportion of those who would receive compensation under any scheme whose diabetes was actually caused by Agent Orange exposure would also be small (i.e., the false positive rate would be high). With crude measures of exposure that would include large numbers of veterans without the degree of exposure needed to cause disease, the SAF would be smaller still, with a correspondingly high proportion mistakenly compensated.

Any available information on the above inputs to the compensation process could restrict the scope of presumptions needed for Agent Orange and type 2 diabetes. Clearly the use of some information on exposure to

Agent Orange would reduce the effect on reduction of the SAF caused by including unexposed veterans. In the absence of better scientific information on Agent Orange exposure and type 2 diabetes, it will not be possible to utilize veteran information on potential modifying factors such as age of exposure, age of disease onset, or latency period to provide strata of SAF, although assumptions might have a role. For example, a hypothetical case could be made to limit the number of years allowable between exposure to Agent Orange and onset of diabetes. Regarding the presence of other diabetes risk factors that modify baseline risk, in the absence of good information on the form of interactions with Agent Orange, an assumption of additivity of risks might be made that could make it possible to provide stratified SAFs. A later age of diabetes onset in this case, for example, would increase baseline risk and reduce the SAF.

The current presumption for Agent Orange and type 2 diabetes has implicit assumptions as to sensitivity and specificity. With a presumption that requires service in Vietnam and diagnosed type 2 diabetes, sensitivity, $TP/(TP + FN)$, is nearly 1.0 as there are essentially no FNs. That is, any Vietnam veteran who got diabetes from Agent Orange exposure will receive compensation. On the other hand, specificity, $TN/(TN + FP)$, is 0 since there are no TNs. That is, no Vietnam veterans whose diabetes was caused by something other than Agent Orange will not be compensated. The positive predictive value of compensation, $TP/(TP + FP)$ is very small because FP is exceedingly large due to the small SAF. That is, only a small fraction of those who receive compensation will actually have had their diabetes caused by exposure. The negative predictive value, $TN/(TN + FN)$, is almost meaningless because both TN and FN are essentially nonexistent. These characteristics of this particular presumption are therefore quite extreme.

The case of radiation and lung cancer presents distinct contrasts to that of Agent Orange and type 2 diabetes. As detailed earlier (see radiation case study in Appendix I), here the case for causation is strong, uncertainty is relatively well estimated, and there is extensive information on dose-response relationships. Information on the effects of other factors, principally smoking and age, is also relatively extensive. However, even in this case there are deficiencies in the state of the information that invite presumptions. These deficiencies include (1) poor individual person-dose estimation; and (2) inadequate information on the form of the radiation interaction model for other risk factors, again principally smoking.

Based on the above information it is clear that the estimated SAF is relatively large for radiation and lung cancer and has less associated uncertainty than most exposures. As noted before, the radioepidemiological tables (NIH, 1985) provide estimated PCs for radiation in lung cancer by exposure dose, age at exposure and at cancer diagnosis, latency, and cigarette smoking history. However, there is little agreement on the form of the radiation-smoking interaction in lung cancer, with initial evidence favoring additive effects and more recent interpretations favoring multiplicative (or submultiplicative) effects (see radiation case study in Appendix I). Because the form of the interaction has a large impact on estimation of the SAF, uncertainty about the form complicates use of an SAF even for lung cancer (see discussion on effects on the positive predictive value below).

The current presumption for radiation and lung cancer also has implicit assumptions as to sensitivity and specificity. Sensitivity, *TP*/(*TP* + *FN*), is good as there will only be a few FNs. That is, most radiation-exposed veterans who get lung cancer from radiation exposure will receive compensation, at least when based on a presumption of exposure. Specificity, *TN*/(*TN* + *FP*) is also good because those with low radiation risk, such as those with low estimated exposure, are less likely to receive compensation, although because of inaccuracies in the estimated exposure, some will (these will be FPs). The positive predictive value of compensation, *TP*/(*TP* + *FP*), is very good because FPs are relatively uncommon because of the large AF. That is, a large fraction of those who receive compensation will actually have had their lung cancer caused by exposure. The negative predictive value, *TN*/(*TN* + *FN*), is also very good because FNs are relatively uncommon. These characteristics of this particular presumption therefore seem to be reasonable.

However, even for the case of radiation and lung cancer, the above assessment of these characteristics is dependent on the way other disease risk factors, for example smoking, are determined to interact with the effect of radiation. For nonsmokers the above assessment is reasonable and does not depend on the form of the interaction. For smokers the assessment varies depending on whether smoking is determined to interact additively or multiplicatively with radiation exposure. With a multiplicative interaction, exposure RR and therefore AF is the same regardless of smoking status. In the additive case, the RR and the AF can vary dramatically by smoking status (see Tables 9-1 and 9-2, above). This will have no effect on sensitivity or specificity, as these are unaffected by the AF. However, positive and negative predictive values will be affected as both change as a function of the AF. Because the AF is substantially smaller in smokers than nonsmokers under an additive model, the positive predictive value is likewise smaller, indicating that for smokers a substantial percentage of those receiving compensation will not have gotten lung cancer as a result of exposure to radiation. The AF (and the PC derived from it) in the radioepidemiological tables is therefore critically dependent on the form of the interaction that is determined to be the case. Therefore, even with better scientific information than is available for any other military exposure, there is still room for presumptions. However, the better the information, the more focused and limited in scope the presumptions can be.

Science and Compensation Presumptions

The inability to identify the disease role of specific military exposures in any *individual* veteran partly motivates the need for compensation presumptions. The scope of a presumption is, in turn, partly determined by the available scientific information and corresponding information on any given veteran. The more scientific information available on the causal relationship between a service exposure and disease, and the more information available on an individual veteran's exposure and disease risk, the more narrow in scope the presumption needs be. The contrasting cases of Agent Orange and type 2 diabetes, and radiation and lung cancer, discussed above serve to make these points.

It is likely that there will be substantial advances in our ability to quantify exposure and other disease risks in individual veterans, perhaps through the use of specific biomarkers of exposure or disease for example, and by exploiting findings from toxicogenetics and toxicogenomics. These advances could possibly refine the scope of presumptions or conceivably do away with the need for some presumptions.

Earlier chapters laid out a framework for determining when a compensation presumption may be considered based on the state of scientific information. The intent in this chapter has been to identify concepts and tools that can be utilized in making decisions as to the form and content of a compensation presumption. These include (1) a set of SAFs that is as refined as the science permits; (2) features of alternative presumptions, such as sensitivity, specificity, and positive predictive value, that characterize and quantify the relative strengths and unavoidable mistakes (and therefore costs) implicit in each presumption; and (3) an appreciation of the relationship between the SAFs and some of these features, namely the positive and negative predictive values.

It has not been the intent here to determine whether a specific presumption and its form are justified or sensible or to identify better alternatives. These are issues on which VA and Congress deliberate. It is hoped, however, that the framework outlined can be used in these deliberations to allow for more rational, science-based decisions about the content of specific presumptions than may have been the case in the past.

REFERENCES

Austin, H., Delzell, E., and Cole, P. 1988. Benzene and leukemia: A review of the literature and a risk assessment. *American Journal of Epidemiology* 127:419-439.

Benichou, J. 2001. A review of adjusted estimators of attributable risk. *Statistical Methods in Medical Research* 10:195-216.

Bruzzi, P., S. B. Green, D. P. Byar, L. A. Brinton, and C. Schairer. 1985. Estimating the population attributable risk for multiple risk factors using case-control data. *American Journal of Epidemiology* 122(5):904-914.

Cox, A. T. 1984. Probability of causation and the attributable proportion of risk. *Risk Analysis* 4(3):221-230.

Cox, A. T. 1987. Statistical issues in the estimation of assigned shares for carcinogenesis liability. *Risk Analysis* 7(1):71-80.

DHHS (Department of Health and Human Services). 2002. 42 CFR Parts 81 and 82. Guidelines for determining the probability of causation and methods for radiation dose reconstruction under the Employees Occupational Illness Compensation Program Act of 2000; Final Rules. *Federal Register* 67(85):22296-22330.

Greenland, S. 1999. Relation of probability of causation to relative risk and doubling dose: A methodologic error that has become a social problem. *American Journal of Public Health* 89:1166-1169.

Greenland, S., and J. M. Robins. 1988. Conceptual problems in the definition and interpretation of attributable fractions. *American Journal of Epidemiology* 128:1185-1197.

Greenland, S., and J. M. Robins. 2000. Epidemiology, justice and the probability of causation. *Jurimetrics* 40:321-340.

Lagakos, S. W., and F. Mosteller. 1986. Assigned shares in compensation for radiation-related cancers. *Risk Analysis* 6(3):345-357.

NCI (National Cancer Institute). 2006. *Lung cancer prevention.* http://www.cancer.gov/cancertopics/pdq/prevention/lung/Patient/page2 (accessed May 23, 2007).

NIH (National Institutes of Health). 1985. *Report of the National Institutes of Health Ad Hoc Working Group to Develop Radioepidemiological Tables. Responding to the congressional mandate under Section 7(b) of the Orphan Drug Act of January 4, 1983 (PL-97-414).* NIH Pub. No. 85-2748. Washington, DC: U.S. Government Printing Office.

NIOSH (National Institute of Occupational Safety and Health). 2007. *Users guide for the Interactive RadioEpidemiological Program (NIOSH-IREP).* Version 5.5.2. http://0-www.cdc.gov.mill1.sjlibrary.org/niosh/ocas/pdfs/irep/irepug0607.pdf (accessed July 28, 2007).

NRC (National Research Council). 1984. *Assigned share for radiation as a cause of cancer, review of radioepidemiologic tables assigning probabilities of causation.* Washington, DC: National Academy Press.

NRC. 2000. *A review of the draft report of the NCI-CDC Working Group to Revise the 1985 Radioepidemiological Tables.* Washington, DC: National Academy Press.

Obuchowski, N. A. 2003. Receiver operating characteristic curves and their use in radiology. *Radiology* 229:3-8.

OEHHA (Office of Environmental Health Hazard Assessment). 2001. *Public health goal for benzene in drinking water.* California Environmental Protection Agency. http://www.oehha.ca.gov/water/phg/pdf/BenzeneFinPHG.pdf (accessed February 7, 2007).

Oh, W. K., Hurwitz, M., D'Amico, A. V., Richie, J. P., Kantoff, P. W. 2003. Neoplasms of the prostate (Ch. 111). In: *Holland-Frei Cancer Medicine* 6, 6th ed. Hamilton, ON: BC Decker.

OSTP (Office of Science Technology and Policy). 1988. *Use of probability of causation by the Veterans Administration in the adjudication of claims of injury due to exposure to ionizing radiation.* OSTP Committee on Interagency Radiation Research and Policy Coordination. Executive Office of the President, Washington, DC.

Presidential Commission. 1990. Ch. 4. Standards and procedures for latent illnesses. *Presidential Commission on Catastrophic Nuclear Accidents: Report to Congress.* Washington, DC.

Robins, J. 2004. Should compensation schemes be based on the probability of causation or expected years of life lost? *Journal of Law and Policy* 12:537-548.

Robins, J. M., and S. Greenland. 1989a. Estimability and estimation of excess and etiologic fractions. *Statistics and Medicine* 8:845-859.

Robins, J., and S. Greenland. 1989b. The probability of causation under a stochastic model for individual risk. *Biometrics* 45:1125-1138.

Robins, J., and S. Greenland. 1991. Estimability and estimation of expected years of life lost due to a hazardous exposure. *Statistics and Medicine* 10:79-93.

Rothman, K. J., and S. Greenland. 1998. *Modern Epidemiology*, 2nd ed. Philadelphia, PA: Lippincott-Raven. Pp. 54-55.

Steenland, K., and B. Armstrong. 2006. An overview of methods for calculating the burden of disease due to specific risk factors. *Epidemiology* 17(5):512-519.

Thomas, D. C. 2000. The probability of causation can be used in an equitable manner to resolve radiation tort claims and design compensation claims. *Radiation Research* 154(6):718-719.

10

Health and Exposure Data Infrastructure to Improve the Scientific Basis of Presumptions

INTRODUCTION

This chapter addresses the implementation of a system of data collection to support surveillance and research, as well as to track the exposures of individual military personnel. The long-term goal is a system that would improve or complete many of the evidence gaps that now lead to presumptions. Information on exposure is needed to conduct studies that will provide data for calculating attributable fractions and for determining exposure groups of particular individuals.

Once a causal relationship has been established or presumed between a specific disease and a type of exposure, it becomes crucial to establish whether the Service member was exposed during military service. When data are not sufficient to describe a specific Service member's service-exposure history, presumptions are needed to give guidance about what to assume as exposure magnitude is considered. One clear path toward reducing the need for presumptions in decision making is to accurately document and provide Service member-specific exposure and health data to those making decisions regarding that Service member's case. Thus individuals determined by an adequate exposure surveillance system not to be exposed to an agent of concern would not be at risk for the particular health outcome(s) caused by that specific exposure. The availability of exposure data would provide evidence to support a veteran's claim that the exposure occurred while in military service. The availability of exposure data will allow more informative epidemiological studies to be performed and a more accurate determination of service-attributable fraction (SAF).

The need for having better exposure data has been recognized repeatedly in numerous external reviews of Department of Defense (DoD) and Department of Veterans Affairs (VA) activities regarding Service member health protection and veteran health care and disability determination (GAO, 1999, 2000a,b, 2005a,b, 2006; IOM, 1996a, 1999b, 2000c).

Detailed health status data collected throughout a Service member's active duty and veteran experience, coupled with individual exposure data collected during that period, would provide the data needed to make better decisions about an individual's likelihood of service-related disease causation and thus minimize the need for presumptions. As the Institute of Medicine (IOM) noted in 1996,

> The DoD, the branches of the armed services, and the DVA should continue to work together to develop, fund, and staff medical information systems that include a single, uniform, continuous, and retrievable electronic medical record for each [S]ervice member. The uniform record should include each relevant health item (including baseline personal risk factors, every inpatient and outpatient medical contact, and all health-related interventions), allow linkage to exposure and other data sets, and have the capability to incorporate relevant medical data from beyond DoD and DVA institutions (e.g., U.S. Public Health Service facilities, civilian medical providers, and other health-care institutions). . . . (IOM, 1996a, p. 10)

DoD and VA have been working together since 1998 to improve sharing of medical information for active-duty military personnel and veterans. The agencies have developed a short-term plan to improve their existing health information systems and a long-term plan to create a modern health information system based on computable data. However, as GAO points out, DoD and VA lack a detailed project management plan to guide their efforts (GAO, 2007).

In 1997, President Clinton issued a directive to DoD and VA "to create a new Force Health Protection Program. Every soldier, sailor, airman, and Marine will have a comprehensive, life-long medical record of all illnesses and injuries they suffer, the care and inoculations they receive, and their exposure to different hazards. These records will help us prevent illness and identify and cure those that occur" (DoD, 2006a, p. 2).

Also in 1997, coincident with the presidential directive described above, DoD issued an instruction describing the "Implementation and Application of Joint Medical Surveillance for Deployments." This document defined initial expectations for more detailed medical surveillance and exposure assessment data collection systems for both deployment and in-garrison or nondeployment settings. This plan laid the groundwork for systems that would "eventually be capable of linking deployment and nondeployment environmental and occupational exposure and data to health hazard and/or health risk assessments to individual medical records and medical outcome databases" (DoD, 1997, p. 5).

The vision for a more comprehensive and continuous surveillance system was articulated in DoD Directive 6490.2 issued in 2004. It proposed that

> Health surveillance systems shall be continuously in effect throughout each [Service member]'s career, capturing data about individual health status; instances of disease and injury; medical interventions such as immunizations, treatments, and preventive medications; and exposures to potential and actual health hazards associated with occupation, deployment, and lifestyle. (DoD, 2004, p. 3)

It also dictated policy that "[s]urveillance data collected on individual [Service member]s during their careers shall be provided to VA upon their separation or retirement from the military" (DoD, 2004, p. 4).

Defining and developing the mechanisms and systems to implement these goals has been an iterative process that has taken years—largely due to the magnitude and complexity of the issues being addressed. Those efforts are now bringing action as a series of systems and expectations are being implemented. DoD Instruction 6490.03 of 2006, which replaced the 1997 DoD Instruction 6490.3, sets clear expectations that deployment exposure assessment and monitoring data be submitted to individual health records and to a DoD-wide database (DOEHRS—the Defense Occupational and Environmental Health Readiness System) (DoD, 2006c, p. 21).

The remainder of this chapter reviews the current state and future plans for DoD and VA collection and use of health and exposure data throughout a Service member's span of service. The availability of such data would enable studies to better understand potential linkages between service-connected exposures and future health status and would reduce reliance on presumptions in decision making.

DOD HEALTH AND EXPOSURE ASSESSMENT DATA COLLECTION

DoD Health Assessment and Medical Surveillance

Overview

Opportunities for health assessments of Service members on active duty occur at obvious service milestones throughout the Service member's span of service. These milestones include the initial medical evaluation at accession, or entry into the service, and subsequent periodic health assessments that continue until separation or retirement from the service. These milestones are displayed in Figure 10-1. Additional surveillance may precede or follow specific deployments with assessments tailored to the particular hazards of a deployment.

Routine Health Assessments Throughout the Span of Service

Elements of the health data collected for each of the assessments performed over the span of a Service member's service are found in Table 10-1. They may include responses to a health history questionnaire, physical examination findings, and laboratory test results. The degree of detail and areas of emphasis in each assessment vary based on the specific point in the span of service or on the purpose of each individual assessment. Generally, a self-completed questionnaire contains a core set of questions regarding physical and mental health, and history of environmental and occupational exposures and stressors. This is intended to follow the recommendations of the U.S. Preventive Health Services Task Force's *Guide to Clinical Preventive Services* (AHRQ, 2006). Data are collected in a combination of written and electronic formats.

All new recruits and enlisted Service members undergo an initial evaluation at the time of accession. This is the most comprehensive of the assessments and provides the baseline set of data that is updated at the time of each future assessment. As in all assessments, the nature of the responses and test results partly determine what additional evaluation or screening is performed. At this time, data from this evaluation are generally saved only in a hard copy format. The Health Assessment Review Tool (HART) is an electronic and standardized implementation of the self-reporting questionnaire that is currently being pilot tested at Ft. Jackson (Army) and San Diego (United States Marine Corps); the HART-A (the accession version) is expected to be more generally available in the next few months (Personal communication, Col. K. Cox and C. Postlewaite, Department of Defense, November 1, 2006).

The periodic health assessments (PHAs) are episodic (generally annual) follow-up evaluations primarily employing self-completed questionnaires. Positive responses on this questionnaire, or additions to previously collected information, trigger a more detailed assessment. In following the U.S. Preventive Health Services Task Force recommendations, the PHAs are ideally targeted based on gender, age, disease risk factors, medical history, and exposure history (DoD, 2006d). The PHA is currently being instituted by the Army, but it has been established in the Navy and Air Force for several years.

The separation, retirement, or deactivation assessment is the final routine evaluation that all Service members undergo. Whereas previously a

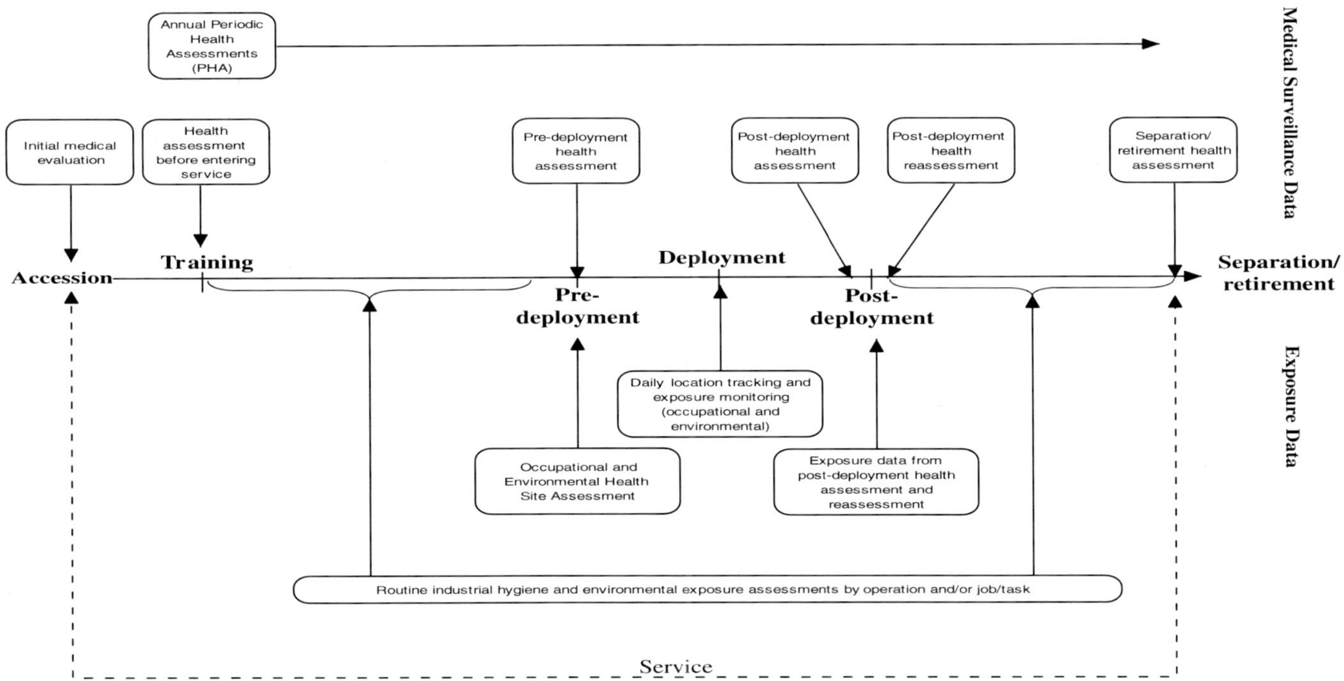

FIGURE 10-1 Timeline for medical surveillance and exposure data collection.

TABLE 10-1 Timeline for Medical Surveillance and Exposure Data Collection

			In Service					
	Accession	After Training Before Service	Throughout Service	Pre-Deployment	Deployment	Post-Deployment	Post-Deployment Reassessment	Separation/ Retirement
Routine Medical Surveillance Data[a]								
Self-Administered Questionnaire								
Family history of chronic diseases	X		X					
Personal habits	X							
Past medical history	X							
Medications	X			X		X		X
Allergies	X							
General health status			X	X		X	X	
Significant events since last periodic health assessment				X				X
On a profile, light duty, or undergoing a medical board				X				
Medical or dental problems				X				X
Pregnancy				X				
Counseling or care for mental health in past year				X				
Questions or concerns about health				X				
Health changes during deployment						X	X	
In sick call during deployment						X	X	

Nights spent as a patient in a hospital during deployment	X	X	X
Vaccinations	X		
Symptoms now or developed anytime during this deployment[b]	X	X	
See anyone wounded, killed, or dead during this deployment	X		
Engaged in direct combat where discharged weapon	X		
During deployment, feel like in great danger of being killed	X		
Interested in receiving help for a stress, emotional, alcohol, or family problem	X	X	X
Little interest or pleasure in doing things	X	X	
Feeling down, depressed, or hopeless	X	X	
Thoughts that you would be better off dead or hurting yourself in some way	X		
Nightmares due to an experience so frightening, horrible, or upsetting	X	X	
Constantly on guard, watchful, or easily startled	X	X	
Numb or detached from others, activities, or your surroundings	X	X	

continued

TABLE 10-1 Continued

			In Service					
	Accession	After Training Before Service	Throughout Service	Pre-Deployment	Deployment	Post-Deployment	Post-Deployment Reassessment	Separation/ Retirement
Self-Administered Questionnaire (continued)								
Concerns of serious conflicts with spouse, family members, or close friends						X	X	
Concerns of hurting or lose control with someone						X		
Having problems if wounded, injured, or assaulted during deployment							X	
Alcohol use							X	
Difficulty working, taking care of things at home, or getting along with other people							X	X
Illnesses or injuries that caused you to miss duty for longer than 3 days								X
Treated by a healthcare provider, admitted to a hospital, or had surgery								X
Injuries or illnesses while on active duty for which you did not seek medical care								X
Other questions or concerns about your health								X

Intend to seek Department of Veterans Affairs disability								X
Laboratory Tests								
Urinalysis (albumin, sugar, HCG)	X	X	X					
H/H	X	X	X					
Blood type	X	X	X					
Drugs and alcohol	X	X	X					
Serum sample	X		X	X		X		
HIV testing	X		X					
CBC	X							
Hemoglobin	X							
Hematocrit	X							
Vaccination status	X							
Clinical Screening and Measurements								
Height	X	X	X					
Weight	X	X	X					
Temperature	X	X	X					
Pulse	X	X	X					
Blood pressure	X	X	X					
Distant vision, near vision	X	X	X					
Refraction by autorefraction or manifest	X	X	X					
Heterophoria	X	X	X					
Color vision	X	X	X					
Depth perception, field of vision, night vision	X	X	X					

continued

TABLE 10-1 Continued

			In Service					
	Accession	After Training Before Service	Throughout Service	Pre-Deployment	Deployment	Post-Deployment	Post-Deployment Reassessment	Separation/Retirement
Clinical Screening and Measurements (continued)								
Intraocular tension	X	X	X					
Audiometer	X	X	X					
Pap smear	X	X	X					
Allergies			X					
Tobacco use			X					
Alcohol abuse and stress management			X					
Chronic illnesses			X					
Medications			X					
Cholesterol			X					
Breast exam, mammogram			X					
Fecal occult blood			X					
Sigmoid			X					
Colonscopy			X					
Immunizations			X					
Clinical Evaluations								
Head, face, neck, and scalp	X	X	X					
Nose, sinuses	X	X	X					
Mouth and throat	X	X	X					
Heart	X	X	X					

Lungs and chest, vascular system	X	X	X
Anus and rectum	X	X	X
Abdomen and viscera	X	X	X
External genitalia	X	X	X
Upper and lower extremities	X	X	X
Spine, musculoskeletal system	X	X	X
Body marks, scars, tattoos	X	X	X
Skin	X	X	X
Neurologic and psychiatric disorders	X	X	X
Pelvis	X	X	X
Endocrine system	X	X	X
Routine Exposure Data[a]			
Industrial Hygiene Exposure Assessment of Operations, Jobs/Tasks			X
Qualitative Exposure Judgments			X
Occupational Exposure Monitoring			X
Routine Environmental Health Programs			X

continued

TABLE 10-1 Continued

			In Service					
	Accession	After Training Before Service	Throughout Service	Pre-Deployment	Deployment	Post-Deployment	Post-Deployment Reassessment	Separation/ Retirement
Environmental Health Site Assessment (EHSA)[c]								
Current use of site, adjoining properties, and surrounding area				X				
Past use of site, adjoining properties, and surrounding area				X				
Geologic, hydrogeologic, hydrologic, meteorologic, and topographic conditions				X				
General description of structures				X				
Roads				X				
Potable water supply				X				
Sewage disposal system				X				
Hazardous materials in connection with identified use				X				
Storage tanks				X				
Odors				X				
Pools of liquid				X				
Drums				X				

Hazardous materials and petroleum products containers	X			
Unidentified substance containers	X			
Heating and cooling	X			
Stains or corrosion	X			
Drains and sumps	X			
Pits, ponds, and lagoons	X			
Stained soil or pavement	X			
Stressed vegetation	X			
Solid waste	X			
Waste water	X			
Well	X			
Septic systems	X			
Daily Location Tracking		X		
OEHS Site Assessments		X		
Environmental Monitoring		X		
Exposure Incident Response		X		
Self-Administered Questionnaire				
DEET insect repellant applied to skin			X	X
Pesticide-treated uniforms			X	X

continued

TABLE 10-1 Continued

			In Service					
	Accession	After Training Before Service	Throughout Service	Pre-Deployment	Deployment	Post-Deployment	Post-Deployment Reassessment	Separation/ Retirement
Self-Administered Questionnaire (continued)								
Environmental pesticides (like area fogging)						X	X	
Flea or tick collars						X	X	
Pesticide strips						X	X	
Smoke from oil fire or burning trash or feces						X	X	
Vehicle or truck exhaust fumes						X	X	
Tent heater smoke						X	X	
JP8 or other fuels						X	X	
Fog oils (smoke screen)						X	X	
Solvents						X	X	
Paints						X	X	
Ionizing radiation						X	X	
Radar/microwaves						X	X	
Lasers						X	X	
Loud noises						X	X	
Excessive vibration						X	X	
Industrial pollution						X	X	
Sand/dust						X	X	
Depleted uranium						X	X	
Days wear MOPPS over garments						X		

Times put on gas mask because of alerts and not because of exercises	X
Ever enter or closely inspect any destroyed military vehicles	X
Exposed to chemical, biological, or radiological warfare agents during deployment	X

[a] Non-routine medical surveillance and exposure data are event driven.

[b] Includes chronic cough, runny nose, fever, weakness, headaches, swollen, stiff or painful joints, back pain, muscle aches, numbness or tingling in hands or feet, skin diseases or rashes, redness of eyes with tearing, dimming of vision, chest pain or pressfainting, lightheadedness, difficulty breathing, still feeling tired after sleeping, difficulty remembering, diarrhea, frequent indigestion, vomiting, ringing of the ears.

[c] This information is used to develop a conceptual site model and may be summarized into a preliminary hazard assessment; SOURCE: ASTM, 2003.

SOURCE: For medical surveillance data: Personal communication, Col. K. Cox and C. Postlewaite, Department of Defense, November 1, 2006; DoD Form 2808 "Report of Medical Examination"; DoD Form 2795 "Predeployment Health Assessment Form"; DoD Form 2796 "Post-Deployment Health Assessment Form"; DoD Form 2900 "Post Deployment Health Reassessment Form"; DoD Form 2697 "Separation and Retirement Medical Assessment." For exposure data: ASTM, 2003; DoD Form 2796 "Post Deployment Health Assessment Form"; DoD Form 2900 "Post Deployment Health Reassessment Form."

retirement evaluation of a career Service member was optional, this has become mandatory since 2005 (Personal communication, Col. K. Cox and C. Postlewaite, Department of Defense, November 1, 2006). The final assessment is performed to document any history of a "limiting" condition. This is determined by a medical evaluation board and may describe the need for "alternative duty" in subsequent employment because of a disability suffered while in the service. The determination of this board addresses the service connectedness of a condition that a Service member may have and thus that Service member's eligibility for VA services.

Nonroutine Health Assessments

Event-driven assessments Health evaluations are also performed in the event of acute health problems or worsening of preexisting conditions. These are focused evaluations that address the specific concern at hand.

Deployment-specific health assessments The predeployment assessment occurs within 60 days of deployment and builds on the PHA. This brief evaluation focuses on interval changes since the most recent PHA, highlighting medications used and any limited duty or short-term disability given. A serum sample is archived and any theater-specific or occupation-specific testing is performed. An HIV test is required if none has been done in the previous 12 months. For deployments lasting less than 30 days, the predeployment assessment is optional as determined by the deployment health authority. Combatant command determines whether additional specific tests will be required, such as cholinesterase levels if deployed into pest management activities or zones, or G6PD enzyme levels. Although not all Service members undergo this assessment, at least 90 percent do (Personal communication, Col. K. Cox and C. Postlewaite, Department of Defense, November 1, 2006).

During deployment there are no generic health assessments. Evaluations are triggered by specific exposures or events, and there may be theater-specific assessments. Also, follow-up may be indicated when environmental sampling suggests a hazard, such as poor water quality. Patient-encounter data are often in electronic format and are captured by the Armed Forces Health Longitudinal Technology Application (AHLTA); sites that are currently not using an electronic data record are planned to have their data entered in the future. Depending on the circumstance, exposures to documented excursions of ambient air, water, or soil concentrations, are also theoretically entered into individual records. Under a new requirement, environmental summaries for all permanent and semi-permanent base camps will be generated according to time and location (Personal communication, Col. K. Cox and C. Postlewaite, Department of Defense, November 1, 2006).

Postdeployment evaluations must occur within 30 days of reployment, although most take place before actually leaving the deployment arena, or while in transit from theater. This evaluation uses a self-reported questionnaire, but also includes a personal interview with a care provider who determines the need for further follow-up. A serum sample is typically obtained when a Service member is at "home." There is documentation of environmental and occupational exposures. Rosters of specific exposure- or event-defined cohorts are assembled based on professional judgment; these are used for purposes of health follow-up or risk communication. Examples include lung function testing following sulfur dioxide exposures or follow-up of those exposed to depleted uranium (Personal communication, Col. K. Cox and C. Postlewaite, Department of Defense, November 1, 2006). Though the impact of combat related stressors on mental health may be significant, structured assessments on symptoms related to emotional stressors, depression, anxiety, posttraumatic stress disorder, and interpersonal difficulties, including hurting someone or losing control, are brief and only assessed at postdeployment period.

HEALTH DATABASES

The above-described assessments generate data that are stored in several databases or formats, thus requiring record linkage, and data entry, for analysis. One primary database is the Defense Medical Surveillance System (DMSS). The DMSS is a relational database that currently contains up-to-date Service member data for all in- and out-patient in-garrison health encounters including acute health events and exposures. It currently has some in-theater encounters provided by AHLTA, but not all. As noted above, HART-A is only now being implemented, so much of the accession evaluation is only present in hard copy form. Also, while standardization is the goal, data collection is not completely standardized across the service branches. AHLTA is the new DoD automated medical records system and clinical data repository; this includes all laboratory data and electronic PHAs. Integration of medical records is clearly a goal in DoD. This is manifested in the current process of establishing an Armed Forces Health Surveillance Center to integrate DMSS, AHLTA, and personnel data (from the Defense Manpower Data Center). Although much of the surveillance health data present in the DMSS are relevant to AHLTA (for example, reportable medical conditions), there is no need for complete overlap (Personal communication, Col. K. Cox and C. Postlewaite, Department of Defense, November 1, 2006).

Troop Tracking and Linking of Individual Exposure and Health Data

Improvements in tracking of troop location are underway, reflecting in part an awareness of the need to perform troop tracking to allow reconstruction of exposure scenarios. A new tracking software, the Defense Theater Accountability Software, which is in limited use, currently requires data entry by hand at the unit level. The Defense Manpower Data Center can currently query records in the DMSS. There is no capability to resolve location within a 24-hour period, as only one 24-hour entry is currently used (Personal communication, Col. K. Cox and C. Postlewaite, Department of Defense, November 1, 2006).

The need to link exposure data with health outcomes is appreciated, but this capability is currently not fully developed. The current situation is driving efforts to construct environmental monitoring summaries for various theaters and locales, and to assign surveillance exposure data to individual health records.

DOD EXPOSURE ASSESSMENT

Overview

Occupational and environmental exposures occur throughout the span of a Service member's service career. In summarizing the exposure assessments needed to cover that experience, we can use the same milestones as were used to describe health assessments. They begin with exposure opportunities in the first months of service immediately following service entry and also proceed in a longitudinal manner through routine garrison experiences through multiple deployments and on through separation or retirement (see Figure 10-1).

Exposure Assessments Throughout the Span of Service

Exposure assessment elements collected for each milestone of the Service member's span of service are summarized in Table 10-1 and may include qualitative exposure judgments, occupational exposure monitoring, and environmental monitoring results. As in the case of health assessments, the degree of detail and areas of emphasis vary based on the specific point in the span of service or a specialized reason for the assessment. Data are collected in a combination of written and electronic formats, but there is significant activity moving DoD toward fully integrated electronic records.

Exposure assessments are made so that appropriate exposure controls can be planned and implemented. In the case of routine operations or low-risk combat scenarios the implementation of these controls is straightforward. Under high-risk combat scenarios, however, it may be difficult or impossible to consistently implement controls for environmental agents as the risks posed by implementing those controls under severe combat conditions may be higher than those posed by the exposures. In each case, however, there is a need to characterize and document exposures to agents from occupational and environmental sources.

Nondeployment Military Bases

The individual services within DoD have had traditional industrial hygiene and environmental health programs in place for many years in military base or installation settings. These programs conduct occupational and environmental exposure risk assessments for routine and nonroutine operations and document results in a variety of service-specific paper and electronic data repositories.

Predeployment

In support of deployment occupational environmental health and safety (OEHS) measures for information/intelligence preparation of the environment, a phase I deployment OEHS assessment is produced for military location(s) of interest that assesses known and/or potential deployment OEH hazards and threats ranging from industrial chemicals, historical contamination, radiation, infectious disease, entomological risks, weapons of mass destruction, and specified intelligence based threats. These assessments are quantitative and also identify any preventive medicine measures and counter-measures and deployment OEH surveillance activities to ensure force health protection measures for deployments. For deployments less than 30 days, some of these activities are performed at the discretion of the operational commander as it is recognized that for special operations and very short deployments they may not all be feasible (DoD, 2006c).

Deployment

OEHS site assessments, exposure assessments, environmental monitoring, exposure incident response (and reports), and daily individual troop locations as determined by global positioning system (GPS) or other means are performed during deployment (see Figure 10-2) (DoD, 2006c). The content and detail included in these assessments vary depending on the length of deployment, the location of deployment, the intensity of combat operations, the number of deployed personnel, and the training of deployed personnel (DoDI 6490.03 2006 [DoD, 2006c]).

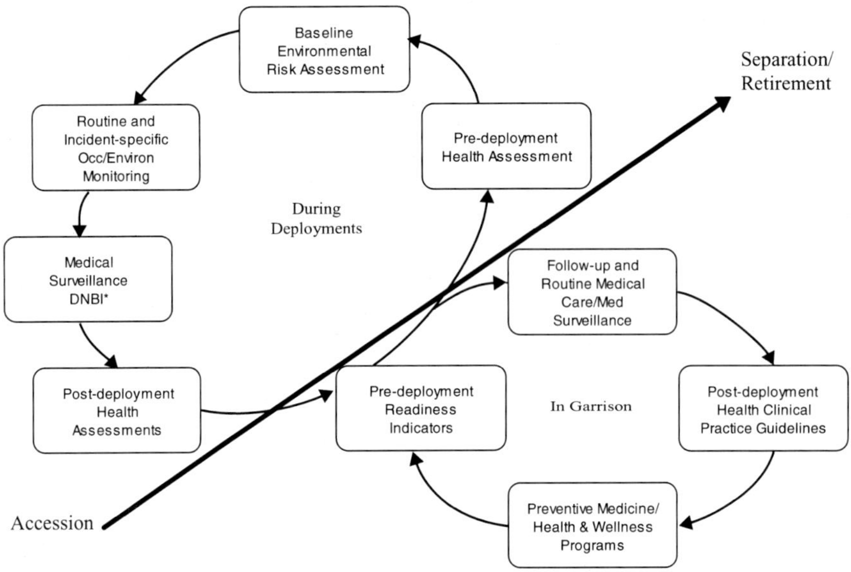

FIGURE 10-2 DoD's deployment health surveillance elements.
*DNBI (disease and nonbattle injury).
SOURCE: Adapted from Postlewaite, 2006.

Postdeployment

Postdeployment assessment activities primarily involve data and report cleanup and submission for central documentation—including documentation of health and exposure data and incidents in individual health records.

EXPOSURE DATABASES

Service Specific

The Army and Navy maintain collected exposure data at their respective occupational health and preventive medicine headquarters, the U.S. Army Center for Health Promotion and Preventive Medicine and the Navy Environmental Health Center respectively. The Air Force retains its data at each individual Air Force base (Table 10-2). Although the Army and Navy have a central headquarters database maintenance system, they also have individual activity databases for exposure data. These individual activity databases are rolled into the headquarters system but are also maintained at

TABLE 10-2 Service-Specific Databases for Exposure

Service	Database	Data Maintenance	Health Hazard Inventory Database	Quantitative Exposure Data	Deployment Exposure Data	In-Garrison Data
Army	HHIM	CHPPM	HHIM	Yes	No	Yes
Army	DESS	USACHPPM	DESS	Yes	Yes	No
Navy	IHIMS	NEHC	NOED	Yes	Yes	Yes
Air Force	CCS	AF Bases	AF-EMIS/ HMMS	Yes	No*	Yes

NOTE: Table conveys the service-specific databases available and where the data are stored.
ABBREVIATIONS: AF-EMIS = Air Force Environmental Management Information System; CCS = Command Core System; CHPPM = U.S. Army Center for Health Promotion and Preventive Medicine; DESS = Deployment Environmental Surveillance System; HHIM = Health Hazard Information Module; HMMS = Hazardous Material Management System; IHIMS = Industrial Hygiene Information Management System; NEHC = Navy Environmental Health Center; NOED = Navy Occupational Exposure Database.
*Some deployment exposure data are currently stored in the Air Force's Global Expeditionary Medical System (GEMS).
SOURCE: Adapted from DoD, 2006a.

the respective individual activities. All data will eventually be consolidated into the DOEHRS program, but individual activity data are also retained at the respective individual sites. Services have indicated that they will retain some of their legacy systems after inclusion of data into DOEHRS. Industrial hygiene exposure data consolidation into DOEHRS is expected to be completed by 2010 with all exposure data entry completed by 2013.

DOEHRS—DEFENSE OCCUPATIONAL AND ENVIRONMENTAL HEALTH READINESS SYSTEM

Overview

DOEHRS is an automated information system designed to replace existing service-specific database collection and storage systems. It supports reduction in redundant data entry between worksites and occupational health clinics. DOEHRS also eliminates redundant exposure data collection through interfaces with clinical, environmental, safety, and personnel automated information systems. The DOEHRS structure is outlined in Figure 10-3.

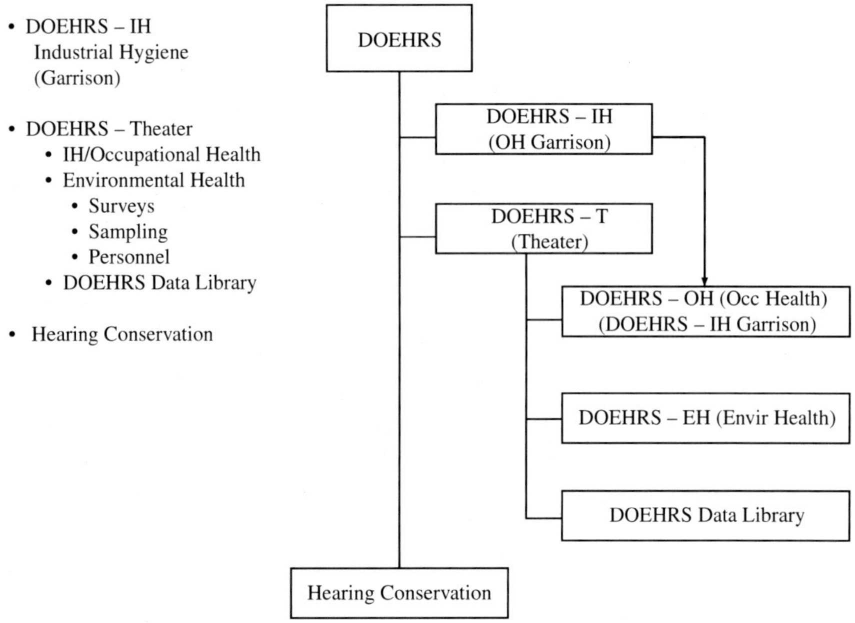

FIGURE 10-3 National Defense Occupational and Environmental Health Readiness System (DOEHRS).
SOURCE: Adapted from Heller, 2006.

According to the DOEHRS student guide,

> The Industrial Hygiene module of DOEHRS, DOEHRS [sic] is a key enabling technology within the presidentially mandated FHP and is further supported by Public Law 105-85. DOEHRS is a comprehensive, automated information system for assembling, comparing, using, evaluating, and storing occupational personnel exposure information, workplace environmental monitoring data, personal protective equipment usage data, observation of work practices data, and employee health hazard educational data. DOEHRS provides information needed by occupational health staff and command surgeons for reporting options to commanders regarding the reduction of health threats. (DoD, 2006b, ch. 1, p. 2)
>
> DOEHRS supports the prevention of illness and injury in DoD military members and civilian employees from exposure to chemical, biological, or physical hazards. Exposures can occur throughout the continuum of military operations, such as industrial maintenance facilities, administrative offices, hospitals, aboard ship, while operating weapon systems in training

> exercises, and while deployed in war fighting or other military operations. DOEHRS prevents illness by identifying potential health hazards; providing and documenting exposures and provides recommendations to commanders, supervisors, and personnel to minimize adverse health effects; and monitoring effectiveness of procedures followed. Interface with other DOEHRS occupational health programs provides medical surveillance for early identification of exposure, treatment, rehabilitation, and follow-up to ensure that no repeated illnesses occur. (DoD, 2006b, ch. 1, p. 3)
>
> DOEHRS maintains longitudinal exposure records for individual workers in DoD. Longitudinal exposure records contain a history of predeployment, deployment, and postdeployment exposure. These records provide a baseline to facilitate postdeployment follow-up. (DoD, 2006b, ch. 1, p. 2)
>
> DOEHRS is scheduled to interface with each service's hazardous material tracking system and laboratory information management systems. DOEHRS is the occupational medicine answer for DoD's medical records system (AHLTA). . . . DOEHRS will be deployed on a Defense Information Systems Agency (DISA) platform in the DISA Defense Enterprise Computing Center Detachment in San Antonio, Texas to support the Army, Navy, Coast Guard, and other agencies. (DoD, 2006b, ch. 1, p. 3)

Initial implementation of this system includes the DOEHRS industrial hygiene module, which supports the DoD industrial hygiene exposure assessment model based on the American Industrial Hygiene Association's "Strategy for Assessing and Managing Occupational Exposures," a state-of-the-art approach developed through consensus of government, industry, and academic industrial hygienists (DoD, 2006b). The approach is applicable to assessing and managing occupational and environmental exposures associated with routine and nonroutine operations that may be encountered in-garrison and during deployment. Core to the approach is the appropriate grouping of individuals into similar exposure groups and the characterization, assessment, and control of exposures common to individuals in those groups (DoD, 2006b).

DOEHRS Implementation and Continuous Improvement

DODI 6490.3 (DoD, 1997, p. 9) set the original intent to integrate exposure records with medical records. DODI 6490.03 (DoD, 2006c, p. 28) directed that exposure data records will be integrated into individual medical records and commits DoD to accomplish the integration. DoD personnel acknowledge that this integration will be a continuous improvement effort as functionalities of DOEHRS are developed (Personal communication, C. Postlewaite et al., Department of Defense, November 21, 2006).

The current version of DOEHRS, version 1.0.5.0, includes the first iterations of the industrial hygiene and theater-focused environmental health sample management capabilities. Many additional requirements were addressed in the DoD planning and programming budget for fiscal year (FY) 2013 (POM 2008-2013).

Because DOEHRS is a platform information system for all services, DODI 6490.03 specified how integration would occur and provided standardized definitions and exclusions for compliance. Recording exposures occurring during deployment is a crucial part of the database with *deployment* defined here as "[t]he relocation of forces and materiel to desired operational areas. Deployment encompasses all activities from origin or home station through destination, specifically including intracontinental United States, intertheater, and intratheater movement legs, staging, and holding areas" (DoD, 2006c, p. 2). This definition allows for home station (in-garrison) delineation of exposure data distinct from deployment data. The use of the term *deployment* for the Navy has different connotations and consequently this instruction addresses that issue: "[s]hipboard operations that are not anticipated to involve operations ashore are exempt from the requirements of this instruction *except* for recording individual daily deployment locations or when potential health threats indicate actions necessary beyond the scope of shipboard occupational health programs or per the decision of the commander exercising operational control" (DoD, 2006c, p. 2).

DOEHRS Current Functionality

DOEHRS is being implemented step-by-step, phasing in each of its functional elements. The hearing conservation portion of DOEHRS has been functional since 1997, as directed by the DoD Instruction 6490.3. (DoD, 1997). Some industrial hygiene exposure data have been collected and entered into the system through the DoD Industrial Hygiene Exposure Assessment Model released in January 2000 (DoD Industrial Hygiene Working Group, 2000). The Navy and Air Force plan to fully implement the industrial hygiene (in-garrison) function by the end of FY 2008. This implementation includes the downloading of currently stored exposure data as applicable. The use of the DOEHRS industrial hygiene functionality for currently collected exposure data will be deployed to all Army installations by March 2007. While deployment data are currently being collected and archived, the deployment exposure data function has not been fully developed or implemented. The Army serves as the DoD lead for deployment occupational and environmental health surveillance data archives (DODI 6490.03, 2006; CJCS Memorandum MCM-0006-02, 2002, under revision). This deployment data with DOEHRS is expected to be fully completed and online in FY 2010 (POM 2008-2013).

As set out in the DoD POM 2008-2013 for DOEHRS, all anticipated requirements and functionalities for the project have been addressed. Funding support is anticipated on a fiscal year basis with new functionalities being developed and implemented on the same fiscal year basis. If fully funded as anticipated, all DOEHRS functionalities will be completed and online by the end of FY 2013. As presented by DoD representatives (Postlewaite, 2006; Personal communication, C. Postlewaite et al., Department of Defense, and reiterated during the teleconference on November 21, 2006), DOEHRS has full funding support by DoD, and DoD is fully committed to DOEHRS full implementation and triservice functioning by the end of FY 2013.

DOEHRS Effectiveness

As proposed and defined, DOEHRS will be a highly effective system for coordinating collected exposure data from both home station (in-garrison) and deployment locales. Combining the Service member's medical records with the consolidated environmental monitoring and personal exposure data in DOEHRS is key to enabling VA to provide necessary health care to these future veterans. A major problem encountered in the current VA health-care provision system is a lack of exposure data. The DOEHRS program has the potential to alleviate this lack of data. However, the data must be provided to VA to be of any use. Currently, there is no avenue to transfer these data from DoD to VA. This avenue of data transference must be developed and supported by both DoD and VA for DOEHRS to fully benefit the veteran. An agency-to-agency coordinating board between DoD and VA would be a starting point. VA is at a distinct disadvantage if it must consistently request the data from DoD.

One barrier to implementation of this system of shared exposure data is the concern that sharing some of these data may compromise the secrecy of troop locations or other combat-specific or national security issues. Although DoD classification for security purposes must be considered, there remains a need to work through this challenge for the benefit of the veteran. Although secrecy is a necessary requirement for the protection of Service members during conflict, a rapid declassification of the collected exposure data is also necessary to provide health care to Service members when needed. Furthermore, if exposure studies are conducted involving secrecy classification, VA must make their health-care providers aware of the possible adverse health effects so that presenting veterans can be properly treated.

DOEHRS, as envisioned, is a project that can greatly benefit DoD and VA when used effectively and competently by both agencies. Full funding to complete development and implementation of DOEHRS is necessary to provide and deliver to VA the exposure data needed for the provision of health care for our nation's veterans.

USE OF HEALTH AND EXPOSURE DATA BY VA

Veteran Care and Disability Support

Overview

The Veterans Health Administration (VHA) is the largest of the three operational administrations of VA and comprises more than 200,000 employees who provide medical, surgical, and rehabilitative care via a system of over 150 hospitals and 1,000 outpatient clinics nationwide. Close to 8 million veterans were enrolled in the VA hospital system in 2005; of those, more than 5.3 million sought and received care (VA, 2006a, pp. 2, 3, 6).

The vast majority of care provided by VHA is through its network of outpatient clinics, which registered more than 57 million visits in 2005. Close to 600,000 inpatients were also treated in hospitals (VA, 2006a, p. 2).

Eligibility

Eligibility for VHA care has been codified into an elaborate hierarchy of eight levels with the first level being the highest priority for care. In this level are veterans with service-connected disabilities rated 50 percent or more or veterans determined by VA to be unemployable due to service-connected conditions (VA, 2007a, p. 2). Lower priority levels of eligibility for VHA care are a function of degree of service-connected disability and income. Importantly, by FY 2005, it was estimated that close to 80 percent of all disabled and low-income veterans had enrolled with VHA for care, and 65 percent sought care and were treated (VA, 2006a, pp. 2-3).

It is also important to note that while incurring a disability during military service is one pathway to eligibility for VA care, the care provided is not limited to that required for the qualifying disability, but rather, that needed for the total care the veteran requires. Following entry into the VA health-care system, a veteran may request an appointment with a primary care physician who can conduct a comprehensive assessment of the veteran's health-care needs.. For veterans in the first level of eligibility, the wait time for this initial appointment is supposed to be less than 30 days (VA, 2007d).

Military Service and Special Eligibility for VA Health Care

On the application form for health benefits required for entry into the VA health-care system, veterans record their service branch, dates of service, and type of discharge. Veterans are also queried about history of injury (Purple Heart awarded), presence of a service-connected disability, percentage of impairment, and a host of questions on specialized exposure opportunities including Agent Orange, radiation, and presence of illness from Gulf War service or spinal cord injury (VA, 2005b).

Seamless Transition

There has been an increased effort on the part of VA to publicize to Service members who are preparing for discharge their eligibility for VA benefits and health care (VA, 2007b). This is true for both those who have not incurred a service-related disability and those who have. A network of field-based VA employees has been sent to the larger military transfer facilities to act as onsite liaisons and offer counseling on benefit eligibility to Service members. Currently, under the seamless transition effort, VA has employees staffed at Landstuhl, Germany, and major military transfer facilities, such as Walter Reed and Eisenhower medical centers. These VA employees assist with disability claims and Service members' transfer to enrollment in the VA system. The VA Secretary also notifies every new veteran by mail of his or her potential eligibility. There is also an attempt, again in the field, when large groups of Service members are separating, to have onsite VA counselors on hand to help with the transition. However, the "seamless transition" appears to be more about communicating eligibility for care and benefits than about the transfer of medical and exposure records. With the exception of Service members who are being discharged from a military transfer facility to a local VA facility with significant residuals of traumatic injuries, the likelihood that a Service member's medical record, much less an exposure record (if one existed), seamlessly passes from DoD to the VA health-care system is remote at best.

Seamless Transfer of DoD Data to VA

The medical records system of the DoD (AHLTA) does not interface easily with VA's (VISTA) systems. Some transfer to VA of both physical and electronic records takes place, but this is generally on a case-by-case basis.

The reports from medical evaluation boards dealing with a Service member's health conditions that render him or her unfit for regular duty or requiring restricted duty (e.g., asthma, insulin-dependent diabetes) are currently relatively crude, impairing their usefulness for decision making regarding service connectedness for VA care. This directly affects the ability of VA to determine care and benefit eligibility assessments and disability evaluations. A postdeployment electronic form—the Health Assessment Form—is under development and uses the Federal Health Information Exchange to transfer information in one direction, between DoD and VA. The plan is to use the Federal Health Information Exchange (FHIE) to allow two-way data transfer (Do, 2006), though currently it provides only for unidirectional flow of information from DoD to VA. The plan is for the FHIE to evolve into the Clinical Health Data Repository (CHDR).

EPIDEMIOLOGIC STUDIES OF VETERANS

Introduction

Epidemiologic studies on the adverse health effects of military service in veterans have covered exposures that have occurred in essentially every war in which U.S. Service members have been deployed, beginning with World War I. Although the largest group of these studies has been carried out in some fashion through VA, some have been supported through the National Institutes of Health (NIH), the Centers for Disease Control and Prevention (CDC), and other funding organizations. In this section, we review the breadth of these studies with a view to understanding the sources of data and the sources of funding. In this way, it is hoped that insights can be gained that might recommend preferred, or even alternative, approaches to carrying out epidemiologic studies on the health of veterans to inform the compensation and disability decision-making process. It is not the primary purpose of this chapter to review these studies with a view to assessing the validity of their findings.

VA has carried out and been involved in many epidemiologic studies addressing the health of veterans. Here we provide an overview of studies that specifically deal with veterans' health in relation to actual or suspected exposures that occurred while they were serving in the U.S. military.

Department of Veterans Affairs Epidemiologic Studies

Veterans Health Administration (VHA) Studies

The VHA funds research studies through its Office of Research and Development. A broad range of health-related studies is supported, including clinical, basic science, and epidemiologic studies. Epidemiologic studies include those on the effects of wartime exposures on veterans' health, including studies on recently returning Service members. For example, in

2005 the Office of Research and Development announced an invitation for research proposals on combat casualty neurotrauma (VA, 2005a), and in 2006 it announced an invitation for research proposals on health studies of veterans returning from Afghanistan and Iraq (VA, 2006b). Other research surveillance activities sponsored by VA include the establishment of several registries. In 2003, the Office of Research and Development created a national registry of veterans with amyotrophic lateral sclerosis to track the health status of veterans with the disease and help recruit research participants (VA, 2003). Strategic planning for VHA-funded research is carried out by the Field Research Advisory Committee.

Two centers for the study of war-related illnesses were established in VA medical centers in 2001, one in Washington, D.C., and one in East Orange, New Jersey. Initially known as the Centers for the Study of War-Related Illnesses, these were subsequently renamed the War-Related Illness and Injury Study Centers (WRIISC). Both have clinical and research responsibilities (VA, 2006c).

The largest and undoubtedly the most substantial body of research on health effects of returned veterans has been carried out by Dr. Han K. Kang and his colleagues at the Environmental Epidemiology Service at the VHA in Washington, D.C., which is now part of the Washington, D.C., WRIISC. Dr. Kang has carried out studies of veterans in the following broad areas: mustard gas exposure, prisoners of war, radiation exposure, Vietnam veterans, Gulf War veterans, and women veterans. A bibliography of Dr. Kang's epidemiologic studies is included in Appendix K-1, organized by these subject areas.

Twin Registry Studies

In 1958, the Medical Follow-Up Agency, with funding by NIH and VA, began a project to identify white male twin pairs who had been in military service during World War II (The National Academy of Sciences [NAS]/National Research Council [NRC] Twin Registry of WWII Military Veteran Twins [SOURCE: http://www.iom.edu/CMS/3795/4907.aspx]). Using state birth records, searches were made by hand against VA files to determine veteran status. Eventually, nearly 16,000 twin pairs were identified. Baseline data were abstracted from VA and military records and a baseline questionnaire was mailed to the twin pairs. Anthropometric and fingerprint data were used to determine zygosity (IOM, 2004b).

A bibliography of research studies based on this NAS/NRC twin registry can be found at http://www.iom.edu/CMS/3795/4907/17038.aspx. A total of 308 published research studies and 7 research reports are based on this registry.

The Vietnam Era Twin (VET) Registry The VET registry was created by VA in the mid-1980s in response to concerns regarding the health effects specifically of exposure to Agent Orange (Goldberg et al., 2002). The registry was built using DoD computerized records and consists of 7,369 male-male twin pairs born between 1939 and 1957, who served from 1965 to 1975 (VA, 2007e). It is now housed in the Seattle Epidemiological Research and Information Center, a joint venture of the Department of Epidemiology at the University of Washington's School of Public Health and Community Medicine and VA (VA, 2007c). Approximately half of the twins are monozygotic, and half are dizygotic (Henderson et al., 1990). Table 10-3 details the research studies that have been completed using the VET registry, or are currently underway.

National Academies' Monographs on Veterans' Health by Theater or Exposure

The National Academies has produced a large number of monographs on veterans' health dealing with exposures during military service dating back to WWI (Table 10-4). These provide useful summaries, assessments, and updates of scientific findings based on studies completed before the publication of each monograph. It is evident that the more recent the exposure, the larger the number of monographs devoted to it.

Non-VA Epidemiologic Studies of Veterans' Health

The Millennium Cohort Study

The Millennium Cohort Study is the largest prospective study of military personnel ever conducted. Sponsored by DoD, and recommended by the IOM Committee on Measuring the Health of Gulf War Veterans (IOM, 1999a, p. 6), the study was initiated in 2001 to evaluate the long-term health effects of military service, particularly operational deployment. More than 110,000 people are enrolled currently, and a total of 140,000 are expected to be enrolled by the end of study recruitment in 2007. Study participants will complete a paper or Web-based questionnaire assessing demographics, medical conditions and symptoms, and health-related behaviors once every 3 years until 2022. Survey data will be linked with data from other military databases on deployment, occupation, vaccinations, health-care utilization, and disability. It is hoped that the cohort data will serve as a foundation upon which additional epidemiologic studies of military personnel might develop, in addition to revealing trends in veterans' health over time (Gray et al., 2002; The Millennium Cohort Study, 2007).

TABLE 10-3 Summary of VET Registry Projects

Study Name	Method of Recruitment	Recruitment Period	Number of Participants	Twin Pairs
Registry construction				
Military Records	Record abstracts	1983-1986	14,750	7,375
Studies of the full registry				
Survey of Health	Mail/telephone follow-up	1987	10,979	4,774
NHLBI VET Study of Cardiovascular Disease	Mail/telephone follow-up	1990	8,169	3,698
Harvard Twin Study of Drug Abuse and Dependence	Telephone	1991-1993	10,979	3,698
Male Health Survey	Mail	1999	5,349	1,615
Studies of selected twins				
Impulsivity and aggression	Mail/telephone follow-up	1992	796	314
Consequences of drug abuse	In-person	1995-1996	254	127
Alcohol and health services use	Telephone	1995	2,936	
Biologic markers for	In-person	1995-1998	322	161
posttraumatic stress disorder (PTSD)	Telephone	1995-1996	2,003	322
Alcohol vulnerability	In-person	1997-1999	760	380
PTSD Sleep study	In-person	Ongoing	11/22	9
	Telephone		207/248	248
Twin-family study of health behaviors	Telephone and mail	Ongoing	533	214
PTSD MRI study 1	In-person	Ongoing	48	45
PTSD MRI study 2	In-person	Ongoing	52	
New studies of selected twins pathological gambling				
Spirituality and PTSD	Mail	Newly funded 2006	510	255
Cardiovascular disease and depression	Mail	Newly funded 2006	320	160
Twins as parents	Telephone and mail	Newly funded 2006	1,060	530

SOURCE: Adapted from VA, 2007c.

TABLE 10-4 National Academies' and VA Medical Monographs on Veterans' Health by Theater or Exposure

Mustard gas exposure	IOM. 1993. *Veterans at risk: The health effects of mustard gas and lewisite.*
Prisoners of war	VA Medical Monographs. 1954. *A follow-up study of World War II prisoners of war* (Cohen and Cooper, 1954). IOM. 1992. *The health of former prisoners of war: Results from the Medical Examination Survey of Former POWs of World War II and the Korean Conflict.*
Other WWII	VA Medical Monographs. 1955. *Tuberculosis in the Army of the United States in World War II.* (Long and Jablon, 1955). VA Medical Monographs. 1961. *A follow-up study of head wounds in World War II* (Walker and Jablon, 1961).
Radiation exposure	NRC. 1985. *Studies of participants in nuclear tests* (Robinette et al., 1985). IOM. 1995a. *Adverse reproductive outcomes in families of atomic veterans: The feasibility of epidemiologic studies.* IOM. 1996b. *Mortality of veteran participants in the CROSSROADS nuclear test.*
Vietnam veterans	IOM. 1994. *Veterans and Agent Orange: Health effects of herbicides used in Vietnam.* IOM. 1996b. *Mortality of veteran participants in the CROSSROADS nuclear test.* IOM. 1997. *Characterizing exposure of veterans to Agent Orange and other herbicides used in Vietnam: Scientific considerations regarding a request for proposals for research.* IOM. 1999c. *Veterans and Agent Orange: Update 1998.* IOM. 2000d. *Veterans and Agent Orange: Herbicide/dioxin exposure and type 2 diabetes.* IOM. 2001b. *Veterans and Agent Orange: Update 2000.* IOM. 2002. *Veterans and Agent Orange: Herbicide/dioxin exposure and acute myelogenous leukemia in the children of Vietnam veterans.* IOM. 2003a. *Characterizing exposure of veterans to Agent Orange and other herbicides used in Vietnam: Interim findings and recommendations.* IOM. 2003b. *Characterizing exposure of veterans to Agent Orange and other herbicides used in Vietnam: Final report.* IOM. 2003d. *Veterans and Agent Orange: Update 2002.* IOM. 2004c. *Veterans and Agent Orange: Length of presumptive period for association between exposure and respiratory cancer.* IOM. 2005b. *Veterans and Agent Orange: Update 2004.*

TABLE 10-4 Continued

Gulf War veterans	IOM. 1995b. *Health consequences of service during the Persian Gulf War: Initial findings and recommendations for immediate action.* IOM. 1996a. *Health consequences of service during the Persian Gulf War: Recommendations for research and information systems.* IOM. 1998a. *Adequacy of the VA Persian Gulf Registry and Uniform Case Assessment Protocol.* IOM. 1998b. *Measuring the health of Persian Gulf veterans: Workshop summary.* IOM. 1999a. *Gulf War veterans: Measuring health.* IOM. 2000a. *The five series study: Mortality of military participants in U.S. nuclear weapons tests.* IOM. 2000b. *Gulf War and health, volume 1: Depleted uranium, pyridostigmine bromide, sarin, vaccines.* IOM. 2001a. *Gulf War veterans: Treating symptoms and syndromes.* IOM. 2003c. *Gulf War and health, volume 2: Insecticide and solvents.* IOM. 2004a. *Gulf War and health: Updated literature review of sarin.* IOM. 2005a. *Gulf War and health, volume 3: Fuels, combustion products, and propellants.* IOM. 2006. *Gulf War and health, volume 4: Health effects of serving in the Gulf War.* IOM. 2007. *Gulf War and health, volume 5: Infectious diseases.*

CDC-Funded Studies

The CDC and its National Center for Environmental Health has supported studies on veterans of Vietnam (SOURCE: http://www.cdc.gov/nceh/veterans/default1.htm) and the Gulf War (SOURCE: http://www.cdc.gov/nceh/veterans/default2.htm). Relating to Vietnam, CDC supported the following studies:

- Vietnam Experience Study
- Postservice Mortality Among Vietnam Veterans Study
- Agent Orange Validation Study
- Selected Cancers Study

On the Gulf War, CDC funded the following studies:

- Health Effects of Exposure to Smoke from Oil Well Fires
- Birth Defects
- Air Force Study
- Health Assessment of Gulf War Veterans from Iowa
- Iowa Asthma Follow-Up Study
- Cognitive Function and Symptom Patterns in Gulf War Veterans

- Defining Gulf War Illness
- Epidemiologic Study of the Occurrence of Amyotrophic Lateral Sclerosis (ALS) among Gulf War Veterans
- Deployment to the Gulf War and Subsequent Development of Cancer

Of these CDC-funded studies, the Vietnam Experience Study was arguably the most influential. A random sample of 7,924 men who enlisted in the period from 1965 to 1971 and who served in Vietnam, and 7,364 non-Vietnam veterans, were interviewed by telephone. Vietnam veterans reported more health problems than non-Vietnam veterans, including less fertility and more health problems in their children. An in-person, comprehensive health evaluation was done on a random subsample of 2,490 Vietnam veterans and 1,972 non-Vietnam veterans. Although the vast majority of comparisons showed no differences, results of this examination showed more hearing loss, lower sperm concentrations, and more depression, anxiety, and PTSD in Vietnam veterans. Offspring of Vietnam veterans did not show increased birth defects (see Appendix K-3) (CDC VES, 1989).

NIH-Funded, Individual Investigator Studies

The NIH has funded a large number of health studies involving veterans through its several research funding mechanisms, and has also collaborated with VHA and CDC in providing funding for research on veterans. Relatively few NIH studies focus on investigating the role of military exposures in disease. Many use a population sample of veterans to gain mechanistic insight into diseases affecting the general population. Others evaluate effectiveness of disease treatment. NIH-funded studies that are relevant to the assessment of military exposure effects are listed in Appendix K-4 by title and year funding was begun.

Observations and Recommendations on Epidemiologic Studies of Veterans

Clearly a large number of epidemiologic studies on health effects of military exposure in veterans have been completed over the years. Many continue to be performed, reflecting the ongoing military engagements in Iraq and Afghanistan. There has been a near-exponential increase in the number of completed health studies and IOM reports in relation to the proximity in time of the specific engagement.

Although the scientific information on military exposures and subsequent health status is extensive, some exposures of concern remain inadequately studied or the relevant studies on these exposures have yielded findings that are inconclusive. It is acknowledged that there may be obstacles to performing rigorous observational studies on the veteran population. Nevertheless, there are at least three other potential reasons for some of the inadequacy in the scientific information: (1) there has been no effective organized approach to setting research priorities; (2) exposure information and exposure metrics are relatively crude for most exposure-disease combinations of interest; and (3) there is no standardized, comprehensive, universal, and accessible source of information on veteran's health outcomes.

Two complementary options for improving the utility of this health research in strengthening the scientific foundations for veterans' compensation are (1) establishing a body that is responsible for strategically managing the research agenda on veterans and military exposures, and (2) developing and maintaining a repository of research on veterans' health to allow an overview of research supported by various funding agencies. Suggestions to facilitate carrying out these studies and to allow more rigorous study of exposure health effects center on exploiting the exposure and health information systems described above. This would require more centralized data storage and improved data access.

VA REGISTRIES

Another public health surveillance tool that can be used to collect and organize health status data of a specific population is a registry. "A registry is an organized system for the collection, storage, retrieval, analysis, and dissemination of information on individual persons who have either a particular disease, a condition (e.g., a risk factor) that predisposes to the occurrence of a health-related event, or prior exposure to substances (or circumstances) known or suspected to cause adverse health effects" (SOURCE: From FAQ on Public Health Registries: www.ncvhs.hhs.gov/9701138b.htm).

Registry data offer a number of valuable uses in public health and medicine, "including estimating the magnitude of a problem," "determining the incidence of disease," "examining trends of disease over time," "identifying groups at high-risk," estimating health service needs, and "conducting research" (SOURCE: www.ncvhs.hhs.gov/9701138b.htm). For some groups of veterans, surveillance could be extended to intermediate markers, such as indicators of physiological functioning, so that adverse effects of exposures could be detected before the level of impairment became sufficient to produce a diagnosed disease. For example, in personnel exposed to respiratory hazards, lung function could be tracked over time to detect a rate of loss beyond that expected on the basis of aging alone.

Registries collect data on individuals who share certain characteristics, typically a specific disease or condition. This information includes demographic and medical information. Registries often seek validation of the data by collecting detailed test results (such as a pathology report from a biopsy or a specific blood test result).

More recently, the registry concept has been applied to follow groups of people who do not share a common disease, but rather, a common exposure history. Examples here would include the National Exposure Registry operated by the Agency for Toxic Substances and Disease Registry (ATSDR), part of CDC. This registry identifies and enrolls persons likely to have been exposed to hazardous environmental toxicants, usually due to the location of the person's residence near a contaminated Superfund site. The registry establishes a pool of persons, potentially at increased risk of health harm, and allows tracking of this group. This tracking enables subsequent contact of the registered persons by health authorities, who may offer health information, opportunities for study participation, or care recommendations. The course of the registrant's health may also be followed over time through periodic surveys performed by the registry (ATSDR, 2003).

VA has used the public health registry concept to identify and track several different groups of veterans. It operates registries that are both disease based, such as the multiple sclerosis (MS) and amyotrophic lateral sclerosis (ALS) registries, and those that are exposure based, such as the Agent Orange and Gulf War registries (see Table 10-5).

Summary of Important Findings and Recommendations

DoD and VA are clearly intent on improving the breadth, depth, and availability of health and exposure data. In addition, there are numerous examples of those data being used to better understand Service member and veteran health and its relationship to exposures. Suggestions follow for ensuring that the data improvements are fully realized and the data fully utilized in Service member–veteran disease prevention and treatment in well-conceived and coordinated surveillance and research efforts and in compensation adjudication and presumptive decision-making. Many of these recommendations are also found in the Committee's overall recommendations in Chapter 13. The Committee presents these suggestions here to tie back into the specific lessons learned from an assessment of the military personnel's and veterans' health and exposure data infrastructure.

1. Ensure that DOEHRS is implemented as planned.

DOEHRS is a major undertaking that has potential for dramatically increasing the availability of exposure data. However, DoD has many important priorities and short-term funding pressures have the potential to delay implementation activities. Due to the importance of these efforts for both DoD and VA, we recommend that additional steps be taken to ensure that DOEHRS is fully implemented as planned. In addition, due to the importance of adequately trained individuals to the success of DOEHRS, we further recommend that these steps specifically include detail on the training of individuals needed to make the accurate professional judgments and generate appropriate exposure data critical to DOEHRS. These additional steps are as follows:

1. Include a specific DoD budget line item for DOEHRS that includes funding for system development and enhancement, system implementation, and training of personnel.
2. Develop clear metrics for tracking the effective deployment and utilization of DOEHRS throughout DoD.
3. Require an annual status report to Congress on DOEHRS development and implementation progress and related training activities.

2. Improve the interface between the electronic health record data systems used by DoD and VA—including capabilities for handling individual exposure information that is included as part of a Service member's health record.

While there are efforts underway to electronically transfer Service member health records from DoD to VA, these efforts are moving slowly and the timeline for completion of a seamless interface is unclear. DoD and VA should increase attention to this effort with a clear integration plan, timetable for implementation, metrics for tracking implementation progress, and annual reporting of metric results.

To date, there has been little discussion regarding the electronic transfer of Service member exposure information to VA. As the inclusion of exposure data in employee health records is a key DoD strategy for ensuring that exposure information is available for individual Service members, this seems a major disconnect. DoD and VA should explicitly include the integration of these individual exposure data into the health record transfer integration plan, implementation timetable, metrics, and annual reporting. Reports on progress of these plans should be included in the annual report to Congress on DOEHRS progress.

3. Develop an interface that allows the VA to access the electronic exposure data systems used by DoD.

DoD is investing heavily in DOEHRS and other improved exposure data systems that are standardized across the various armed services. In our interviews with people responsible for development and deployment of these systems we did not encounter anyone with knowledge of activities by DoD or VA to develop a VA interface with these systems that will allow use of the Service member-specific and longitudinal exposure data by VA.

TABLE 10-5 VA Health Registries

Registry Management Purpose	Number of Veterans	Basis for Enrollment	Source of Data	Type of Data
Agent Orange Registry[a] (Started in 1978) Managed by the Environmental Agents Service To identify medical problems associated with Agent Orange exposure	408,811 400,849 men 7,962 women	Service in Vietnam, Korea, or otherwise exposed	Dates, areas of service, possible Agent Orange exposure, birth defect data	Purely voluntary; data from Agent Orange Registry exams; veterans are well informed of the existence of registry exams

Data Collected	Selected Publications from Registry
Demographics: Race/ethnicity; martial status; gender; current military status; branch of service; service in either/or Vietnam or Korea; dates of last two periods of service if other than Vietnam or Korea; full medical history, including information about the family, occupation, social history noting tobacco, alcohol, and drug use; civilian exposure to possible toxic agents; psychosocial history Medical history: Assessment of own health; date of registry examination; complaints/symptoms (coders are asked to enter ICD-9 codes on form); chest X ray (if determined to be medically necessary); complete blood count; comprehensive metabolic panel or blood chemistries and enzyme studies; urinalysis; hepatitis C screening Exposure: Exposure to Agent Orange (definitely yes, not sure, definitely no); handling or spraying Agent Orange; not directly sprayed but in a recently sprayed area; exposed to herbicides other than Agent Orange; directly sprayed with Agent Orange; ate food/drink that could have been sprayed with Agent Orange	Bullman TA, Kang HK. 1994. Posttraumatic stress disorder and the risk of traumatic deaths among Vietnam veterans. Journal of Nervous and Mental Disorder 182:604-610. Bullman TA, Watanabe KK, Kang HK. 1994. Risk of testicular cancer associated with surrogate measures of Agent Orange exposure among Vietnam veterans on the Agent Orange Registry. Annals of Epidemiology 4:11-16. Bullman TA, Kang HK, Thomas TL. 1991. Posttraumatic stress disorder among Vietnam veterans on the Agent Orange Registry: A case control analysis. Annals of Epidemiology 1:505-512.

continued

TABLE 10-5 Continued

Registry Management Purpose	Number of Veterans	Basis for Enrollment	Source of Data	Type of Data
Gulf War Registry[b] (Started in 1992) Managed by the Environmental Agents Service To identify medical problems associated with exposures in the Persian Gulf	97,002 87,074 men 9,928 women	Service in SW Asia (1990 to present) Operation Enduring Freedom (OEF) veterans not included because they are in Afghanistan	Exposures of concern, combat experiences, birth defect data	Purely voluntary; data from Gulf War Registry exams

Data Collected	Selected Publications from Registry
Demographics: Race/ethnicity; marital status; gender; occupation; current military status; branch of service; military service in Persian Gulf area; dates and MOS of last two periods of service Medical history: Family history; occupational history; social history including tobacco, alcohol, drug use; civilian exposure(s) history to possible toxic agent; psychosocial history; military service in Persian Gulf area; dates and military occupational specialty (MOS) of last two periods of service Medical history: Psychosocial conditions; review of systems; complaints and symptoms (coders asked to include ICD-9 codes on form); time of onset of the symptoms or conditions; intensity; degree of physical incapacitation; details of any treatment received; complete blood count; blood and serum screening tests; urinalysis; pulmonary function, sperm counts, or other diagnostic studies if medically indicated	Miller R, Costigan, Young H, Kang H, Salager N, Crawford H, Page W, Thaul S. 2006. Patterns of health care seeking of Persian Gulf War Registry members prior to deployment. Military Medicine 171:370-375. Gray GC, Gackstetter GD, Kang HK, Graham JT, Scott KC. 2004. After more than 10 years of Gulf War veteran medical evaluation, what have we learned? American Journal of Preventive Medicine 26:443-452. Hallman WK, Kipen HM, Diefenbach M, Boyd K, Kang H, Leventhal H, Wartenber D. 2003. American Journal of Public Health 93:624-629. Smith TC, Smith B, Ryan MA, Gray GC, Hooper TI, Heller JM, Dalager NA, Kang HK, Gackstetter GD. 2002. Ten years and 100,000 participants later: Occupational and other factors influencing participation in US Gulf War health registries. Journal of Occupational and Environmental Medicine 44:758-768. Murphy FM, Kang HK, Dalager NA. 1999. The health status of Gulf War veterans: Lessons learned from the Department of Veterans Affairs health registry. Military Medicine 164:327-331. Kipen HM, Hallman W, Kang HK, et al. 1999. Prevalence of chronic fatigue and chemical sensitivities in Gulf Registry veterans. Archives of Environmental Health 54:313-318.

continued

TABLE 10-5 Continued

Registry Management Purpose	Number of Veterans	Basis for Enrollment	Source of Data	Type of Data
Gulf War Registry (continued)				
Ionizing Radiation Registry[c] (Started in 1986) Managed by the Environmental Agents Service To identify medical problems associated with ionizing radiation exposure	23,624 23,472 men 152 women	Set up for WWII and Cold War veterans Service in Hiroshima and Nagasaki, gaseous diffusion plants, and area K25 in United States; nuclear weapons testing	Receipt of nasopharyngeal treatment, birth defect data, diagnoses if possible radiogenic-related diseases, disability claims	Purely voluntary; data from Ionizing Radiation Registry exams
ALS Registry Managed by the Epidemiologic Research and Information Center in Durham, NC To identify and characterize veterans with ALS	1,602	Diagnoses of ALS within VA health-care system and self-referrals	Health-care utilization, ALS Functional Rating Scale every 6 months	Data from existing VA files and self-referrals; a consecutive registry

Data Collected	Selected Publications from Registry
Exposure: Exposure to environmental factors (smoking cigarettes, years of smoking cigarettes, number of packs smoked per day, years smoked); while in the Gulf exposure to smoke from oil fires, fumes from tent heaters, cigarette smoke (passive from others), diesel and/or other petrochemical fumes, and burning trash/feces; skin exposure to diesel; chemical agent-resistant compounds; other paint or solvent and/or petrochemical substances; depleted uranium; microwaves; personal pesticide use; nerve gas or other nerve agent Demographics: Family; occupation; tobacco, alcohol, and drug use Medical History: Psychosocial conditions; time of the onset of the veteran's symptoms or conditions; intensity of symptoms or conditions; degree of physical incapacitation; details of any treatment received; chest X ray (if medically necessary), complete blood count; basic metabolic panel and comprehensive metabolic panel or equivalent blood chemistries and enzyme studies; urinalysis	Gray GC, Hawksworth AW, Smith TC, Kang HK, et al. 1998. Gulf War veterans' health registries. Who is most likely to seek evaluation? American Journal of Epidemiology 148:343-349. Blanck RR, Hiatt J, Hyams KC, Kang HK, et al. 1995. Unexplained illnesses among Desert Storm Veterans: A search for causes, treatment, and cooperation. Archives of Internal Medicine 155:262-268.
	Kasarkis EJ, Dominic K, Oddone EZ. 2004. The National Registry of Veterans with Amyotrophic Lateral Sclerosis: Department of Veterans Affairs Cooperative Studies Program (CSP). Amyotrophic Lateral Sclerosis & Other Motor Neuron Disorders 5(Supplement 1):129-132.

continued

TABLE 10-5 Continued

Registry Management Purpose	Number of Veterans	Basis for Enrollment	Source of Data	Type of Data
MS Registry (Started in 1998) Managed by the MS Center of Excellence East in Baltimore, MD, and the MS Center of Excellence West in Portland, OR, and Seattle, WA, to identify and characterize veterans with MS	31,946	Diagnoses of MS within the VA health-care system	Health-care utilization, health economic data	Data from existing VA files; a consecutive registry
Cancer Registry (Started in 1995) Managed by the Program Office for Oncology in Washington, DC To identify and characterize veterans with cancer, analysis of specific therapies and outcomes, and resource allocation	356,174	Diagnoses of cancer within the VA health-care system	Possible cancer risk factors, cancer identification, prognosis factors, treatment data, follow-up, and recurrence	Compilation of cancer registries at each VA facility; a consecutive registry

Data Collected	Selected Publications from Registry
	Culpepper WJ, Mhrmantraut M, Wallin MT, Flannery K, Bradham DD. 2006. Veteran Health Administration multiple sclerosis surveillance registry: The problem of case-finding from administrative databases. Journal of Rehabilitation Research and Development 43(1):17-24.

continued

TABLE 10-5 Continued

Registry Management Purpose	Number of Veterans	Basis for Enrollment	Source of Data	Type of Data
HIV Registry (Started in 1983) Managed by the Center for Quality Management in Public Health in Palo Alto, CA To track overall trends in HIV-related outcomes, health-care utilization planning, quality improvement of care	54,000	Diagnoses of HIV within the VA health-care system	Possible risk factors, lab results, pharmacy use	Data from existing VA files; a consecutive registry
Hepatitis C Registry (Started in 1996) Managed by the Center for Quality Management in Public Health in Palo Alto, CA To track overall trends in hepatitis C-related outcomes, health-care utilization planning, quality improvement of care	253,160	Diagnoses of hepatitis C within the VA health-care system	Liver biopsy data, lab results, pharmacy use	Data from existing VA files; a consecutive registry

Data Collected	Selected Publications from Registry

continued

TABLE 10-5 Continued

Registry Management Purpose	Number of Veterans	Basis for Enrollment	Source of Data	Type of Data
Depression Registry (Started in 2001)[d] Managed by the Serious Mental Illness Treatment, Research, and Evaluation Center in Ann Arbor, MI To identify and characterize veterans with depression; monitor and evaluate care	690,867 (in FY 2005)	Diagnoses of depression within the VA health-care system	Health-care utilization, Global Assessment Functioning Scores, medication use, health-care costs	Data from existing VA files; an annual registry
Psychoses Registry[e] (Started in 1988) Managed by the Serious Mental Illness Treatment, Research, and Evaluation Center in Ann Arbor, MI To identify and characterize veterans with psychoses; monitor and evaluate care	239,304 (in FY 2005)	Diagnoses of psychoses within the VA health-care system	Healthcare utilization, Global Assessment Functioning Scores, medication use, health-care costs	Data from existing VA files; a consecutive registry

[a] More information can be found at http://www1.va.gov/vhapublications/ViewPublication.asp?pub_ID=77.
[b] More information can be found at http://www.vethealth.cio.med.va.gov/Pubs/1303.2GWHB-05.pdf.
[c] More information can be found at http://www1.va.gov/irad/docs/IRADHANDBOOK012006.PDF.

Data Collected	Selected Publications from Registry
Demographics: Age, gender; race/ethnicity; marital status; VISN analyses; service connection; VERA patient class, homelessness, access to medical care Medical History: Inpatient and outpatient services uses; medication and services use; health-care costs; primary care treatment; mortality; psychiatric comorbidities (depression alone or depression with an anxiety disorder other than PTSD); depression and substance abuse; depression and PTSD; other complicated depression; medical comorbidities (peripheral vascular disease, chronic obstructive pulmonary disease, diseases of the digestive system, liver disease, genitourinary symptoms, arthritis, injury and poisoning); Global Assessment of Functioning (GAF)	
Demographics: Age, gender, race; martial status Medical History: Pharmacy and medical services use; cost; diagnoses (total, schizophrenia, bipolar, other); GAF scores; mortality; VERA patient class; homelessness; service connection; access to health care; inpatient psychiatric care; inpatient rehabilitation; inpatient domiciliary care; inpatient nursing home care; outpatient care	

[d] More information can be found at http://www.hsrd.ann-arbor.med.va.gov/documents/2002NARDEP.pdf.
[e] More information can be found at http://www.hsrd.ann-arbor.med.va.gov/documents/3rdAnnual_psychosisVHA.pdf.
SOURCE: Derived from [a] DoD/VHA, 2000; [b] DoD/VHA, 2005; [c] DoD/VHA, 2006; Kang, 2006; [d] SMITREC, 2002; [e] SMITREC, 2001.

VA should move quickly to develop plans for interfaces to these new DoD exposure data systems. This should not require massive new data systems within VA but instead consist of appropriate interfaces and views to the data within DoD systems that are accessible by the VA. The first step would be a VA team embedded with DoD implementation team at the Army's CHPPM where they can examine the system capabilities and data structures so that appropriate interfaces can be defined and developed to meet the needs of VA.

Recommendation: Conduct a critical evaluation of Gulf War troop tracking and environmental exposure monitoring data so that improvements can be made in this key DoD strategy for characterizing exposures during deployment.

Characterizing exposures during intense combat deployment scenarios is the most challenging aspect of DoD's efforts to characterize Service member exposures throughout their military service. An important part of the current strategy is a combination of troop tracking and environmental monitoring such that overlaying of troop location with the location of environmental monitoring results will enable the characterization of troop exposures. The success of this approach depends directly on the detail of both the troop tracking and the environmental monitoring. More frequent measurement and recording of troop location coupled with more frequent (e.g., time and location) environmental exposure monitoring will allow more accurate characterization of individual exposures. The current goal is to record troop location at least once every 24 hours. Minimal environmental monitoring requirements are less clear. In particular, monitoring during shorter deployments (less than 30 days) may be sporadic as requirements vary depending on the predeployment risk assessment, the availability of appropriate medical personnel, and the commander's discretion (DOD Instruction 6490.03 [DoD, 2006c]).

DoD should undertake a detailed review of this strategy using data from the Gulf War and subsequent deployments in Afghanistan and Iraq to determine limitations to the current approach and identify opportunities for improvement. The review should consist of the formation of exposure matrices for a group of randomly selected Service members who served in that theater using data available on troop location, environmental measurements, and exposure data in individual health records. Gaps in those exposure matrices should then be examined to identify data limitations so that strategies can be developed for future approaches that minimize those limitations.

4. Develop DoD policy to ensure that classification/declassification (secrecy) issues are managed appropriately for both DoD and the veteran.

There are clearly times when national security or mission success depends on maintaining secrecy regarding certain aspects of a Service member's military experience. However, every effort should be made to find mechanisms for characterizing Service member exposure and health histories in manners that do not interfere with the broader issues of national security or mission success. DoD should develop procedures that ensure full or partial declassification of sensitive information for the timely provision of that Service member's or veteran's health care. When such declassification is not possible, DoD should establish procedures whereby blinded data relevant to the Service member's health and exposure history are provided.

In some instances where national security and secrecy issues cannot be resolved, DoD and VA may need to establish mechanisms involving experts with appropriate security clearances to monitor affected registry cohorts for potential health outcomes and define surveillance or research activities that may need to be conducted within appropriate secrecy clearances. An interagency agreement could be developed between DoD and VA addressing the secrecy issue. Since both agencies have used the classification system in the past this agreement would address the policy development process and the exchange of classified information between the two agencies. The process would include establishment of a joint DoD-VA board comprised of individuals who have sufficient security clearance to discuss classified data. The access to classified information process would be contained in a written document outlining a mechanism to identify, monitor, track, and medically treat individuals who were part of research activities involving human subjects and whose research design and results have been classified.

Recommendation: Establish registries of Service members and veterans based on exposure, deployment, and disease histories.

Recommendation: DoD and VA should establish and implement mechanisms to identify, monitor, track, and medically treat individuals involved in research and other activities that have been classified and are secret.

5. Strengthen the assessment of psychological stressors and symptoms.

Psychological and combat-related stressors may detrimentally impact the long-term mental and emotional well-being of military personnel and should be thoroughly assessed at key points during the military career of men and women. Currently, basic clinical evaluations for neurological and psychiatric disorders are made at accession, after training, and throughout the service career. Very brief structured assessments for some psychiatric symptoms occur during the post-deployment periods only.

Assessment of exposure to combat and of psychological stress during deployment is a particularly challenging element of the Committee's proposed approach to tracking factors influencing the health of veterans. Scales have been developed to assess exposures during combat and the validity and reliability of these instruments has been assessed (Friedman et al., 1986; Janes et al., 1991; Keane et al., 1989; Laufer et al., 1984; Lund et al., 1984; Wessely et al., 2003). These instruments have been used in investigations of Vietnam veterans (Buydens-Branch et al., 1990; Frueh et al., 2005; Green et al., 1989; Yehuda et al., 1992) and more recently for personnel deployed in Iraq and Afghanistan (Hoge et al., 2004). A 2004 study carried out by military investigators addressed mental health problems and combat duty in personnel deployed to Iraq and Afghanistan (Hoge et al., 2004). This study demonstrates the feasibility of investigations directed at troops in relation to combat deployment. A follow-up study of Vietnam veterans, the National Vietnam Veterans Readjustment Study, incorporated an exposure measure based on military records (Dohrenwend et al., 2006). Onset of posttraumatic stress disorder (PTSD) was associated with combat exposure, with evidence for a positive close-response relationship.

These studies show that combat exposure and related stress can be measured. They also show the feasibility of informative research on neuropsychiatric disorders among veterans. Further development will be needed to achieve the type of surveillance proposed by the Committee.

Psychiatric disorders, particularly PTSD, depression, and alcohol abuse and dependence are common. More data systematically collected using validated and structured instruments pre- and post-deployment will aid DoD and the VA to better identify stressors that may predispose individuals to develop these disorders, identify Service members to whom early intervention should be provided, and track individuals exposed to emotional trauma and with psychiatric symptoms in specialized registries.

A number of brief validated instruments are available for PTSD, major depression, and alcohol abuse and dependence—three common psychiatric disorders experienced by veterans. A dedicated, face-to-face interview by an experienced clinician, recognized to be the most valid method of assessing PTSD, is likely not feasible in the post-deployment or separation/retirement medical evaluations. While a host of instruments are available for assessing PTSD, realistically the only feasible instruments that might be useful in this context would be one of several available screening questionnaires. These include (1) the 4-question Primary Care PTSD Screen (Prins et al., 2003), (2) a 7-question scale keyed to the DSM-IV criteria for PTSD (Breslau et al., 1999), (3) the 17-question PTSD Symptom Scale Self-Report (Coffey et al., 1998), (4) the Screen for Posttraumatic Stress Symptoms (Carlson, 2001), and (5) the PTSD subscale of the large Psychiatric Diagnostic Screening Questionnaire (Zimmerman and Mattia, 2001). Only the first of these, the Primary Care PTSD Screen, has been validated on combat veterans. Also, while these screening instruments may be useful in identifying veterans who may have PTSD, they are not adequate for diagnosing PTSD.

There are also a host of screening instruments for major depression including the 2 item Prime-MD, the 9 item Patient Health Questionnaire, and the 20 item Centers for Epidemiological Studies Depression (CES-D) scale, among others. Alcohol abuse and dependence can be screened with a number of instruments including the RAPS-QF, the AUDIT, and the CAGE, among others. These instruments vary in length and sensitivity and specificity in different populations.

Studies that employ these screening instruments for prospective research will need to account for some degree of misclassification of the health outcome. In spite of these shortcomings, data from a screening instrument on an unselected population of veterans obtained in a systematic manner would be very valuable for the type of prospective studies envisioned in this report to better understand service-related morbidity.

6. Establish registries of Service members and veterans based on exposure, deployment, and disease histories.

The Committee recommends that VA and Congress consider the initiation and prospective follow-up of specific veteran populations who may share a common exposure history as a viable surveillance tool. Creating a registry that may include initial demographic, exposure, and health information is a reasonable interim response to veterans with unexplained or underexplained health complaints that are temporally but not scientifically related to military service.

A registry would allow the formation of a pool of veterans who are linked by some shared attribute of military service, such as combat campaign, theater location, or catastrophic event (e.g., Khamisiyah, Iraq), to be identified and actively followed forward through regular follow-up contacts from the registry staff. Trends in health of the registrants could be followed forward, and communication with registrants about new health information or treatment recommendations could be facilitated. As well, the registrants could be invited to participate in scientific studies to elucidate the cause or proposed mechanism of health harm they may have experienced. Such a model is being used to follow the World Trade Center responders, workers, and neighborhood population. This model differs somewhat from existing VA registries (e.g., Gulf War or Agent Orange) in that these tend to be cross-sectional assessments, with little regular follow-up or interaction with staff.

Although registry costs can be high, so are the costs of presumptions. Enrollment in a registry may offer the veteran access to some of the medical services a presumption provides, but under a different mechanism that could allow time for the clinical and epidemiologic evidence to accumulate so as to make a more evidence-based decision about a presumption.

Recommendation: Develop a plan for an overall integrated surveillance strategy for the health of Service members and veterans.

It is critical that DoD and VA work together to define a common strategy for integrated health surveillance of Service members and veterans. Fully leveraging the Service member-veteran exposure and health data is critical to the full understanding of disease etiology and causation, the establishment of relative risk, the adjudication of disability claims, and the treatment of disease. It is also critical to appropriate deliberations regarding presumptions in disability decision making.

The need for surveillance can be identified at any point in a Service member's or veteran's experience history. Surveillance studies begun during a Service member's service career may need to extend into his or her post-service experience. Data needs for the specific surveillance activity may have been generated during either the Service member experience or the veteran experience or both. Therefore this activity must be jointly well managed by DoD and VA. A strong central organization, staffed jointly by DoD and VA with external expert advisors, should be given responsibility for the ongoing evaluation of health and exposure data quality, the regular review of registry and surveillance activities, the definition of surveillance and research strategies, and the coordination of surveillance and research projects. This joint DoD-VA Service member and veteran exposure and health surveillance organization would have broad responsibility for oversight of all DoD and VA surveillance and research activities whether they are conducted internally or externally by those organizations.

Recommendation: Improve the data linkage between the electronic health record data systems used by DoD and VA—including capabilities for handling individual Service member exposure information that is included as part of the individual's health record.

Although there are efforts underway to electronically transfer Service member health records from DoD to VA, these efforts are moving slowly and the timeline for completion of a seamless interface is unclear. DoD and VA should increase attention to this effort with a clear integration plan, timetable for implementation, metrics for tracking implementation progress, and annual reporting of metric results.

To date there has been little discussion regarding electronic transfer of Service members' exposure information in their health records to VA. As the inclusion of exposure data in employee health records is a key DoD strategy for ensuring that exposure information is available for individual Service members, this appears to be a major weakness in the system. DoD and VA should explicitly include the integration of these individual exposure data into the health record transfer integration plan, implementation timetable, metrics, and annual reporting. Reports on progress of these plans should be included in the annual report to Congress on DOEHRS progress.

Recommendation: Ensure implementation of the DoD strategy for improved exposure assessment and exposure data collection.

The DOEHRS program is a major undertaking that has potential for dramatically increasing the availability of exposure data. However, DoD has many important priorities, and short-term funding pressures have the potential to delay implementation activities. Because of the importance of these efforts, not only to DoD but to VA as well, we recommend that additional steps be taken to ensure that DOEHRS is fully implemented as planned. In addition, because of the importance of adequately trained individuals to the success of DOEHRS, we further recommend that these steps specifically include detail on the training of individuals needed to make the accurate professional judgments and generate appropriate exposure data critical to DOEHRS. These additional steps are as follows:

1. Include a specific DoD budget line item for DOEHRS that includes funding for system development and enhancement, system implementation, and training of personnel.
2. Develop clear metrics for tracking the effective deployment and utilization of DOEHRS throughout DoD.
3. Require an annual status report to Congress on DOEHRS development and implementation progress and related training activities.

Recommendation: Develop a data interface that allows VA to access the electronic exposure data systems used by DoD.

DoD is investing heavily in DOEHRS and other improved exposure data systems that are standardized across the various armed services. In the Committee's interviews with people responsible for development and deployment of these systems, we did not encounter anyone with knowledge of activities by DoD or VA to develop a VA interface with these systems that will allow use of the Service member-specific and longitudinal exposure data by VA.

VA should move quickly to develop plans for interfaces to these new DoD exposure data systems. This should not require massive new data systems within VA but instead consist of appropriate interfaces and views to the data within DoD systems that are accessible by VA. The first step would be a VA team embedded within the DoD implementation team at the Army's Center for Health Promotion and Preventive Medicine where the VA team can examine the system capabilities and data structures so that appropriate interfaces can be defined and developed to meet the needs of VA.

Recommendation: Consider interim interventions for affected veterans while data are collected or more thoroughly analyzed to resolve scientific uncertainty.

It can take significant time to collect and analyze data needed to adequately resolve scientific uncertainty in establishing causal relationships between exposure and disease. VA should consider interim interventions in instances where veterans are severely affected during the time it takes to conduct the needed research. These measures might consist of provisional health care for affected veterans during the interim period.

REFERENCES

AHRQ (Agency for Healthcare Research and Quality). 2006. *Guide to clinical preventive services. Recommendations of the U.S. Preventive Services Task Force.* AHRQ Publication No. 06-0588. Rockville, MD: AHRQ.

ASTM (American Society for Testing and Materials). 2003. *Standard guide for environmental health site assessment process for military deployments. Designation E 2318-03.* West Conshohocken, PA: ASTM International.

ATSDR (Agency for Toxic Substances and Disease Registry). 2003. *What Is the National Exposure Registry (NER)?* http://www.atsdr.cdc.gov/NER/index.html (accessed April 6, 2007).

Breslau, N., E. L. Peterson, R. C. Kessler, L. R. Schultz. 1999. Short screening scale for DSM-IV posttraumatic stress disorder. *American Journal of Psychiatry* 156(6):908-911.

Buydens-Branch, N. D., and M. Branchey. 1990. Duration and intensity of combat exposure and posttraumatic stress disorder in Vietnam veterans. *Journal of Nervous and Mental Disease* 178:582-587.

Carlson, E. B. 2001. Psychometric study of a brief screen for PTSD: Assessing the impact of multiple traumatic events. *Assessment* 8(4):431-441.

CDC VES (Centers for Disease Control and Prevention Vietnam Experience Study). 1989. *Health status of Vietnam veterans. Synopsis.* Vol. 1. Atlanta, GA: Centers for Disease Control. http://www.cdc.gov/nceh/veterans/default1c.htm (accessed April 9, 2007).

Coffey, S. F., B. S. Dansky, S. A. Falsetti, M. E. Saladin, K. T. Brady. 1998. Screening for PTSD in a substance abuse sample: Psychometric properties of a modified version of the PTSD Symptom Scale Self-Report. Posttraumatic stress disorder. *Journal of Traumatic Stress* 11(2):393-399.

Cohen, B. M., and M. Z. Cooper. 1954. *A follow-up study of World War II prisoners of war.* VA Medical Monograph. Washington, DC: U.S. Government Printing Office.

Do, N. 2006. *DoD and Veterans Affairs: Health information sharing*. Paper presented at the third meeting of the IOM's Committee on the Evaluation of the Presumptive Disability Decision-Making Process for Veterans, San Antonio, TX.

DoD (Department of Defense). 1997. *Instruction 6490.3: Implementation and application of joint medical surveillance for deployments*. Fort Sam Houston, TX: Army Medical Department Center and School.

DoD. 2004. *Directive 6490.2: Comprehensive health surveillance*.

DoD. 2006a. *Defense Occupational and Environmental Health Readiness System (DOEHRS): Implementation and training (I&T) plan*. PLN-002. Washington, DC: DOEHRS Project Management Office.

DoD. 2006b. *Defense Occupational and Environmental Health Readiness System (DOEHRS)*. Student Guide Version 1.0.2.0. Washington, DC: DOEHRS Project Management Office.

DoD. 2006c. *Instruction 6490.03: Deployment health*.

DoD. 2006d. *Periodic health assessment policy for active duty and selected reserve members. Memorandum for Assistant Secretary of the Army, Assistant Secretary of the Navy, Assistant Secretary of the Air Force*. HA Policy 06-006. Washington, DC: Department of Defense.

DoD Industrial Hygiene Working Group. 2000. *DoD industrial hygiene exposure assessment model*. Report 2000-1. https://www.denix.osd.mil/denix/Public/News/Army/DOHP/Occhealth/Documents/IHEAM/ihassessmodelv8.html (accessed July 28, 2007).

DoD/VHA (Veterans Health Administration). 2000. *VHA Directive 1302: Agent Orange Registry (AOR) Program*. Washington, DC: Department of Veterans Affairs/Veterans Health Administration. http://www1.va.gov/vhapublications/ViewPublication.asp?pub_ID=77 (accessed April 6, 2007).

DoD/VHA. 2005. *VHA Handbook 1303.2: Gulf War (Including Operation Iraqi Freedom) Registry (GWR) Program—(formerly Persian Gulf Registry [GWR] Program)*. Washington, DC: Department of Veterans Affairs/Veterans Health Administration. http://www.vethealth.cio.med.va.gov/Pubs/1303.2GWHB-05.pdf (accessed April 6, 2007).

DoD/VHA. 2006. *Ionizing Radiation Registry (IRR) Program procedures*. Washington, DC: Department of Veterans Affairs/Veterans Health Administration. http://www1.va.gov/irad/docs/IRADHANDBOOK012006.PDF (accessed April 9, 2007).

Dohrenwend, B. P., J. B. Turner, N. A. Turse, B. G. Adams, K. C. Koenen, and R. Marshall. 2006. The psychological risks of Vietnam for U.S. veterans: A revisit with new data and methods. *Science* 313:979-982.

Friedman, M. J., C. K. Schneiderman, A. N. West, and J. A. Corson. 1986. Measurement of combat exposure, posttraumatic stress disorder, and life stress among Vietnam combat veterans. *American Journal of Psychiatry* 143:537-539.

Frueh, B. C., J. D. Elhai, A. L. Grubaugh, J. Monnier, T. B. Kashdan, J. A. Sauvageot, M. B. Hamner, B. G. Burkett, and G. W. Arana. 2005. Documented combat exposure of U.S. veterans seeking treatment for combat-related post-traumatic stress disorder. *British Journal of Psychiatry* 186:467-472.

GAO (Government Accountability Office). 1999. *Veterans' benefits claims: Further improvements needed in claims-processing accuracy. Report to the ranking minority member, Committee on Veterans' Affairs, House of Representatives*. GAO/HEHS-99-35. Washington, DC: Government Accountability Office. http://www.gao.gov/archive/1999/he99035.pdf (accessed February 14, 2007).

GAO. 2000a. *Veterans Benefits Administration: Problems and challenges facing disability claims processing: Testimony before the Subcommittee on Oversight and Investigations, Committee on Veterans' Affairs, House of Representatives, Statement of Cynthia A. Bascetta, Association Director, Veterans' Affairs and Military Health Care Issues, Health, Education, and Human Services Division.* GAO/T-HEHS/AIMD-00-146. Washington, DC: Government Accountability Office. http://www.gao.gov/new.items/h100146t.pdf (accessed February 14, 2007).

GAO. 2000b. *Veterans' benefits: Promising claims-processing practices need to be evaluated. Report to ranking minority member, Committee on Veterans' Affairs, House of Representatives.* GAO/HEHS-00-65. Washington, DC: Government Accountability Office. http://www.gao.gov/archive/2000/he00065.pdf (accessed February 14, 2007).

GAO. 2005a. *DoD and VA systematic data sharing would help expedite servicemembers' transition to VA services: Testimony before the Subcommittee on Oversight and Investigations, Committee on Veterans' Affairs, House of Representatives. Statement of Cynthia A. Bascetta. Director, Health Care—Veterans' Health and Benefits Issues.* GAO-05-722T. Washington, DC: Government Accountability Office. http://www.gao.gov/new.items/d05722t.pdf (accessed February 14, 2007).

GAO. 2005b. *Veterans' Benefits: Further changes in VBA's field office structure could help improve disability claims processing: Report to congressional requesters.* GAO-06-149. Washington, DC: Government Accountability Office. http://www.gao.gov/new.items/d06149.pdf (accessed February 14, 2007).

GAO. 2006. *VA and DoD health care: Opportunities to maximize resource sharing remain. Report to congressional committees.* GAO-06-315. Washington, DC: Government Accountability Office. http://www.gao.gov/new.items/d06315.pdf (accessed February 14, 2007).

GAO. 2007. *VA and DoD are making progress in sharing medical information, but remain far from having comprehensive electronic medical records.* GAO-07-1108T. Washington, DC: Government Accountability Office. http://www.gao.gov/new.items/d071108t.pdf (accessed July 27, 2007).

Goldberg, J., B. Curran, M. E. Vitek, W. G. Henderson, and E. J. Boyko. 2002. The Vietnam Era Twin Registry. *Twin Research* 5(5):476-481.

Gray, G. C., K. B. Chesbrough, M. A. Ryan, P. Amoroso, E. J. Boyko, G. D. Gackstetter, T. I. Hooper, J. R. Riddle, Millennium Cohort Study Group. 2002. The millennium cohort study: A 21-year prospective cohort study of 140,000 military personnel. *Military Medicine* 167(6):483-488.

Green, B. L., J. D. Lindy, M. C. Grace, and G. C. Gleser. 1989. Multiple diagnosis in posttraumatic stress disorder. The role of war stressors. *Journal of Nervous and Mental Disease* 177:329-335.

Heller, J. M. 2006. *Deployment health surveillance: Past, current, and future operations.* Paper presented at the second meeting of the IOM's Committee on the Evaluation of Presumptive Disability Decision-Making Process for Veterans, Washington, DC.

Henderson, W. G., S. Eisen, J. Goldberg, W. R. True, J. E. Barnes, and M. E. Vitek. 1990. The Vietnam Era Twin Registry: A resource for medical research. *Public Health Reports* 105(4):368-373.

Hoge, C. W., C. A. Castro, S. C. Messer, D. McGurk, D. I. Cotting, and R. L. Koffman. 2004. Combat duty in Iraq and Afghanistan, mental health problems, and barriers to care. *New England Journal of Medicine* 351:13-22.

IOM (Institute of Medicine). 1992. *The health of former prisoners of war.* Washington, DC: National Academy Press.

IOM. 1993. *Veterans at risk: The health effects of mustard gas and lewisite.* Washington, DC: National Academy Press.

IOM. 1994. *Veterans and Agent Orange: Health effects of herbicides used in Vietnam*. Washington, DC: National Academy Press.

IOM. 1995a. *Adverse reproductive outcomes in families of atomic veterans: The feasibility of epidemiologic studies*. Washington, DC: National Academy Press.

IOM. 1995b. *Health consequences of service during the Persian Gulf War: Initial findings and recommendations for immediate action*. Washington, DC: National Academy Press.

IOM. 1996a. *Health consequences of service during the Persian Gulf War: Recommendations for research and information systems*. Washington, DC: National Academy Press.

IOM. 1996b. *Mortality of veteran participants in the CROSSROADS nuclear test*. Washington, DC: National Academy Press.

IOM. 1997. *Characterizing exposure of veterans to agent orange and other herbicides used in Vietnam: Scientific considerations regarding a request for proposals for research*. Washington, DC: National Academy Press.

IOM. 1998a. *Adequacy of the VA Persian Gulf registry and uniform case assessment protocol*. Washington, DC: National Academy Press.

IOM. 1998b. *Measuring the health of Persian Gulf veterans: Workshop summary*. Washington, DC: National Academy Press.

IOM. 1999a. *Gulf War veterans: Measuring health*. Washington, DC: National Academy Press.

IOM. 1999b. *Strategies to protect the health of deployed forces: Medical surveillance, record keeping, and risk reduction*. Washington, DC: National Academy Press.

IOM. 1999c. *Veterans and Agent Orange: Update 1998*. Washington, DC: National Academy Press.

IOM. 2000a. *The five series study: Mortality of military participants in U.S. nuclear weapons tests*. Washington, DC: National Academy Press.

IOM. 2000b. *Gulf War and health, volume 1: Depleted uranium, pyridostigmine bromide, sarin, vaccines*. Washington, DC: National Academy Press.

IOM. 2000c. *Protecting Those Who Serve: Strategies to Protect the Health of the Deployed U.S. Forces*. Washington, DC: National Academy Press.

IOM. 2000d. *Veterans and Agent Orange: Herbicide/dioxin exposure and type 2 diabetes*. Washington, DC: National Academy Press.

IOM. 2001a. *Gulf War veterans: Treating symptoms and syndromes*. Washington, DC: National Academy Press.

IOM. 2001b. *Veterans and Agent Orange: Update 2000*. Washington, DC: National Academy Press.

IOM. 2002. *Veterans and Agent Orange herbicide/dioxin exposure and acute myelogenous leukemia in the children of Vietnam veterans*. Washington, DC: National Academy Press.

IOM. 2003a. *Characterizing exposure of veterans to Agent Orange and other herbicides used in Vietnam: Interim findings and recommendations*. Washington, DC: The National Academies Press.

IOM. 2003b. *Characterizing exposure of veterans to Agent Orange and other herbicides used in Vietnam: Final Report*. Washington, DC: The National Academies Press.

IOM. 2003c. *Gulf War and health, volume 2: Insecticides and solvents*. Washington, DC: The National Academies Press.

IOM. 2003d. *Veterans and Agent Orange: Update 2002*. Washington, DC: The National Academies Press

IOM. 2004a. *Gulf War and health: Updated literature review of sarin*. Washington, DC: The National Academies Press.

IOM. 2004b. *Studies of U.S. veterans twins*. http://www.iom.edu/CMS/3795/4907.aspx (accessed February 14, 2007).

IOM. 2004c. *Veterans and Agent Orange: Length of presumptive period for association between exposure and respiratory cancer.* Washington, DC: The National Academies Press.

IOM. 2005a. *Gulf War and health, volume 3: Fuels, combustion products, and propellants.* Washington, DC: The National Academies Press.

IOM. 2005b. *Veterans and Agent Orange: Update 2004.* Washington, DC: The National Academies Press.

IOM. 2006. *Gulf War and health, volume 4: Health effects of serving in the Gulf War.* Washington, DC: The National Academies Press.

IOM. 2007. *Gulf War and health, volume 5: Infectious diseases.* Washington, DC: The National Academies Press.

Janes, G. R., J. Goldberg, S. A. Eisen, and W. R. True. 1991. Reliability and validity of a combat exposure index for Vietnam era veterans. *Journal of Clinical Psychology* 47:80-86.

Kang, H. 2006 (July 27). *VA health registries.* Paper presented at the second meeting of the IOM's Committee on the Evaluation of the Presumptive Disability Decision-Making Process for Veterans, Washington, DC.

Keane, T. M., J. A. Fairbank, J. M. Caddell, R. T. Zimering, K. L. Taylor, and C. A. Mora. 1989. Clinical evaluation of a measure to assess combat exposure. *Psychological Assessment* 1:53-55.

Laufer, R. S., M. S. Gallops, and E. Frey-Wouters. 1984. War stress and trauma: The Vietnam veteran experience. *Journal of Health and Social Behavior* 25:65-85.

Long, E. R., and S. A. Jablon. 1955. *Tuberculosis in the army of the United States in World War II.* VA Medical Monograph. Washington, DC: U.S. Government Printing Office.

Lund, M., D. Foy, C. Sipprelle, and A. Strachan. 1984. The Combat Exposure Scale: A systematic assessment of trauma in the Vietnam War. *Journal of Clinical Psychology* 40:1323-1328.

The Millennium Cohort Study. 2007. http://www.millenniumcohort.org/about.php (accessed July 24, 2007).

Postlewaite, C. 2006. *Overview: DoD deployment and installation-based occupational/environmental health programs.* Paper presented at the second meeting of the IOM's Committee on the Evaluation of the Presumptive Disability Decision-Making Process for Veterans, Washington, DC

Prins, A., P. Ouimette, R. Kimerling, R. P. Cameron, D. S. Hugelshofer, J. Shaw-Hegwer, A. Thrailkill, F. D. Gusman, and J. I. Sheikh. 2004. The primary care PTSD screen (PC–PTSD): Development and operating characteristics. *Primary Care Psychiatry* 9(1):9-14.

Robinette, C. D., S. Jablon, and T. L. Preston. 1985. *Studies of participants in nuclear tests.* Washington, DC: National Academy Press.

SMITREC (Serious Mental Illness Treatment Research and Evaluation Center). 2001. *Care for veterans with psychosis in the VHA FY01: 3rd Annual National Psychosis Registry Report.* Ann Arbor, MI: Serious Mental Illness Treatment Research and Evaluation Center, Health Services Research and Development Center of Excellence. http://www.hsrd.ann-arbor.med.va.gov/documents/3rdAn0nual_psychosisVHA.pdf (accessed April 6, 2007).

SMITREC. 2002. *Specialty care for veterans with depression in the VHA: 2002 National Registry for Depression (NARDEP) Report.* Ann Arbor, MI: Serious Mental Illness Treatment Research and Evaluation Center, Health Services Research and Development Center of Excellence. http://www.hsrd.ann-arbor.med.va.gov/documents/2002NARDEP.pdf (accessed April 6, 2007).

VA (Department of Veterans Affairs). 2003. *Press release. VA begins registry for Lou Gehrig's Disease.* http://www.research.va.gov/news/press_releases/lou-gehrig-021803.cfm (accessed April 5, 2007).

VA. 2005a. *Office of Research and Development Program announcement. Request for applications in combat casualty neurotrauma*. http://www.research.va.gov/funding/solicitations/docs/neurotrauma.pdf (accessed April 5, 2007).

VA. 2005b. *VA Form 10-10EZ. Application for health benefits*. https://www.1010ez.med.va.gov/sec/vha/1010ez/Form/vha-10-10ez.pdf (accessed April 5, 2007).

VA. 2006a. *Fact sheet: Facts about the Department of Veterans Affairs*. Washington, DC: Department of Veterans Affairs. http://www1.va.gov/OPA/fact/docs/vafacts.pdf (accessed April 9, 2007).

VA. 2006b. *Office of Research and Development Program announcement. Deployment health: OEF/OIF veteran research issues*. http://www.research.va.gov/funding/solicitations/docs/Deployment_Health_2006.pdf (accessed April 5, 2007).

VA. 2006c. *VA WRIISC-DC-Veterans Affairs War-Related Illness and Injury Study Center in Washington, DC*. http://www.va.gov/WRIISC-DC/ (accessed April 5, 2007).

VA. 2007a. *Federal benefits for veterans and dependents*. Washington, DC: Department of Veterans Affairs. http://www1.va.gov/opa/vadocs/fedben.pdf (accessed April 5, 2007).

VA. 2007b. *Seamless transition home*. http://www.seamlesstransition.va.gov/ (accessed April 5, 2007).

VA. 2007c. Seattle Epidemiologic Research and Information Center. http://www.eric.seattle.med.va.gov/index.html (accessed April 6, 2007).

VA. 2007d. *VA health care eligibility and enrollment: Getting care*. http://www.va.gov/healtheligibility/gettingcare/ (accessed April 5, 2007).

VA. 2007e. *Vietnam Era Twin Registry: Identification of Vietnam era veteran twins*. http://www.eric.seattle.med.va.gov/VETR/identification_of_twins.html (accessed April 6, 2007).

Walker, A. E., and S. Jablon. 1961. *A follow-up study of head wounds in World War II*. VA Medical Monograph. Washington, DC: U.S. Government Printing Office.

Wessely, S., C. Unwin, M. Hotopf, L. Hull, K. Ismail, V. Nicolaou, and A. David. 2003. Stability of recall of military hazards over time. Evidence from the Persian Gulf War of 1991. *British Journal of Psychiatry* 183:314-322.

Yehuda, R., S. M. Southwick, and E. L. Giller, Jr. 1992. Exposure to atrocities and severity of chronic posttraumatic stress disorder in Vietnam combat veterans. *American Journal of Psychiatry* 149:333-336.

Zimmerman, M., and J. I. Mattia. 2001. The Psychiatric Diagnostic Screening Questionnaire: Development, reliability, and validity. *Comprehensive Psychiatry* 42(3):175-189.

11

Governmental Classification and Secrecy

BACKGROUND

Secrecy surrounds many facets of homeland security issues and, in general, is of concern to national security. Many scientific studies conducted during the two world wars through the Cold War were classified, and many are still not declassified. Studies dealing with warfare gases and radiation were classified during the time of the studies and remain classified today. This classification makes appropriately informed treatment of the involved veterans with adverse health effects difficult, if not impossible, and impedes research on the consequences of exposures. The recent declassification of mustard gas and lewisite studies conducted during World War II and numerous radiation studies documented that classification greatly deterred treatment of health effects affecting the volunteers who played key roles during these studies. To many citizens, the idea of secrecy in government is linked with "national security secrets" or "classified information." The system of classification occupies a special place in governmental secrecy. Classified information is accessible only to those who have been "cleared" following investigation and who agree to abide by the rules regarding access to this information; violation of these rules can result in severe criminal penalties. These rules can greatly hinder medical treatment of individuals who have been exposed during classified activities.

The authority to classify information derives from legislation and from Presidential executive order. In 1917, Congress passed the Espionage Act to address wartime spying (SOURCE: http://www.firstworldwar.com/source/espionageact1918.htm; Gathering, Transmitting or Losing Defense Information. 2007. 18 U.S.C. § 793; Gathering, or Delivering Defense Information to Aid Foreign Government. 2007. 18 U.S.C. § 794), and further legislation providing for military secrets was enacted in 1938 (Photographing and Sketching Defense Installations. 2007. 18 U.S.C. § 795; Use of Aircraft for Photographing Defense Installations. 2007. 18 U.S.C. § 796; Publication and Sale of Photographs of Defense. 2007. 18 U.S.C. § 797; Quist, 2002). In 1940 President Franklin D. Roosevelt issued the first executive order on classification, which was based on the authorization of the 1938 law enacted to protect military installations and equipment (Truman, 1950). The regulations that interpreted the World War I law declared that secrets could be kept not only for national security reasons but also for other reasons. In 1936, for example, the Army issued rules that provided for Secret, Confidential, and Restricted information. The definition of Confidential provided that

> A document will be classified and marked "Confidential" when the information it contains is of such nature that its disclosure, *although not endangering our national security,* might be prejudicial to the interests or prestige of the Nation, an individual, or any governmental activity, or be of advantage to a foreign nation. (Classification, 1936; emphasis added)

Similarly, data could be classified Secret if release "might endanger the national security or cause serious injury to the interests or prestige of the Nation, an individual, or any government activity"(Classification, 1936).

The use of classification and secrecy by the government is detailed exquisitely by the history of the formation of the Atomic Energy Commission and the development of the atomic bomb during World War II. The Advisory Committee on Human Radiation Experiments (ACHRE) Report (ACHRE, 1995) provides an extremely detailed chronology of the development of the classification scheme and the use of secrecy by the government as it relates to any aspect of radiation work. The history of use of the secrecy classification for radiation studies is outlined in Appendix L-1.

Especially during times of national crisis the general public and the government take security seriously. The concern about national security has evolved considerably over the evolutionary period of classification. During World War II and the development of the atomic bomb under the Manhattan Project, considerable emphasis was placed on wartime secrecy. Secrecy and the oath of secrecy were extended not only to the actual participating scientists and staff but to families of these individuals. Appendix L-1 provides an overview of the secrecy concerns surrounding these projects. During this developmental time period, considerable emphasis was placed on secrecy surrounding the use of human volunteers, and that emphasis remains today. Some materials still remain classified today under the umbrella of national security.

The historical development of the classification systems used during the atomic bomb era revealed that more than national security was a concern for classifying some material as secret. Concerns revolving around prestige, public relations, and governmental embarrassment were also used to invoke the secrecy umbrella. In public, some officials stated that national security was the paramount concern, while in private they endorsed the concerns involving prestige, public relations, and embarrassment (ACHRE, 1995). Declassification of materials has been slow, and many documents are still being withheld because of these expressed concerns.

Although Appendix L-1 addresses the history of classification in relationship to the birth of the Atomic Energy Commission (AEC), the recent declassification of some of the World War II mustard gas and lewisite studies reveals that radiation studies were not the only studies classified for national security concerns (IOM, 1993). A more current example of this classification usage is the recent declassification of some of the SHAD (Shipboard Hazard and Defense) Project data, studies that were conducted and classified in the 1960s (SOURCE: http://www.deploymentlink.osd.mil/shad/factSheets.jsp). In view of these two chemical examples, concern arises as to how many other studies were classified secret and have not yet been declassified, leading potentially to the withholding of needed medical care from human participants in the studies.

Although the written history addresses the experiences of the AEC (see Appendix L-1), the issues of secrecy and classification obviously could be extrapolated to other areas of research that would involve human subjects. Pertinent areas of concern in this regard would involve the use of chemical warfare agents for both prevention of injuries and possible use in tactical defense. The use of mustard agents and lewisite in studies addressing protective measures during and following World War II is a prime example of human subject use that was classified and remains partially classified today. Results from some of these studies were not declassified until the early 1990s at the insistence of an Institute of Medicine (IOM) study (IOM, 1993), and some studies remain classified today.

The use of chemical warfare agents and simulants in the 1960s is a further example of retaining human studies under the umbrella of secret classification. In a series of tests under the project list of SHAD, Navy ships were exposed to chemical or biological agents or simulants to establish protective measures and decontamination efficiency for machinery and personnel (SOURCE: http://www.deploymentlink.osd.mil/shad/index.jsp; http://www1.va.gov/shad/; Brown, 2003). The numerous tests were classified as secret and have only been recently partially declassified, again at the insistence of an IOM study (IOM, 1993). In this example, the Department of Defense (DoD) allowed IOM and the Department of Veterans Affairs (VA) personnel who possessed sufficient security clearance levels to review the documents and release selected pieces of information. It must be noted, however, that not all of the classified SHAD data have been declassified; only those parts that identify personnel involved, for which records were kept by DoD, and the agents or simulants they were potentially or actually exposed to have been declassified. These examples then bring to the forefront: How many other human use studies have been, or are being, conducted and are classified secret? In an August 2006 information letter released by the Veterans Health Administration (VHA) (VHA, 2006, p. 2), more than 250 chemicals were identified as chemicals of potential concern related to human use studies.

DoD classification authority derives primarily from Presidential order. Currently the DoD Information Security Program (DoD, 1997) is the program used for classification and is based on Executive Order 12958 (Clinton, 1995) and its subsequent amendment Executive Order 13292 (Bush, 2003) addressing classified national security information. The current national security classification system is "designed primarily to protect the confidentiality of military, foreign policy, and intelligence information. It deals with only a small slice of the government information that requires protection although it drives the government's security apparatus and most of its costs . . . the classification system, largely unchanged since the Eisenhower administration, has grown out of control. More information is being classified and for extended periods of time. Security rules have proliferated, becoming more complex yet remaining unrelated to the threat" (Pike, 2002).

Today's classification system "starts with three levels of classification (Confidential, Secret, and Top Secret), often referred to collectively as collateral national security information. Layered on top of these three levels are at least nine additional protection categories. These include DoD Special Access Programs, Department of Energy (DOE) Special Access Programs, Director of Central Intelligence Sensitive Compartmented Information Programs, and other material controlled by special access or bigot lists such as the war plans of the Joint Chiefs of Staff and the operational files and source information of the CIA Operations Directorate. Further complicating the system are restrictive markings and dissemination controls such as ORCON (originator controlled dissemination and extraction of information), WNINTEL (warning notice, intelligence sources and methods), NOFORN (not releasable to foreign nationals), and NOCONTRACT (not releasable to contractors)" (Pike, 2002).

LEVELS OF CLASSIFICATION

Policies governing DoD's classification program are implemented through the Information Security Program (DoD, 1997). This regulation implements Executive Order 12958 (Clinton, 1995), "Classified National Security Information," and has been codified at 32 CFR Part 159 (DoD Information Security Program. 2001. 32 C.F.R. § 159). "A security clearance is a determination that a person is eligible for access to classified information. 'Need to know' is a determination made by a possessor of classified information that a prospective recipient, in the interest of national security, has a requirement for access to, or knowledge, or possession of the classified information in order to accomplish lawful and authorized government purposes" (Pike, 2002). Current levels of classification are broadly contained under the headings of Unclassified, Limited, Confidential, Secret, Top Secret, Limited Dissemination (LIMDIS), Special Access Program (SAP), and Sensitive Compartmented Information (SCI) (Pike, 2002). Appendix L-2 provides a discussion of each of the categories of unclassified and classified information control.

> No person may have access to classified information unless that person has been determined to be trustworthy and unless access is essential to the accomplishment of lawful and authorized government purposes, that is, the person has the appropriate security clearance and a need to know. Further, cleared personnel may not have access until they have been given an initial security briefing. Procedures are established by the head of each DoD component to prevent unnecessary access to classified information. (Pike, 2002)

> There must be a demonstrable need for access to classified information before a request for a personnel security clearance can be initiated. The number of people cleared and granted access to classified information is maintained at the minimum number that is consistent with operational requirements and needs. No one has a right to have access to classified information solely by virtue of rank or position. The final responsibility for determining whether an individual's official duties require possession of or access to any element or item of classified information, and whether the individual has been granted the appropriate security clearance by proper authority, rests upon the individual who has authorized possession, knowledge, or control of the information and not upon the prospective recipient. (Pike, 2002)

SECRECY AND MEDICAL RESEARCH

Numerous aspects of medical research have been classified on the basis of national security and have only recently been brought to public light. The

ACHRE Report (ACHRE, 1995) enumerated numerous radiation studies conducted during and after World War II which were classified, and some still have not been declassified. Although the Espionage Act of 1918 really began the era of national security classification, more and more documents have been classified with each new Presidential administration (ACHRE, 1995; Quist, 2002). Today the system is complicated and burdensome to use as discussed above. Medical research is still conducted and classified under the aegis of national security. This secrecy classification can establish hindrances in the medical care provided to the participants in these studies. All institutions that participate in medical research have some degree of classification for their projects, depending upon funding sponsor, subject, and agents used. Much of the current research on modern nerve agents, for example, is classified at the secret and above levels, even though there are many unclassified documents on nerve agents available to the public (IOM, 1993). And while DoD participates extensively in classified medical research studies, VA has not been excluded from such activities. Chapter 13 of the ACHRE Report outlined VA participation in maintenance of "confidential" files regarding radiation studies:

> VA, similarly, was able to provide fragments of information that show that "confidential" files were kept in anticipation of potential radiation liability claims. However, neither the VA, nor the DOE and DoD (who evidently were parties to this secret record keeping), have been able to determine exactly what secret records were kept and what rules governed their collection and availability. (ACHRE, 1995, ch. 13)

(As explained in Chapter 10 of the ACHRE Report, VA concluded that a "confidential" division contemplated in relation to secret record keeping was not activated.)

> VA publications did contain lists of several thousand (nonclassified) human experiments conducted at VA facilities; however, the information was quite fragmentary, and further information could not be readily retrieved (if it still exists) on the vast majority of these experiments. Thus, in looking for answers to questions about the secrecy of data on human experiments and intentional releases, we find record-keeping practices that leave questions about both what secrets were kept and what rules governed the keeping of secrets. (ACHRE, 1995, ch. 13)

Medical research involving human subjects must follow certain ethical and standard practice guidelines such as those established by the Nuremberg Code of 1947 (Trials of War Criminals Before the Nuremberg Military Tribunals, 1949). The 10 key elements of the Nuremberg Code are outlined in Appendix L-3.

Some medical research studies conducted prior to the Nuremburg Code implementation might not have followed the precepts of the code. Congressional inquiries during 1975 and 1976 requested that the Army Inspector General review the use of human volunteers in chemical agent research (IOM, 1993). An excerpted summary of this review (Taylor and Johnson, 1975) is presented in Appendix L-4. While this report concentrated on psychochemical testing conducted during the period 1950-1975, it also addressed the history of chemical warfare testing using human volunteers and the degree of compliance with the Nuremberg Code (IOM, 1993). The overriding conclusion from this report was that the secrecy applied to research using human volunteers "left ample room for misinterpretation, lack of knowledge about [guidelines governing human volunteers] and outright disregard for established policies and guidelines" (Taylor and Johnson, 1975, as referenced in IOM, 1993, p. 379). Concern regarding these conclusions remains today.

The issue of secrecy hindering medical treatment for veterans is amply exhibited in the IOM report *Veterans at Risk: The Health Effects of Mustard Gas and Lewisite* (IOM, 1993). Serious concerns were enumerated in the report over the secrecy issue demonstrated by DoD. These expanded concerns are presented in Appendix L-5.

CONCLUSIONS AND RECOMMENDATIONS FROM IOM'S *VETERANS AT RISK* REPORT

In *Veterans at Risk* (IOM, 1993), emphasis was placed on (1) the lack of exposure data, (2) the continuing dependence and reliance on secrecy by DoD, (3) serious ethical questions regarding the use of human volunteers, (4) total absence of long-term medical surveillance of participants, and (5) in some cases inadequate short-term follow-up even though medical knowledge was available as early as 1933 that exposure to mustard gas or lewisite could produce adverse health problems.

The oath of secrecy taken by participants, and enforced by potential punishment protocols if broken, resulted in continual and escalating cases of health impairment among the human volunteers in these chemical agent studies. The Taylor and Johnson report contains specific statements addressing the issue of secrecy and the participants who took the secrecy oath. An overarching conclusion stated in the report addressed future DoD research with human subjects. These future studies must be conducted following a set of ethical principles that mirror those that non-DoD researchers must follow. The 1975 Army Inspector General report (Taylor and Johnson, 1975) concludes that the mantle of secrecy gives implicit permission to researchers to stretch the boundaries of ethical guidelines in DoD human research under the guise of national security.

VA acknowledges that it must, at times, request exposure data from DoD in order to make a compensation decision. These exposure data may or may not be classified by DoD, and DoD has the option of releasing the data to VA. If the data are classified, DoD may not release them to VA citing national security issues (as stated during Do, 2006, and Freeman, 2006). This failure to release exposure data hinders medical treatment to the veteran. The potential for negative impact on the veteran population is demonstrated in the August 2006 VHA information letter released to health-care providers and the public (VHA, 2006). In this letter, VHA indicated that there may be in excess of 250 additional chemical agents that were used or tested in the chemical warfare arena. The Committee does not know if there are data available on each of these chemicals or if the data are unclassified. DoD is the only organization that can provide those answers. DoD has acknowledged that some 250 additional chemicals might fall under this concern (VHA, 2006). If chemical studies have been classified, DoD is not obligated to inform VA about the studies under the umbrella of national security concerns. As discussed above in the levels of classification, there are many levels under which exposure data could be classified. And, if DoD were to impose the restriction on VA that they must identify which data and under which level of classification the data fall before they release the data to VA, this would hinder access to important information useful for the care of veterans. Not withstanding national security issues, VA must have access to all exposure data to fully provide health care to veterans. A high level of cooperation between both agencies is necessary to provide maximum support to the veteran population.

SUMMARY

In view of the history of human subject use in various DoD and other agency studies, a mechanism is needed to protect the health of our veterans and their families. A joint effort between DoD and VA must be initiated to develop a mechanism to monitor human studies and provide health-protection measures to those individuals involved. Foremost would be the identification of all Service members involved in the studies. Secondly, the chemical, biological, infectious, and radiological agents used during the studies must be identified so that potential adverse health effects and treatments can be determined. Thirdly, accurate exposure assessment data must be collected and made available to appropriate scientists to be used in determining treatment regimens. As is the case in issues of this concern, the "dose makes the poison." Fourthly, national security concerns must be maintained while providing the necessary health support to veterans and their families.

These areas of concern should be addressed by the formation of, and effective and intelligent use of, a joint DoD-VA board to develop and implement policy areas surrounding national security and human subject research. Paramount to the effectiveness of the board, would be membership of individuals with sufficient security clearance to address national security, DoD weapons and tactical areas, and medical concerns, including exposure assessment. The major undertakings of this board would be the following:

- Identifying any human-use study
- Developing a registry of Service members involved in the studies
- Developing a tracking mechanism to maintain contact with the Service members involved in the studies
- Providing periodic medical evaluations or surveillance of Service members involved in the studies
- Determining appropriate medical treatment if an adverse health effect is detected
- Developing a mechanism to make information public as necessary
- Keeping the veteran, and family as applicable, fully informed regarding potential health effects of the materials that were used in the studies

Recommendation

DoD and VA should establish and implement mechanisms to identify, monitor, track, and medically treat individuals involved in research and other activities that have been classified and are secret.

There are clearly times when national security or mission success depends on maintaining secrecy regarding certain aspects of a Service member's military experience. However, every effort should be made to find mechanisms for characterizing Service member exposure and health histories in manners that do not interfere with the broader issues of national security or mission success. DoD should develop procedures that ensure full or partial declassification of sensitive information for the timely provision of that Service member's or veteran's health care. When such declassification is not possible, DoD should establish procedures whereby blinded data relevant to the Service member's health and exposure history are provided.

In some instances where national security and secrecy issues cannot be resolved, DoD and VA may need to establish mechanisms involving experts with appropriate security clearances to monitor affected registry cohorts for potential health outcomes and define surveillance or research activities that may need to be conducted within appropriate secrecy clearances. An interagency agreement could be developed between DoD and VA addressing the secrecy issue. As both agencies have used the classification system in the past, this agreement would address the policy development process and the exchange of classified information between the two agencies. The process would include establishment of a joint DoD-VA board composed of individuals who have sufficient security clearance to discuss classified data. The access to the classified information process would be contained in a written document outlining a mechanism to identify, monitor, track, and medically treat individuals who were part of research activities involving human subjects and whose research design and results have been classified.

REFERENCES

ACHRE (Advisory Committee on Human Radiation Experiments). 1995. *Final report.* Washington, DC: Government Printing Office. http://hss.energy.gov/healthsafety/ohre/roadmap/achre/report.html (accessed March 7, 2007).

Brown, M. 2003. *VA charge to the IOM Oversight Committee on the Study of the Health of Participants in Project SHAD (Shipboard Hazard and Defense).* Washington, DC: Department of Veterans Affairs. http://www1.va.gov/shad/docs/VA_Charge_IOM_on_the_Health_Study_of_SHAD.pdf (accessed March 7, 2007).

Bush, G. W. 2003. Executive order 13292: Further amendment to executive order 12958, as amended, classified national security information. *Federal Register* 68(60):15315-15334. http://a257.g.akamaitech.net/7/257/2422/14mar20010800/edocket.access.gpo.gov/2003/pdf/03-7736.pdf (accessed March 7, 2007).

Classification. 1936. *Dictionary of Unites States Army terms: Army regulation 320-5. Attachment 2.* Washington, DC: Government Printing Office. http://www.gwu.edu/~nsarchiv/radiation/dir/mstreet/commeet/meet14/brief14/tab_d/br14d1b.txt (accessed March 7, 2007).

Clinton, W. J. 1995. Executive order 12958: Classified national security information. *Federal Register* 60(76):19825-19843. http://frwebgate.access.gpo.gov/cgi-bin/getdoc.cgi?dbname=1995_register&docid=fr20ap95-135.pdf (accessed March 7, 2007).

Do, N. 2006. *DoD and Veterans Affairs: Health information sharing.* Paper presented at the third meeting of the IOM's Committee on the Evaluation of the Presumptive Disability Decision-Making Process for Veterans, San Antonio, TX.

DoD (Department of Defense). 1997. *Information Security Program.* DoD 5200.1-R. Washington, DC: Office of the Assistant Secretary of Defense/Command, Control, Communications, and Intelligence. http://www.fas.org/irp/doddir/dod/5200-1r/ (accessed March 7, 2007).

Freeman, C. 2006. *Department of Veterans Affairs/Department of Defense: Health data systems interoperability.* A presentation to the Institute of Medicine Committee on the Evaluation of the Presumptive Disability Decision-Making Process for Veterans, San Antonio, TX.

IOM (Institute of Medicine). 1993. *Veterans at risk: The health effects of mustard gas and lewisite.* Washington, DC: National Academy Press.

Pike, J. 2002. *Security and classification.* Gloucester, MA: Granite Island Group, Technical Surveillance Counter Measures. http://www.tscm.com/classification.html (accessed April 10, 2007).

Quist, A. S. 2002. *Introduction, history, and adverse impacts*. Vol. 1. Oak Ridge, TN: Oak Ridge Classification Associates, LLC. http://www.fas.org/sgp/library/quist/index.html (accessed March 7, 2007).

Taylor, J. R., and W. N. Johnson. 1975. *Research report concerning the use of volunteers in chemical agent research*. DAIG-IN 21-75. Washington, DC: Department of the Army, Office of the Inspector General and Auditor General.

Trials of war criminals before the Nuremberg military tribunals. 1949. *Control Council Law* 10(2):181-182. http://www.copernicusgroup.com/irbForms/NurembergCode.pdf (accessed March 7, 2007).

Truman, H. S. 1950. *Executive order 10104: Defining certain vital military and naval installations and equipment as required protection against the general dissemination of information relative thereto*. http://www.presidency.ucsb.edu/ws/index.php?pid=59321 (accessed April 10, 2007).

VHA (Veterans Health Administration). 2006. *Under Secretary for Health Information Letter: Potential health effects among veterans involved in military chemical warfare agent experiments conducted from 1955 to 1975*. Information letter 10-2006-010. Washington, DC: Department of Veterans Affairs. http://www1.va.gov/environagents/docs/USHInfoLetterIL10-2006-010.pdf (accessed March 7, 2007).

12

The Way Forward

INTRODUCTION

In previous chapters of this report, the Committee examined and described Congress' and the Department of Veterans Affairs' (VA's) past and present approaches to establishing presumptions. The case studies illustrate the application of the current approach, as well as approaches taken previously, and point to multiple points in the process of establishing presumptions that, in the Committee's view, should be modified by its participants (Chapter 5). The Committee set out principles related to evidence evaluation and causal inference as a foundation for setting in place an approach that is as firmly grounded as possible in the relevant base of scientific evidence for particular exposures and health outcomes (Chapters 6-9). The Committee also addressed the task of more comprehensively tracking the exposures of those serving in the military and prospectively monitoring military personnel and veterans for disease occurrence so that the risks of exposures can be assessed more systematically (Chapter 10) and so that exposures subject to secrecy can be considered (Chapter 11).

Based on the case studies and other information that was gathered, the Committee has concluded that there is a basis for making changes to the present approach. Building on the conceptual foundation developed in these earlier chapters, the Committee addresses the second part of its charge in this chapter and recommends a framework for establishing presumptions in the future.

The Committee suggests that its recommended framework be considered as a model to guide the evolution from the current approach toward that proposed by the Committee. The Committee recognizes that specific elements of its proposal (e.g., the call for carrying out exposure assessments and making exposure estimates) are not fully practicable for all relevant exposures at present and would take time to develop and implement. However, feasibility of specific elements of its proposal should be enhanced with future methodologic developments. The Committee believes that its approach can be applied to the full range of factors (e.g., chemical, biological, infectious, physical, and psychological) that may adversely affect the health of military personnel and veterans. The Committee does not intend that its approach be applied retrospectively to existing presumptions. The Committee is aware that policy or other concerns could lead Congress or VA to modify or even reject some of the Committee's recommendations. Congress and VA may find alternative processes to achieve the overall objective of the Committee's recommendations: an evidence-based approach to making presumptive disability decisions. However, the Committee suggests that its proposal will prove feasible and practical over time, that many of the elements in its proposal can and should be implemented without delay, and that the Committee's proposal would significantly improve the presumptive disability decision-making process for veterans.

Out of necessity, the Committee also makes some recommendations related to the implementation of its proposed approach. The Committee makes specific recommendations with regard to proposed advisory and review committees that will likely require congressional authorization, and the Committee recommends that VA would need to make adjustments in its overall approach to the presumptive disability decision-making process in order to follow the Committee's recommendations.

The Committee's recommended approach (Figure 12-1) has multiple new elements: a process for proposing exposures and illnesses for review; a systematic evidence review process incorporating a new evidence classification scheme and quantification of the extent of disease attributable to an exposure; a transparent decision-making process by VA; and an organizational structure to support the process. In using the term "exposure," the Committee defines exposure in a broad manner to include chemical, biological, infectious, physical and psychological stressors. We also call for a comprehensive approach to tracking exposures of military personnel and monitoring their health while in service and subsequent to service. The tracking should cover the full spectrum of exposures relevant to future risk for disease, including chemical, biological, infectious, physical and psychological stressors. The Committee's recommendations are based in a framework that sets out this evidence-based process (Figure 12-1).

The proposed process includes the engagement of two panels: An Advisory Committee and a Science Review Board. The Advisory Committee would be advisory to VA and would consider proposals for the review

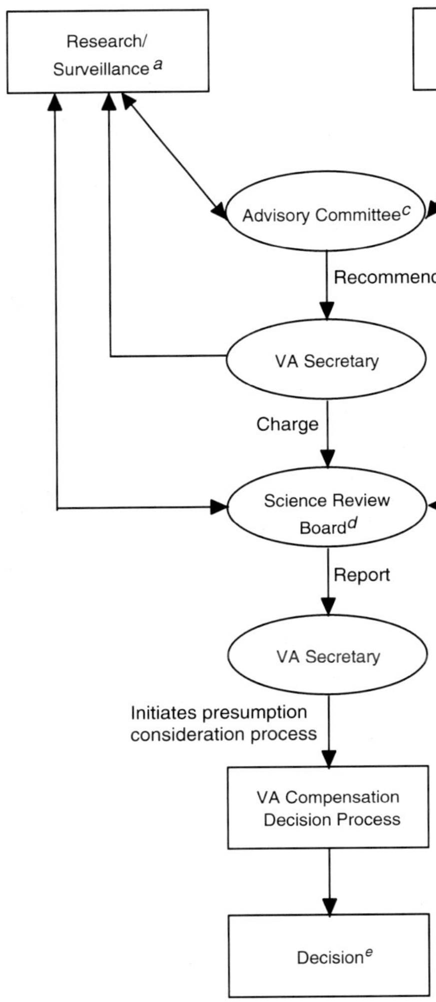

FIGURE 12-1 Proposed framework for future presumptive disability decision-making process for veterans.

[a] Includes research for classified or secret activities, exposures, etc.

[b] Includes veterans, veterans service organizations, federal agencies, scientists, general public, etc.

[c] This committee screens stakeholders' proposals and research in support of evaluating evidence for presumptions and makes recommendations to the VA Secretary when full evidence review or additional research is appropriate.

[d] The board conducts a two-step evidence review process (see report text for further detail).

[e] Final presumptive disability compensation decisions are made by the Secretary, Department of Veterans Affairs, unless legislated by Congress.

of exposures and illnesses that might be the basis for presumptions and recommend to the VA Secretary exposures and illnesses needing further consideration. The Science Review Board, which would be independent from VA, would conduct a comprehensive evaluation of the evidence for causation and, if warranted by the level of evidence in support of causation, estimate the service-attributable fraction of disease.

The Committee calls for the implementation of a health and exposure surveillance system such that veterans' health would be seamlessly tracked from entry into the service through retirement or separation and on to death. The resulting evidence on service-caused risks to health would be one critical component of the foundation of evidence for decision making, along with other sources of evidence, including studies of other populations, toxicologic studies, and other research. The accumulating evidence would undergo periodic review in a transparent and uniform fashion to gauge the strength of evidence in support of general causation and for determination of individual causation, drawing on the exposure data and perhaps other information. This review, carried out by the Science Review Board, would classify the strength of evidence for general causation in a standardized classification scheme as input into a compensation process by VA. VA, also deliberating in a transparent fashion based on established principles, would render a decision by the VA Secretary with regard to a presumption. The process includes a mechanism for stakeholders to propose exposures and illnesses for potential presumptions. These would be considered by the Advisory Committee.

GENERAL FRAMEWORK: THE ADVISORY COMMITTEE AND THE SCIENCE REVIEW BOARD

In the Committee's view, a change in the processes for the entities involved in the presumptive disability decision-making process is needed. In its recommendations for Congress, the Committee proposes the creation of an Advisory Committee and a Science Review Board.

The Advisory Committee would serve as an advisory committee to VA and consider the wide range of exposures and illnesses that might be a basis for presumptions. It would also consider research needs and assist VA in strategic research planning. The Science Review Board (independent from VA) would evaluate the evidence for causation and, if warranted, estimate the attributable fraction of disease in veterans due to exposure.

The role of the Advisory Committee would be to gather suggestions from all stakeholders (i.e., veterans service organizations, veterans, scientists, policy makers, and others) regarding specific exposures and illnesses that might be considered for comprehensive evaluation as potential presumptions, and to recommend to the VA Secretary those exposures and illnesses worthy of further consideration. This committee would also advise on research to be carried out by various entities.

The role of the Science Review Board would be to weigh the evidence on general causation of disease (including data from a wide range of sources) and to provide recommendations to the VA Secretary regarding presumptions. One critical element in the deliberations of the Science Review Board would be evidence from monitoring the veterans themselves. The health of military personnel should be seamlessly tracked from entry into the service through retirement or separation and on to death. This accumulating evidence would undergo periodic review by the Science Review Board in a transparent and consistent manner. The Science Review Board would also consider evidence from studies of nonveteran populations, toxicological studies, and basic science research. The Science Review Board would provide VA with input for its presumptive decisions, including a summary report of the available scientific evidence in a standardized classification scheme. VA would then render its decision with regard to a presumption through a transparent process of deliberation for potential compensation.

PRINCIPLES FOR THE PRESUMPTIVE DISABILITY DECISION-MAKING PROCESS FOR VETERANS

This section describes the principles that should be incorporated into this process at every level. VA's decision to make a presumption may involve weighing difficult and incomplete scientific evidence, in the context of veterans' concerns and society's obligations to the affected veterans as well as potential costs. Although the potential complexity of the presumptive disability decision-making process may make a complete codification difficult, the underlying principles can be clearly expressed.

Our country has long recognized that veterans make great sacrifices through their service, including being willing to risk their lives in combat. Historically, presumptions established by Congress and VA have acknowledged the special responsibilities of the government to injured veterans. Recent military conflicts have brought new concerns that extend beyond combat injury and that reflect the potential for delayed adverse consequences of complex combat exposures from chemical, biological, infectious, physical, and psychological stressors. The principles underlying presumptive disability decision making are critical for its success, and consequently the Committee calls for Congress and VA to affirm certain principles that underlie decision making around presumptions. The Committee recommends the following six principles as such a foundation:

1. Stakeholder inclusiveness
2. Evidence-based decisions

3. Transparency
4. Flexibility
5. Consistency
6. Causation, not just association, as the target for decision making

Each of these principles is discussed in detail below.

Stakeholder Inclusiveness

The Committee was impressed with the number of groups who expressed intense interest in the Committee's deliberations and in this report. The Committee's meetings were attended by representatives of veterans service organizations and by individual veterans. Optimal decision making has to include input from such stakeholders who will be affected by the process. Veterans and their families already have some input to VA through the political process. However, the Committee sees a need for more active solicitation of stakeholder input, not just into decisions on specific presumptions but more generally with regard to VA's overall process for making presumptions. It is with this principle in mind that the Committee recommends the creation of the Advisory Committee, separate from but advisory to VA, to consider exposures and diseases for which comprehensive scientific evaluation and possible presumptions may be warranted. Among others, this entity should consult with: representatives of veterans service organizations; veterans; veterans' families; medical personnel at VA who are engaged in the research, diagnosis, and treatment of conditions at issue; and personnel at the Department of Defense (DoD) who are knowledgeable about pertinent exposures and exposure data.

Evidence-Based Decisions

Over the last several decades, there has been a strong movement to ground clinical medicine and public health in an evidence-based framework for decision making. The systematic and consistent capture and analysis of all relevant evidence is central in this approach. Many previous IOM committees addressing scientific issues that would later be used by Congress or VA in establishing presumptions have followed structured approaches, typically evaluating all relevant observational studies on particular hazards faced by veterans and interpreting the findings in a broad biomedically grounded framework. However, while some of these reviews evaluated additional available toxicological or mechanistic evidence, they did not incorporate this evidence when reaching conclusions about the available scientific evidence for the relationship. The Committee recommends giving more consideration to toxicological investigation in general and to mechanisms of action in particular. The overall presumptive disability decision-making process needs to be grounded in the full extent of the scientific evidence available.

Although previous IOM committees have appropriately considered all available epidemiologic evidence on veterans, both domestic and foreign, as well as relevant studies from civilian populations, the available studies may be limited for many agents. In spite of efforts over the years by VA, the Medical Follow-Up Agency at IOM, and other federal and non-federal organizations to address critical health matters for veterans, the array of studies and findings is lacking as a basis for establishing well-grounded scientific presumptive disability decisions for many health outcomes. With the principle of evidence-based decisions in mind, this Committee also recommends that veterans be more effectively monitored, both in their military exposures and in relevant health outcomes throughout their lifetimes.

Transparency

Transparency in decision making is critical to the perception of fairness. The Committee strongly recommends that more emphasis be put on assuring transparency at every stage of the presumptive disability decision-making process. There are multiple stakeholders concerned with every specific presumption, including veterans who are already ill, those potentially at risk of illness, veterans service organizations, and the general public. Transparency means that each step of decision making should have a clear and known basis; stakeholders should be able to fully understand how decisions about presumptions are made, and the basis for those decisions, with reference to documented details of the presumptive disability decision-making process. VA has expressed concern that transparency could compromise internal discussion and affect decision-making deliberations; any unanticipated, adverse consequences of transparency should be noted and implications considered.

Flexibility

Scientific evidence is not static, and it often is less than certain. Given that the scientific basis for presumptive decisions will change over time, the Committee recommends that VA should be able to adjust future decisions when such change is scientifically justified. This does not mean that the Committee recommends that benefits previously granted should be terminated. The Committee is aware that disabled veterans and their families are often dependent on such payments and that it could create a hardship to remove them, a matter that VA disability policy recognizes in other situations. There should be a process of ongoing data collection so that relevant new findings are recognized and taken into account as quickly as possible. Differing approaches to assisting affected veterans might be used as evidence is accumulating. For example, when causation is very uncertain, a decision might be made by VA to award medical care to the veterans possibly harmed, leaving open the possibility of future financial compensation if the evidence strengthens over time.

Another aspect of flexibility is ongoing improvement of the decision-making process. At present, the Committee found little indication that VA assesses the performance of its own presumptive disability decision-making process or seeks to improve it. Even if VA were to adopt the decision-making structure recommended by the Committee (see Figure 12-1), it would also be necessary to set up mechanisms for evaluating VA's internal process over time. The Committee recommends that VA establish ongoing monitoring and evaluation to allow the decision-making process to be refined and improved. An information-gathering process would be needed for this purpose; consideration might also be given to appointment of an external committee to provide independent guidance on quality improvement, or the Advisory Committee could provide this function.

For the short term, as a new approach is implemented, careful review and evaluation may be particularly critical. Consequently, Congress may choose to be involved in the assessment and change the process as well, particularly as there is a transition from the current approach to a new process.

Consistency

One lesson from the case studies is that there is no firm consistency in the basis for presumptive decisions, possibly contributing to a perception by some of arbitrariness in the presumptive disability decision-making process. VA has offered a description of its internal processes as they have evolved over the last 15 years with regard to the receipt and consideration of IOM's Agent Orange and Gulf War reports. The materials from VA do not describe a standard protocol by which various internal groups respond to an IOM report. Although the Committee lacks full information on VA's processes, the Committee was left with the impression that better structure and documentation of its approach are needed. The Committee recommends that VA take steps to ensure that the bases for its internal decision making are explicit and applied consistently from case to case. To achieve consistency, consideration should be given to procedures for each element of the process within VA: evidence review, decision making, and implementation. For some elements of the process, models are already available, as in the instance of previous IOM Agent Orange and Gulf War committees.

Causation, Not Just Association

One of the most critical matters, in the Committee's view, is clarifying the basis for making a decision to compensate veterans for service-related disability. The Committee recommends that causation, not just association, should be the basis of presumptive compensation. The justification for this recommendation is provided below.

Presumptive disability decisions are based on two judgments: (1) that a group of veterans was *exposed* to a potentially harmful agent or condition during service, and (2) that the agent or condition *is able to cause* disease leading to disability. The second proposition states a causal association, and not merely an association for which causation has not been established. An association between an exposure and outcome can be good evidence for a causal claim, but it is not the same as a causal claim.

The history of presumptions for Agent Orange illustrates the need to be clear on this point. The Veterans' Dioxin and Radiation Exposure Compensation Standards Act of 1984 (Public Law 98-542. 98th Cong., 2d Sess.) used language of both association and causation in describing the evidence required for presumptions. Initially, VA interpreted the law as requiring a certain threshold of evidence for causation, and as a result denied presumptions between Agent Orange and all diseases except chloracne. Veterans interpreted the intent of the law differently, and a district court sided with the veterans finding the Act ambiguous and interpreting *congressional intent* as establishing a threshold of evidence for an association (*Nehmer v. United States Veterans' Administration*, 1989. Henderson, T. E. United States District Court for the Northern District of California Case Number C86-6160 TEH).

The Agent Orange Act of 1991 (Public Law 102-4. 102d Cong., 1st Sess.) led the VA to provide the following charge to IOM in making scientific determinations:

- whether a statistical association with herbicide exposure exists, taking into account the strength of the scientific evidence and the appropriateness of the statistical and epidemiologic methods used to detect the association;
- the increased risk of the disease among those exposed to herbicides during service in the Republic of Vietnam during the Vietnam era; and
- whether there exists a plausible biological mechanism or other evidence of a causal relationship between herbicide exposure and the disease.

VA contracted with IOM to provide a biennial review of the scientific evidence, and VA provided each of the IOM Agent Orange committees (IOM, 1994, 1996, 1999, 2001, 2003b, 2005b) the 3-point charge contained in the Agent Orange Act. IOM reports on Agent Orange (IOM, 1994, 1996, 1999, 2001, 2003b, 2005b) generally stated that the committees were unable to address the second point of their charge and did not use evidence from the third point of their charge to incorporate into the overall strength of evidence decision on association. The first IOM Agent Orange committee (IOM, 1994) established categories for the strength of evidence based on an *association* (sufficient, limited/suggestive, inadequate/insufficient, and no association) that have been used by subsequent IOM Agent Orange committees (IOM, 1996, 1999, 2000b, 2001, 2003b, 2005b).

Based in part upon IOM's categorization of limited/suggested evidence of an association between exposure to Agent Orange and a specific health outcome—without scientific research on increased risk in exposed veterans (second point of charge), or robust evidence for a plausible biological mechanism (third point of charge), VA has presumptively service-connected several health outcomes to Agent Orange since 1994. In the example of type 2 diabetes, the scientific basis for the presumption was not evidence of a causal connection, but far more limited evidence of an association. Of course, the Committee recognizes that Congress and VA may choose to presumptively service-connect health outcomes for which the evidence for causation is weak; however, the basis for making such a decision should be made explicit.

In recommending a shift from association to causation as the underlying basis for compensation decisions, the Committee notes that such a shift would not necessarily raise the bar for establishing a presumption. It should be noted here that previous IOM committees reviewing mustard gas and lewisite (IOM, 1993) and the Gulf War (IOM, 2000a, 2003a, 2005a, 2006, 2007) each used a causal categorization in their reports. A more thorough consideration of mechanistic evidence of causation could actually reduce the need for evidence of an association. For example, in *Gulf War and Health* (IOM, 2003a, p. 330) IOM found that "there is inadequate/insufficient evidence to determine whether an association exists between chronic exposure to benzene and myelodysplastic syndromes" in veterans even though many toxicologists and hematologists view the *overall* evidence as strongly supportive of a causal relationship in rodents.

The Committee recommends a scheme for the classification of evidence for causation in the following section.

STRUCTURE AND ACTIVITIES OF THE PRESUMPTIVE DISABILITY DECISION-MAKING PROCESS

The Committee proposes a transparent, public process through which diseases or health conditions potentially caused or aggravated by military service and the putative causal agents (e.g., chemical, biological, infectious, physical, and psychological stressors) would be nominated for review and, given sufficient information and numbers of veterans affected, formally evaluated to determine if the evidence for causality supports consideration of presumptive service connection by VA. The process would be fully transparent and the outcomes of the evaluation made available in a timely manner.

The Committee recommends that Congress create an Advisory Committee to VA. This Advisory Committee would be composed of scientific experts and veterans' representatives who would identify and recommend to the VA Secretary health conditions and agents (i.e., chemical, biological, infectious, physical, and psychological stressors) for referral to and comprehensive evaluation by the independent Science Review Board. In turn, the Science Review Board's findings and report would be provided to the VA Secretary for consideration in establishing presumptive compensation decisions.

The Advisory Committee

An Advisory Committee, chartered by Congress, is needed to identify potential exposures during military service, and related disabilities caused by these exposures, and to refer these topics for comprehensive review to the Science Review Board. This permanent committee would receive proposals for review, screen the available scientific information and research, and give priority to proposals based on the nature and extent of evidence supporting the relationship. The Advisory Committee would be composed of veterans' representatives and recognized and credible experts in relevant fields, for example epidemiology, industrial hygiene, toxicology, occupational medicine, public health, military surveillance and databases, and exposure assessment. The Advisory Committee would be supported by VA and other federal staff with appropriate backgrounds and expertise to assist the committee. The Advisory Committee would review the initial assessment, give priorities, and make recommendations for proceeding with the full, comprehensive scientific review to the VA Secretary. The VA Secretary would have the authority to select conditions and agents for comprehensive scientific review by the Science Review Board.

Open Proposal Process

Health conditions and causative agents or circumstances would be proposed for review based on evidence of a connection between the condition and military service, and evidence that a sizable or well-defined group of veterans is likely to be affected. Concerns as to the need for a presumption might arise from the health surveillance of veterans or active military personnel, laboratory research discoveries, or findings from occupational studies of exposures and health effects (e.g., by the International Agency for Research on Cancer [see Chapter 8]). Proposals from any source on behalf of affected veterans (e.g., veterans, veterans' families, veterans service organizations, VA, DoD, other governmental bodies, researchers, or the general public) would be accepted. Proposals along with supporting information would be tracked and evaluated on a scheduled basis.

Screening of Proposals

An initial review of the evidence would be performed by professional VA staff in support of the Advisory Committee. The purpose of the screen would be to determine whether there is a minimum amount of evidence suggesting that the condition could have been caused or aggravated by military service, or of military exposure to the putative causal agent, and also to gauge the extent and nature of the evidence supporting the proposal. The process of proposal review would be structured to be responsive to stakeholders of varying expertise and capabilities, and include the gathering of additional evidence beyond that submitted with the proposal.

Prioritization

Those exposures found to, at a minimum, have some positive evidence of a relationship to health conditions and adequate data to initiate review would be candidates for full evaluation. Higher priority would be given to the conditions and causative agents or circumstances with the strongest evidence, affecting the largest numbers of veterans, and leading to the most severe health consequences.

Advisory Committee Review

The Advisory Committee would review materials assembled by the VA staff and other input from stakeholders and the general public to make recommendations to the VA Secretary for full, comprehensive scientific review by the Science Review Board. The process used by the Advisory Committee, which would be subject to the Federal Advisory Committee Act, and the rationale for recommendations would be documented and transparent. The process would also provide opportunities for input by stakeholders during the Advisory Committee's review of proposals. To assist the Advisory Committee in developing recommendations, it is important that VA improve its data collection processes to track claims filed by veterans for benefits so that environmental exposure issues connected with new claims can be identified quickly.

The VA Secretary

Ultimately, the decision regarding which topics deserve full, comprehensive scientific evaluation resides with VA. VA would take the Advisory Committee recommendations under advisement, and consider the nature and extent of evidence, number of veterans potentially affected, severity of the conditions, public comment, and potentially other factors to decide the topics that would proceed to the Science Review Board for full, comprehensive scientific evaluation. Transparency at this stage by VA is critical. The VA Secretary would be required to respond to the Advisory Committee's recommendations, providing an explanation for his or her decisions, a copy of which would be filed with Congress on an annual basis.

In the Committee's proposed presumptive disability decision-making process, VA would receive the full, comprehensive scientific evaluation, as described below, from the Science Review Board. We recommend that VA establish a uniform and transparent process for making decisions with regard to presumptions following receipt of such evidence reviews. The process should incorporate the principles embodied in this Committee's proposed approach. VA procedures should be established with input from the many concerned stakeholders. Its protocols should acknowledge who would be accountable for considering the reports of the Science Review Board and a description of how the reports would be used. A clear and comprehensive evidence-based rationale should be offered for all decisions and made public.

Science Review Board

For the process of comprehensive scientific review of the evidence to be successful, it must be regarded as credible by veterans, the general public, and the scientific community. It is essential that the process be objective, transparent, and of the highest scientific quality, reflecting scientific consensus among acknowledged experts at the time of the review. The Science Review Board is envisioned as following a transparently operated, adequately funded and staffed process in which outside experts, with various disciplinary backgrounds serving as needed, would conduct the full, comprehensive scientific evaluation. Rereview of cases would be conducted as new evidence would emerge, and further research would be encouraged when important hypotheses are unresolved by the available scientific evidence.

An independent Science Review Board would be authorized by Congress and funded by VA. The group would have expertise in the key disciplines needed to weigh the causal evidence and determine the service-attributable fraction. Ad hoc members could be added when specialized expertise was needed or issues of secrecy would need to be addressed. Members of the

Science Review Board would serve as independent experts, and without conflicts of interest. The Science Review Board would be housed in an organization or institution that would ensure its credibility, its sustained growth, and consistent efforts and products.

A staff of professionals with expertise in relevant disciplines would be needed to support the Science Review Board. Staff would seek out and compile relevant information, solicit input from outside organizations, and assist in report writing and in developing and finalizing recommendations from the Science Review Board.

Public and Other Requests for Relevant Data

VA would publicly announce in the *Federal Register* the health conditions and putative causal agents that would undergo full, comprehensive scientific review by the Science Review Board. In the initial preparations for the evidence review, a request for information on the evidence for and against causal relationship for the particular condition and agent or circumstance would be announced, for example in the *Federal Register* and on VA's website. Relevant data may also be requested from DoD, organizations within VA, or other knowledgeable organizations, by project staff or the Science Review Board.

Two-Step Process of Evidence Utilization

The Committee recommends a two-step process for evaluation of scientific evidence by the Science Review Board. Step one would involve a systematic review of relevant data to determine the strength of evidence for causation, using one of four categories as presented in Chapter 8:

1. *Sufficient*: The evidence is sufficient to conclude that a causal relationship exists.
2. *Equipoise and Above*: The evidence is sufficient to conclude that a causal relationship is at least as likely as not, but not sufficient to conclude that a causal relationship exists.
3. *Below Equipoise*: The evidence is not sufficient to conclude that a causal relationship is at least as likely as not, or is not sufficient to make a scientifically informed judgment.
4. *Against*: The evidence suggests the lack of a causal relationship.

The scientific review would include all relevant evidence using existing systematic review models. The Science Review Board would develop standard operating procedures, which would be reviewed and updated on a regular basis, and outline the protocol by which evidence would be reviewed and categorized. The evidence gathered and reviewed would be similar in nature to that supporting cancer or reproductive toxicity evaluations by the National Toxicology Program's Center for the Evaluation of Risks to Human Reproduction, the National Toxicology Program's *Report on Carcinogens*, the International Agency for Research on Cancer, and the U.S. Environmental Protection Agency. The public and stakeholders would be encouraged to provide input into the scientific review process.

If the evidence for causation were categorized as *Sufficient* or at *Equipoise and Above*, then we anticipate that VA would consider a presumptive service connection based upon causal evidence categorization and the service-attributable fraction if available (to be estimated in the second step of the process, described below). As is current VA policy, if the evidence is at *Equipoise*, the benefit of the doubt would be given to the veteran, and a presumptive service connection would be considered. If the evidence were categorized as *Against*, then we anticipate that VA would not consider a presumptive service connection. If, however, the evidence were categorized as *Below Equipoise*, then we anticipate that VA would, after carefully considering the prospects and recommendations for future research, decide on an appropriate time frame for the subsequent scientific review of the evidence, with the expectation that the evidence would then be sufficient to resolve matters either for or against the causal claim at that time. Such information would be considered by the Advisory Committee serving in its capacity as overseer of the overall process and advisor to the VA Secretary.

If the VA Secretary were to decide that a presumption would not be established for evidence categorized as *Below Equipoise* or, for other reasons, for evidence categorized as *Equipoise and Above*, then during the period of further evidence development and gathering and prior to the subsequent scientific review of the evidence, VA should consider providing some support to potentially affected veterans, such as providing provisional access to medical care.

As evidence accumulates, the balance might move to strengthen or to weaken the case for causality. Importantly, the Science Review Board should be free to upgrade the level of evidence, to downgrade the level of evidence, or to leave it as the same categorization. For evidence that has reached the classification of *Sufficient*, we would not anticipate a potential lowering of the classification, if the original determination was correctly made and based on sound scientific evidence.

If the strength of the evidence reaches *Sufficient* or *Equipoise and Above*, then the evaluation would move to step two, the calculation of the service-attributable fraction of disease when required information and data are available. This calculation is independent of the classification of the strength of evidence for causation, and the magnitude of the service-attributable fraction is not considered in the application of the four-level schema for categorizing evidence. Rather, the service-attributable fraction would be of value for decision making, giving an understanding of the scope of the population to be covered by a presumption.

In step two, the Science Review Board would consider the extent of exposure among veterans and subgroups of veterans, as well as dose-response relationships. When such information is available, the board would estimate the service-attributable fraction and its related uncertainty. The purpose of step two is to convey the impact of the exposure on veterans as a whole for the purpose of decision making and planning, but not to serve inappropriately as an estimate of probability of causation for individuals. Some exposures may contribute greatly to the disease burden of veterans, while other exposures (even with a known causal effect) may have a small impact overall. This additional information would be useful to VA in its decision making as to whether a presumption should be made for the veteran population in general, for subgroups, or not at all. When service-attributable fraction data are not available, the VA may consider presumptions on the information contained in step one.

Periodic Reevaluation of Evidence

All but the most conclusive evaluations would be subject to rereview and updating. Rereviews could follow a fixed cycle, for example every 5, 7, or 10 years. Rereview and updating could also be triggered by new compelling scientific information, in which case outside parties could make nominations to the Advisory Committee for reconsideration by the Science Review Board.

EXAMPLE OF APPLICATION IN CURRENT CONFLICTS

The Committee's framework is intended for prospective application during peace- and wartime and for in-garrison exposures as well as those experienced in wartime theatres. The potential utility of the recommended approach might be considered by applying it retrospectively to the case studies or prospectively to the current conflicts in Iraq and Afghanistan. For the purposes of this hypothetical illustration we use the current conflicts, although in establishing the framework we drew on lessons learned from the case studies regarding such matters as secrecy (e.g., mustard gas and lewisite), lack of ongoing epidemiological surveillance (e.g., cardiovascular disease in amputees), and insufficient exposure information (e.g., Agent Orange and Gulf War in 1990).

With regard to the current military actions in Iraq and Afghanistan, the conflicts have been marked by the hostility of the environments with ubiquitous threats to military personnel and widespread use of improvised explosive devices (IEDs) bringing risk of maiming and death. The level of psychological stress has increased risk for posttraumatic stress disorder (PTSD) and the IEDs have led to high rates of limb loss and traumatic brain injury (TBI). Additionally, many of the deployed personnel are in the National Guard and Reserves and have faced unexpected disruption of their civilian lives from one or several deployments during the course of the current conflicts.

How might a full implementation of the Committee's proposed framework prove useful for the purpose of presumptive disability decision making for veterans of the current conflicts in Iraq and Afghanistan? We call for systematic and ongoing exposure assessment that would extend beyond chemical, biological, and physical stressors to psychological stress; with suitable instruments, exposures to stress would be estimated among samples of various at-risk groups of individuals, as the basis for future observation for onset of PTSD or other disorders in relation to exposure. For chemical exposures, industrial hygiene approaches could also be used for exposed groups of individuals, again as the basis for assigning exposures to various groups. Stored blood samples from pre- and post-deployment examinations could also be used to indicate and assess exposures to chemical agents, to assess immune responses to infectious agents, or to measure other biomarkers of exposure or of injury. For all deployed personnel, geographic location and duties could serve as the basis for assigning potential exposures to groups of individuals.

Information on future disease risks in relation to exposure could be obtained through follow-up via health status and exposure data records linkage to VA, DoD, and other data systems, including the National Health Index for mortality. Special cohorts (e.g., registries) could be constructed to identify and track particular exposed groups with greater intensity and focused outcome assessment. Service members with TBI should be identified and tracked, for example, for level of functioning and quality of life. Risk for PTSD might be monitored in groups with greater and lesser levels of stress.

A general consequence of the Committee's approach would be continuous monitoring of health outcomes among those who had been deployed to the zones of current conflict in Iraq and Afghanistan. Comparison of disease risks in those deployed to those not deployed in these areas could signal any potential increased risk and lead to more focused assessment and review of exposure and health outcomes concerns, including review by the Advisory Committee.

In the event that the Advisory Committee determined that an evidence evaluation was needed, the Science Review Board would be able to use the findings of the exposure and health tracking system. Evidence would be available directly from the tracking of veterans that would be included in the review along with other relevant information. If indicated by the classification of strength of evidence, the service-attributable fraction should be estimable. The size of the exposed, and hence eligible, pool of veterans would be known with some degree of certainty. The evidence review conducted by the Science Review Board would be reported back to VA, so that the VA Secretary could make a determination as to whether a service-connection presumption would be established. These activities would follow the transparent process laid out by the Committee, possibly increasing confidence in the decisions made.

SECRECY AND THE PRESUMPTIVE DISABILITY DECISION-MAKING PROCESS

Research involving individuals exposed to chemical, biological, or radiological agents is often classified for security reasons, and information related to clandestine missions is also classified. This classification can be detrimental to the long-term health status of our veterans, who maintain the oath of secrecy. So long as information remains classified—which can be for a long period of time—these veterans cannot openly investigate or inquire about the relationships between their disease or health condition and the exposures they received. Although secrecy must be applied and maintained for obvious homeland security and national defense reasons, this designation must not be used to deny or forestall necessary medical treatment for afflicted individuals. As made clear by the case study of mustard gas and lewisite (see Appendix I), veterans may be harmed by exposures from classified activities. It is absolutely necessary for DoD and VA to develop, implement, and maintain a policy program that addresses the issues of health maintenance and national security for our veterans. The case study of mustard gas and lewisite illustrates the opportunity for harm to occur in research volunteers because of secrecy (see Appendix I).

Regarding the processes for science review proposed here, review would be particularly challenging when classified or secret information is involved. Nonetheless, the Committee recommends that DoD and VA develop a process for ensuring that exposures sustained in the course of classified or secret activities are not excluded from the presumptive disability decision-making process. Our Committee can make only general comments on this matter. For some issues involving classified and secret information, consultants with appropriate expertise and security clearance might be added to the Advisory Committee and Science Review Board. They could review the classified or secret information and provide information or recommendations for the decision process in a format that would not violate the government's need for secrecy. This variation in process would be clearly and openly described.

Perhaps in some circumstances, no element of the relationship between military exposure and the condition could be divulged. This circumstance would call for a separate special process to protect government secrecy as well as provide fair treatment for affected veterans.

ADDITIONAL DATA FOR DECISION MAKING

To make the best possible decisions regarding compensation for veterans, it is necessary to go beyond the published literature. In this section we will consider several sources of data that would greatly enhance the presumptive disability decision-making process for veterans.

At present, research on the health of veterans is conducted in a variety of venues. Examples include the following:

- Intramural research of the War-Related Illness and Injury Study Center assesses the health consequences of deployment to a combat theater.
- The Medical Follow-Up Agency of IOM's Board on Military and Veterans Health carries out targeted epidemiologic research on health of military personnel.
- Extramural research related to the health of veterans may be funded by VA through its extramural research program or by the National Institutes of Health.

Although investigators at the War-Related Illness and Injury Study Center have a track record of productivity, the Committee anticipates that substantial additional capacity for multidisciplinary research will be needed as better surveillance methods are put into place and new hypotheses are generated.

The approach to research should be driven by a sustained and iterative planning process that strategically identifies and addresses emerging questions. Issues needing investigation might be identified through surveillance findings, stakeholder input, or findings emerging in research conducted beyond VA. VA needs a process that strategically addresses research needs to ensure that presumptions are evidence-based to the best extent possible. In the Committee's recommendations, we call for an Advisory Committee that would provide guidance to VA in developing and maintaining a targeted and strategic research planning process. The reviews carried out by the Science Review Board would also highlight gaps that need to be addressed through research.

REFERENCES

IOM (Institution of Medicine). 1993. *Veterans at risk: The health effects of mustard gas and lewisite*. Washington, DC: National Academy Press.

IOM. 1994. *Veterans and Agent Orange: Health effects of herbicides used in Vietnam*. Washington, DC: National Academy Press.

IOM. 1996. *Veterans and Agent Orange: Update 1996*. Washington, DC: National Academy Press.

IOM. 1999. *Veterans and Agent Orange: Update 1998*. Washington, DC: National Academy Press.

IOM. 2000a. *Gulf War and health, volume 1: Depleted uranium, pyridostigmine bromide, sarin, vaccines*. Washington, DC: National Academy Press.

IOM. 2000b. *Veterans and Agent Orange: Herbicide/dioxin exposure and type 2 diabetes*. Washington, DC: National Academy Press.

IOM. 2001. *Veterans and Agent Orange: Update 2000*. Washington, DC: National Academy Press.

IOM. 2003a. *Gulf War and health, volume 2: Insecticides and solvents*. Washington, DC: The National Academies Press.

IOM. 2003b. *Veterans and Agent Orange: Update 2002*. Washington, DC: The National Academies Press.

IOM. 2005a. *Gulf War and health, volume 3: Fuels, combustion products, and propellants*. Washington, DC: The National Academies Press.

IOM. 2005b. *Veterans and Agent Orange: Update 2004*. Washington, DC: The National Academies Press.

IOM. 2006. *Gulf War and health, volume 4: Health effects of serving in the Gulf War*. Washington, DC: The National Academies Press.

IOM. 2007. *Gulf War and health, volume 5: Infectious diseases*. Washington, DC: The National Academies Press.

13

Recommendations

In meeting its charge, the Committee has heard presentations and received information from past and present congressional staff members as well as representatives of the Department of Veterans Affairs (VA), the Department of Defense (DoD), the Institute of Medicine (IOM), various stakeholder groups (e.g., veterans service organizations [VSOs]), individual veterans and the general public. The Committee has reviewed an extensive amount of information including (but not limited to): documents provided by the Veterans' Disability Benefits Commission, public laws and their supporting House and Senate committee reports, *Federal Register* notices, VA documents (i.e., cost estimates), DoD documents, and IOM reports that have been commissioned by VA and DoD. The Committee has completed case studies that analyze a wide variety of circumstances in which presumptions have been established by Congress and VA. Additionally, the Committee has considered how to use scientific evidence in guiding the process for making decisions that impact the compensation of veterans. It has covered the evaluation of evidence for inferring association and causation as well as the quantification of the contribution of an agent to disease causation in populations and the extension of this quantification to individuals.

Based on its extensive evaluation of the current process for establishing presumptive disability decisions and its consideration of alternative approaches, the Committee has a series of recommendations for an approach that is both more strongly grounded in scientific evidence and more responsive and open to veterans. Chapter 12 describes that process. We propose a transformation of the current presumptive disability decision-making process for veterans. We recognize that considerable time will be needed to implement some of these recommendations and will require investment in tracking the exposures and health of current military service men and women as well as veterans. Progress depends on greater research capacity and changes in the evaluation and use of scientific evidence in making compensation decisions. The Committee finds that there are sufficient remediable shortcomings within the current process to warrant immediate action as Congress and VA move toward implementation of a new approach. The Committee concluded that improvements are needed throughout the presumptive disability decision-making process. The recommendations that follow are based on the Committee's proposed framework for making presumptive decisions (see Chapter 12). We list the recommendations in relation to the appropriate body. In recommending the organizational structure below, the Committee recognizes that Congress and VA might pursue alternative structures to achieve the Committee's overall goal of having an evidence-based presumptive disability decision-making process. However, the Committee believes that its proposal is feasible and practical over time, many of the elements in its proposal can and should be implemented without delay and that the Committee's proposal would significantly improve the presumptive disability decision-making process for veterans.

CONGRESS

Recommendation 1. Congress should create a formal advisory committee (Advisory Committee) to VA to consider and advise the VA Secretary on disability-related questions requiring scientific research and review to assist in the consideration of possible presumptions.

The investigation and evaluation of the relationships of exposures during military service and subsequent disabilities experienced by veterans have not been sufficiently prompt and comprehensive. To assure that research and review are timely and on target, the Committee recommends creation of an Advisory Committee to VA composed of veterans and recognized experts in disciplines such as epidemiology, toxicology, exposure assessment and biostatistics to identify and assess issues for referral to the VA Secretary and then to the Science Review Board, which would carry out the subsequent full, comprehensive scientific evaluation of the evidence (see Recommendation 2).

In the Committee's recommended approach, the Advisory Committee has two key roles: screening exposures and illnesses proposed for review for possible presumptive compensation, and providing guidance to VA on research needs and planning. The multidisciplinary Advisory Committee should include stakeholder representatives and have a permanent staff to support its function.

The Advisory Committee would also receive the proposals for exposures and illnesses of concern made by stakeholders and other groups. With staff, the Advisory Committee would evaluate the candidates for potential presumptions and make recommendations to the VA Secretary as to whether a full, comprehensive scientific review by the Science Review Board should be carried out. Recommendations made to the VA Secretary and his or her responses thereto should be reported to Congress on an annual basis. To assist the Advisory Committee, a VA tracking system should be developed to identify filed disability claims that suggest the need for further investigation of the relationship linking exposures to health conditions during service. Additionally, claims filed and decided following the creation of a presumption should be tracked to validate previous estimates of case load and to project future claims arising secondarily from the primary condition for service connection.

Recommendation 2. Congress should authorize a permanent independent review body (Science Review Board) operating with a well-defined process that will use evaluation criteria as outlined in this Committee's recommendations to evaluate scientific evidence for VA's use in considering future service-connected presumptions.

Current statutory authority for independent evaluation of scientific evidence for potential service-connected presumptions has too often resulted from ad hoc responses to the pressing questions of the moment. Absent a permanent committee and staff to consider and evaluate the evidence relevant to particular potential presumptions, approaches to evaluation have not been uniform and have not always provided VA with evidence syntheses that fully used the available evidence. The implementation of the Science Review Board, or a comparable entity, is central to the Committee's recommended changes to the presumptive disability decision-making process.

The Science Review Board would implement a well-defined, consistent, and transparent evidence-based approach as described in this report. It should be housed within an organization or institution that can assure the highest level of credibility for its process and reports. The existence of a permanently staffed body would also allow it to be proactive rather than reactive to veterans' concerns.

Recognizing that the development of sufficient scientific evidence to warrant a positive presumptive decision does not always occur quickly, Congress should also consider granting VA discretionary authority to provide provisional medical treatment to veterans while research findings are pending.

DEPARTMENT OF VETERANS AFFAIRS

Recommendation 3. VA should develop and publish a formal process for consideration of disability presumptions that is uniform and transparent and clearly sets forth all evidence considered and the reasons for the decisions reached.

Pursuant to statute, VA is directed to make decisions concerning the establishment of service-connected presumptions for Agent Orange determined on the basis of sound medical and scientific evidence. In making such decisions, VA is required to consider pertinent reports from the National Academy of Sciences and "all other sound medical and scientific information and analyses available" (Agent Orange Act of 1991. Public Law 102-4. 102d Cong., 1st Sess.).

The Committee found that VA (1) has no formal published rules governing this process, (2) does not thoroughly disclose and discuss what "other" medical and scientific information it considered, and (3) publishes abbreviated and insufficiently informative explanations of why a presumption was or was not granted.

The closed nature of VA practices does not foster public understanding of the reasoning behind the VA's decisions; the Committee believes that a move by VA to a more transparent process would better meet the expectations of the nation's veterans and of the public at large. The Committee recommends that VA promulgate, without delay, a more formal procedure for establishing presumptive disability decisions. The procedure needs to be transparent and consistent with the practices of federal regulatory agencies. The word "uniform" in the recommendation refers to a process that works in a consistent fashion with regards to its procedures and outcomes; in other words, given a similar body of evidence for different diseases, the end result of the process should be similar. Members of internal working groups should be disclosed; all evidence considered should be disclosed; and a thorough discussion of the weight attached to the evidence considered should be published so that veterans and the public have a clear understanding of the basis for the decision reached.

SCIENCE REVIEW BOARD

The recommendations that follow are directed toward the proposed, future Science Review Board, the entity to be established in the Committee's proposed approach.

Recommendation 4. The Committee recommends that the goal of the presumptive disability decision-making process be to ensure compen-

sation for veterans whose diseases are *caused by* military service and that this goal must serve as the foundation for the work of the Science Review Board. The Committee recommends that the Science Review Board implement its proposed two-step process.

Previous IOM Agent Orange committees have focused on strength of evidence for an association when causal language has also been included in their charge (IOM, 1994, 1996, 1999, 2000b, 2001, 2003b, 2005b). Agent Orange legislation calls for establishing the presence of an "association" between exposure and disease; however, the enabling legislation also called for consideration of study bias and biologic mechanisms, which address the underlying question of causation (Agent Orange Act of 1991. Public Law 102-4. 102d Cong., 1st Sess.). IOM Gulf War committees have established evidence categorizations based upon both causation and association (IOM, 2000a, 2003a, 2005a, 2006, 2007). The enabling legislation for Gulf War actions did not specify the strength of evidence to be used in scientific reviews (Veterans' Benefits Improvements Act of 1994. Public Law 103-446. 103rd Cong., 2d Sess., codified as Compensation for Disabilities Occurring in Persian Gulf War Veterans. 2006. 38 U.S.C. § 1117; Omnibus Consolidated and Emergency Supplemental Appropriations Act of 1998 (Part II). Public Law 105-277. 105th Cong., 2d Sess.). The IOM committee that evaluated mustard gas and lewisite based its evidence categorization solely upon causation (IOM, 1993). The Committee therefore recommends that the focus be shifted to the question most fundamental to presumptions, namely whether a military exposure is able to cause a disease.

Recommendation 5. The Committee recommends that the Science Review Board use the proposed four-level classification scheme, as follows, in the first step of its evaluation. The Committee recommends that a standard be adopted for "causal effect" such that if there is at least as much evidence in favor of the exposure having a causal effect on the frequency or severity of disease as there is evidence against, then a service-connected presumption will be considered.

The Committee recognizes that gathering and synthesizing the evidence necessary to prove a causal effect can be daunting, but expert groups have repeatedly done so using replicable approaches and standard classification schemes. The Science Review Board should adopt a written protocol for evidence review and apply the Committee's recommended four-level scheme:

1. *Sufficient*: The evidence is sufficient to conclude that a causal relationship exists.
2. *Equipoise and Above*: The evidence is sufficient to conclude that a

causal relationship is at least as likely as not, but not sufficient to conclude that a causal relationship exists.

3. *Below Equipoise*: The evidence is not sufficient to conclude that a causal relationship is at least as likely as not, or is not sufficient to make a scientifically informed judgment.

4. *Against*: The evidence suggests the lack of a causal relationship.

Using this scheme, the Committee recommends that the presumption of a causal effect be considered when an expert scientific evaluation finds the evidence considered in support of a causal effect to be at least as strong as the evidence against. We express this criterion as "*Equipoise and Above.*"

Recommendation 6. The Committee recommends that a broad spectrum of evidence, including epidemiologic, animal, and mechanistic data, be considered when evaluating causation.

Past decisions on presumptions have sometimes been based largely on epidemiologic evidence. The Committee recommends that evidence to evaluate causation be derived not only from epidemiologic studies of veterans and other exposed groups, but also from toxicological studies of animals or tissue, mechanistic studies of biological mechanisms related to the exposure or the disease process, and any other relevant scientific evidence. There are a number of existing approaches used by other organizations that the Science Review Board should consider.

Recommendation 7. When the causal evidence is at Equipoise and Above or Sufficient, the Committee recommends that an estimate also be made of the size of the causal effect among those exposed.

In past evaluations, the primary question has been whether there is an association between an exposure and disease. The Committee recommends that future evaluations should, in addition, provide an estimate of the strength of this association. In the crudest setting, this may be a simple ratio of the risk among the exposed compared with the risk among the unexposed (the relative risk). More sophisticated estimates may also be made, for example when there are dose-response data that can be applied to levels of military exposure.

Recommendation 8. The Committee recommends that, as the second part of the two-step evaluation, the relative risk and exposure prevalence be used to estimate an attributable fraction for the disease in the military setting (i.e., service-attributable fraction).

The relative risk can be used to make a rough estimate of the fraction of diseased persons exposed in the military setting whose disease was actually caused by their military exposure. Although this number is only roughly approximate, it does provide an estimate of the burden of disease caused by the military exposure and could be useful for projecting future costs. This estimate may be useful to VA in its decision-making process and to the veterans themselves in assessing the need for a presumption.

DEPARTMENT OF DEFENSE AND THE DEPARTMENT OF VETERANS AFFAIRS

The following recommendations are intended to improve the evidence on exposures and health status of veterans:

Recommendation 9. Inventory research related to the health of veterans, including research funded by DoD and VA, and research funded by the National Institutes of Health and other organizations.

Recommendation 10. Develop a strategic plan for research on the health of veterans, particularly those returning from conflicts in the Gulf and Afghanistan.

Models are available for planning major long-term research agendas that are intended to identify critical gaps in the availability of evidence. For example, a National Research Council committee provided a national agenda for research on airborne particles (NRC, 1998) that was used by the Environmental Protection Agency to initiate and track a major research program.

Recommendation 11. Develop a plan for augmenting research capability within DoD and VA to more systematically generate evidence on the health of veterans.

Recommendation 12. Assess the potential for enhancing research through record linkage using DoD and VA administrative and health record databases.

Recommendation 13. Conduct a critical evaluation of Gulf War troop tracking and environmental exposure monitoring data so that improvements can be made in this key DoD strategy for characterizing exposures during deployment.

Characterizing personnel exposures during deployment depends extensively on a system of troop location tracking and environmental monitoring that can be coordinated to characterize Service members' exposures. This approach is relatively new and, while promising, faces some key limitations as currently implemented that may significantly affect the degree to which the approach can adequately characterize individual Service member exposures. Experience acquired during the Gulf War, and subsequent uses of tracking systems in Afghanistan and Iraq, offer important opportunities to evaluate effectiveness so that refinements can be implemented.

Recommendation 14. Establish registries of Service members and veterans based on exposure, deployment, and disease histories.

Creating registries of Service members based on common groupings that may be important for future health surveillance or research is most easily performed at the time the Service members are together in those groupings. Making lists years after the common experience can lead to inaccuracies from lost records and recall bias. Groupings for registries can be based on many characteristics, including common exposures, common jobs, common deployment experiences, or common illnesses.

Recommendation 15. Develop a plan for an overall integrated surveillance strategy for the health of Service members and veterans.

DoD and VA need to work together to define a common strategy for integrated health surveillance of Service members and veterans. The need for surveillance can be identified at many points along a veteran's service to post-service experience. Surveillance studies that are initiated during a Service member's service career may need to extend beyond the period of military service. Data requirements for the specific surveillance activity may have been generated during military service, after military service, or both.

Recommendation 16. Improve the data linkage between the electronic health record data systems used by DoD and VA—including capabilities for handling individual Service member exposure information that is included as part of the individual's health record.

There is immediate benefit to be gained by a robust electronic sharing of military health records, including exposure information, by DoD with VA. DoD has mandated inclusion of service exposure records into its health records. Military health records are a routine part of VA's approach to assessing veteran health and disability. The final link in the chain is the complete transfer of those exposure and health records from DoD to VA.

Recommendation 17. Ensure implementation of the DoD strategy for improved exposure assessment and exposure data collection.

DoD has an ambitious and robust plan for improving the breadth and depth of its exposure evaluations and in consolidating records and approaches. These data would be especially useful for the longitudinal characterization of Service member exposures. Given the importance of the success of this initiative to the future understanding of service-related exposures, it is critical that the plan be fully implemented. The Committee recommends that the Veterans' Disability Benefits Commission work through Congress to establish a specific DoD budget line for the Defense Occupational and Environmental Health Readiness System (DOEHRS) implementation, including the appropriate training of personnel in exposure assessment and in use of the system, and that Congress receive annual reports from DoD on the status of DOEHRS development and implementation.

Recommendation 18. Develop a data interface that allows VA to access the electronic exposure data systems used by DoD.

DoD continues to invest heavily in electronic systems for documenting exposures experienced by Service members during their military service. These data are critical to VA's ability to manage veteran health and disabilities and to the presumptive disability decision-making process, yet VA has direct access to little of DoD's data. DoD and VA should begin to work together immediately to assess the available systems and to define and construct appropriate interfaces for these systems. The Committee recommends that the Veterans' Disability Benefits Commission work through Congress to establish specific DoD and VA budget lines to enable the development and implementation of a data interface that allows electronic access between DoD and VA records, and that Congress receive annual reports from DoD and VA on the development and implementation efforts.

Recommendation 19. DoD and VA should establish and implement mechanisms to identify, monitor, track, and medically treat individuals involved in research and other activities that have been classified and are secret.

The major requirements for interaction between DoD and VA regarding classified activities would be the following:

- Prospectively identify classified studies and activities involving humans.

- Develop a registry of Service members involved in the studies and activities.
- Develop a tracking mechanism to maintain contact with the Service members involved.
- Provide periodic medical evaluations and surveillance of Service members involved.
- Determine appropriate medical treatment if an adverse health effect is detected.
- Develop a mechanism to make information public as necessary.
- Keep the veterans, and families as applicable, fully informed regarding potential health effects of the materials that were used in the studies and activities.

The Advisory Committee, mentioned previously, could be assigned to oversee these functions.

REFERENCES

IOM. 1993. *Veterans at risk: The health effects of mustard gas and lewisite*. Washington, DC: National Academy Press.

IOM. 1994. *Veterans and Agent Orange: Health effects of herbicides used in Vietnam*. Washington, DC: National Academy Press.

IOM. 1996. *Veterans and Agent Orange: Update 1996*. Washington, DC: National Academy Press.

IOM. 1999. *Veterans and Agent Orange: Update 1998*. Washington, DC: National Academy Press.

IOM. 2000a. *Gulf War and health, volume 1: Depleted uranium, pyridostigmine bromide, sarin, vaccines*. Washington, DC: National Academy Press.

IOM. 2000b. *Veterans and Agent Orange: Herbicide/dioxin exposure and type 2 diabetes*. Washington, DC: National Academy Press.

IOM. 2001. *Veterans and Agent Orange: Update 2000*. Washington, DC: National Academy Press.

IOM. 2003a. *Gulf War and health, volume 2: Insecticides and solvents*. Washington, DC: The National Academies Press.

IOM. 2003b. *Veterans and Agent Orange: Update 2002*. Washington, DC: The National Academies Press.

IOM. 2005a. *Gulf War and health, volume 3: Fuels, combustion products, and propellants*. Washington, DC: The National Academies Press.

IOM. 2005b. *Veterans and Agent Orange: Update 2004*. Washington, DC: The National Academies Press.

IOM. 2006. *Gulf War and health, volume 4: Health effects of serving in the Gulf War*. Washington, DC: The National Academies Press.

IOM. 2007. *Gulf War and health, volume 5: Infectious diseases*. Washington, DC: The National Academies Press.

NRC (National Research Council). 1998. *Research priorities for airborne particulate matter: I. Immediate priorities and a long-range research portfolio*. Washington, DC: National Academy Press.

Appendix A

Statement of the Veterans' Disability Benefits Commission to the Institute of Medicine's Committee on the Presumptive Disability Decision-Making Process, May 31, 2006

The Veterans' Disability Benefits Commission created by Public Law 108-136 is charged with studying the benefits provided to compensate and assist veterans for disabilities attributable to military service. The Commission was mandated to consult with the Institute of Medicine (IOM) of the National Academy of Sciences with respect to the medical aspects of contemporary disability compensation policies. The Commission will evaluate and assess:

- The appropriateness of benefits
- The appropriateness of the level of those benefits
- The appropriate standard(s) for determining whether the disability should be compensated

In order to meet the three goals above, the Commission produced a list of 31 research questions to be answered during its investigation. IOM has established four committees that will address some of these questions in whole or in part. Your Committee will research and report on presumptions. Another committee, the Committee on Medical Evaluation of Veterans for Disability Compensation, was created to research and report on several aspects of compensation policies. IOM also established two committees to deal with various aspects of PTSD including diagnosis, treatment, and compensation. The Commission encourages your Committee to collaborate with the other three committees since there are many areas of overlapping and complementary interests.

The Commission consists of 13 members who were appointed by the President and the leaders of Congress. Twelve of the Commissions have served in the military. Nine members have combat experience. Combined, the members have over 260 years of military experience. The establishing statute requires that seven members have received combat decorations such as the Silver Star or higher. The Commission is charged to submit its report by October 1, 2007, to the President and Congress.

The Commission is looking forward to receiving expert advice from your Committee regarding the process by which presumptions of service connections are established. The Commission asks that you evaluate the current model used to determine diseases that qualify for service connection on a presumptive basis, and if appropriate, propose improvements in the model.

The Commission requests that your Committee assess the overall process used to establish a presumption. Currently, in determining if a herbicide disease should have a presumption established, the Secretary must determine that the results upon which the presumption is based are statistically significant, are capable of replication, and withstand peer review.

The Commission previously provided IOM an analysis of the history of presumptions completed by the VA Office of General Counsel in 1993. The Commission also provided an analysis completed this year by Mr. Donald Zeglin, legal consultant to the Commission, which summarized the General Counsel analysis and analyzed decisions on presumptions that occurred since the completion of the General Counsel analysis.

A presumptive condition is an injury or illness in which VA presumes a relationship exists between service and the conditions being claimed. A recurring theme within the compensation program has been the expansion of the definition of service connection, mainly under the presumption basis.

In general terms, presumptions shift the burden of proof from the veteran to the Government. Among the earliest presumptions, not dealing with service connection, are the presumption of sound condition upon entry on active military duty, the presumption relating to aggravation of pre-existing conditions during service, and the presumption of death after an absence of seven years.

In many instances, presumptions of service connection have been created when the manifestation of disability is remote from the veteran's service. This could be because medical science could not determine the origin or cause of some disabilities such as multiple sclerosis or how long the time period should be between exposure to the origin and initial diagnosis. In some cases, delayed onset is recognized as a feature of a disability such as posttraumatic stress disorder. In other cases, evidence supporting the need for a presumption can only be obtained through epidemiological studies of the frequency of disease among groups of people and research into the effects of various exposures on health.

Some presumptions were mandated by statute and some of those were based more on a political decision than a scientific decision. Often, the basis for presumption consisted of a combination of expert opinion, advocacy from organizations and individuals, and Congress' sense of justice, rather than scientific evidence.

The Commission would like you to thoroughly assess the processes used in the past and at the current time to make decisions on presumptions. In some cases, you may find that the processes are ad hoc in nature, varying from time to time and depending on the political and management philosophies of those involved. An understanding of past processes will be very instructive in deciding what the most appropriate process should be in the future.

The Commission is aware, as is the Institute of Medicine, that several presumptions were approved because it was not possible to document exposure to biological, chemical, radiological, or other environmental agents by accurate information on the exact locations to which military service members were assigned during precise periods of time. This lack of information prevented definitive studies. Your Committee may be able to provide substantive advice concerning how to ensure that this situation is not repeated in the future. Currently everyone who served in Vietnam is presumed to have been exposed to dioxin from Agent Orange. Do we have a better way of making these determinations?

A review of the history of the process for some presumption determinations indicates that many years can elapse between the onset of the disease and the establishment of the presumption. Examples of this include diseases associated with herbicide exposure during Vietnam service and experimental exposure to mustard gas during WWII service. Such long periods of time without compensation have no doubt resulted in significant hardship for many veterans and their families. What are the factors that contribute to these long periods of elapsed time? What can be done about these factors to improve the result?

Agent Orange, Radiation, and Gulf War Syndrome have resulted in a rapidly growing area of environmental presumptions that have prompted some to raise questions about the disability compensation program. War often affects men and women in profound ways that are not easily explainable or treatable. Many veterans experience problems/diseases that they attribute to chemical or radiation exposure. Leaving aside questions of the possible effect of psychic injuries inflicted by war on these questions, it seems that science cannot easily or quickly resolve these issues particularly where (1) chemical/radiation exposure levels are often unknowable or difficult to ascertain and (2) the effect of exposure on diseases experienced is scientifically unsettled.

Notwithstanding this uncertainty, the intense emotions surrounding those genuinely suffering and the perceived unfairness of forcing veterans to "prove" the environments or places where they served related to their possible exposure has led Congress and the Executive Branch to create presumptions. Certain studies (not even necessarily involving veterans), for example, showing that those exposed to dioxin have slightly higher rates of diabetes or prostate cancer, have resulted in an inexorable push to compensate all veterans with diabetes/prostate cancer even if it is likely that dioxin exposure is a determinative factor in only a small percentage of cases. Since it is impossible to know what role dioxin played in any particular case, all Vietnam veterans with diabetes and prostate cancer have been and are being granted presumptive service connection. Is this presumption fully supported by medical evidence? What amount of increase in occurrence rate is enough to warrant compensation? What approaches could be considered to alleviate this costly result?

Your Committee should consider if a different methodology should be used in determining causal relationships other than the environmental aspect used for the current method. Should the Committee on Presumptions review the Gulf War Illness presumptions? Should there be a defined process in place at VA to review and establish presumptions? Should the same or a different process be used periodically to review existing presumptions?

The Commission also requests that your Committee provide advice, from an epidemiological and statistical standpoint, on what strength of evidence would be the appropriate requirement when the Secretary of Veterans Affairs considers whether to establish a presumption. Currently, in determining if a herbicide disease should have a presumption established, the Secretary must determine that the results upon which the presumption is based are statistically significant, are capable of replication, and withstand peer review. And, an association is considered positive if the credible evidence for the association is equal to or outweighs the credible evidence against the association. Should the standards for inferential statistical evidence in finding an association between causative factors and disabilities change? From whom should VA accept sound medical and scientific information to analyze and to consider whether a condition be added as a presumption?

Are medical advancements occurring so rapidly and new medical findings becoming available so quickly that a formal regulatory process for presumption impedes decision making? How could a regulatory process react in a timely manner to the accelerating changes in medical science? Is a significant change in the methodology used to establish a presumption something to be considered?

During your Committee's review, the Commission would ask you to analyze all key documents and literature regarding presumptions to include all legislative and committee reports. We also encourage you to review published research on and medical studies of disease exposure and the subsequent development of those diseases.

Requesting your Committee to study these issues underlining the research question should not be taken as directing any disposition or finding with respect to the research question. Rather the Commission is asking that particular attention be focused on the issue.

SUMMARY

The Commission recognizes the challenges that the Committee on Presumptive Disability Decision Making Process faces in dealing with this issue. Your Committee has been asked to help ensure that future veterans are granted service connection under a presumption basis based on the best scientific evidence available. Your advice is crucial. The Commission anticipates that you will provide suggestions that will improve the processes that establish future presumptions. Presumptions are intended to protect a service member from being denied service connection for a disease or injury because he/she is unable to confirm the incurrence of the injury during combat or exposure to the disease through no fault of his or her own. To the extent possible, suggestions that will avoid the necessity for many future presumptions by ensuring that exposure of service members is documented and scientific evidence is made available would be important.

Having a method of granting service connection quickly and fairly based on a presumption is of critical importance to our disabled veterans and their surviving spouses. A through review of the present processes is needed. The presumptions must also be understandable to raters to allow for uniform and equitable application to veterans' claims regardless of where the rating is prepared. Ensuring that future presumption processes reflect the then current medical knowledge about the causal relationship would benefit entire veteran community.

Your suggestions will be considered by the Commission in determining the appropriateness of benefits, the appropriateness of the level of such benefits, and the appropriate standard or standards for determining whether a disability or death of a veteran should be compensated.

The Commission will consider the Committee's findings and suggestions in framing its response to the charge from Congress and the President.

We look forward to hearing the results of your Committee's deliberations in the coming months.

Appendix B

Committee on Evaluation of the Presumptive Disability Decision-Making Process for Veterans Open Session Meeting Agendas

Committee Meeting #1
May 31, 2006
Keck Center of the National Academies
Washington, D.C.

AGENDA

Wednesday, May 31 Room 201

8:30 a.m. Closed Session (Committee Members and IOM Staff Only)
10:30 a.m. Open Session Begins
10:30 a.m. Welcome and Introductory Remarks, Introduction of Committee Member and Attendees
Jonathan Samet, M.D., M.S., Committee Chair
10:40 a.m. Expectations of the Study Sponsor
Commissioner John Grady (Member, Veterans' Disability Benefits Commission)
11:00 a.m. An Overview of the Disability Benefits Program and Presumptions Affecting Veterans' Benefits
Thomas Pamperin, M.B.A. (Assistant Director for Policy, Compensation and Pension Service, Department of Veterans Affairs)
11:45 a.m. Legislative and Regulatory History of Presumptions
David Barrans, J.D. (Deputy Assistant General Counsel, Office of General Counsel, Department of Veterans Affairs)

12:15 p.m.	Lunch
1:15 p.m.	The Role of Science in Establishing VA Disability Compensation Policies *Mark Brown, Ph.D. (Director, VA's Environmental Agents Service, Office of Public Health and Environmental Hazards, Department of Veterans Affairs)*
1:45 p.m.	Presumptions in VA's Disability Program—The Effect *Thomas Pamperin, M.B.A. (Assistant Director for Policy, Compensation and Pension Service, Department of Veterans Affairs)*
2:05 p.m.	PANEL Q&A—VA Presenters and Committee Members
2:45 p.m.	Break
3:00 p.m.	An Examiner's Use of the Clinician's Guide and How Examiners Are Selected and Trained by VHA *Patrick Joyce, M.D., J.D., M.P.H. (Chief Physician, Compensation and Pension Program, VA Medical Center, Washington, D.C.)*
3:45 p.m.	Making Decisions Based on Medical Evidence *Bradley Flohr (Chief of Advisory Review Staff, Compensation and Pension Service)*
4:15 p.m.	Public Comments (Attendees will be given the opportunity to make brief remarks to the Committee Members)
5:15 p.m.	Open Session Ends
5:15 p.m.	Closed Session (Committee Members and IOM Staff Only)
6:15 p.m.	Adjourn

Committee Meeting #2
July 27, 2006
Keck Center of the National Academies
Washington, D.C.

AGENDA

Thursday, July 27 Room 101

8:30 a.m.	Closed Session (Committee Members and IOM Staff Only)
9:00 a.m.	Open Session Begins
9:00 a.m.	Welcome and Introductory Remarks, Introduction of Committee Members and Attendees *Jonathan Samet, M.D., M.S., Committee Chair*

9:10 a.m.	Summary of Recent IOM Studies Conducted for VA *Rose Marie Martinez, Sc.D. (Director, Board on Population Health and Public Health Practice, Institute of Medicine)*
9:45 a.m.	VA Health Care Utilization Among Operation Iraqi Freedom/ Operation Enduring Freedom Veterans *Han K. Kang, Dr.P.H. (Director, Environmental Epidemiology Service, Department of Veterans Affairs)*
10:15 a.m.	Overview of VA Registries *Han K. Kang, Dr.P.H. (Director, Environmental Epidemiology Service, Department of Veterans Affairs)*
10:45 a.m.	Break
11:00 a.m.	Assessing Environmental and Occupational Exposures—VA Disability and Compensation Policies *Lawrence R. Deyton, M.S.P.H., M.D. (Chief Officer, Public Health and Environmental Hazards, Department of Veterans Affairs)*
12:00 p.m.	Lunch
1:00 p.m.	Overview of DoD Deployment and Installation-Based Occupational and Environmental Health Programs *R. Craig Postlewaite, D.V.M., M.P.H. (Senior Analyst, Environmental Health Surveillance, DoD Deployment Health Support Directorate)*
1:20 p.m.	Deployment Health Surveillance: Past, Current, and Future Operations *Jack M. Heller, Ph.D. (Director, Health Risk Management, U.S. Army Center for Health Promotion and Preventive Medicine)*
2:05 p.m.	DoD Occupational Health Exposure Assessment Processes *John Seibert, C.I.H., C.S.P. (Assistant for Safety, Health and Fire Protection, Office of the Deputy Under Secretary of Defense for Installations and Environment)*
2:50 p.m.	Break
3:00 p.m.	Panel Discussion with DoD Representatives
4:00 p.m.	Public Comments from Veterans Service Organizations The American Legion *Cathy Wiblemo, M.H.A. (Deputy Director, Veterans Affairs and Rehabilitation Division)* AMVETS *Jim Doran (National Service Director)* United Spinal Association *Leonard Selfon, Esq. (National Service Director)*

	Veterans of Foreign Wars of the United States *Quentin Kinderman (Deputy Director, National Legislative Service)* Vietnam Veterans of America *Rick Weidman (Executive Director for Policy and Government Affairs)*
4:30 p.m.	Public Comments from Attendees (Attendees will also be given the opportunity to make brief remarks to the Committee Members)
5:00 p.m.	Open Session Ends
5:15 p.m.	Closed Session (Committee Members and IOM Staff Only)
6:00 p.m.	Adjourn

Committee Meeting #3
October 4, 2006
Emily Morgan Hotel
705 East Houston Street
San Antonio, Texas

AGENDA

Wednesday, October 4 Emily Morgan Hotel (Room 2)

7:30 a.m.	Closed Session (Committee Members and IOM Staff Only)
8:00 a.m.	Open Session Begins
8:00 a.m.	Welcome and Introductory Remarks, Introduction of Committee Members and Attendees *Jonathan M. Samet, M.D., M.S., (Chair, Committee on Evaluation of the Presumptive Disability Decision-Making Process for Veterans)*
8:10 a.m.	Presentations from Past Congressional Staffers *Laura Petrou* *Patrick Ryan, J.D.* *Edward Scott, J.D.* *Chris Yoder*
9:10 a.m.	Panel Q&A—Panel Presenters and Committee Members
9:50 a.m.	Break
10:00 a.m.	DoD and Veterans Affairs: Health Information Sharing *Nhan Do, M.D., M.S., F.A.C.P. (Information Manager, Medical Informatics, TricareManagement Activity)* *Cliff Freeman, M.A., M.S. (Director, VA/DoD Health IT Sharing Program)*

10:30 a.m.	Panel Q&A—Health IT Presenters and Committee Members
11:00 a.m.	Public Comments from Veterans Service Organizations Public Comments from Attendees (Attendees will also be given the opportunity to make brief remarks to the Committee Members) *Comments from LTG James Terry Scott, U.S. Army (Ret.) (Chairman, Veterans Disability Benefits Commission)* *Closing Comments from Jonathan M. Samet, M.D., M.S. (Chair, Committee on Evaluation of the Presumptive Disability Decision-Making Process for Veterans)*
12:00 p.m.	Open Session Ends
1:00 p.m.	Closed Session (Committee Members and IOM Staff Only)
6:00 p.m.	Adjourn

Appendix C

Glossary

a priori—Proceeding from a known or assumed cause to a necessarily related effect; based on a hypothesis or theory rather than on experiment or experience; made before or without examination and not supported by factual study.

Accession—Entry into the service.

Acidosis—A pathologic state characterized by an increase in the concentration of hydrogen ions in the arterial blood above the normal level, 40 nmol/L, or pH 7.4; may be caused by an accumulation of carbon dioxide or acidic products of metabolism, or by a decrease in the concentration of alkaline compounds. (Stedman's medical dictionary 28th ed., 2005)

Acneiform (or acneform) lesions—Lesions resembling acne. (Stedman's medical dictionary 28th ed., 2005)

Active duty—(A) Full-time duty in the Armed Forces, other than active duty for training; (B) Full-time duty (other than for training purposes) as a commissioned officer of the Regular or Reserve Corps of the Public Health Service (i) on or after July 29, 1945, or (ii) before that date under circumstances affording entitlement to "full military benefits" or (iii) at any time, for the purposes of chapter 13 of this title (38 U.S.C.S. § 1301 et seq.); (C) Full-time duty as a commissioned officer of the National Oceanic and Atmospheric Administration or its predecessor organization the Coast and Geodetic Survey (i) on or after July 29, 1945, or (ii) before that date (I) while on transfer to one of the Armed Forces, or (II) while, in time of war or national emergency declared by the President, assigned to duty on a project for one of the Armed Forces in an area determined by the Secretary of Defense to be of immediate military hazard, or (III) in the Philippine Islands on December 7, 1941, and continuously in such islands thereafter, or (iii) at any time, for the purposes of chapter 13 of this title (38 U.S.C.S. § 1301 et seq.); (D) Service as a cadet at the United States Military, Air Force, or Coast Guard Academy, or as a midshipman at the United States Naval Academy; and (E) Authorized travel to or from such duty or service. (Definitions. 2006. 38 U.S.C. § 101.)

Active duty for training—(A) Full-time duty in the Armed Forces performed by Reserves for training purposes; (B) Full-time duty for training purposes performed as a commissioned officer of the Reserve Corps of the Public Health Service (i) on or after July 29, 1945, or (ii) before that date under circumstances affording entitlement to "full military benefits," or (iii) at any time, for the purposes of chapter 13 of this title (38 U.S.C.S. § 1301 et seq.); (C) In the case of members of the National Guard or Air National Guard of any State, full-time duty under section 316, 502, 503, 504, or 505 of title 32 (32 U.S.C.S. § 316, 502, 503, 504, or 505), or the prior corresponding provisions of law; and (D) Duty performed by a member of a Senior Reserve Officers' Training Corps program when ordered to such duty for the purpose of training or a practice cruise under chapter 103 of title 10 (10 U.S.C.S. § 2101 et seq.) for a period of not less than four weeks and which must be completed by the member before the member is commissioned; and (E) Authorized travel to or from such duty. The term does not include duty performed as a temporary member of the Coast Guard Reserve. (Definitions. 2006. 38 U.S.C. § 101.)

Active military, naval, or air service—(A) Active duty; (B) any period of active duty for training during which the individual concerned was disabled or died from a disease or injury incurred or aggravated in line of duty; and (C) Any period of inactive duty training during which the individual concerned was disabled or died—(i) from an injury incurred or aggravated in line of duty; or (ii) from an acute myocardial infarction, a cardiac arrest, or a cerebrovascular accident occurring during such training. (Definitions. 2006. 38 U.S.C. § 101.)

Acute myelogenous leukemia (AML)—A form of leukemia characterized by an uncontrolled proliferation of myelopoietic cells in the bone marrow and in extramedullary sites, and the presence of large numbers of immature and mature granulocytic forms in various tissues (and organs) and in the circulating blood.

Acute nonlymphocytic leukemia (ANLL)—Any of several forms of myelogenous leukemia marked by an abnormal increase in the number of immature white blood cells; risk of disease is increased among people who have been exposed to massive doses of radiation.

Addison's anemia (also known as primary anemia, pernicious anemia)—A chronic progressive anemia of older adults (occurring more frequently during the fifth and later decades, rarely before 30 years of age), due to the failure of absorption of vitamin B_{12}, usually resulting from a defect of the stomach accompanied by mucosal atrophy and associated with lack of secretion of "intrinsic" factor; characterized by numbness and tingling, weakness, and a sore smooth tongue, as well as dyspnea after slight exertion, faintness, pallor of the skin and mucous membranes, anorexia, diarrhea, loss of weight, and fever; laboratory studies usually reveal greatly decreased red blood cell counts, low levels of hemoglobin, numerous characteristically oval shaped macrocytic erythrocytes (color index greater than normal, but not truly hyperchromic), and hypo- or achlorhydria, in association with a predominant number of megaloblasts and relatively few normoblasts in the bone marrow; the leukocyte count in peripheral blood may be less than normal, with relative lymphocytosis and hypersegmented neutrophils; a low level of vitamin B_{12} is found in peripheral red blood cells; administration of vitamin B_{12} results in a characteristic reticulocyte response, relief from symptoms, and an increase in erythrocytes, provided that pernicious anemia is not complicated by another disease; the condition is not actually "pernicious," as it was prior to the availability of therapy with vitamin B_{12}. At least two autosomal recessive forms are known. In one there is a defect of intrinsic factor and in the other a defective absorption of vitamin B_{12} from the intestine. (Stedman's medical dictionary 28th ed., 2005)

Additive model—A model in which the combined effect of several factors is the sum of the effects that would be produced by each of the factors in the absence of the others. For example, if factor X adds *x* percent to risk in the absence of Y, and if factor Y adds *y* percent to risk in the absence of X, an additive model states that the two factors together will add $(x + y)$ percent to risk. (Last, 2001)

Adult fibrosarcoma—A sarcoma of relatively low malignancy consisting chiefly of spindle-shaped cells that tend to form collagenous fibrils.

Agent Orange—An herbicide and defoliant consisting of 2,4,5-trichlorophenoxyacetic acid, 2,4-dichlorophenoxyacetic acid, and dioxin, that was widely used during the Vietnam War; it has been shown to produce residual postexposure carcinogenic and teratogenic effects in humans. (Stedman's medical dictionary 28th ed., 2005)

Alveolar (alveolus)—A small cell, cavity, or socket. (1) Syn: *pulmonary alveolus.* (2) One of the terminal secretory portions of an alveolar or racemose gland. (3) One of the honeycomb pits in the wall of the stomach. (4) Syn: *tooth socket.* (Stedman's medical dictionary 28th ed., 2005)

Ambient air—The surrounding or encompassing air; pertaining to the environment in which an organism or apparatus functions.

Amebiasis—Infection with the protozoon *Entamoeba histolytica*. (Stedman's medical dictionary 28th ed., 2005)

Amebic dysentery—An inflammation of the intestine caused by infestation with *Entamoeba histolytica*. Marked by dysentery, abdominal pain, and erosion of the intestinal wall.

Amputation—The cutting off of a limb or part of a limb, the breast, or other projecting part.

Amyloidosis—A disease characterized by extracellular accumulation of amyloid in various organs and tissues of the body; may be primary or secondary.

Amyotrophic lateral sclerosis (ALS)—A rare fatal progressive degenerative disease that affects pyramidal motor neurons, usually begins in middle age, and is characterized especially by increasing and spreading muscular weakness. Also known as Lou Gehrig's disease. (Stedman's medical dictionary 28th ed., 2005)

Anemia—Any condition in which the number of red blood cells/mm^3, the amount of hemoglobin in 100 ml of blood, and/or the volume of packed red blood cells/100 ml of blood is less than normal; clinically, generally pertaining to the concentration of oxygen-transporting material in a designated volume of blood, in contrast to total quantities as in oligocythemia, oligochromemia, and oligemia. Anemia is frequently manifested by pallor of the skin and mucous membranes, shortness of breath, palpitations of the heart, soft systolic murmurs, lethargy, and tendency to fatigue. (Stedman's medical dictionary 28th ed., 2005)

Angioendotheliomatosis—Proliferation of endothelial cells within blood vessels. (Stedman's medical dictionary 28th ed., 2005)

Angiosarcoma—A rare malignant neoplasm occurring most often in soft tissues; believed to originate from the endothelial cells of blood vessels; microscopically composed of spindle-shaped cells, some of which line small spaces resembling vascular clefts. (Stedman's medical dictionary 28th ed., 2005)

Anthrax—Infection by the bacterium *Bacillus anthracis*, which in humans is caused by infected animals or animal products, and ingestion or inhalation of spores of the bacterium. The most common naturally occurring form of human anthrax is the cutaneous, and both the inhalational and the gastrointestinal forms are quite rare. Anthrax in animals occurs throughout the world, primarily in herbovores, especially cattle, horses, goats, and sheep. (Stedman's medical dictionary 28th ed., 2005)

Anxiety neurosis—Apprehension of danger and dread accompanied by restlessness, tension, tachycardia, and dyspnea unattached to a clearly identifiable stimulus.

Aplastic anemia—Anemia characterized by a greatly decreased formation of erythrocytes and hemoglobin, usually associated with pronounced granulocytopenia and thrombocytopenia, as a result of hypoplasticity or aplasticity of bone marrow. (Stedman's medical dictionary 28th ed., 2005)

Appendectomy—Surgical removal of the appendix. (Stedman's medical dictionary 28th ed., 2005)

Armed Forces—The United States Army, Navy, Marine Corps, Air Force, and Coast Guard, including the reserve components thereof. (Definitions. 2006. 38 U.S.C. § 101.)

Arrhythmia—Loss or abnormality of rhythm; denoting especially an irregularity of the heartbeat. (Stedman's medical dictionary 28th ed., 2005)

Arteriosclerosis—Hardening of the arteries; types generally recognized are: atherosclerosis, Mönckeberg arteriosclerosis, and arteriolosclerosis. (Stedman's medical dictionary 28th ed., 2005)

Arthritis—Inflammation of a joint or a state characterized by inflammation of joints. (Stedman's medical dictionary 28th ed., 2005)

Asbestosis—Pneumoconiosis due to inhalation of asbestos fibers suspended in the ambient air; sometimes complicated by pleural mesothelioma or bronchogenic carcinoma; ferruginous bodies are the histologic hallmark of exposure to asbestos. (Stedman's medical dictionary 28th ed., 2005)

Assay—(1) The quantitative or qualitative evaluation of a substance for impurities, toxicity, etc.; the results of such an evaluation. (2) To examine; to subject to analysis. (3) Test of purity; trial. (Stedman's medical dictionary 28th ed., 2005)

Assigned share—For two groups of people that are alike, except that one group is exposed and the other is not exposed, the excess number of cases in the exposed group expressed as a fraction of the total number of cases in the exposed group.

Association—Statistical dependence between two or more events, characteristics, or other variables. An association is present if the probability of occurrence of an event or characteristic, or the quantity of a variable, is related to the occurrence of one or more other events, the presence of one or more other characteristics, or the quantity of one or more other variables. The association between two variables is described as positive when higher values of a variable are associated with higher values of another variable. In a negative association, the occurrence of higher values of one variable is associated with lower values of the other variable. An association may be fortuitous or may be produced by various other circumstances; the presence of an association does not necessarily imply a causal relationship. If the use of the term *association* is confined to situations in which the relationship between two variables is statistically significant, the terms *statistical association* and *statistically* *significant association* become tautological. However, ordinary usage is seldom so precise at this. The terms *association* and *relationship* are often used interchangeably. Associations can be broadly grouped under two headings, noncausal and causal. (Adapted from Last, 2001)

Asthma—An inflammatory disease of the lungs characterized by reversible (in most cases) airway obstruction. Originally, a term used to mean "difficult breathing"; now used to denote bronchial asthma. (Stedman's medical dictionary 28th ed., 2005)

Atherosclerosis—Arteriosclerosis characterized by irregularly distributed lipid deposits in the intima of large and medium sized arteries, causing narrowing of arterial lumens and proceeding eventually to fibrosis and calcification. Lesions are usually focal and progress slowly and intermittently. Limitation of blood flow accounts for most clinical manifestations, which vary with the distribution and severity of lesions. (Stedman's medical dictionary 28th ed., 2005)

Atrophy—A wasting of tissues, organs, or the entire body, as from death and reabsorption of cells, diminished cellular proliferation, decreased cellular volume, pressure, ischemia, malnutrition, lessened function, or hormonal changes. (Stedman's medical dictionary 28th ed., 2005)

Attributable fraction (AF)—Fraction of disease in the population that would not have occurred had the exposure not occurred. A term sometimes used to refer to the attributable fraction in the population, and sometimes to the attributable fraction among the exposed (Last, 2001). The AF may be best understood by seeing how it is calculated: $AF = (R_1 - R_0) / R_1$, where R_1 is the rate of a disease (typically incidence rate) in an exposed population and R_0 is the rate in that same population if unexposed. AF, then, is the fraction of the rate of disease in the exposed that is due to exposure. Dividing numerator and denominator by R_0, since R_1/R_0 is the relative risk (RR), produces the more familiar expression, $AF = (RR - 1) / RR$. See Population attributable fraction.

Avitaminosis—Properly, hypovitaminosis. (Stedman's medical dictionary 28th ed., 2005)

Bacillary dysentery (also known as shigellosis)—Infection with *Shigella dysenteriae*, *Shingella flexneri*, or other organisms. (Stedman's medical dictionary 28th ed., 2005)

Bancroft[ian] filariasis—Filariasis caused by *Wuchereria bancrofti*. (Stedman's medical dictionary 28th ed., 2005)

Bari Harbor Disaster—On December 2, 1943, German Junkers Ju 88 bombers attacked the port of Bari, a key supply center for Allied forces fighting their way up the Italian peninsula. Several Allied ships were sunk in the overcrowded harbor, including *John Harvey*, which was carrying mustard gas, intended for use if German forces initiated chemical warfare. The presence of the gas was highly classified, and authorities ashore had no knowledge of it. This increased the number of fatalities, since physicians—who had no idea that they were dealing with the effects of mustard gas—prescribed treatment proper for those suffering from exposure and immersion, which proved fatal in many cases.

Basophil—(1) A cell with granules that stain specifically with basic dyes. (2) Syn: *basophilic.* (3) A phagocytic leukocyte of the blood characterized by numerous basophilic granules containing heparin and histamine and leukotrines; except for its segmented nucleus, it is morphologically and physiologically similar to the mast cell though they originate from different stem cells in the bone marrow. (Stedman's medical dictionary 28th ed., 2005)

Bayes' Theorem—A theorem for probability first derived and described by Thomas Bayes (1702-1761), an English clergyman and mathematician, in his Essay Towards Solving a Problem in the Doctrine of Chances (1763, published posthumously). In epidemiology, the theorem is often used to obtain the probability of disease in a group of people with some characteristic on the basis of the overall rate of that disease (the *prior probability* of disease) and the likelihoods of that characteristic in healthy and diseased individuals. The most familiar application is in clinical decision analysis, where it is used for estimating the probability of a particular diagnosis given the appearance of some symptoms or test results. A simplified version of the theorem is

$$P(D|S)=\frac{P(S|D)P(D)}{P(S|D)P(D)+P(S|\bar{D})P(\bar{D})}$$

where D = disease, S = symptom, and $\bar{D}$ = no disease. The probability of disease given the symptom is the *posterior probability.* The probability of disease before knowing of the presence or absence of the symptom is the *prior probability*. The formula emphasizes what clinical intuition often overlooks, namely, that the probability of disease *given* the symptom depends not only on how characteristic that symptom is of the disease but also on how frequent the disease is among the population being served.

The theorem can also be used for estimating exposure-specific rates from case-control studies if there is added information about the overall rate of disease in that population.

The theorem is sometimes presented in terms of the odds of disease before knowing the symptom (*prior odds*) and after knowing the symptom (*posterior odds*). (Adapted from Last, 2001)

Bayesian approach—A method of statistical inference that begins with the state of knowledge, i.e., the facts, prior to an exposure or an intervention, and augments this with the study data to yield the state of knowledge posterior to the study.

Benzene—The basic six-carbon ring structure in most aromatic compounds; a highly toxic hydrocarbon from light coal tar oil; used as a solvent. (Stedman's medical dictionary 28th ed., 2005)

Beriberi—A specific nutritional deficiency syndrome occurring in endemic form in eastern and southern Asia, sporadically in other parts of the world without reference to climate, and sometimes in alcoholic patients, resulting mainly from a dietary deficiency of thiamin; the "dry" form is characterized by painful polyneuropathy that involves both large and small somatic nerve fibers, as well as autonomic nerve fibers, the initial symptom is burning feet, and later symptoms consist of painful parathesias in the distal upper limbs as well, weakness and atrophy of the feet and hands, and distal atrophic skin and hair loss; the "wet" form is characterized by edema resulting from a high-output form of heart failure, but usually there is evidence of a coexisting polyneuropathy as well. (Stedman's medical dictionary 28th ed., 2005)

Beryllium disease—Various conditions resulting from exposure to beryllium and its compounds or alloys.

Bias—Deviation of results or inference from the truth, or process leading to such deviation; any trend in the collection, analysis, interpretation, publication, or review of data that can lead to conclusions that are systematically different from the truth. Among the ways in which deviation from the truth can occur, are the following:

1. Systematic (one-sided) variation of measurements from the true values (syn: *systematc error*)
2. Variation of statistical summary measures (means, rates, measurements of association, etc.) from their true values as result of systematic variation of measurements, other flaws in data collection, or flaws in study design or analysis
3. Deviation of inferences from the truth as a result of flaws in study design, data collection, or the analysis or interpretation of results
4. A tendency of procedures (in study design, data collection, analysis, interpretation, review, or publication) to yield results or conclusions that depart from the truth
5. Prejudice leading to the conscious or unconscious selection of study procedures that departs from the truth in a particular direction or to one-sidedness in the interpretation of results

The term *bias* does not necessarily carry an imputation of prejudice or other subjective factor, such as the experimenter's desire for a particular outcome.This differs from conventional usage, in which bias refers to a partisan point of view. (Adapted from Last, 2001)

Biological plausibility—The criterion that an observed, presumably or putatively causal association is coherent with previously existing biological or medical knowledge. This judgment should be used cautiously since it could impede development of new knowledge that does not fit existing ideas. (Last, 2001)

Bipolar disorder—An affective disorder characterized by the occurrence of alternating manic, hypomanic, or mixed episodes and with major depressive episodes. The DSM specifies the commonly observed patterns of bipolar I and bipolar II disease and cyclothymia. (Stedman's medical dictionary 28th ed., 2005)

Black lung—A form of pneumoconiosis, common in coal miners, characterized by deposits of carbon particles in the lung. (Stedman's medical dictionary 28th ed., 2005)

Black water fever—Hemoglobinuria resulting from severe hemolysis occurring in falciparum malaria. (Stedman's medical dictionary 28th ed., 2005)

Bonus Expeditionary Forces—About 20,000 WWI veterans, their families, and other affiliated groups who demonstrated in Washington, D.C., during the spring and summer of 1932 seeking immediate payment of a "bonus" granted by the Adjusted Service Certificate Law of 1924 for payment in 1945.

Bradford Hill criteria—Heuristic criteria for interpreting when evidence supports moving beyond observed association to causation. The criteria include strength of association, consistency, specificity, temporality, dose-response, plausibility, coherence, experimental evidence, and analogy. Named after Sir Austin Bradford Hill.

Bradley Commission—Formed in 1987 in response to concerns regarding the quality and quantity of the history taught in American classrooms.

Brain hemorrhage (cerebral hemorrhage)—Hemorrhage into the substance of the cerebrum, usually in the region of the internal capsule by the rupture of the lenticulostriate. (Stedman's medical dictionary 28th ed., 2005)

Brain thrombosis (cerebral thrombosis)—Clotting of the blood in a cerebral vessel. (Stedman's medical dictionary 28th ed., 2005)

Bronchiectasis—Chronic dilation of bronchi or bronchioles as a sequel of inflammatory disease or obstruction often associated with heavy sputum production.

Bronchiolo-alveolar carcinoma—A relatively uncommon lung cancer which is a type of non-small cell lung cancer.

Bronchitis—Inflammation of the mucous membranes of the bronchi. (Stedman's medical dictionary 28th ed., 2005)

Buccal cavity—That part of the mouth bounded anteriorally and laterally by the lips and the cheeks, posteriorly and medially by the teeth and/or gums, and above and below by the reflection of the mucosa from the lips and cheeks to the gums. (Stedman's medical dictionary 28th ed., 2005)

Buerger's disease—Thromboangiitis (thromboangiitis—an inflammation of the blood vessels associated with thrombosis) of the small arteries and veins of the extremities and especially the feet resulting in occlusion, ischemia, and gangrene.

Bulbar—(1) Relating to a bulb. (2) Relating to the rhombencephalon (hindbrain). (3) Bulb-shaped; resembling a bulb. (Stedman's medical dictionary 28th ed., 2005)

Burden of persuasion—The duty upon a party in a legal proceeding to persuade the fact-finder to decide for that party on an assertion of fact.

Burden of proof—The duty of proving a disputed assertion or charge.

Butadiene—A flammable gaseous open-chain hydrocarbon used in making synthetic rubbers.

Cacodylic acid—Arsenical contact herbicide that defoliates or desiccates a wide variety of plant species. (Stedman's medical dictionary 28th ed., 2005)

Calculi (Calculus)—A concretion formed in any part of the body, most commonly in the passages of the biliary and urinary tracts; usually composed of salts of inorganic or organic acids, or of other material such as cholesterol. (Stedman's medical dictionary 28th ed., 2005)

Cancer—General term frequently used to indicate any of various types of malignant neoplasms, most of which invade surrounding tissues, may metastasize to several sites, and are likely to recur after attempted removal and to cause death of the patient unless adequately treated; especially, any such carcinoma or sarcoma, but, in ordinary usage, especially the former. (Stedman's medical dictionary 28th ed., 2005)

Cannikin—A nuclear device detonated beneath Amchitka Island, Alaska, in 1971.

Carcinogen—Any cancer-producing substance or organism, such as polycyclic aromatic hydrocarbons, or agents such as in certain types of irradiation. (Stedman's medical dictionary 28th ed., 2005)

Carcinoma—Any of various types of malignant neoplasm derived from epithelial cells, chiefly glandular (adenocarcinoma) or squamous (squamous cell carcinoma); the most commonly occurring kind of cancer. (Stedman's medical dictionary 28th ed., 2005)

Cardiovascular disease—Any abnormal condition characterized by dysfunction of the heart and blood vessels.

Case-control study—An epidemiologic study design in which a population sample is defined on the basis of whether (cases) or not (controls) a disease (or other endpoint) is present; cases and controls are then compared with respect to disease risk factors, typically exposure.

Cataracts (posterior subcapsulary)—Complete or partial opacity of the ocular lens. (Stedman's medical dictionary 28th ed., 2005)

Causal association—An association between two events or characteristics that arises because one causes the other.

Causal inference—Examining the structure and results of many investigations in an attempt to assess and, if possible, eliminate all possible noncausal reasons for observed associations.

Causal pathway—A sequence mechanism, possibly involving several intermediate factors, by which one factor causes another.

Causation—The relating of causes to the effects they produce. A relationship between events (specific, or individual causation) or between variables (general, or population level causation) in which an outside intervention to change the cause would result in a change in the effect.

Child—Except for purposes of chapter 19 of this title (38 U.S.C.S. § 1901 et seq.) (other than with respect to a child who is an insurable dependent under section 1965[10][B] of such chapter [38 U.S.C.S. § 1965(10)(B)] and section 8502[b] of this title [38 U.S.C.S. § 8502(b)]) a person who is unmarried and—(i) who is under the age of eighteen years; (ii) who, before attaining the age of eighteen years, became permanently incapable of self-support; or (iii) who, after attaining the age of eighteen years and until completion of education or training (but not after attaining the age of twenty-three years), is pursuing a course of instruction at an approved educational institution; and who is a legitimate child, a legally adopted child, a stepchild who is a member of a veteran's household or was a member at the time of the veteran's death, or an illegitimate child but, as to the alleged father, only if acknowledged in writing signed by him, or if he has been judicially ordered to contribute to the child's support or has been, before his death, judicially decreed to be the father of such child, or if he is otherwise shown by evidence satisfactory to the Secretary to be the father of such child. A person shall be deemed, as of the date of death of a veteran, to be the legally adopted child of such veteran if such person was at the time of the veteran's death living in the veteran's household and was legally adopted by the veteran's surviving spouse before August 26, 1961, or within two years after the veteran's death; however, this sentence shall not apply if at the time of the veteran's death, such person was receiving regular contributions toward the person's support from some individual other than the veteran or the veteran's spouse, or from any public or private welfare organization which furnishes services or assistance for children. A person with respect to whom an interlocutory decree of adoption has been issued by an appropriate adoption authority shall be recognized thereafter as a legally adopted child, unless and until that decree is rescinded, if the child remains in the custody of the adopting parent or parents during the interlocutory period. A person who has been placed for adoption under an agreement entered into by the adopting parent or parents with any agency authorized under law to so act shall be recognized thereafter as a legally adopted child, unless and until such agreement is terminated, if the child remains in the custody of the adopting parent or parents during the period of placement for adoption under such agreement. A person described in clause (ii) of the first sentence of this subparagraph who was a member of a veteran's household at the time the person became 18 years of age and who is adopted by the veteran shall be recognized as a legally adopted child of the veteran regardless of the age of such person at the time of adoption. (B) For the purposes of subparagraph (A) of this paragraph, in the case of an adoption under the laws of any jurisdiction other than a State (as defined in section 101[20] of this title [para. (20) of this section] and including the Commonwealth of the Northern Mariana Islands)—(i) a person residing outside any of the States shall not be considered to be a legally adopted child of a veteran during the lifetime of such veteran (including the purposes of this subparagraph a Commonwealth Army veteran or new Philippine Scout, as defined in section 3566 of this title (38 U.S.C.S. § 3566) unless such person—(I) was less than eighteen years of age at the time of adoption; (II) is receiving one-half or more of such person's annual support from such veteran; (III) is not in the custody of such person's natural parent, unless such natural parent is such veteran's spouse; and (IV) is residing with such veteran (or in the case of divorce following adoption, with the divorced spouse who is also an adoptive or natural parent) except for periods during which such person is residing apart from such veteran (or such divorced spouse) for purposes of full-time attendance at an educational institution or during which such person or such veteran (or such divorced spouse) is confined in a hospital, nursing home, other health-care facility, or other institution; and (ii) a person shall not be considered to have been a legally adopted child of a veteran as of the date of such veteran's death and thereafter unless—(I) at any time within the one-year period immediately preceding such veteran's death, such veteran was entitled to and was receiving a dependent's allowance or similar monetary benefit under this title for such person; or (II) for a period of at least one year prior to such veteran's death, such person met the requirements of clause (i) of this subparagraph. (Definitions. 2006. 38 U.S.C. § 101.)

Chloracne—An acnelike eruption due to occupational contact, by inhalation or ingestion or through the skin, with certain chlorinated compounds (naphthalenes and diphenyls) used as insulators, insecticides, fungicides, and herbicides, including Agent Orange; keratinous plugs (comedones) form in the pilosebaceous orifices, and various sized small papules (2 to 4 mm) develop. (Stedman's medical dictionary 28th ed., 2005)

Chlorophenols—Several substitution products obtained by the action of chlorine on phenol; used as antiseptics. (Stedman's medical dictionary 28th ed., 2005)

Cholecystitis—Inflammation of the gallbladder. (Stedman's medical dictionary 28th ed., 2005)

Cholera—An acute epidemic infectious disease caused by the bacterium *Vibrio cholerae*. A soluble toxin elaborated in the intestinal tract by the bacterium activates the adenylate cylase of the mucosa, causing active secretion of an isotonic fluid resulting in profuse watery diarrhea, extreme loss of fluid and electrolytes, and dehydration and collapse, but no gross morphologic change in the intestinal mucosa. (Stedman's medical dictionary 28th ed., 2005)

Chondrosarcoma—A malignant neoplasm derived from cartilage cells, occurring most frequently in pelvic bones or near the ends of long bones, in middle-aged and older people; most chondrosarcomas arise de novo, but some may develop in a preexisting benign cartilaginous lesion. (Stedman's medical dictionary 28th ed., 2005)

Chronic fatigue syndrome—A disorder of uncertain cause that is characterized by persistent profound fatigue usually accompanied by impairment in short-term memory or concentration, sore throat, tender lymph nodes, muscle or joint pain, and headache unrelated to any preexisting medical condition.

Chronic multisymptom illness—Chronic illness characterized by a complex of multiple symptoms. More common in deployed Gulf War I (1991) veterans than in non-deployed veterans.

Chronic obstructive pulmonary disease—Comprised of two related diseases (chronic bronchitis and emphysema); chronic obstruction of the flow of air through the airways and out of the lungs, and the obstruction generally is permanent and progressive over time.

Cirrhosis of the liver—A chronic degenerative disease of the liver in which the lobes are covered with fibrous tissue, the parenchyma degenerates, and the lobules are infiltrated with fat. Caused by any of various chronic progressive conditions affecting the liver.

Class Action—A legal action undertaken by one or more plaintiffs on behalf of themselves and all other persons having an identical interest in the alleged wrong.

Classification—Assignment to predesignated classes on the basis of perceived common characteristics (e.g., exposure). A means of giving order to a group of disconnected facts.

Clofibrate—An antilipemic agent that reduces plasma levels of cholesterol, triglycerides, and uric acid; used in the treatment of hypercholesterolemia and atherosclerosis.

Coccidioidomycosis—A variable, benign, severe, or sometimes fatal systemic mycosis due to inhalation of arthroconidia of *Coccidioides immitis*. In benign forms of the infection, the lesions are limited to the upper respiratory tract, lungs, and near lymph nodes; in a low percentage of cases, the disease disseminates to other visceral organs, meninges, bones, joints, and skin and subcutaneous tissues. (Stedman's medical dictionary 28th ed., 2005)

Cohort study—An epidemiologic study design in which a population sample of persons is defined on the basis of some characteristic, typically exposure, and then observed for occurrence of disease events, e.g., death. Comparisons are made between those with varying degrees of exposure or other characteristics.

Compensation—A monthly payment made by the Secretary to a veteran because of service-connected disability, or to a surviving spouse, child, or parent of a veteran because of the service-connected death of the veteran occurring before January 1, 1957. (Definitions. 2006. 38 U.S.C. § 101.)

Confidence interval (CI)—The computed interval with given probability—e.g., 95%—that the true value of a variable such as a mean, proportion, or rate is contained within the interval. (Last, 2001)

Confounder—A variable that can cause or prevent the outcome of interest, is not in the causal pathway between the exposure and the disease on a causal pathway from the cause to the effect, and is associated with the factor under investigation (e.g., exposure). Confounders can create associations between two variables that are not themselves causally related; these associations are often referred to as spurious associations.

Conjunctivitis—Inflammation of the conjunctiva. (Stedman's medical dictionary 28th ed., 2005)

Corneal opacities—Dense, thick white areas in the cornea, through which one cannot see.

Corpuscular—Relating to a corpuscle. (1) A small mass or body. (2) A blood cell. (Stedman's medical dictionary 28th ed., 2005)

Cortisol—The principal glucocorticoid produced by the zona fasciculata of the adrena cortex. It promotes gluconeogenisis and lipolysis, suppresses protein synthesis, inhibits inflammatory and immune responses, and has mild mineralocorticoid (e.g., hypernatremic, kaliuretic, antidiuretic) effects. Most plasma cortisol is bound to transcortin and albumin. Synthetic cortisol administered as a drug is usually known by the alternative name hydrocortisone. (Stedman's medical dictionary 28th ed., 2005)

Counterfactual—A measure in which at least one of the two circumstances in the definition of variables must be contrary to fact. An example is a hypothetical control group that represents what the distribution of exposure would have been if past events had been different from what they actually were. In a *case-specular* study design, the counterfactual control group comprises (imaginary) dwellings on the opposite side of the street from the dwellings occupied by the cases. The purpose is to asses what the exposure would have been in these hypothetical dwellings. The counterfactual difference in past exposure must be defined precisely to facilitate unambiguous calculating of variables in the hypothetical control group. (Adapted from Last, 2001)

Covariate—A possible confounder that is to be adjusted in a statistical analysis—a variable that is considered to be possibly associated with the outcome under study and may or may not be of direct interest to the study. A covariate may be a confounding variable, an effect modifier, or unrelated to the outcome or the exposure.

Crossover study—A method of comparing two or more treatments or interventions in which the subjects or patients, upon completion of the course of one treatment, are switched to another. In the case of two randomly allocated treatments, A and B, half the subjects are randomly allocated to receive these in the order of A, B, and half to receive them in the order of B, A.

CROSSROADS (Operation)—An atmospheric nuclear weapons test series conducted in the summer of 1946 in the Marshall Islands.

Cross-sectional study—An epidemiologic study design in which the relationship between diseases (or other health endpoints) and health-related characteristics is examined as they exist in a defined population at one particular time. The interpretation of associations in cross-sectional studies is limited by the fact that the time order cannot be determined. Thus, an association between A and B may be because A caused B, or B caused A.

Defoliate—To cause the leaves of a plant, tree, or forest to fall off, especially by the use of chemicals.

Dehydroepiandrosterone (DHEA)—A steroid secreted chiefly by the adrenal cortex, but also by the testis; it is the principal precursor of urinary 17-ketosteroids. Weakly androgenic itself, it is metabolized to delta-5 androstenediol, a hormone with both androgenic and estrogenic effects, and is one of the precursors of testosterone. Serum levels are elevated in adrenal virilism. It may function as a neurotransmitter. DHEA secretion begins during fetal life, reaches a peak in the 3rd decade, and declines steadily thereafter; the level at age 80 is only 10-20 percent of the peak level. This decline has been speculatively associated with the changes of aging. Commercial formulations of DHEA are marketed as dietary supplements, although this substance is neither a nutrient nor a component of the human food chain. Available from health food stores in 10-, 25-, and 50-mg capsules, DHEA has been promoted for the prevention of degenerative diseases including atherosclerosis, Alzheimer's dementia, and parkinsonism, and other effects of aging. None of the alleged benefits have been demonstrated in large, randomized clinical trials. Long-term administration to postmenopausal women has been associated with insulin resistance, hypertension, and reduction of LDL cholesterol. An analysis of 16 preparations of DHEA by high-performance liquid chromatography showed a variation in content from 0 to 150 percent of the labeled strength; only 7 products fell between the expected 90-110 percent of labeled strength. (Stedman's medical dictionary 28th ed., 2005)

Department—Department of Veterans Affairs. (Definitions. 2006. 38 U.S.C. § 101.)

Dependency and indemnity compensation—A monthly payment made by the Secretary to a surviving spouse, child, or parent (A) because of a service-connected death occurring after December 31, 1956, or (B) pursuant to the election of a surviving spouse, child, or parent, in the case of such a death occurring before January 1, 1957. (Definitions. 2006. 38 U.S.C. § 101.)

Depleted uranium—A modestly radioactive heavy metal used in projectiles and armament.

Depressive neurosis—A mental state or chronic mental disorder characterized by feelings of sadness, loneliness, despair, low self-esteem, and self-reproach; accompanying signs include psychomotor retardation or less frequently agitation, withdrawal from social contact, and vegetative states such as loss of appetite and insomnia. (Stedman's medical dictionary 28th ed., 2005)

Dermatitis—Inflammation of the skin. (Stedman's medical dictionary 28th ed., 2005)

Dermatofibrosarcoma protuberans—A relatively slowly growing dermal neoplasm consisting of one or several firm nodules that are usually covered by dark red-blue skin, which tends to be fixed to the palpable masses; histologically, the neoplasm resembles a cellular dermatofibroma with a pronounced storiform pattern; metastases are unusual, but the incidence of recurrence is fairly high. (Stedman's medical dictionary 28th ed., 2005)

Diabetes insipidus—Chronic excretion of very large amounts of pale urine of low specific gravity, causing dehydration and extreme thirst; ordinarily results from inadequate output of pituitary antidiuretic hormone;

the urine abnormalities may be mimicked as a result of excessive fluid intake, as in psychogenic polydipsia. Several types exist: central, neurohypophyseal, and nephrogenic. Autosomal dominant, X-linked, and even autosomal recessive forms have been described. (Stedman's medical dictionary 28th ed., 2005)

Diabetes mellitus—A chronic metabolic disorder in which utilization of carbohydrate is impaired and that of lipid and protein enhanced; it is caused by an absolute or relative deficiency of insulin and is characterized, in more severe cases, by chronic hyperglycemia, glycosuria, water and electrolyte loss, ketoacidosis, and coma; long-term complications include neuropathy, retinopathy, nephropathy, generalized degenerative changes in large and small blood vessels, and increased susceptibility to infection. (Stedman's medical dictionary 28th ed., 2005)

Diabetes Type 1—A condition characterized by high blood glucose levels caused by a total lack of insulin. Occurs when the body's immune system attacks the insulin-producing beta cells in the pancreas and destroys them. The pancreas then produces little or no insulin. Type 1 diabetes develops most often in young people but can appear in adults. (Stedman's medical dictionary 28th ed., 2005)

Diabetes Type 2—A condition characterized by high blood glucose levels caused by either a lack of insulin or the body's inability to use insulin efficiently. Type 2 diabetes develops most often in middle-aged and older adults but can appear in young people. (Stedman's medical dictionary 28th ed., 2005)

2,4-Dichlorophenoxyacetic acid—An herbicide, more toxic to broad-level dicotyledonous plants (weeds) than to monocotyledonous ones (grains and grass), used with 2,4,5-trichlorophenoxyacetic acid as a constituent of Agent Orange.

Dioxin—A contaminant in the herbicide 2,4,5-T; it is potentially toxic, teratogenic, and carcinogenic.

Direct causation—There are no intervening causes between an act and the resulting harm.

Disability Compensation—A benefit paid to a veteran because of injuries or diseases that happened while on active duty, or were made worse by active military service; also paid to certain veterans disabled from VA health care.

Discharge or release—(A) Retirement from the active military, naval, or air service, and (B) The satisfactory completion of the period of active military, naval, or air service for which a person was obligated at the time of entry into such service in the case of a person who, due to enlistment or reenlistment, was not awarded a discharge or release from such period of service at the time of such completion thereof and who, at such time, would otherwise have been eligible for the award of a discharge or release under conditions other than dishonorable. (Definitions. 2006. 38 U.S.C. § 101.)

Disfigure—To impair (as in physicality) by deep and persistent injuries.

Distal amputation—An amputation situated away from the center of the body, or from the point of origin.

Dizygotic twins—Relating to twins derived from two separate zygotes, i.e., bearing the same genetic relationship as full sibs but sharing a common intrauterine environment. (Stedman's medical dictionary 28th ed., 2005)

Dose-response—The relationship of risk for observed outcomes (responses) in a population with varying levels of an agent or characteristic, often an exposure.

Dosimeter—A device for measuring doses of radiations (as X-rays).

Double blind design—A procedure of assignment to study (or treatment) and control (or placebo) groups in which neither the investigator nor the study subject has knowledge of the group to which the subject was assigned.

Doubling dose—The dose of a causal factor required to increase the risk of disease twofold.

Dracontiasis (also known as Dracunculosis)—Infection with *Dracunculus medinensis.* (Stedman's medical dictionary 28th ed., 2005)

Dysentery—A disease marked by frequent watery stools, often with blood and mucus, and characterized clinically by pain, tenesmus, fever, and dehydration. (Stedman's medical dictionary 28th ed., 2005)

Dysthymic disorder—(1) A chronic disturbance of mood characterized by mild depression or loss of interest in usual activities. (2) A DSM diagnosis is established when the specified criteria are met. (Stedman's medical dictionary 28th ed., 2005)

Ectomesenchymoma—A rare tumor that may arise in the brain or soft tissue.

Edema—(1) An accumulation of an excessive amount of watery fluid in cells or intercellular tissues. (2) At the gross level, used to describe the physical sign commonly likened to swelling or increased girth that often accompanies the accumulation of fluid in a body part, most often a limb. (Stedman's medical dictionary 28th ed., 2005)

Effect modifier—A factor that modifies the effect on a health outcome of a putative causal factor under study. For example, age is an effect modifier for many conditions, and immunization status is an effect modifier for the consequences of exposure to pathogenic organisms. (Adapted from Last, 2001)

Electrocardiogram—Graphic record of the heart's integrated action currents obtained with the electrocardiograph displayed as voltage changes over time. (Stedman's medical dictionary 28th ed., 2005)

Emphysema—(1) Presence of air in the interstices of the connective tissue of a part. (2) A condition of the lung characterized by increase beyond the normal in the size of air spaces distal to the terminal bronchiole (those parts containing alveoli), with destructive changes in their walls and reduction in their number. Clinical manifestation is breathlessness on exertion, due to the combined effect (in varying degrees) of reduction of alveolar surface for gas exchange and collapse of smaller airways with trapping of alveolar gas in expiration; this causes the chest to be held in the position of inspiration ("barrel chest"), with prolonged expiration and increased residual volume. Symptoms of chronic bronchitis often, but not necessarily, coexist. Two structural varieties are panlobular (panacina) emphysema and centrilobular (centriacinar) emphysema; paracicatricial, paraseptal, and bullous emphysema are also common. (Stedman's medical dictionary 28th ed., 2005)

Encephalitis—Inflammation of the brain. (Stedman's medical dictionary 28th ed., 2005)

Encephalitis lethargica residuals—Any diffuse inflammation of the brain occurring in epidemic form.

Endocarditis—Inflammation of the endocardium. (Stedman's medical dictionary 28th ed., 2005)

Endocrinopathy—A disorder in the function of an endocrine gland and the consequences thereof. (Stedman's medical dictionary 28th ed., 2005)

Entitlement—A right to benefits specified especially by law or contract; a government program providing benefits to members of a specified group and funds supporting or distributed by such a program; belief that one is deserving of certain privileges.

Eosinophil—A polymorphonuclear leukocyte characterized by many large or prominent, refractile, cytoplasmic granules that are fairly uniform in size and bright yellow-red or orange when treated with Wright or similar stains; the nuclei are usually larger than those of neutrophils, do not stain as deeply, and characteristically have two lobes (a third lobe is sometimes interposed on the connecting strand of chromatin); these leukocytes are motile phagocytes with distinctive antiparasitic functions; they also phagocytose antigen-antibody complexes. (Stedman's medical dictionary 28th ed., 2005)

Epidemiology—The study of the distribution and determinants of illnesses or diseases in specified populations, and the application of this study to control of health problems. "Study" includes surveillance, observation, hypothesis testing, analytic research, and population experiments. "Distribution" refers to analysis by time, place, and classes of persons affected. (Adapted from Last, 2001)

Epilepsies—Any of various disorders marked by abnormal electrical discharges in the brain and typically manifested by sudden brief episodes of altered or diminished consciousness, involuntary movements, or convulsions.

Epithelioid leiomyosarcoma—An uncommon neoplasm of smooth muscle in which the cells are polygonal in shape. It usually develops in the stomach.

Epithelioid sarcoma—Malignant mesenchymal tumor showing nodular granulomalike growth of eosinophilic epithelioid and spindle cells palisading around the centrally located necrotic areas. Two subtypes are recognized: a classic distal and fibromalike form. Tumors typically occur in the subcutaneous tissue along the tendons and the fascia. (Stedman's medical dictionary 28th ed., 2005)

Equipoise—A state of uncertainty about the benefit or harm that may result from a suspected causal factor, in which evidence for and against the causal association is equally balanced.

Erythrocyte—A mature red blood cell. (Stedman's medical dictionary 28th ed., 2005)

Escherichia coli—A species that occurs normally in the intestines of man and other vertebrates, is widely distributed in nature, and is a frequent cause of infections of the urogenital tract and of diarrhea in infants. Enteropathogenic strains (serovars) of *Escherichia coli* cause diarrhea due to enterotoxin, the production of which seems to be associated with a transferable episome; the type species of the genus. (Stedman's medical dictionary 28th ed., 2005)

Etiology—Literally, the science of causes, causality; in common usage, cause. See also Causality; Pathogenesis. (Last, 2001)

Ewing's tumor—A malignant neoplasm that occurs usually before the age of 20 years, about twice as frequently in males, and in about 75 percent of patients involves bones of the extremities, including the shoulder girdle, with a predilection for the metaphysis; histologically, there are conspicuous foci of necrosis in association with irregular masses of small, regular, rounded, or ovoid cells (2–3 times the diameter of erythrocytes), with very scanty cytoplasm. (Stedman's medical dictionary 28th ed., 2005)

Exanthema—A skin eruption occurring as a symptom of an acute viral or coccal disease, as in scarlet fever or measles. (Stedman's medical dictionary 28th ed., 2005)

False negative error—The mistake made in accepting a null hypothesis in the presence of a causal association (type I error, alpha error). In the context of diagnostic tests or criteria (or compensation), the number (or percentage) diagnosed not to have the condition who in fact had it.

False positive error—The mistake made in rejecting a null hypothesis in the absence of a causal association (type II error, beta error). In the context of diagnostic tests or criteria (or compensation), the number (or percentage) diagnosed with the condition who in fact did not have it.

Fasting blood glucose—Measures the amount of glucose in your blood after you have not eaten for at least eight hours. It is often done to check for diabetes.

Fibromyalgia—A common syndrome of chronic widespread soft-tissue pain accompanied by weakness, fatigue, and sleep disturbances; the cause is unknown. (Stedman's medical dictionary 28th ed., 2005)

Fibrosarcoma—A malignant neoplasm derived from deep fibrous tissue, characterized by bundles of immature proliferating fibroblasts arranged in a distinctive herringbone pattern with variable collagen formation, which tends to invade locally and metastasize by the bloodstream. (Stedman's medical dictionary 28th ed., 2005)

Fibrous histocytoma—A cutaneous nodule that is painless, round, firm, gray or red, elevated, and commonly found on the extremities.

Filariasis—Presence of filariae in the tissues of the body or in blood (microfilaremia) or tissue fluids (microfilariasis), occurring in tropical and subtropical regions; living worms cause minimal tissue reaction, which may be asymptomatic, but death of the adult worms leads to granulomatous inflammation and permanent fibrosis causing obstruction of the lymphatic channels from dense hyalinized scars in the subcutaneous tissues; the most serious consequence is elephantiasis or pachyderma. (Stedman's medical dictionary 28th ed., 2005)

Five Series Study—Included Operations GREENHOUSE, UPSHOT-KNOTHOLE, CASTLE, REDWING, and PLUMBBOB; these were chosen for a study of atomic veterans to represent tests at both the Nevada Test Site and the Pacific Proving Grounds.

Flat-rate pension—A uniform pension or one based on years of service.

Follicle-stimulating hormone—An acidic glycoprotein hormone of the anterior pituitary that stimulates the graafian follicles of the ovary and assists subsequently in follicular maturation and the secretion of estradiol; in the male, it stimulates the epithelium of the seminiferous tubules and is partially responsible for inducing spermatogenesis. (Stedman's medical dictionary 28th ed., 2005)

Formaldehyde—A pungent gas, HCHO; used as an antiseptic, disinfectant, and histologic fixative, usually in an aqueous solution. (Stedman's medical dictionary 28th ed., 2005)

Former prisoner of war—A person who, while serving in the active military, naval or air service, was forcibly detained or interned in line of duty—(A) By an enemy government or its agents, or a hostile force, during a period of war; or (B) By a foreign government or its agents, or a hostile force, under circumstances which the Secretary finds to have been comparable to the circumstances under which persons have generally been forcibly detained or interned by enemy governments during periods of war. (Definitions. 2006. 38 U.S.C. § 101.)

Frostbite—Local tissue destruction resulting from exposure to extreme cold; in mild cases, it results in superficial, reversible freezing followed by erythema and slight pain (frostnip); in severe cases, it can be painless or paresthetic and result in blistering, persistent edema, and gangrene. Frostbite is currently treated by rapid rewarming. (Stedman's medical dictionary 28th ed., 2005)

Gallstone—A concretion in the gallbladder or a bile duct, composed chiefly of a mixture of cholesterol, calcium bilirubinate, and calcium carbonate, occasionally as a pure stone composed of just one of these substances. (Stedman's medical dictionary 28th ed., 2005)

Ganglionar neuroma—A tumor composed of a solid mass of ganglia and nerve fibers. Usually found in abdominal tissues.

Gardner's syndrome—Multiple polyposis predisposing to carcinoma of the colon; also multiple tumors, osteomas of the skull, epidermoid cysts, and fibromas; autosomal dominant inheritance, caused by mutation in the adenomatous polyposis coli gene (APC) on chromosome 5q. This disorder is allelic to familial adenomatous polyposis (FAP). (Stedman's medical dictionary 28th ed., 2005)

Garrison—A military post; a permanent military installation.

Gastroenteritis—Inflammation of the mucous membrane of both stomach and intestine. (Stedman's medical dictionary 28th ed., 2005)

Gastrointestinal disorder—A disorder relating to the stomach and intestines.

Generalizability—The degree to which the inference drawn from a study can be extended to a different population. Such generalization is warranted when appropriate account is taken of the study methods, the representativeness of the study sample, and the nature of the population from which it is drawn. (Adapted from Last, 2001)

Geneva Convention—One of a series of agreements concerning the treatment of prisoners of war and of the sick, wounded, and dead in battle first made at Geneva, Switzerland, in 1864 and subsequently accepted in later revisions by most nations.

Genitourinary—Relating to the organs of reproduction and urination collectively. (Stedman's medical dictionary 28th ed., 2005)

Genotoxicity—Denoting a substance that by damaging DNA may cause mutation or cancer. (Stedman's medical dictionary 28th ed., 2005)

Glomus tumor—A vascular neoplasm composed of specialized pericytes (sometimes termed glomus cells), usually in single encapsulated nodular masses that may be several millimeters in diameter and occur almost exclusively in the skin, often subungually in the upper extremity; it is exquisitely tender and may be so painful that patients voluntarily immobilize an extremity, sometimes leading to atrophy of muscles; multiple glomus tumors occur, sometimes with autosomal dominant inheritance. Tumors with cavernous spaces lined by glomus cells are called *glomangiomas*. (Stedman's medical dictionary 28th ed., 2005)

Goldenhar syndrome—A syndrome characterized by epibulbar dermoids, preauricular appendages, micrognathia, and vertebral and other anomalies. (Stedman's medical dictionary 28th ed., 2005)

Gout—A disorder of purine metabolism, occurring especially in men, characterized by a raised but variable blood uric acid level and severe recurrent acute arthritis of sudden onset resulting from deposition of crystals of sodium urate in connective tissues and articular cartilage; most cases are inherited, resulting from a variety of abnormalities of purine metabolism. The familial aggregation is for the most part galtonian with a threshold of expression determined by the solubility of uric acid. However, gout is also a feature of the Lesch-Nyhan syndrome, an X-linked disorder. (Stedman's medical dictionary 28th ed., 2005)

Gulf War—A conflict (August 2, 1990–February 28, 1991) between Iraq and a coalition force of approximately 30 nations led by the United States and mandated by the United Nations in order to liberate Kuwait.

Gulf War Syndrome—A syndrome of various health problems experienced by U.S. military personnel after serving in the Persian Gulf conflict of 1991; includes fatigue, musculoskeletal pain, headaches, dyspnea, memory loss, and diarrhea; thought to be related to exposure to low levels of neurotoxins, including sarin, pesticides, and pyridostigmine bromide (the latter supplied to troops as a protective anti-toxin). (Stedman's medical dictionary 28th ed., 2005)

Hansen's disease (also known as Leprosy)—A chronic granulomatous infection caused by *Mycobacterium leprae* affecting the cooler body parts, especially the skin, peripheral nerves, and testes. Leprosy is classified into two main types, lepromatous and tuberculoid, representing extremes of immunologic response. (Stedman's medical dictionary 28th ed., 2005)

HARDTACK (Operation)—A series of 72 nuclear tests conducted by the United States in 1958; HARDTACK I was carried out in the Pacific Ocean at Bikini Atoll, Enewetak Atoll, and Johnston Island; HARDTACK II was carried out at the Nevada Test Site.

Heart disease—An abnormal organic condition of the heart or of the heart and circulation.

Helminthiasis—The condition of having intestinal vermiform parasites. Syn: *helminthism*, *invermination*. (Stedman's medical dictionary 28th ed., 2005)

Hemangiopericytoma—An uncommon vascular, usually benign, neoplasm composed of round and spindle cells that are derived from the pericytes and surround endothelium-lined vessels; malignant hemangiopericytomas are difficult to distinguish microscopically from the benign. (Stedman's medical dictionary 28th ed., 2005)

Hematocrit—(1) Percentage of the volume of a blood sample occupied by cells. (2) Obsolete term for a centrifuge or device for separating the cells and other particulate elements of the blood from the plasma. (Stedman's medical dictionary 28th ed., 2005)

Hemochromatosis—A disorder of iron metabolism characterized by excessive absorption of ingested iron, saturation of iron-binding protein, and deposition of hemosiderin in tissue, particularly in the liver, pancreas, and skin; cirrhosis of the liver, diabetes (bronze diabetes), bronze pigmentation of the skin, and, eventually heart failure may occur; also can result from administration of large amounts of iron orally, by injection, or in forms of blood transfusion therapy. (Stedman's medical dictionary 28th ed., 2005)

Hemoglobin (Hb)—The red respiratory protein of erythrocytes, consisting of approximately 3.8 percent heme and 96.2 percent globin, with a molecular weight of 64,450, which as oxyhemoglobin (HbO_2) transports oxygen from the lungs to the tissues where the oxygen is readily released and HbO_2 becomes Hb. When Hb is exposed to certain chemicals, its normal respiratory function is blocked; e.g., the oxygen in HbO_2 is easily displaced by carbon monoxide, thereby resulting in the formation of fairly stable carboxyhemoglobin (HbCO), as in asphyxiation resulting from inhalation of exhaust fumes from gasoline engines. When the iron in Hb is oxidized from the ferrous to the ferric state, as in poisoning with nitrates and certain other chemicals, a nonrespiratory compound, methemoglobin (MetHb), is formed.

In humans there are at least five kinds of normal Hb: two embryonic Hb's (Hb Gower-1, Hb Gower-2), fetal (Hb F), and two adult types (Hb A, Hb A_2). There are two α globin chains containing 141 amino acid residues, and two of another kind (β, γ, δ, ε, or ζ), each containing 146 amino acid residues in four of the Hb's. Hb Gower-1 has two ζ chains and two ε chains. The production of each kind of globin chain is controlled by a structural gene of similar Greek letter designation; normal individuals are homozygous for the normal allele at each locus. Substitutions of one amino acid for another in the polypeptide chain can occur at any codon in any of the five loci and have resulted in the production of many hundreds of abnormal Hb types, most of no known clinical significance. In addition, deletions of one or more amino acid residues are known, as well as gene rearrangements due to unequal crossing over between homologous chromosomes. Newly discovered abnormal Hb types are first assigned a name, usually the location where discovered, and a molecular formula is added when determined. (Stedman's medical dictionary 28th ed., 2005)

Hemoglobinuria (paroxysmal)—The presence of hemoglobin in the urine, including certain closely related pigments that are formed from slight alteration of the hemoglobin molecule; when present in sufficient quantities, they result in the urine being colored in shades varying from light reddish-yellow to fairly dark red. (Stedman's medical dictionary 28th ed., 2005)

Hemophilia—An inherited disorder of blood coagulation characterized by a permanent tendency to hemorrhages, spontaneous or traumatic, because of a defect in the blood coagulating mechanism. (Stedman's medical dictionary 28th ed., 2005)

Hemorrhagic—Relating to or marked by hemorrhage. (Stedman's medical dictionary 28th ed., 2005)

Hepatitis B—A virus disease with a long incubation period (usually 50-160 days), caused by a hepatitis B virus, a DNA virus and member of the family *Hepadnaviridae*, usually transmitted by injection of infected blood or blood derivatives or by use of contaminated needles, lancets, or other instruments; clinically and pathologically similar to viral hepatitis type A, but there is no cross-protective immunity; HB_sAg is found in the serum and the hepatitis delta virus occurs in some patients. May lead to acute or chronic liver disease. Syn: *viral hepatitis type b.* (Stedman's medical dictionary 28th ed., 2005)

Herbicide—An agent used to destroy or inhibit plant growth.

Heterozygous—Having different alleles at one locus on the pair of chromosomes present at the diploid state; for example, having a normal beta globin gene (coding for normal hemoglobin, HbA) at locus p15.5 on one chromosome 11 and an abnormal gene (coding for sickle-cell hemoglobin, Hb S) at the same locus on the other chromosome 11. (Stedman's medical dictionary 28th ed., 2005)

Hirsutism—Presence of excessive bodily and facial hair, usually in a male pattern, especially in women; may be present in normal adults as an expression of an ethnic characteristic or may develop in children or adults as the result of androgen excess due to tumors or drugs, or of nonandrogenetic or other drugs. (Stedman's medical dictionary 28th ed., 2005)

Hodgkin's disease—A disease marked by chronic enlargement of the lymph nodes, often local at the onset and later generalized, together with enlargement of the spleen and often of the liver, no pronounced leukocytosis, and commonly anemia and continuous or remittent (Pel-Ebstein) fever; considered to be a malignant neoplasm of lymphoid cells of uncertain origin (Reed-Sternberg cells), associated with inflammatory infiltration of lymphocytes and eosinophilic leukocytes and fibrosis; can be classified into lymphocytic predominant, nodular sclerosing, mixed cellularity, and lymphocytic depletion type. (Stedman's medical dictionary 28th ed., 2005)

Homozygous—Having identical alleles at one or more loci. (Stedman's medical dictionary 28th ed., 2005)

Hydrocephalus—A condition marked by an excessive accumulation of fluid resulting in dilation of the cerebral ventricles and raised intracranial pressure; may also result in enlargement of the cranium and atrophy of the brain. (Stedman's medical dictionary 28th ed., 2005)

Hypercoagulability—Abnormally increased coagulability. (Stedman's medical dictionary 28th ed., 2005)

Hyperglycemia—An abnormally high concentration of glucose in the circulating blood, seen especially in patients with diabetes mellitus. (Stedman's medical dictionary 28th ed., 2005)

Hyperinsulinemia—Increased levels of insulin in the plasma due to increased secretion of insulin by the beta cells of the pancreatic islets. Decreased hepatic removal of insulin is a cause in some patients, although hyperinsulinism usually is associated with insulin resistance and is commonly found in obesity in association with varying degrees of hyperglycemia. Syn: *hyperinsulinism.* (Stedman's medical dictionary 28th ed., 2005)

Hyperlipidemia—Elevated levels of lipids in the blood plasma. There are several types of hyperlipidemia; one is associated with a deficiency of α-aminoadipic semialdehyde synthase. (Stedman's medical dictionary 28th ed., 2005)

Hyperpigmentation—An excess of pigment in a tissue or part. (Stedman's medical dictionary 28th ed., 2005)

Hypertension—High blood pressure; transitory or sustained elevation of systemic arterial blood pressure to a level likely to induce cardiovascular damage or other adverse consequences. Hypertension has been arbitrarily defined as a systolic blood pressure above 140 mm Hg or a diastolic blood pressure above 90 mm Hg. Consequences of uncontrolled hypertension include retinal vascular damage (Keith-Wagener-Barker changes), cerebrovascular disease and stroke, left ventricular hypertrophy and failure, myocardial infarction, dissecting aneurysm, and renovascular disease. An underlying disorder (e.g., renal disease, Cushing's syndrome, pheochromocytoma) is identified in fewer than 10 percent of all cases of hypertension. The remainder, traditionally labeled "essential" hypertension, probably arise from a variety of disturbances in normal pressure-regulating mechanisms (which involve baroreceptors, autonomic influences on the rate and force of cardiac contraction and vascular tone, renal retention of salt and water, formation of angiotensin II under the influence of renin and angiotensin-converting enzyme, and other factors known and unknown), and most are probably genetically conditioned. (Stedman's medical dictionary 28th ed., 2005)

Hypertrophy—General increase in bulk of a part of organ, not due to tumor formation. Use of the term may be restricted to denote greater bulk through increase in size, but not in number, of cells or other individual tissue elements. (Stedman's medical dictionary 28th ed., 2005)

Hypochondriasis—A morbid concern about one's own health and exaggerated attention to any unusual bodily or mental sensations; a delusion that one is suffering from some disease for which no physical basis is evident. (Stedman's medical dictionary 28th ed., 2005)

Hypomania—A mild degree of mania. (Stedman's medical dictionary 28th ed., 2005)

Hypothyroidism—Diminished production of thyroid hormone, leading to clinical manifestations of thyroid insufficiency, including low metabolic rate, tendency to weight gain, somnolence, and sometimes myxedema. (Stedman's medical dictionary 28th ed., 2005)

Hysteria—Denoting maladies involving physical symptoms that seem better explained by psychological factors. The concept of hysteria is historically differentiated into somatization disorder and conversion disorder, both of which are considered types of somatoform disorders in the DSM. The current ICD-10, however, places conversion disorder with dissociative disorders, not with somatoform disorders. (Adapted from Stedman's medical dictionary 28th ed., 2005)

Inactive duty training—(A) Duty (other than full-time duty) prescribed for Reserves (including commissioned officers of the Reserve Corps of the Public Health Service) by the Secretary concerned under section 206 of title 37 (37 U.S.C.S. § 206) or any other provision of law; (B) Special additional duties authorized for Reserves (including commissioned officers of the Reserve Corps of the Public Health Service) by an authority designated by the Secretary concerned and performed by them on a voluntary basis in connection with the prescribed training or maintenance activities of the units to which they are assigned; and (C) Training (other than active duty for training) by a member of, or applicant for membership (as defined in section 8140[g] of title 5 [5 U.S.C.S. § 8140(g)]) in, the Senior Reserve Officers' Training Corps prescribed under chapter 103 of title 10 (10 U.S.C.S. § 2101 et seq.). In the case of a member of the National Guard or Air National Guard of any State, such term means duty (other than full-time duty) under sections 316, 502, 503, 504, or 505 of title 32 (32 U.S.C.S. § 316, 502, 503, 504, or 505), or the prior corresponding provisions of law. Such term does not include (i) work or study performed in connection with correspondence courses, (ii) attendance at an educational institution in an inactive status, or (iii) duty performed as a temporary member of the Coast Guard Reserve. (Definitions. 2006. 38 U.S.C. § 101.)

Incidence—The number of instances of illness commencing, or of persons falling ill, during a given period in a specified population. More generally, the number of new events, e.g., new cases of disease in a defined population, within a specified period of time. The term incidence is sometimes wrongly used to denote incidence rate. Syn: *incident number*. (Last, 2001)

Indemnity—A security against hurt, loss, or damage; exemption from incurred penalties or liabilities.

Influenza—An acute infectious respiratory disease, caused by influenza viruses, which are found in the family Orthomyxoviridae, in which the inhaled virus attacks the respiratory epothelial cells of susceptible persons and produces a cararrhal inflammation; characterized by sudden onset, chills, fever of short duration (3-4 days), severe prostration, headache, muscle aches, and a cough that usually is dry and may be followed by secondary bacterial infections that can last up to 10 days. The disease commonly occurs in epidemics, sometimes in pandemics, which develop quickly and spread rapidly; mortality rate is usually low, but may be high in cases with secondary bacterial pneumonia, particularly in the elderly and those with underlying debilitating diseases; strain-specific immunity develops, but mutations in the virus are frequent, and the immunity usually does not affect antigenically different strains. (Stedman's medical dictionary 28th ed., 2005)

Information bias (observational bias)—A flaw in measuring exposure or outcome data that results in different quality (accuracy) or information between comparison groups. (Last, 2001)

Instrumental variable—A factor related directly to the putative cause, but independent of all potential confounders, used to estimate the strength of causal influence even in the presence of confounding.

Instrumental variable (IV) estimation—In linear regression, used when the error distribution cannot be considered independent of the regressor's distribution.

Interaction—(1) The interdependent operation of two or more causes to produce or prevent an effect. *Biological interaction* means the interdependent operation of two or more causes to produce, prevent, or control disease. (2) Differences in the effects of one or more factors according to the level of the remaining factor(s). (Last, 2001) In epidemiology, synonymous with effect modification (see Effect modification).

Ionizing radiation—Either particle radiation or electromagnetic radiation in which an individual particle/photon carries enough energy to ionize an atom or molecule by completely removing an electron from its orbit; if enough occur, can be very destructive to living tissue and can cause DNA damage and mutations. (Last, 2001)

Irritable bowel syndrome (IBS)—A condition characterized by gastrointestinal signs and symptoms including constipation, diarrhea, gas, and bloating, all in the absence of organic pathology. Associated with uncoordinated and inefficient contractions of the large intestine. (Stedman's medical dictionary 28th ed., 2005)

Ischemic heart disease—Deficient supply of blood to the heart that is due to obstruction of the inflow of arterial blood (as by the narrowing of arteries by spasm or disease).

Jaundice—A yellowish staining of the integument, sclerae, deeper tissues, and excretions with bile pigments, resulting from increased levels in the plasma. (Stedman's medical dictionary 28th ed., 2005)

Kala-azar—(1) A chronic disease, occurring in India, China, Pakistan, the Mediterranean littoral, the Middle East, South and Central America, Asia, and Africa caused by *Leishmania donovani* and transmitted by the bite of an appropriate species of sandfly of the genus *Phlebotomus* or *Lutzomyia;* the organisms grow and multiply in macrophages, eventually causing them to burst and liberate amastigote parasites that then invade other macrophages; proliferation of macrophages in the bone marrow causes crowding out of erythroid and myeloid elements, resulting in leukopenia, and anemia, splenomegaly, and hepatomegaly, which are characteristic, along with enlargement of lymph nodes; fever, fatigue, malaise, and secondary infections also occur; different strains of *L. donovani* occur; *L. infantum* in Eurasia, *L. chagasi* in Latin America. (2) Visceral leishmaniasis caused by *Leishmania tropica*, cultured from bone marrow aspirates of some military patients following the Gulf War. Syn: *visceral leishmaniasis*. (Stedman's medical dictionary 28th ed., 2005)

Kaposi's sarcoma—A multifocal malignant neoplasm of primitive vasoformative tissue, occurring in the skin and sometimes in lymph nodes or viscera, consisting of spindle cells and irregular small vascular spaces frequently infiltrated by hemosiderin-pigmented macrophages and extravasated red cells; clinically manifested by cutaneous lesions consisting of reddish-purple to dark-blue macules, plaques, or nodules; seen most commonly in men over 60 years of age and, in AIDS patients, as an opportunistic disease associated with human herpes virus 8 infection. (Stedman's medical dictionary 28th ed., 2005)

Keratitis—Inflammation of the cornea. (Stedman's medical dictionary 28th ed., 2005)

Korean conflict—The period beginning on June 27, 1950, and ending on January 31, 1955. (Definitions. 2006. 38 U.S.C. § 101.)

K-Z syndrome (POW syndrome)—Marked by severe, permanent psychological scars and nonspecific physical problems and is attributed to organic brain disease.

Laryngeal cancer—Cancer of the organ of voice production, the part of the respiratory tract between the pharynx and the trachea.

Laryngitis—Inflammation of the mucous membrane of the larynx. (Stedman's medical dictionary 28th ed., 2005)

Leiomyosarcoma—A malignant neoplasm derived from smooth (non-striated) muscle. (Stedman's medical dictionary 28th ed., 2005)

Leishmaniasis—Infection with a species of *Leishmania* resulting in a clinically ill-defined group of diseases traditionally divided into four major types: (1) visceral leishmaniasis (kala-azar); (2) Old World cutaneous leishmaniasis; (3) New World cutaneous leishmaniasis; (4) mucocutaneous leishmaniasis. Each is clinically and geographically distinct and each has in recent years been subdivided further into clinical and epidemiological categories. Transmission is by various sandfly species of the genus *Phlebotomus* or *Lutzomyia.* (Stedman's medical dictionary 28th ed., 2005)

Leprosy (Hansen's disease)—(1) A chronic granulomatous infection caused by *Mycobacterium leprae* affecting the cooler body parts, especially the skin, peripheral nerves, and testes. Leprosy is classified into two main types, lepromatous and tuberculoid, representing extremes of immunologic response. (Stedman's medical dictionary 28th ed., 2005)

Leukemia—Progressive proliferation of abnormal leukocytes found in hemopoietic tissues, other organs, and usually in the blood in increased numbers. Leukemia is classified by the dominant cell type, and by duration from onset to death. This occurs in *acute leukemia* within a few months in most cases, and is associated with acute symptoms including severe anemia, hemorrhages, and slight enlargement of the lymph nodes or the spleen. The duration of *chronic leukemia* exceeds one year, with a gradual onset of symptoms of anemia or marked enlargement of the spleen, liver, or lymph nodes. (Stedman's medical dictionary 28th ed., 2005)

Lewisite—A war gas; a vesicant, a lung irritant like mustard gas; a systemic poison entering the circulation through the lungs or skin, and a mitotic poison arresting mitosis in the metaphase. Dimercaprol is the antidote. (Stedman's medical dictionary 28th ed., 2005)

Likelihood ratio—The ratio of the likelihood of the observed data in a sample for two competing hypotheses about the true unknown characteristic ("parameter value") of the population sampled; or comparison of various model conditions to assess which model provides the best fit. Likelihood ratios are used to evaluate screening and diagnostic tests in clinical epidemiology. (Last, 2001)

Limited/suggestive evidence—From the IOM series Veterans and Agent Orange; "evidence is suggestive of an association between herbicides and the outcome but is limited because chance, bias, and confounding could not be ruled out with confidence. For example, at least one high-quality study shows a positive association, but the results of other studies are inconsistent."

Line of duty—All that is authorized, required, or normally associated with some field of responsibility.

Linear relationship—The condition in which a given variable changes by an absolute constant amount with each unit change in another variable.

Liposarcoma—A malignant neoplasm of adults that occurs especially in the retroperitoneal tissues and the thigh, usually deep in the intermuscular or periarticular planes; histologically, liposarcoma is a large tumor that may be composed of well-differentiated fat cells or may be dedifferentiated, either myxoid, round-celled, or pleomorphic, usually in association with a rich network of capillaries; recurrences are common, and dedifferentiated liposarcoma metastasizes to the lungs or serosal surfaces. (Stedman's medical dictionary 28th ed., 2005)

Loiasis—A chronic disease caused by the filarial nematode *Loa loa*, with symptoms and signs first occurring approximately 3-4 years after a bite by an infected tabanid fly. When the infective larvae mature, the adult worms move about in an irregular course through the connective tissue of the body (as rapidly as 1 cm per minute), frequently becoming visible beneath the skin and mucous membranes; e.g., in the back, scalp, chest, inner surface of the lip, and especially on the conjunctiva. The worms provoke hyperemia and exudation of fluid, often a host response to the worm products, a Calabar or fugitive swelling that causes no serious damage and subsides as the parasites move on; the patient is annoyed by the "creeping" in the tissues and intense itching, as well as occasional pain, especially when the swelling is in the region of tendons and joints. Most patients have marked eosinophilia of 10-40 percent. (Stedman's medical dictionary 28th ed., 2005)

Long Shot—A nuclear device detonated beneath Amchitka Island, Alaska, in 1965.

Longitudinal study—See Cohort study.

Lung epithelium—The purely cellular avascular layer covering the lung's internal surfaces.

Lung fibrosis—Formation of fibrous tissue as a reparative or reactive process, as opposed to formation of fibrous tissue as a normal constituent of the lung.

Lung pleura (visceral pleura)—The serous membrane investing the lungs and dipping into the fissures between the lobes of the lungs. (Stedman's medical dictionary 28th ed., 2005)

Lupus erythematosus (systemic)—An inflammatory connective tissue disease with variable features, frequently including fever, weakness and fatigability, joint pains or arthritis resembling rheumatoid arthritis, diffuse erythematous skin lesions on the face, neck, or upper extremities, with liquefaction degeneration of the basal layer and epidermal atrophy, lymphadenopathy, pleurisy or pericarditis, glomerular lesions, anemia, hyperglobulinemia, and a positive LE cell test result, with serum antibodies to nuclear protein and sometimes to double-stranded DNA and other substances. (Stedman's medical dictionary 28th ed., 2005)

Luteinizing hormone (lutropin)—One of two glycoprotein hormones that stimulate the final ripening of the follicles and the secretion of progesterone by them, their rupture to release the egg, and the conversion of the ruptured follicle into the corpus luteum. Syn: *lutropin.* (Stedman's medical dictionary 28th ed., 2005)

Lymphocyte—A white blood cell formed in bone marrow and distributed throughout the body in lymphatic tissue (e.g., lymph nodes, spleen, thymus, tonsils, Peyer patches), where it undergoes proliferation. In normal adults, lymphocytes make up 22-28 percent of the total number of leukocytes in the circulating blood. Lymphocytes are generally small (7-8 μm), although larger forms (10-20 μm) occur frequently. With Wright or similar stain, the nucleus is colored a deep purple-blue and is composed of dense aggregates of chromatin within a sharply defined nuclear membrane; the nucleus usually is round, but may be slightly indented, and is eccentrically situated within a relatively small amount of light blue cytoplasm that ordinarily contains no granules; especially in larger forms, the cytoplasm may be fairly abundant and include several fine granules of bright red-violet; unlike granules of the myeloid series of cells, those in lymphocytes do not yield a positive oxidase or peroxidase reaction. Lymphocytes are divided into two principal groups, T and B cells, based on their function and on characteristics of their surface molecules. Null cells, which include natural killer cells, represent a small percentage of the lymphocyte population. (Stedman's medical dictionary 28th ed., 2005)

Lymphohaematopoietic cancer—Cancer of the lymph (a clear, transparent, sometimes faintly yellow and slightly opalescent fluid that is collected from the tissues throughout the body, flows in the lymphatic vessels, and is eventually added to the venous blood circulation) and the blood cells.

Lymphoma—Any neoplasm of lymphoid or reticuloendothelial tissues, in general use, synonymous with malignant lymphoma; present as apparently solid tumors composed of cells that appear primitive or resemble lymphocytes, plasma cells, or histiocytes. Lymphomas appear most frequently in the lymph nodes, spleen, or other normal sites of lymphoreticular cells; may invade other organs or manifest as leukemia. Lymphomas are now classified by histology, immunophenotype, and cytogenic analysis, according to cell or origin (B or T cells) and degree of maturation. The current World Health Organization (WHO) classification of lymphoid neoplasms is based on the Revised European-

American Lymphoma (REAL) classification and effectively replaces older schemes such as the Working Formulation and Rappaport classification, which were based solely on morphology. (Stedman's medical dictionary 28th ed., 2005)

Malaria—A disease caused by the presence of the sporozoan *Plasmodium* in human or other vertebrate red blood cells, usually transmitted to humans by the bite of an infected female mosquito of the genus *Anopheles* that previously sucked the blood from a person with malaria. Human infection begins with the exoerythrocytic cycle in liver parenchyma cells, followed by a series of erythrocytic schizogenous cycles repeated at regular intervals; production of gametocytes in other red cells provides future gametes for another mosquito infection; characterized by episodic severe chills and high fever, prostration, occasionally fatal termination. (Stedman's medical dictionary 28th ed., 2005)

Malnutrition (including optic atrophy)—Faulty nutrition resulting from malabsorption, poor diet, or overeating. (Stedman's medical dictionary 28th ed., 2005)

Manhattan Project—The project to develop the first nuclear weapons during World War II by the United States, the United Kingdom, and Canada. Refers specifically to the period of the project from 1942 to 1946.

Measurement error/bias—Systematic error arising from inaccurate measurements (or classification) of subjects of study variable(s).

Melioidosis—An infectious disease of rodents in India and Southeast Asia that is caused by *Pseudomonas pseudomallei* and is communicable to humans. The characteristic lesion is a small caseous nodule, found generally throughout the body, which breaks down into an abscess; symptoms vary according to the tracts or organs involved. (Stedman's medical dictionary 28th ed., 2005)

Mesenchymoma—Rarely used term for a neoplasm in which there is a mixture of mesenchymal derivatives, other than fibrous tissue. A benign mesenchymoma may contain foci of vascular, muscular, adipose, osteoid, osseous, and cartilaginous tissue; such neoplasms are sometimes classed under a compounded name, e.g., angioleiomyolipoma, and the like, but the broader term may be preferred. A malignant mesenchymoma may also occur as a similar mixture of two or more types of mesenchymal cells that are malignant (other than fibrous tissue cells). (Stedman's medical dictionary 28th ed., 2005)

Mesothelioma—A rare neoplasm derived from the lining cells of the pleura and peritoneum, which grows as a thick sheet covering the viscera, and is composed of spindle cells or fibrous tissue that may enclose gland-like spaces lined by cuboidal cells. (Stedman's medical dictionary 28th ed., 2005)

Meta-analysis—A statistical synthesis of the data from separate but similar, i.e., comparable, studies, leading to a quantitative summary of the pooled results. In the biomedical sciences, the systematic, organized, and structured evaluation of a problem of interest, using information (commonly in the form of statistical tables or other data) from a number of independent studies of the problem. A frequent application has been the pooling of results from a set of randomized controlled trials, none in itself necessarily powerful enough to demonstrate statistically significant differences, but in aggregate capable of doing so. Meta-analysis has a qualitative component, i.e., application of predetermined criteria of quality (e.g., completeness of data, absence of biases) and a quantitative component, i.e., integration of the numerical information. The aim is to integrate the findings, pool the data, and identify the overall trend of results. An essential prerequisite is that the studies must stand up to critical appraisal, and various biases, e.g., *publication bias*, must be allowed for. (Last, 2001)

Mexican border period—The period beginning on May 9, 1916, and ending on April 5, 1917, in the case of a veteran who during such period served in Mexico, on the borders thereof, or in the waters adjacent thereto. (Definitions. 2006. 38 U.S.C. § 101.)

Milrow—A nuclear device detonated beneath Amchitka Island, Alaska, in 1969.

Misclassification—The erroneous classification of an individual, value, or an attribute into a category other than that to which it should be assigned. The probability of misclassification may be the same in all study groups (nondifferential misclassification) or may vary between groups (differential misclassifications). (Last, 2001)

Model averaging—Computing the average of a parameter from a model.

Monocyte—A relatively large mononuclear leukocyte (16-22 μm in diameter), that normally constitutes 3-7 percent of the leukocytes of the circulating blood, and is normally found in lymph nodes, spleen, bone marrow, and loose connective tissue. When treated with the usual dyes, monocytes manifest an abundant pale blue or blue-gray cytoplasm that contains numerous, fine, dustlike, red-blue granules; vacuoles are frequently present; the nucleus is usually indented, or slightly folded, and has a stringy chromatin structure that seems more condensed where the delicate strands are in contact. Monocytes that leave the blood stream and enter the connective tissue spaces are called macrophages. (Stedman's medical dictionary 28th ed., 2005)

Mononucleosis—Presence of abnormally large number of mononuclear leukocytes in the circulating blood, especially with reference to forms that are not normal. (Stedman's medical dictionary 28th ed., 2005)

Monozygotic twins—Twins resulting from one zygote that at an early stage of development becomes separated into independently growing cell aggregations giving rise to two individuals of the same sex and identical genetic constitution. (Stedman's medical dictionary 28th ed., 2005)

Multiple myeloma—An uncommon disease that occurs more frequently in men than in women and is associated with anemia, hemorrhage, recurrent infections, and weakness. Ordinarily, it is regarded as a malignant neoplasm that originates in bone marrow and involves chiefly the skeleton, with clinical features attributable to the sites of involvement and to abnormalities in formation of plasma protein; characterized by numerous diffuse foci or nodular accumulations of abnormal or malignant plasma cells in the marrow of various bones (especially the skull), causing palpable swellings of the bones, and occasionally in extraskeletal sites; radiologically, the bone lesions have a characteristic punched-out appearance. The myeloma cells produce abnormal proteins in the serum and urine; those formed in any one example of multiple myeloma are different from other myeloma proteins, as well as from normal serum proteins, the most frequent abnormalities in the metabolism of protein being (1) the occurrence of Bence Jones proteinuria, (2) a great increase in monoclonal γ-globulin in the plasma, (3) the occasional formation of cryoglobulin, and (4) a form of primary amyloidosis. The Bence Jones protein is not a derivative of abnormal serum protein, but seems to be formed de novo from amino acid precursors. (Stedman's medical dictionary 28th ed., 2005)

Multiple regression model—Given data on an outcome variable y and more than one possible predictive variables x_1, x_2, etc., regression analysis involves finding the "best" mathematical model (within some restricted class of models) to describe y as a function of the x's, or to predict y from the x's. Not to be confused with multivariate analysis.

Multiple sclerosis (MS)—Common demyelinating disorder of the central nervous system, causing patches of sclerosis (plaques) in the brain and spinal cord; occurs primarily in young adults, and has protean clinical manifestations, depending upon the location and size of the plaque; typical symptoms include visual loss, diplopia, nystagmus, dysarthria, weakness, paresthesias, bladder abnormalities, and mood alterations; characteristically, the plaques are "separated in time and space" and clinically the symptoms show exacerbations and remissions. (Stedman's medical dictionary 28th ed., 2005)

Multiplicative model—A model in which the joint effect of two or more causes is the product of their individual effects. For instance, if factor a multiplies risk by the amount a in the absence of factor b, and factor b multiplies risk by the amount b in the absence of factor a, the combined effect of factors a and b on risk is $a \times b$. (Last, 2001)

Multivariate model—A model where the variation in several variables is studied simultaneously; in statistics, any analytic method that allows the simultaneous study of two or more dependent variables.

Mustard gas—An irritant, vesicant, oily liquid used especially as a chemical weapon.

Mutagenic—Promoting mutation.

Myasthenia gravis—A disorder of neuromuscular transmission marked by fluctuating weakness and fatigue of certain voluntary muscles, including those innervated by brainstem motor nuclei; caused by a marked reduction in the number of acetylcholine receptors in the postsynaptic membrane of the neuromuscular junction, resulting from an autoimmune mechanism. (Stedman's medical dictionary 28th ed., 2005)

Mycosis (mycoses)—Any disease caused by a fungus. (Stedman's medical dictionary 28th ed., 2005)

Myelitis—(1) Inflammation of the spinal cord. (2) Inflammation of the bone marrow. (Stedman's medical dictionary 28th ed., 2005)

Myelodysplastic syndrome (MDS)—A heterogeneous group of clonal hematopoietic stem cell disorders characterized by the presence of dysplastic changes in one or more of hematopoietic lineages. The common clinical picture may include anemia, infections, and bleeding problems. Occurs generally in elderly patients, or those with prior exposure to leukemogenic agents. Transformation rates to acute leukemia range from 10 to 80 percent. Cytogenetic abnormalities are associated with a poor prognosis. (Stedman's medical dictionary 28th ed., 2005)

Myocarditis—Inflammation of the muscular walls of the heart. (Stedman's medical dictionary 28th ed., 2005)

Nasopharyngeal cancer—Cancer of the nose or naval cavity and the pharynx.

National Childhood Vaccine Injury Act—Enacted in 1986 to reduce the potential financial liability of vaccine makers due to vaccine injury claims; created the National Vaccine Injury Compensation Program to provide a federal no-fault system for compensating vaccine-related injuries or death.

Necessary cause—A causal factor whose presence is required for the occurrence of a given effect.

Negative predictive value (NPV)—The probability that a person with a negative test does not have the disease or condition (Last, 2001); specifically, the ratio of those who are identified by a test not to have the condition who in fact do not have it, divided by all those identified by a test not to have the condition (i.e., true negatives, divided by the sum of true negatives and false negatives). See Positive predictive value.

Nephritis—Inflammation of the kidneys. (Stedman's medical dictionary 28th ed., 2005)

Nephrolithiasis—Presence of renal calculi. (Stedman's medical dictionary 28th ed., 2005)

Neuropsychiatric disease—A disease of both neurology (nervous system) and psychiatry (mental disorders).

Neutrophil—(1) A mature white blood cell in the granulocytic series, formed by myelopoietic tissue of the bone marrow (sometimes also in extramedullary sites), and released into the circulating blood, where they normally represent 54-65 percent of the total number of leukocytes. When stained with the usual Romanovsky type of dyes, neutrophils are characterized by (a) a dark purple-blue nucleus, lobated (three to five distinct lobes joined by thin strands of chromatin), and with a rather coarse network of fairly dense chromatin; and (b) a cytoplasm that is faintly pink (sharply contrasted with the nucleus) and contains numerous fine pink or violet-pink granules, i.e., not acidophilic or basophilic (as in eosinophils or basophils). The precursors of neutrophils, in order of increasing maturity, are: myeloblasts, promyelocytes, myelocytes, metamyelocytes, and band forms. Although the terms neutrophilic leukocytes and neutrophilic granulocytes include younger cells in which neutrophilic granules are recognized, the two expressions are frequently used as synonyms for neutrophils, which are mature forms unless otherwise indicated by a modifying term, such as immature neutrophil. (2) Any cell or tissue that manifests no special affinity for acid or basic dyes, i.e., the cytoplasm stains approximately equally with either type of dye. (Stedman's medical dictionary 28th ed., 2005)

Nodule—A small node; in skin, a node up to 1.0 cm in diameter, solid, with palpable depth; a pulmonary or pleural lesion seen on a radiographic image as a well-defined, discrete, roughly circular opacity 2-30 mm in diameter. (Stedman's medical dictionary 28th ed., 2005)

Non-Hodgkin's lymphoma (NHL)—A lymphoma other than Hodgkin's disease, classified by Rappaport into a nodular or diffuse tumor pattern and by cell type; a working or international formulation separates such lymphomas into low-, intermediate-, and high-grade malignancy and into cytologic subtypes reflecting follicular center cell or other origin. (Stedman's medical dictionary 28th ed., 2005)

Nonlymphocytic leukemia—A malignant neoplasm of blood-forming tissues characterized by the uncontrolled proliferation of immature granular leukocytes. The risk of the disease is increased among people who have been exposed to massive doses of radiation.

Non-service-connected—With respect to disability or death, that such disability was not incurred or aggravated, or that the death did not result from a disability incurred or aggravated, in line of duty in the active military, naval, or air service. (Definitions. 2006. 38 U.S.C. § 101.)

Normalized data—Data that are continuous and have a symmetrical distribution, both tails extend to infinity; the arithmetic mean, mode, and median are identical; the distribution shape is completely determined by the mean and standard deviation.

Null hypothesis—The statistical hypothesis that one variable has no association with another variable or set of variables, or that two or more population distributions do not differ from one another; states that the results observed in a study, experiment, or test are no different from what might have have occurred as a result of the operation of chance alone. (Last, 2001)

Nursing home care—The accommodation of convalescents or other persons who are not acutely ill and not in need of hospital care but who require nursing care and related medical services. (Definitions. 2006. 38 U.S.C. § 101.)

Obesity—An excess of subcutaneous fat in proportion to lean body mass. Excess fat accumulation is associated with increase in the size (hypertrophy) as well as the number (hyperplasia) of adipose tissue cells. Obesity is variously defined in terms of absolute weight, weight-height ratio, distribution of subcutaneous fat, and societal and esthetic norms. Measures of weight in proportion to height include relative weight (RW, body weight divided by median desirable weight for a person of the same height and medium frame according to actuarial tables), body mass index (BMI, kg/m^2), and ponderal index (kg/m^3). These do not differentiate between excess adiposity and increased lean body mass. In contrast, subscapular and triceps skinfold measurements and determination of the waist-to-hip ratio help define the regional deposition of fat and differentiate the more medically significant central obesity from peripheral obesity in adults. No single cause can explain all cases of obesity. Ultimately it results from an imbalance between energy intake and energy expenditure. While faulty eating habits related to failure of normal satiety feedback mechanisms may be responsible for some cases, many obese persons neither consume more calories nor eat different proportions of foodstuffs than nonobese persons. Contrary to popular belief, obesity is not caused by disorders of pituitary, thyroid, or adrenal gland metabolism. However, it is often associated with hyperinsulinism and relative insulin resistance. Studies of obese twins strongly suggest the presence of genetic influences on resting metabolic rate, feeding behavior, changes in energy expenditures in response to overfeeding, lipoprotein lipase activity, and basal rate of lipolysis. Environmental factors associated with obesity include socioeconomic status, race, region of residence, season, urban living, and being part of a smaller family. The prevalence of obesity is greater when weight is measured during winter rather than summer. Obesity is much more common in the southeastern United States, although the northeastern and midwestern states also have high rates, a phenomenon independent of race, population density, and season. (Stedman's medical dictionary 28th ed., 2005)

Observational study—An epidemiologic study that does not involve any experimental intervention, such as randomizing exposure or treatment.

Obstructive pulmonary disease—A progressive and irreversible condition characterized by diminished inspiratory and expiratory capacity of the lungs.

Occult blood—Blood in the feces in amount too small to be seen but detectable by chemical tests. (Stedman's medical dictionary 28th ed., 2005)

Ochronosis—A rare, autosomal recessive disease characterized by alkaptonuria with pigmentation of the cartilages and sometimes tissues such as muscle, epithelial cells, and dense connective tissue; may affect also the sclera, mucous membrane of the lips, and skin of the ears, face, and hands, and cause standing urine to be dark-colored and contain pigmented casts; pigmentation is thought to result from oxidized homogentisic acid, and cartilage degeneration results in osteoarthritis, particularly of the spine. (Stedman's medical dictionary 28th ed., 2005)

Odds ratio (OR)—The ratio of two odds, often used in case-control studies as an estimate of relative risk. Consider the following notation for the distribution of a binary exposure and a disease in a population or a sample.

	Exposed	Unexposed
Disease	*a*	*b*
No disease	*c*	*d*

The odds ratio (cross-product ratio) is *ad*/*bc*. Syn: *cross-product ratio, relative odds*. (Adapted from Last, 2001)

Onchocerciasis—Infection with *Onchocerca* (especially *O. volvulus*, a filarial nematode transmitted from person to person by black flies of the genus *Simulium*), marked by nodular swellings forming a fibrous cyst enveloping the coiled parasites (onchocercoma); microfilariae move freely out of the nodule and escape into the intercellular lymph in the dermis. Dermatologic changes often develop, especially in Africa, resulting in intense pruritus, scaly or lichenoid skin, depigmentation, and destruction of elastic fibers. Most important are the ocular complications that may develop after a long chronic course, with blindness frequently occurring in advanced cases, caused by the presence of living or dead microfilariae seen by slitlamp biomicroscopy. (Stedman's medical dictionary 28th ed., 2005)

Operation Ranch Hand—The military code name for the spraying of herbicides from U.S. Air Force aircraft in Southeast Asia from 1962 through 1971.

Operation TOP HAT—Conducted in Fort McClellan, Alabama, in 1953; used Chemical Corps personnel in tests of decontamination methods for biological welfare agents, sulfur mustard, and nerve gases.

Ophthalmological changes—Changes concerned with the eye, its disease, and refractive errors.

Organic disease of the nervous system (organic disease)—A disease in which there are anatomic or pathophysiologic changes in some bodily tissue or organ, in contrast to a functional disorder; particularly one of psychogenic origin. (Stedman's medical dictionary 28th ed., 2005)

Organic residuals of frostbite—Any detectable or observable changes due to frostbite.

Oroya fever (also known as bartonellosis and carrion)—A generalized, acute, febrile, endemic, and systemic form of bartonellosis; marked by high fever, rheumatic pains, progressive, severe anemia, and albuminuria. (Stedman's medical dictionary 28th ed., 2005)

Osteitis (Paget's disease)—Inflammation of bone. (Stedman's medical dictionary 28th ed., 2005)

Osteoarthritis—Arthritis characterized by erosion of articular cartilage, either primary or secondary to trauma or other conditions, which becomes soft, frayed, and thinned with eburnation of subchondral bone and outgrowths of marginal osteophytes; pain and loss of function result; mainly affects weight-bearing joints, is more common in old people and animals. (Stedman's medical dictionary 28th ed., 2005)

Osteomalacia—A disease in adults characterized by a gradual softening and bending of the bones with varying severity of pain; softening occurs because the bones contain osteoid tissue that has failed to calcify because of lack of vitamin D or renal tubular dysfunction; more common in women than in men, osteomalacia often begins during pregnancy. (Stedman's medical dictionary 28th ed., 2005)

Osteopathy—(1) Any disease of bone. (2) A school of medicine based upon a concept of the normal body as a vital machine capable, when in correct adjustment, of making its own remedies against infections and other toxic conditions; practitioners use the diagnostic and therapeutic measures of conventional medicine in addition to manipulative measures. (Stedman's medical dictionary 28th ed., 2005)

Osteoporosis—Reduction in the quantity of bone or atrophy of skeletal tissue; an age-related disorder characterized by decreased bone mass and loss of normal skeletal microarchitecture, leading to increased susceptibility to fractures. (Stedman's medical dictionary 28th ed., 2005)

Osteosarcoma—The most common and malignant of bone sarcomas, which arises from bone-forming cells and affects chiefly the ends of long bones. Its greatest incidence is in the age group between 10 and 25 years. (Stedman's medical dictionary 28th ed., 2005)

Paget's disease—(1) A generalized skeletal disease, frequently familial, of older persons in which bone resorption and formation are both increased, leading to thickening and softening of bones (e.g., the skull), and bending of weight-bearing bones; Syn: *osteitis deformans.* (2) A disease of elderly women, characterized by an infiltrated, somewhat eczematous lesion surrounding and involving the nipple and areola, and associated with subjacent intraductal cancer of the breast and infiltration of the lower epidermis by malignant cells. (3) Syn: *extramammary Paget's disease.* (Stedman's medical dictionary 28th ed., 2005)

Palsy—Paralysis or paresis. (Stedman's medical dictionary 28th ed., 2005)

Paralysis agitans—Obsolete term for parkinsonism. (Stedman's medical dictionary 28th ed., 2005)

Paranoia—A severe but relatively rare mental disorder characterized by the presence of systematized delusions often of a persecutory character involving being followed, poisoned, or harmed by other means, in an otherwise intact personality. (Stedman's medical dictionary 28th ed., 2005)

Parathyroid adenoma—Tumors of the parathyroid glands, which are located in the neck and help regulate calcium metabolism.

Parent—A father, a mother, a father through adoption, a mother through adoption, or an individual who for a period of not less than one year stood in the relationship of a parent to a veteran at any time before the veteran's entry into active military, naval, or air service or if two persons stood in the relationship of a father or a mother for one year or more, the person who last stood in the relationship of father or mother before the veteran's last entry into active military, naval, or air service (except for purposes of chapter 19 of this title [38 U.S.C.S. § 1901 et seq.]). (Definitions. 2006. 38 U.S.C. § 101.)

Parkinson's disease (also called paralysis agitans, parkinsonism)—(1) A neurologic syndrome usually resulting from deficiency of the neurotransmitter dopamine as the consequence of degenerative, vascular, or inflammatory changes in the basal ganglia; characterized by rhythmic muscular tremors, rigidity of movement, festination, droopy posture, and masklike facies. (2) A syndrome similar to parkinsonism. Some features seen with Parkinson disease that occur with other disorders (e.g., progressive supranuclear palsy) or as a side effect of certain medications. (Stedman's medical dictionary 28th ed., 2005)

Parsimonious model—A model with as few parameters as possible.

Pathogenesis—The postulated mechanisms by which the etiologic agent produces disease. The difference between *etiology* and pathogenesis should be noted: The etiology of a disease or disability consists of the postulated causes that initiate the pathogenetic mechanisms; control of these causes might lead to prevention of the disease. (Last, 2001)

Pellagra—An affection characterized by gastrointestinal disturbances, erythema (particularly of exposed areas) followed by desquamation, and nervous and mental disorders; may occur because of a poor diet, alcoholism, or some other disease causing impairment of nutrition; commonly seen when corn (maize) is a main nutrient in the diet, resulting in a deficiency of niacin. (Stedman's medical dictionary 28th ed., 2005)

Pension—A monthly or other periodic payment made by the Secretary to a veteran because of service, age, or non-service-connected disability, or to a surviving spouse or child of a veteran because of the non-service-connected death of the veteran. (Definitions. 2006. 38 U.S.C. § 101.)

Peptic ulcer (gastric or duodenal)—An ulcer of the alimentary mucosa, usually in the stomach or duodenum, exposed to gastric secretion. (Stedman's medical dictionary 28th ed., 2005)

Period of war—The Spanish-American War, the Mexican border period, World War I, World War II, the Korean conflict, the Vietnam era, the Persian Gulf War, and the period beginning on the date of any future declaration of war by the Congress and ending on the date prescribed by Presidential proclamation or concurrent resolution of the Congress. (Definitions. 2006. 38 U.S.C. § 101.)

Peripheral arterial hemodynamics—Blood circulation outside the arteries.

Peripheral nerve disease—See Peripheral neuropathy.

Peripheral neuropathy (acute and subacute)—A disease or degenerative state of the peripheral nerves in which motor, sensory, or vasomotor nerve fibers may be affected and which is marked by muscle weakness and atrophy, pain, and numbness.

Peripheral vasculature—Affecting extremities and abdominal blood vessels.

Persian Gulf War—The period beginning on August 2, 1990, and ending on the date thereafter prescribed by Presidential proclamation or by law. (Definitions. 2006. 38 U.S.C. § 101.)

Pharynx—The superior expanded portion of the alimentary tract, between the mouth and nasal cavities (superiorly and anteriorly) and the esophagus (inferiorly); consisting of the nasopharynx, oropharynx, and laryngopharynx, the first two being shared with the respiratory tract; the pharynx is distinct from the rest of the alimentary tract in that it is composed exclusively of voluntary skeletal muscle arranged in outer circular and inner longitudinal layers. (Stedman's medical dictionary 28th ed., 2005)

Phenoxyherbicides—Related to the growth hormone indoleacetic acid;

when sprayed on broad-leaf plants they induce rapid and uncontrolled growth, eventually killing them.

Phenytoin—An anticonvulsant used in the treatment of generalized tonic clonic and complex partial epilepsy. (Stedman's medical dictionary 28th ed., 2005)

Picloram—A systemic herbicide used for control of woody plants and a wide range of broad-leaved weeds.

Pinta—A disease caused by a spirochete *Treponema carateum*, endemic in Mexico and Central America, and characterized by a small primary papule followed by an enlarging plaque and disseminated secondary macules of varying color called pintids that finally become white. (Stedman's medical dictionary 28th ed., 2005)

Plague—(1) Any disease of wide prevalence or of excessive mortality. (2) An acute infectious disease caused by the bacterium *Yersinia pestis* and marked clinically by high fever, toxemia, prostration, a petechial eruption, lymph node enlargement, pneumonia, or hemorrhage from the mucous membranes; primarily a disease of rodents, transmitted to humans by fleas that have bitten infected animals. In humans the disease takes one of four clinical forms: bubonic plague, septicemic plague, pneumonic plague, or ambulant plague. (Stedman's medical dictionary 28th ed., 2005)

Platelet—An irregularly shaped disklike cytoplasmic fragment of a megakaryocyte that is shed in the marrow sinus and subsequently found in the peripheral blood, where it functions in clotting. A platelet contains granules in the central part (granulomere) and, peripherally, clear protoplasm (hyalomere), but no definite nucleus; is about one-third to one-half the size of an erythrocyte; and contains no hemoglobin. (Stedman's medical dictionary 28th ed., 2005)

Plutonium (Pu)—A transuranium artificial radioactive element, atomic no. 94, atomic wt. 244.064. The best-known α-emitting isotope is ^{239}Pu (half-life 24,110 years) which, like ^{235}U, is fissionable and can be used in atomic bombs and nuclear power plants; ^{238}Pu (half-life 87.74 years) is used as an energy source in pacemakers. Pu ions are bone-seekers; ingestion is a radiation hazard, as with radium and radiostrontium. (Stedman's medical dictionary 28th ed., 2005)

Pneumonia—Inflammation of the lung parenchyma characterized by consolidation of the affected part, the alveolar air spaces being filled with exudated, inflammatory cells, and fibrin. Most cases are due to infection by bacteria or viruses, a few to inhalation of chemicals or trauma to the chest wall, and a small minority to rickettsias, fungi, and yeasts. Distribution may be lobar, segmental, or lobular; when lobular and in associated with bronchitis, it is termed bronchopneumonia. (Stedman's medical dictionary 28th ed., 2005)

Polycythemia (erythremia)—A condition marked by an abnormal increase in the number of circulating red blood cells.

Polydipsia—Excessive thirst that is relatively prolonged. (Stedman's medical dictionary 28th ed., 2005)

Polyuria—Excessive excretion of urine resulting in profuse and frequent micturition. (Stedman's medical dictionary 28th ed., 2005)

Population attributable fraction (PAF)—PAF is the attributable fraction (AF) in the entire population rather than in just the exposed population. To calculate PAF, AF in the exposed is multiplied by the fraction of the entire population that is exposed (i.e., by the prevalence of exposure). See Attributable fraction.

Porphyria cutanea tarda (PCT)—Familial or sporadic porphyria characterized by liver dysfunction and photosensitive cutaneous lesions, with bullae, hyperpigmentation, and scleroderma-like changes in the skin and increased excretion of uroporphyrin; caused by a deficiency of uroporphyrinogen decarboxylase induced in sporadic cases by chronic alcoholism; autosomal dominant inheritance in familial cases. (Stedman's medical dictionary 28th ed., 2005)

Portability—The degree to which the relative risk estimated from one population can be properly applied to another population.

Positive predictive value (PPV)—The probability that a person with a positive test is a true positive (i.e., does have the disease or condition); specifically, the ratio of those who are identified by a test to have the condition who in fact have it, divided by all those identified by a test to have the condition (i.e, true positives, divided by the sum of true positives and false positives). See Negative predictive value.

Posterior subcapsular cataracts—A cataract involving the cortex at the posterior pole of the lens. (Stedman's medical dictionary 28th ed., 2005)

Postirradiation osteosarcoma—Osteosarcoma after radiation therapy; see Osteosarcoma.

Post-traumatic stress disorder (PTSD)—(1) Development of characteristic long-term symptoms following a psychologically traumatic event that is generally outside the range of usual human experience; symptoms include persistently reexperiencing the event and attempting to avoid stimuli reminiscent of the trauma, numbed responsiveness to environmental stimuli, a variety of autonomic and cognitive dysfunctions, and dysphoria. (2) A DSM diagnosis that is established when the specified criteria are met. (Stedman's medical dictionary 28th ed., 2005)

Presumption—A procedural device that dictates that once basic fact A is established, the existence of fact B must be assumed unless the presumed fact is rebutted.

Prevalence—The ratio of the number of those with a given condition in a population (or sample) divided by the number of the entire population (or sample).

Prima facie—At first view; on the first appearance; legally sufficient to establish a fact or a case unless disproved.

Prisoner of War—A combatant who is imprisoned by an enemy power during or immediately after an armed conflict.

Probability distribution—For a discrete (non-continuous) random variable, the function that given the probabilities that the variable equals each of a sequence of possible values; examples include the binomial and Poisson distributions. For a continuous random variable, often used synonymously with the probability density function; an example is the normal distribution. (Adapted from Last, 2001)

Probability of causation (PC)—The fraction of disease risk *in an exposed individual* that is due to the exposure. This is expressed as $(r_{1i} - r_{0i}) / r_{1i}$, where r_{1i} is the disease risk in individual i if exposed and r_{0i} is the disease risk in that same individual if unexposed (i.e., the counterfactual). PC is also often defined as the probability that the exposure caused the disease in an exposed individual. PC has also been used to refer to the AF when AF is applied to individuals, but this usage is incorrect. Since we can know neither r_{1i} nor r_{0i}, and there is substantial variation in these across individuals in even relatively homogeneous populations, for any individual AF cannot be known to be a good estimate of PC.

Proportionate recovery—A defendant compensates a claimant for a fraction of his/her injury that represents the defendant's statistical share in that injury.

Prosthetics—The art and science of making and adjusting artificial parts of the human body. (Stedman's medical dictionary 28th ed., 2005)

Prothrombin—A glycoprotein, molecular weight approximately 72,500, formed and stored in the parenchymal cells of the liver and present in blood in a concentration of approximately 20 mg/100 ml. In the presence of thromboplastin and calcium ion, prothrombin is converted to thrombin, which in turn converts fibrinogen to fibrin, this process resulting in coagulation of blood; a deficiency of prothrombin leads to impaired blood coagulation. (Stedman's medical dictionary 28th ed., 2005)

Proximal limb amputations—An amputation of a limb situated nearest the trunk or the point of origin.

Psychoneurosis—A mental or behavioral disorder of mild or moderate severity; formerly a classification of neurosis that included hysteria, psychasthenia, neurasthenia, and the anxiety and phobic disorders. (Stedman's medical dictionary 28th ed., 2005)

Psychosis (psychoses)—(1) A mental and behavioral disorder causing gross distortion or disorganization of a person's mental capacity, affective response, and capacity to recognize reality, communicate and relate to others to the degree of interfering with a person's capacity to cope with the ordinary demands of everyday life. The psychoses are divided into two major classifications according to their origins: those associated with organic brain syndromes (e.g., Korsakoff's syndrome); and those less clearly organic and having some functional component(s) (e.g., the schizophrenias, bipolar disorder). (2) Generic term for any of the so-called insanities, the most common forms of which are the schizophrenias. (3) A severe emotional and behavioral disorder. (Stedman's medical dictionary 28th ed., 2005)

Purpura—A condition characterized by hemorrhage into the skin. Appearance of the lesions varies with the type of purpura, the duration of the lesions, and the acuteness of the onset. The color is first red, gradually darkens to purple, fades to a brownish yellow, and usually disappears in 2-3 weeks; color of residual permanent pigmentation depends largely on the type of unabsorbed pigment of the extravasated blood; extravasations may occur also into the mucous membranes and internal organs. (Stedman's medical dictionary 28th ed., 2005)

Putative cause—A commonly accepted or assumed cause.

***P*-value**—The probability that a test statistic (such as relative risk) would be as extreme as or more extreme than observed if the null hypothesis were true. The letter *P*, followed by the abbreviation n.s. (not significant) or by the symbol < (less than) or > (greater than) and a decimal notation, such as 0.01, 0.05, is a statement of the probability that the difference observed could have occurred by chance if the groups were really alike, i.e., under the null hypothesis.

Investigators may arbitrarily set their own significance levels, but in most biomedical and epidemiologic work, a study result whose probability value is less than 5 percent ($P < 0.05$) or 1 percent ($P < 0.01$) is considered sufficiently unlikely to have occurred by chance to justify the designation "statistically significant." (Adapted from Last, 2001)

Pyridostigmine bromide—A cholinesterase inhibitor useful in the treatment of the disorder of neuromuscular transmission.

Radioepidemiological Tables—Developed by the National Institutes of Health working group in 1985; serve as a reference tool providing probability of causation estimates for individuals with cancer who were exposed to ionizing radiation.

Radiogenic disease—A disease that may be induced by ionizing radiation.

Radionuclide—An isotope of artificial or natural origin that exhibits radioactivity. (Stedman's medical dictionary 28th ed., 2005)

Radium—A metallic element, atomic no. 88, extracted in very minute quantities from pitchblende; ^{226}Ra, its longest-lived isotope, is produced as an intermediate in the uranium series by the emission of an α particle from thorium-230 (ionium); ^{226}Ra emits α particles and gamma rays with a half-life of 1,599 years breaking down to ^{222}Rn; chemically, it is an alkaline earth metal with properties similar to those of barium. Its therapeutic action is similar to that of x-rays, since the α emission is filtered out. (Stedman's medical dictionary 28th ed., 2005)

Randomized clinical (or controlled) trial (RCT)—An experiment in which subjects in a population are randomly allocated into groups, usually called study and control groups, to receive or not to receive an experimental preventive or therapeutic procedure, maneuver, or intervention. The results are assessed by rigorous comparison of rates of disease, death, recovery, or other appropriate outcome in the study and control groups. Randomized controlled trials are generally regarded as the most scientifically rigorous method of hypothesis testing available. (Last, 2001)

Rating schedule—Certain criteria and/or levels of disability are required for entitlement to ancillary and special purpose benefits.

Raynaud's syndrome—Idiopathic paroxysmal bilateral cyanosis of the digits due to arterial and arteriolar contraction; caused by cold or emotion. Syn: *Raynaud Syndrome.* (Stedman's medical dictionary 28th ed., 2005)

Readjustment Counseling Program—Services provided to combat veterans in the effort to make a satisfying transition from military to civilian life.

Receiver operator characteristics (ROC) curve—(1) A plot of percentage of true positive results versus percentage of false positive results, typically used in assessing the value of a diagnostic test. (2) A graphic means for assessing the ability of a screening or diagnostic test to discriminate between healthy and diseased persons. (Adapted from Stedman's medical dictionary 28th ed., 2005)

Registry—An organized system for the collection, storage, retrieval, analysis and dissemination of information on individual persons who have either a particular disease, a condition that predisposes to the occurrence of a health-related event, or prior exposure to substances known or suspected to cause adverse health effects (definition from www.ncvhs.hhs.gov/9701138b.htm).

Relative risk (RR)—(1) The ratio of the risk of disease or death among the exposed compared to the risk among the unexposed. (2) Alternatively, the ratio of the cumulative incidence rate in the exposed to the cumulative incidence rate in the unexposed, i.e., the rate ratio. (3) The term *relative risk* has also been used synonymously with *odds ratio* and, in some biostatistical articles, has been used for the ratio of *force of morbidity*. The use of the term *relative risk* for several different quantities arises from the fact that for "rare" diseases (e.g., neonatal mortality in infants under 1,500-g birth weight), the approximations do not hold. (Last, 2001)

Reserve—A member of a reserve component of one of the Armed Forces. Reserve component: With respect to the Armed Forces—(A) The Army Reserve; (B) The Navy Reserve; (C) The Marine Corps Reserve; (D) The Air Force Reserve; (E) The Coast Guard Reserve; (F) The Army National Guard of the United States; and (G) The Air National Guard of the United States. (Definitions. 2006. 38 U.S.C. § 101.)

Residual confounding—Confounding that persists after incomplete or unsuccessful attempts to account or adjust for it.

Retirement—Leaving the military after at least 20 years of active service.

Reverse causality—An association that arises when the purported cause is actually the effect (A is thought to cause B, when in fact B causes A). See Cross-sectional study.

Rhabdomyosarcoma—A malignant neoplasm derived from skeletal (striated) muscle, occurring in children or, less commonly, in adults; classified as embryonal alveolar (composed of loose aggregates of small round cells) or pleomorphic (containing rhabdomyoblasts). (Stedman's medical dictionary 28th ed., 2005)

Rheumatoid arthritis—A generalized disease, occurring more often in women, that primarily affects connective tissue; arthritis is the dominant clinical manifestation, involving many joints, especially those of the hands and feet, accompanied by thickening of articular soft tissue, with extension of synovial tissue over articular cartilages, which become eroded; the course is variable but often is chronic and progressive, leading to deformities and disability. (Stedman's medical dictionary 28th ed., 2005)

Rickets—A disease due to vitamin D deficiency and characterized by overproduction and deficient calcification of osteoid tissue, with associated skeletal deformities, disturbances in growth, hypocalcemia, and sometimes tetany; usually accompanied by irritability, listlessness, and generalized muscular weakness; fractures are frequent. (Stedman's medical dictionary 28th ed., 2005)

Risk estimate—Combining risk characterization, dose-response relationships, and exposure estimates to quantify the risk level in a specific population. The end result is a qualitative and quantitative statement about the health effects expected and the proportion and number of affected people in a target population. Sometimes used as a general term for effect measure in an epidemiological analysis. (Adapted from Last, 2001)

Roentgenogram (radiograph)—A negative image on photographic film made by exposure to x-rays or gamma rays that have passed through matter or tissue. (Stedman's medical dictionary 28th ed., 2005)

Saccharin—In dilute aqueous solutions it is 300 to 500 times sweeter than sucrose; used as a sweetening agent.

"Safe" dose—A threshold below which there is no increase in risk.

Sandfly fever—An infectious but not contagious disease occurring in the Balkan Peninsula and other parts of southern Europe, caused by several viruses in the family Bunyaviridae apparently introduced by the bite of the sandfly, *Phlebotomus papatasii;* symptoms resemble those of dengue but are less severe and of shorter duration. Syn: *Phlebotomus fever.* (Stedman's medical dictionary 28th ed., 2005)

Sarcoidosis—A systemic granulomatous disease of unknown cause, especially involving the lungs with resulting interstitial fibrosis, but also involving lymph nodes, skin, liver, spleen, eyes, phalangeal bones, and parotid glands; granulomas are composed of epithelioid and multinucleated giant cells with little or no necrosis. (Stedman's medical dictionary 28th ed., 2005)

Sarcoma—A connective tissue neoplasm, usually highly malignant, formed by proliferation of mesodermal cells. (Stedman's medical dictionary 28th ed., 2005)

Sarin—A nerve poison similar to diisopropyl fluorophosphate and tetraethyl pyrophosphate; a very potent irreversible cholinesterase inhibitor and a more toxic nerve gas than tabun or soman. (Stedman's medical dictionary 28th ed., 2005)

Schistosomiasis—Infection with a species of *Schistosoma;* manifestations of this often chronic and debilitating disease vary with the infecting species but depend in large measure upon tissue reaction (granulation and fibrosis) to the eggs deposited in venules and in the hepatic portals, the latter resulting in portal hypertension and esophageal varices, as well as liver damage leading to cirrhosis. (Stedman's medical dictionary 28th ed., 2005)

Schizoaffective disorder—(1) An illness manifested by an enduring major depressive, manic, or mixed episode along with delusions, hallucinations, disorganized speech and behavior, and negative symptoms of schizophrenia. In the absence of major depressive, manic, or mixed episode, there must be delusions or hallucinations for several weeks. (2) A DSM diagnosis that is established when the specific criteria are met. (Stedman's medical dictionary 28th ed., 2005)

Schizophrenia—A term coined by Bleuler, synonymous with and replacing *dementia praecox*, denoting a common type of psychosis, characterized by abnormalities in perception, content of thought, and thought process (hallucinations and delusions) and by extensive withdrawal of interest from other people and the outside world, with excessive focusing on one's own mental life. Now considered a group or spectrum of disorders rather than a single entity, with distinction sometimes made between process schizophrenia and reactive schizophrenia. The "split" personality of schizophrenia, in which individual psychic components or functions split off and become autonomous, is popularly but erroneously identified with multiple personality, in which two or more relatively complete personalities dominate by turns the psychic life of a patient. (Stedman's medical dictionary 28th ed., 2005)

Schizophreniform disorder—(1) A disorder with essential features that are identical to those of schizophrenia, with the exception that the duration including prodromal, active, and residual phases is shorter than 6 months. (2) A DSM diagnosis that is established when the specific criteria are met. (Stedman's medical dictionary 28th ed., 2005)

Schwannoma—A benign, encapsulated neoplasm in which the fundamental component is structurally identical to a syncytium of Schwann cells; the neoplastic cells proliferate within the endoneurium, and the perineurium forms the capsule. The neoplasm may originate from a peripheral or sympathetic nerve, or from various cranial nerves, particularly the eighth nerve; when the nerve is small, it is usually found (if at all) in the capsule of the neoplasm; if the nerve is large, the neurilemoma may develop within the sheath of the nerve, the fibers of which may then spread over the surface of the capsule as the neoplasm enlarges. Microscopically, neurilemoma is composed of combinations of two patterns, Antoni types A and B, either of which may be predominant in various examples of neurilemomas. (Stedman's medical dictionary 28th ed., 2005)

Scleroderma—Thickening and induration of the skin caused by new collagen formation, with atrophy of pilosebaceous follicles; either a manifestation of progressive systemic sclerosis or localized (morphea). (Stedman's medical dictionary 28th ed., 2005)

Sclerosis—In neuropathy, induration of nervous and other structures by a hyperplasia of the interstitial fibrous or glial connective tissue. (Stedman's medical dictionary 28th ed., 2005)

Scurvy—A disease marked by inanition, debility, anemia, and edema of the dependent parts; a spongy condition sometimes with ulceration of the gums and loss of teeth, hemorrhages into the skin from the mucous membranes and internal organs, and poor wound healing; due to a diet lacking vitamin C. (Stedman's medical dictionary 28th ed., 2005)

Seamless transition—The commitment of DoD and VA to work closely in harmonizing the medical records of Service members for a smooth transition from DoD care to VA care.

Secretary—Secretary of Veterans Affairs; Secretary concerned (A) The Secretary of the Army, with respect to matters concerning the Army; (B) The Secretary of the Navy, with respect to matters concerning the Navy; or the Marine Corps; (C) The Secretary of the Air Force, with respect to matters concerning the Air Force; (D) The Secretary of Homeland Security, with respect to matters concerning the Coast Guard; (E) The Secretary of Health and Human Services, with respect to matters concerning the Public Health Service; and (F) The Secretary of Commerce, with respect to matters concerning the National Oceanic and Atmospheric Administration or its predecessor organization the Coast and Geodetic Survey. (Definitions. 2006. 38 U.S.C. § 101.)

Selection bias—In a case-control study, occurs when the chance of being selected as a case or a control is influenced by exposure status. In a cohort study, occurs when the chance of participation in a study as exposed or non-exposed is influenced by disease status. Also, error due to systematic differences in characteristics between those who take part in a study and those who do not. Selection bias can invalidate conclusions and generalizations that might otherwise be drawn from such studies.

Sensitivity—The proportion of truly diseased persons in the screened population who are correctly identified as diseased by the screening test; a measure of the probability of correctly diagnosing a case, or the probability that any given case will be identified by the test; specifically, the ratio of those who are identified by a test to have the condition who in fact have it, divided by all those who have the condition (i.e., true positives, divided by the sum of true positives and false negatives).

Sensitivity analysis—A method to determine the robustness of a result by examining the extent to which the result is affected by changes in methods, values of variables, or assumptions. (Adapted from Last, 2001)

Separation—Left the military before 20 years; cannot apply for retirement benefits (Source: Personal communication, Col. K. Cox, Department of Defense, January 5, 2007):

1. The act of keeping apart or dividing, or the state of being held apart.
2. In dentistry, the process of gaining slight spaces between the teeth preparatory to treatment. (Stedman's medical dictionary 28th ed., 2005)

Service-attributable disability—Disability caused by a veteran's service.

Service-attributable fraction (SAF)—The attributable fraction (AF) when the specific exposure is military service (see Attributable fraction); in other words, the proportion of a disease attributable to military service.

Service-connected—With respect to disability or death, that such disability was incurred or aggravated, or that the death resulted from a disability incurred or aggravated, in line of duty in the active military, naval, or air service. (Definitions. 2006. 38 U.S.C. § 101.)

Seveso study—The study of a population exposed to dioxin from an industrial accident that occurred in 1976 in a small manufacturing plant in the Lombardy region in Italy.

Shared psychotic disorder—A mental disorder in which a delusion develops in a person in a relationship with another person with an established delusion. (Stedman's medical dictionary 28th ed., 2005)

Shigellosis—Bacillary dysentery caused by bacteria of the genus *Shigella*, often occurring in epidemic patterns; an opportunistic infection of person with AIDS. (Stedman's medical dictionary 28th ed., 2005)

Sliding scale pension—A pension based on income level.

Spanish-American War—(A) The period beginning on April 21, 1898, and ending on July 4, 1902, (B) Includes the Philippine Insurrection and the Boxer Rebellion, and (C) In the case of a veteran who served with the United States military forces engaged in hostilities in the Moro Province, means the period beginning on April 21, 1898, and ending on July 15, 1903. (Definitions. 2006. 38 U.S.C. § 101.)

Specificity—The proportion of truly nondiseased persons who are correctly identified by the screening test; a measure of the probability of correctly identifying a nondiseased person with a screening test; specifically, the ratio of those who are identified by a test to not have the condition who in fact do not have it, divided by all those who do not have the condition (i.e., true negatives, divided by the sum of true negatives and false positives).

Spouse—A person of the opposite sex who is a wife or husband. (Definitions. 2006. 38 U.S.C. § 101.)

Spurious association—A noncausal association due to chance, bias, failure to control for extraneous variables, confounding, etc. (see Confounder).

Squamous cell carcinoma—A malignant neoplasm derived from stratified squamous epithelium, but which may also occur in sites such as bronchial mucosa where glandular or columnar epithelium is normally present; variable amounts of keratin are formed, in relation to the degree of differentiation, and, if the keratin is not on the surface, it may accumulate in the neoplasm as a keratin pearl; in instances in which the cells are well differentiated, intercellular bridges may be observed between adjacent cells. (Stedman's medical dictionary 28th ed., 2005)

Stakeholder—One with an interest or share in an undertaking or enterprise.

State—Each of the several States, Territories, and possessions of the United States, the District of Columbia, and the Commonwealth of Puerto Rico. For the purpose of section 2303 and chapters 34 and 35 of this title (38 U.S.C.S. § 2303, 3451 et seq., and 3500 et seq.), such term also includes the Canal Zone. (Definitions. 2006. 38 U.S.C. § 101.)

State home—A home established by a State (other than a possession) for veterans disabled by age, disease, or otherwise who by reason of such disability are incapable of earning a living. Such term also includes such a home which furnishes nursing home care for veterans. (Definitions. 2006. 38 U.S.C. § 101.)

Stratum (strata)—Subsamples according to specified criteria, such as age groups, socioeconomic status, etc.

One of the layers of differentiated tissue, the aggregate of which forms any given structure, such as the retina or the skin. (Stedman's medical dictionary 28th ed., 2005)

Stroke—(1) Any acute clinical event, related to impairment of cerebral circulation, that lasts more than 24 hours. (2) A harmful discharge of lightning, particularly one that affects a human being. (3) A pulsation. (4) To pass the hand or any instrument gently over a surface. See also stroking. (5) A gliding movement over a surface. (Stedman's medical dictionary 28th ed., 2005)

Subcapsular cataracts—A cataract in which the opacities are concentrated beneath the capsule. (Stedman's medical dictionary 28th ed., 2005)

Sufficient cause—The minimum set of conditions, factors, or events needed to produce a given outcome. (Adapted from Last, 2001)

Sufficient component causes model—A model that postulates disease resulting from any of several sufficient causal constellations, each of which comprises components that are all necessary to make them a complete cause.

Sulfur mustard—Cytotoxic vesicant chemical warfare agent with the ability to form large blisters on exposed skin (e.g., mustard gas).

Surveillance—Continuous monitoring of disease occurrence within a population.

Surviving spouse—A person of the opposite sex who was the spouse of a veteran at the time of the veteran's death, and who lived with the veteran continuously from the date of marriage to the date of the veteran's death (except where there was a separation which was due to the misconduct of, or procured by, the veteran without the fault of the spouse) and who has not remarried or (in cases not involving remarriage) has not since the death of the veteran, and after September 19, 1962, lived with another person and held himself or herself out openly to the public to be the spouse of such other person (except for purposes of chapter 19 of this title [38 U.S.C.S. § 1901 et seq.]). (Definitions. 2006. 38 U.S.C. § 101.)

Synovial sarcoma—A rare malignant tumor of synovial origin, most commonly involving the knee joint and composed of spindle cells usually enclosing slits or pseudoglandular spaces that may be lined by radially disposed epitheliallike cells. (Stedman's medical dictionary 28th ed., 2005)

Syringomyelia—The presence in the spinal cord of longitudinal cavities lined by dense, gliogenous tissue, that are not caused by vascular insufficiency. Syringomyelia is marked clinically by pain and paresthesia, followed by muscular atrophy of the hands and analgesia with thermoanesthesia of the hands and arms, but with the tactile sense preserved; later marked by painless whitlows, spastic paralysis in the lower extremities, and scoliosis of the lumbar spine. Some cases are associated with low-grade gliomas or vascular malformations of the spinal cord. (Stedman's medical dictionary 28th ed., 2005)

Systematic error—One-sided variation of measurements from the true values; see also Bias.

Systemic lupus erythematosus—An inflammatory connective tissue disease with variable features, frequently including fever, weakness and fatigability, joint pains or arthritis resembling rheumatoid arthritis, diffuse erythematous skin lesions on the face, neck, or upper extremities, with liquefaction degeneration of the basal layer and epidermal atrophy, lymphadenopathy, pleurisy or pericarditis, glomerular lesions, anemia, hyperglobulinemia, and a positive LE cell test result, with serum antibodies to nuclear protein and sometimes to double-stranded DNA and other substances. (Stedman's medical dictionary 28th ed., 2005)

Testosterone—The most potent naturally occurring androgen, formed in greatest quantities by the interstitial cells of the testes, and possibly secreted also by the ovary and adrenal cortex; may be produced in nonglandular tissues from precursors such as androstenedione; used in the treatment of hypogonadism, cryptorchism, certain carcinomas, and menorrhagia. (Stedman's medical dictionary 28th ed., 2005)

2,3,7,8-Tetrachlorodibenzo-*p*-dioxin (TCDD)—See Dioxin.

Theater—A specific geographic area within which armed conflict occurs.

Thromboangiitis obliterans (Buerger's disease)—Inflammation of the entire wall and connective tissue surrounding medium-sized arteries and veins, especially of the legs of young and middle-aged men; associated with thrombotic occlusion and commonly resulting in gangrene. (Stedman's medical dictionary 28th ed., 2005)

Thyroid nodular disease—Presence of palpable thyroid nodules. These nodules may be solitary or one or more within a multi-nodular thyroid. Most are benign, colloid nodules.

Thyroxine—The *l*-isomer is the active iodine compound existing normally in the thyroid gland and extracted therefrom in crystalline form for therapeutic use; also prepared synthetically; used for the relief of hypothyroidism, cretinism, and myxedema. (Stedman's medical dictionary 28th ed., 2005)

Tolman Committee—Also known as the Committee on Declassification; appointed by General Groves in 1944 to study the declassification of Manhattan Project research.

Tonsillectomy—Removal of the entire tonsil. (Stedman's medical dictionary 28th ed., 2005)

Tort litigation—Legal proceeding for a wrongful act other than a breach of contract for which relief may be obtained in the form of damages or an injunction.

Toxicant—Any poisonous agent, specifically alcohol or other poison, causing symptoms of what is popularly called intoxication. (Stedman's medical dictionary 28th ed., 2005)

Toxicogenomics—A scientific subdiscipline that combines toxicology (the study of the nature and effects of poisons) with genomics (the investigation of the way that our genetic makeup translates into biological functions).

Transparency—Characterized by visibility or accessibility of information, especially concerning business practices.

2,4,5-Trichlorophenoxyacetic acid—An herbicide and defoliant synthesized by condensation of chloracetic acid and 2,4,5-trichlorophenol, used as the principal constituent of Agent Orange.

Triglyceride—Glycerol esterified at each of its three hydroxyl groups by a fatty (aliphatic) acid. Syn: *triacylglycerol.* (Stedman's medical dictionary 28th ed., 2005)

Trypanosomiasis—Any disease caused by a trypanosome. (Stedman's medical dictionary 28th ed., 2005)

Tuberculosis (TB)—A specific disease caused by infection with *Mycobacterium tuberculosis*, the tubercle bacillus, which can affect almost any tissue or organ of the body, the most common seat of the disease being the lungs. Primary tuberculosis is typically a mild or asymptomatic local pulmonary infection. Regional lymph nodes may become involved, but in otherwise healthy people generalized disease does not immediately develop. A cell-mediated immune response arrests the spread of organisms and walls off the zone of infection. Infected tissues and lymph nodes may eventually calcify. The tuberculin skin test becomes positive within a few weeks, and remains positive throughout life. Organisms in a primary lesion remain viable and can become reactivated months or years later to initiate secondary tuberculosis. Progression to the secondary stage eventually occurs in 10-15 percent of people who have had primary tuberculosis. The risk of reactivation is increased by diabetes mellitus, HIV infection, silicosis, and various systemic or malignant conditions, as well as in alcoholics, IV drug abusers, nursing home residents, and those receiving adrenocortical steroid or immunosuppressive therapy. Secondary or reactivation tuberculosis usually results in a chronic, spreading lung infection, most often involving the upper lobes. Minute granulomas (tubercles), just visible to the naked eye, develop in involved lung tissue, each consisting of a zone of caseation necrosis surrounded by chronic inflammatory cells (epithelioid histiocytes and giant cells). These lesions, which give the disease its name, are also found in other tissues (lymph nodes, bowel, kidney, skin) to which the disease may spread. Rarely, reactivation results in widespread dissemination of tubercles throughout the body (miliary tuberculosis). The symptoms of active pulmonary tuberculosis are fatigue, anorexia, weight loss, low-grade fever, night sweats, chronic cough, and hemoptysis. Local symptoms depend on the parts affected. Active pulmonary tuberculosis is relentlessly chronic and, if untreated, leads to progressive destruction of lung tissue. Cavities form in the lungs, and erosion into pulmonary blood vessels can result in life-threatening hemorrhage. Gradual deterioration of nutritional status and general health culminates in death due to wasting, infection, or multiple organ failure. Variant syndromes (tuberculous lymphadenitis in children, severe systemic disease in persons with AIDS) are caused by organisms of the *Mycobacterium avium-intracellulare* complex (MAIC). The diagnosis of TB is based on tuberculin skin testing (negaitive in 20 percent of people with active TB), imaging studies (computed tomography is more sensitive than standard chest radiography in detecting pleural effusion, miliary disease, and cavitation), and the finding of the causative organism in sputum of tissue specimens by acid-fast or fluorochrome staining, nucleic acid amplification, or culture. (Stedman's medical dictionary 28th ed., 2005)

Tumors—(1) Any swelling or tumefaction. (2) Syn: *neoplasm.* (3) One of the four signs of inflammation (t., calor, dolor, rubor) enunciated by Celsus. (Stedman's medical dictionary 28th ed., 2005)

Malignant tumor—A tumor that invades surrounding tissues, is usually capable of producing metastases, may recur after attempted removal, and is likely to cause death of the host unless adequately treated. (Stedman's medical dictionary 28th ed., 2005)

Type I presumptions—Shifts both the burden of production and the burden of persuasion.

Type II presumptions—Establishment of the basic fact does not shift to the opponent the burden of persuading the adjudicator that the presumed fact does not exist. The opponent of the presumption only has to produce evidence that is contrary to or meets the presumption.

Ulcer—A lesion through the skin or a mucous membrane resulting from loss of tissue, usually with inflammation. (Stedman's medical dictionary 28th ed., 2005)

Ulceration—(1) The formation of an ulcer. (2) An ulcer or aggregation of ulcers. (Stedman's medical dictionary 28th ed., 2005)

Uncertainty—The state of being indeterminate, not certain to occur, not reliable, not having certain knowledge, or not clearly identified or defined.

Undiagnosed illness (or unexplained illness)—A constellation of symptom complaints; was called "Gulf War Syndrome."

Vaccine Injury Table—Lists and explains injuries/conditions that are presumed to be caused by vaccines and covered under the National Vaccine Injury Compensation Program.

Valvulitis—Inflammation of a valve, especially a heart valve. (Stedman's medical dictionary 28th ed., 2005)

Vesicant—An agent that produces a vesicle. (Stedman's medical dictionary 28th ed., 2005)

Veteran—A person who served in the active military, naval, or air service, and who was discharged or released therefrom under conditions other than dishonorable. (Definitions. 2006. 38 U.S.C. § 101.)

Veteran of any war—Any veteran who served in the active military, naval, or air service during a period of war. (Definitions. 2006. 38 U.S.C. § 101.)

Vietnam era—(A) The period beginning on February 28, 1961, and ending on May 7, 1975, in the case of a veteran who served in the Republic of Vietnam during that period. (B) The period beginning on August 5, 1964, and ending on May 7, 1975, in all other cases. (Definitions. 2006. 38 U.S.C. § 101.)

Viral exanthemas—A skin eruption occurring as a symptoms of an actual viral disease.

von Recklinghausen's neurofibromatosis (Type I neurofibromatosis)—Characterized clinically by the combination of patches of hyperpigmentation and cutaneous and subcutaneous tumors. The hyperpigmented skin areas, present from birth and found anywhere on the body surface, can vary markedly in size and color—the dark brown ones are called café-au-lait spots. The multiple cutaneous and subcutaneous tumors, called neurofibromas, can develop anywhere along the peripheral nerve fibers, from the roots distally. Neurofibromas can become quite large, causing a major disfigurement, eroding bone, and compressing various peripheral nerve structures; a small hamartoma (Lisch nodule) can be found in the iris of almost all patients. Has autosomal dominant inheritance, with the gene locus on chromosome 17q11, and is caused by mutation in the NF1 gene that encodes neurofibromin. Syn: *Type I neurofibromatosis*. (Stedman's medical dictionary 28th ed., 2005)

World War I—(A) The period beginning on April 6, 1917, and ending on November 11, 1918, and (B) In the case of a veteran who served with the United States military forces in Russia, means the period beginning on April 6, 1917, and ending on April 1, 1920. (Definitions. 2006. 38 U.S.C. § 101.)

World War II—The period beginning on December 7, 1941, and ending on December 31, 1946 (except for purposes of chapters 31 and 37 of this title [38 U.S.C.S. § 3100 et seq. and 3701 et seq.]). (Definitions. 2006. 38 U.S.C. § 101.)

Yaws—An infectious tropical disease caused by *Treponema pertenue* and characterized by the development of crusted granulomatous ulcers on the extremities; may involve bone, but, unlike syphilis, does not produce central nervous system or cardiovascular pathology. (Stedman's medical dictionary 28th ed., 2005)

Yellow fever—A tropical mosquito-borne viral hepatitis, due to yellow fever virus, a member of the family Flaviviridae, with an urban form transmitted by *Aedes aegypti*, and a rural, jungle, or sylvatic form from tree-dwelling mammals by various mosquitoes of the *Haemagogus* species complex; characterized clinically by fever, slow pulse, albuminuria, jaundice, congestion of the face, and hemorrhages, especially hematemesis; used to occur in epidemics mainly in port cities, especially in late summer, with 20-40 percent case fatality rates; immunity to reinfection accompanies recovery. (Stedman's medical dictionary 28th ed., 2005)

LEGISLATION

1818	Service Pension Law
1862	General Pension Act
1862	Homestead Act
1890	Dependent Pension Act
1917	War Risk Insurance Act Amendments
1918	Vocational Rehabilitation Act
1924	World War Adjustment Compensation Act
1933	Economy Act
1943	Disabled Veterans' Rehabilitation Act
1944	Servicemen's Readjustment Act (GI Bill of Rights)
1950	Vocational Rehabilitation Act
1952	Veteran's Readjustment Assistance Act (Korean GI Bill)
1954	War Claims Act Amendments
1959	Veterans' Pension Act
1978	Veterans Disability Compensation and Survivor Act
1979	The Veterans Health Care Amendments
1979	Veterans Health Program Extension and Improvement Act
1981	Former Prisoners of War Benefits Act
1981	Veterans' Health Care, Training, and Small Business Loan Act
1984	The Veterans Dioxin and Radiation Exposure Compensation Standards Act (VDRECSA)
1984	Veterans' Compensation and Program Improvements Amendments

1984 Veterans' Dioxin and Radiation Exposure Compensation Standards Act
1986 Veterans Benefits Improvement and Health Care Authorization Act
1988 The Radiation-Exposed Veterans Compensation Act (REVCA)
1988 Veterans Benefits and Services Act
1990 The Radiation Exposure Compensation Act (RECA)
1991 Agent Orange Act
1994 Persian Gulf War Veterans' Benefit Act
2000 Veterans Millennium Health Care and Benefits Act
2003 Veterans Benefits Act